FEELING MEMORY

THE COLUMBIA ORAL HISTORY SERIES

THE COLUMBIA ORAL HISTORY SERIES

EDITED BY MARY MARSHALL CLARK, AMY STARECHESKI, KIMBERLY SPRINGER, AND PETER BEARMAN

FEELING MEMORY

Remembering Wartime
Childhoods in France

LINDSEY DODD

Columbia University Press
New York

Columbia University Press
Publishers Since 1893
New York   Chichester, West Sussex
cup.columbia.edu

Library of Congress Cataloging-in-Publication Data
Names: Dodd, Lindsey, author.
Title: Feeling memory : remembering wartime childhoods in France / Lindsey Dodd.
Description: New York : Columbia University Press, [2023] |
    Includes bibliographical references.
Identifiers: LCCN 2022052314 | ISBN 9780231209182 (hardback) |
    ISBN 9780231209199 (trade paperback) | ISBN 9780231557818 (ebook)
Subjects: LCSH: World War, 1939-1945—Children—France. |
    Children—France—Social conditions—20th century. | Memory—France. |
    World War, 1939-1945—Social aspects—France.
Classification: LCC D810.C4 D68328 2023 | DDC 940.530830944—dc23/eng/20230210
LC record available at https://lccn.loc.gov/2022052314

Printed and bound by CPI Group (UK) Ltd, Croydon, CR0 4YY

Cover design: Elliott S. Cairns
Cover image: AFP via Getty Images

For Ann and John Dodd

CONTENTS

ACKNOWLEDGMENTS

My very warmest thanks are due to all my family, friends, and colleagues who have supported the progress and completion of this book. In particular, I could not do what I do without the continuously enriching love, support, conversation, and confidence of those closest to me, in particular Benjamin Bâcle, Clare Forder, and my parents, Ann and John Dodd. I thank my excellent current and former colleagues in the History Department at the University of Huddersfield, particularly Rebecca Gill, Katherine Lewis, Rob Ellis, Barry Doyle, and Pat Cullum, as well as my hardworking coeditors of the journal *Oral History*. I owe a debt of intellectual gratitude to both Sian Sullivan and Todd Reeser for shifting my ideas around.

The whole of this book was drafted while I was a Fellow at the Collegium de Lyon in 2018–2019, an academic year like no other for so many wonderful reasons, not least the good friends I made in that short time. I express my sincere thanks to the Collegium de Lyon, and particularly to Hervé Joly, for the gift I received through my fellowship that was so precious to me: time. The interviewing I undertook in 2009 was funded by the Arts and Humanities Research Council as part of the "Bombing, States and People in Western Europe" project (AH/E007740/1). The interviewing I completed in 2016–2018, as well as my archival listening trip in 2016, was made possible by the Arts and Humanities Research Council/Labex Passés dans le Présent bilateral funding venture, which supported the project "Disrupted Histories, Recovered Pasts: A Cross-Disciplinary Analysis and Cross-Case Synthesis of Oral Histories and History in Post-Conflict and Postcolonial Contexts" (AH/N504579/1).

My gratitude also extends to the Oral History Series editors at Columbia University Press and the editorial team there, who received my manuscript with enthusiasm and supported its completion.

Finally, no oral history is possible without the courage of the people who share their memories with archives and researchers, often without knowing what may become of them. Thanks, first, to the interviewers and archives who have thought to collect stories and have let me listen to them, and particularly to Julien Rocipon and Philippe Béquia for their friendly generosity. As for the interviewees, sharing memories is a deeply personal and risky endeavor. I cannot thank them enough for how they have enriched my understanding and knowledge. To those people I interviewed personally, thank you for your great goodwill and kind hospitality, for the lunches, cakes, and coffees. And to all of the interviewees who volunteered to be recorded, your stories and experiences inspire everything that follows.

It is possible that these people may not like, or might not have liked (many are no longer with us), what I have written about them. I am certain that I get them wrong at times; how could I not? I make no secret that this is my interpretation of their stories, just one approach of any number that are possible. I hope that they would ultimately recognize that, right or wrong, I am interested in their worlds, I think their memories matter, and I have done my best to listen.

CHRONOLOGY

July 1914–November 1918	The First World War, also known as the Great War and, for many of these interviewees, *la guerre de '14* (the 1914 war).
January 30, 1933	Hitler is named Chancellor of Germany.
February 6, 1934	Demonstrations turn to riots in Paris, largely sparked by right-wing French leagues.
May 1936–April 1938	Period in power of the Popular Front government, a left-wing coalition that included the French Communist Party, the French Section of the Workers' International, and the Radical Party.
September 1938	Munich Crisis. Partial mobilization in France. Appeasement of Hitler by British prime minister Neville Chamberlain and French prime minister Édouard Daladier. Munich Agreement signed on September 30, 1938.
August 23, 1939	Molotov-Ribbentrop Pact signed between Germany and the Soviet Union.
September 3, 1939	France declares war on Germany. Full mobilization in France.
September 1939–May 1940	Period known as the "Phoney War" (*la drôle de guerre*). Hitler focuses his attention on his eastern front.
May 10, 1940	Nazi invasion of France, Belgium, the Netherlands, and Luxembourg.

May–June 1940	Civilian exodus in France. Refugees from Belgium, the Netherlands, and Luxembourg flood into France. They join refugees from northern France and then Paris fleeing the oncoming German Wehrmacht and the violence of battle. Refugees are strafed and bombed on the roads.
June 4, 1940	Fall of Dunkirk, following the evacuation of the British Expeditionary Force and some French troops.
June 10, 1940	Italy declares war on France.
June 16, 1940	Prime Minister Paul Reynaud resigns. Marshal Philippe Pétain provides interim leadership.
June 17, 1940	Pétain broadcasts on the radio that the French army must cease combat.
June 18, 1940	Rebel officer Charles de Gaulle broadcasts from London that the flame of French resistance will not be extinguished, calling for military personnel to join him.
June 22, 1940	The Armistice is signed, dividing France into Free and Occupied zones, with the French government seat at Vichy, not far from the demarcation line between zones.
July 10, 1940	The Third Republic votes to end itself and pass control to Pétain as head of the French State. Pierre Laval is vice president of the Council of Ministers, acting as de facto prime minister. Lawmaking and policy developments start to create the authoritarian, conservative, exclusionary National Revolution.
October 3, 1940	First Jewish Statute is promulgated. Anti-Semitic laws created autonomously by the French government debar Jews from certain professions, among other restrictions.
December 13, 1940	Pierre Laval leaves government.
May 14, 1941	Roundup of 3,747 Jewish men in Paris with foreign nationality.

June 2, 1941 — Second Jewish Statute is promulgated. Vichy further restricts Jewish rights and lives.

June 22, 1941 — Operation Barbarossa begins. Hitler invades the Soviet Union, thus ending the terms of the Molotov-Ribbentrop Pact which had officially restricted communist resistance.

August 1941 — Communist escalation of resistance activity and attacks on German personnel in France.

August 20-24, 1941 — French police conduct raids beginning in the eleventh arrondissement of Paris in retaliation for resistance activity. More than four thousand Jewish men are arrested and interned in Drancy, marking the opening of this internment camp just north of Paris. It will act as a transit camp, holding Jews prior to their deportation. A total of 67,400 Jews will be deported from Drancy.

October 25, 1941 — Former prefect Jean Moulin reaches Charles de Gaulle and the Free French in London with news of growing internal resistance movements and networks operating clandestinely in France.

December 7, 1941 — Japanese attack on Pearl Harbor: United States enters the war.

January 1, 1942 — Jean Moulin parachutes back into France to make contact with leaders of resistance movements and networks.

January 20, 1942 — The Wannsee Conference takes place outside Berlin, at which Reinhard Heydrich presents plan for the systematic mass murder of Europe's Jewish population.

March 3–4, 1942 — The British Royal Air Force (RAF) bombs the Renault plant at Boulogne-Billancourt in the western suburbs of Paris, targeting an industrial target in the French capital for the first time.

April 18, 1942	Pierre Laval returns to government as prime minister.
June 7, 1942	Jews over the age of six in the Occupied Zone must wear the yellow star.
June 22, 1942	In a radio broadcast, Laval desires the victory of Germany, without which, he says, communism will triumph in Europe. French collaboration with Nazi Germany steps up a gear.
July 16–17, 1942	Roundup of Jews in Paris (known as the Vel d'Hiv) by the French police: 13,152 people including more than 4,000 children are rounded up and incarcerated in the winter cycling stadium in Paris.
August 26, 1942	6,584 Jews in the Free Zone are rounded up. Some are taken to Rivesaltes internment camp near Perpignan, which acts as a transit camp holding Jews prior to their deportation. This is the only roundup that took place in a region not occupied by the Germans.
November 8–16, 1942	Operation Torch. The Allies land in North Africa.
November 11, 1942	In response to the Allied landings, the Germans invade and occupy the former Free Zone, which is henceforth called the Southern Zone.
January 30, 1943	Creation of the Milice, an all-French right-wing paramilitary force, to hunt down resistance fighters and Jews.
February 16, 1943	The Service du Travail Obligatoire (Forced Labor Service—STO) is organized: all young men (and later older ones and women) are requisitioned for forced labor in Germany. Many dodge the draft, hiding out in the countryside and sometimes joining the maquis (rural resistance guerrilla fighters), whose numbers now grow.
February 1943	Heavy Allied bombing of the German submarine pens built at ports along the French

	Atlantic coast (Bordeaux, La Pallice, Saint-Nazaire, Lorient, Brest). Lorient is area bombed ("carpet bombed"), but the submarine pens remain intact. Civilian populations are evacuated.
March 20, 1943	Jean Moulin returns to France on Charles de Gaulle's orders to attempt to unite the different resistance movements and networks behind de Gaulle.
April 4, 1943	The U.S. Army Air Force (USAAF) bombs the Renault plant at Boulogne-Billancourt. Many schools are closed and the evacuation of children is ordered. The first convoy of children from Boulogne-Billancourt goes to the Creuse department, arriving late April. Many more children from the Paris region are subsequently evacuated to rural France across 1943–1944.
May 27, 1943	Jean Moulin orchestrates the first meeting of the Conseil national de la Résistance (National Resistance Council—CNR) clandestinely in Paris.
June 21, 1943	Jean Moulin is arrested near Lyon, tortured severely, and dies while being deported.
January–April 1944	The Allied High Command puts the "Transportation Plan" into action: the heavy bombing of rail and infrastructure targets across the north of France in preparation for landings.
April 6, 1944	Arrest and subsequent deportation of forty-four Jewish refugee children from the children's home at Izieu, not far from Lyon, and their adult carers.
June 6, 1944	D-Day: Allied landings in Normandy begin.
June 10, 1944	Massacre of 643 French civilians by the Germans at Oradour-sur-Glane.
August 19–25, 1944	Battle for the liberation of Paris, which is declared on August 25, 1944. Dismantling of

	the Vichy government thereafter. Charles de Gaulle heads the new Provisional Government of the French Republic. France rejoins the war under de Gaulle on the side of the Allies.
August–September 1944	Siege of Brest. General Ramcke surrenders on September 19, 1944. Other towns and cities follow different patterns of liberation and have different liberation dates.
May 8, 1945	Victory in Europe (V-E) Day.
August 14–15, 1945	Japan surrenders following the atomic bombing of Hiroshima and Nagasaki. The end of the Second World War.
October 27, 1946–October 4, 1958	Period of the French Fourth Republic.
December 19, 1946–July 20, 1954	French troops fight in the First Indochina War.
November 1, 1954–March 19, 1962	French troops fight in the Algerian War of Independence.
October 4, 1958	The French Fifth Republic is established under a new constitution drafted by Charles de Gaulle, who becomes its president in December 1958.
December 19, 1964	Jean Moulin's ashes are transferred to and interred in the Panthéon in Paris.
May 2–June 23, 1968	Period of civil unrest in France known as May '68, including demonstrations, strikes, and the occupation of factories and universities.
April 28, 1969	Charles de Gaulle resigns as president of the Fifth Republic.
November 9, 1970	Charles de Gaulle dies.
July 16, 1995	President Jacques Chirac apologizes for the French government's complicity in the Holocaust.

A NOTE ON TRANSCRIPTION AND TRANSLATION

A ll interviews used in this study were recorded in French. All extracts from them rely on my own translation, sometimes with advice from native French speakers, and take a generous approach to vernacular expression. One of oral history's great strengths is its ability to convey voice; what is lost in any translated oral history is not just voice but the quirks of dialect and personal intonation. I have tried, as far as my skills permit, to translate in the spirit of the mood of the interview and to convey the buoyancy or reticence of interviewees through a combination of vernacular English, punctuation, and, on occasion, authorial interjection. Translating oral history is a creative, intuitive process, and my intention was to stay true to what I understood the speaker's intention to be, and to convey their meaning as far as was possible. While my own vernacular comes from southeast England, and my original translations reflected this, some alterations to U.S. English have been made by the publisher. In transcribed extracts, the following points should be noted:

- I have used an ellipsis like this . . . to signify that speech has been cut from an extract.
- I have used square brackets to demonstrate any insertion of authorial comments or sense-making explanations, such as [she laughs sadly].
- If a speaker left a phrase dangling, I have used, at the end of a sentence,—. During the flow of speech, I have used—, to show an incomplete phrase or expression.
- I have used the interjection "eh" as a rough equivalent of *hein* in French. This is one of the most frequent interjections; it can be used in a

questioning, interrogatory way or as an emphatic point maker. It is very important in providing cadence and rhythm to French vernacular speech.

- I have translated *ben* in French as "well" (as in *ben, oui*: "well, yes") or as "erm" or "um" when it functions as a marker of hesitancy (*ben—, je ne sais pas*: "erm—, I don't know").
- I have not translated the French interjection *oh là là*. It should be noted that this is not used archly (as in the English "ooh la la!" with a wink of an eye) but indicates surprise, dismay, exasperation, or shock, with a slow shake of the head or rolling of the eyes. It has something in common with "oh dear," "oh my," "my goodness," "dear me," or, in U.S. English, "oh boy."

FEELING MEMORY

INTRODUCTION

This book is made of memories. It is a book about remembering, recounting, and communicating the past and about listening. It is about the nature and characteristics of these memories. It is also about the variety of experiences children had during the Second World War in France and about the similarities and singularities of these. It explores how individual remembering is socially and culturally shaped at both macro and micro levels, how remembering takes place in time and space, and it emphasizes the ongoingness of the past as it reverberates into the present. It sees feeling as fundamental to the processes of remembering, listening, and seeking both to understand and to be understood. It is, therefore, concerned with the ways that feelings about the past—the emotions of history—circulate between individuals, groups, and within and across societies. Importantly, it seeks to know not just about feeling but through feeling and thus makes a strong claim for the value of affective knowledge inside historical inquiry and research more broadly. It takes the French experience of the Second World War as its example, but its principles extend beyond.

Before going any further, it is worth pointing out what this book is not. Or rather, what it is not directly. It is not a book about the Vichy government's policies toward children and childhood nor about children's responses to Vichy, although these do come into it. The Vichy government is the name given to the conservative, authoritarian, anti-Semitic government led by Marshal Philippe Pétain from July 1940, which came into power following the French defeat at the hands of Hitler's Germany. Nor is this book about such structures of childhood as school, family, and health, although these are very present. It does not propose a chronological account of the events of the war as lived by children, but these are often reflected. It is not about French collective memory of the war or the politics of war memory in France, yet these underpin the ways people talk about the past. It is not about the persecution of Jewish children nor about child trauma, although these particularities of experience have an important place. It is not, strictly, a history of children in wartime France. While this may have been its original intention, a shift in emphasis grew out of its sources. This book is based solely on the recorded oral narratives—or, as I will call them, the memory stories—of more than a hundred people who were children in France during the Second World War. It can be read both as an affective exploration of having been a child in war and as a reflective study of remembering.

This duality stems from two basic questions that began the research. First, what was it like to be a child in France during the Second World War? Second, how can we, as historians, get at that that experience "from the inside out"?[1] I take this to mean an attempt to access the internal perspective of the historical actors, more than a description of their external worlds. These questions derive from an ideological positioning: as an oral historian—not just a historian who sometimes uses oral (spoken) sources—I have a long-standing interest in histories from below. By that I mean the histories of populations who struggle to exist in traditional history writing as subjects in their own lives. I consider children, given their relationship to (adult) power, to be a population of this kind.[2] Second, I am interested in methodologies that not only reveal historical actors as agents but also enable their participation, to some degree, in constructing histories of the times they lived through. In my case, this occurs to a lesser degree than in some coproduced research, but it rests on including and valuing the interviewees' own interpretations alongside my own. Third, I am convinced of the importance of everyday life as central to human experience as the site where agency is enacted. Thus, I am interested in the re-creation of past lived experience not just because I am curious about how other people lived in general terms, but because under-standing the other is imperative to constructing inclusive, progressive societies.

Oral history is well suited to thinking about children's everyday lives and the lifeworlds of ordinary (nonelite) people and to engaging with sites of agency, past and present. I do not balk at the word *ordinary* to describe nonelite people.[3] *Ordinary* may well mean lacking in distinctive features, or somehow normal. This could appear to quash individual differences, diminish personal achievements, and endorse a currency of normativity that could become hegemonic or other-wise exclusionary. This is far from the intention of this book, as will become apparent. The meaning I give to *ordinary* recognizes as a normal condition of humanity both the wide-ranging differences in subject positions that people inhabit, in multiple and shifting combinations, and the existence of highly individuated subjectivities. My emphasis lies in their quality of being nonelite. The term *ordinary* thus enables us to gather all sorts of people together who may have little else in common except that they are unlikely to be indexed in standard history books, have encyclopedia entries in their names, or be known beyond the circles of family, profession, and pastime. By lack of distinction I mean that they were not individually responsible for the kind of decision making that shifts national destinies, not that they are indistinguishable from one another or lack distinction in their own spheres of achievement.

All history, as Keith Jenkins has argued, is a question of ideology, epistemology, and methodology.[4] My two research questions were not just determined by an ideological position; they generated the epistemological basis of my research (what I seek to know) and suggested the methodological imperatives (how I can know it). "What was it like to be a child" raises three issues. First, that of the *child*: children are typically defined by age although, as has been well established in childhood studies, the category "child" is culturally determined.[5] However, for the purposes of this study, I have confined myself to people who were fourteen years old and younger during the period of the Second World War. In theory, then, the eldest could have been born in late 1924 to still be fourteen years old in September 1939 when war broke out. I did not set a lower age limit, but interviewees needed to have memories of the period. A couple of the interviewees remember the war only as flashes from their toddler years. I was keen not to get mired in questions of age, which is something of a red herring in terms of experience. Two seven-year-olds may have less in common with each other than a seven-year-old does with a child five years her senior, depending on circumstances such as position in the sibling line, social class, cultural background, historical circumstances, generation, and so on. The second issue is *a child*: which child or children am I writing about? My interest here was not some children or all children but *any* children. I sought variety. I did not want a sample overdetermined as representative according to impersonal criteria; this would have involved discarding some of the precious memory stories. *Any* children provided scope for the scattering of situations that I expected to lead to a broad range. Indeed, this corpus of stories does cover a range of ages, localities, and situations: children in the country, in towns, and in cities; children in Occupied France and the Free Zone; children separated from families or with them; children well off or poor; Jewish children persecuted, hunted, or hidden; some children orphaned, some bombed. There are stories of children playing, working, eating, thinking, doing, and feeling.

The third issue, raised by the question "What was it like," concerns the exploration of qualitative experience. Mark Salber Phillips notes that the question "What was it like," when asked of the past, may be seen by "serious" historians as a "layman's question." Historians should rather ask things like: How did a particular phenomenon change over time? What continuities exist across or between periods or places? What was the effect of such and such events on such and such objects (e.g., people, policies) and vice versa? What factors in the social or cultural or political or economic landscape produced outcome x or y? These structural questions are the stock-in-trade of the professional historian. "What was it like" seeks something different. Phillips notes that some historians have more recently become interested in these ideas. Events and explanations, he says, have given way "somewhat" to a kind of "intimate anthropology" of other times.[6] Thoughts, feelings, physical sensations, and the objects, practices, and textures of everyday life have come into the picture, often via interdisciplinary frameworks. "What was it like" seeks experience: it is phenomenological. It is an "articulation of the realm of 'how one lives' " on the day-to-day plane; how we "move across . . . relationships . . . , where you can move and make new connections, what matters and in what ways."[7] This question therefore derives from my interest in the preoccupations of children's daily lives in practical, relational, spatial, and affective ways, in the ordinary and the extraordinary dimensions of life in war, and in the multiplicity of standpoints such a question presupposes.

The second research question asked how historians can get at childhood experience in the past "from the inside out."[8] It is an epistemological question: How can we—or, indeed, can we—know what it was like to have been a child in wartime France? We could seek knowledge of the experience reflected in the documentary evidence stacked in archives about children and childhood: school records, health records, and so on. But I am more interested the idea of "from the inside out"—that is, deriving from somewhere inside the bodies or minds of the historical actors. One point of access might be the relatively uncommon written or paper sources created by children in the past: children's letters, drawings, and diaries. These are rare, selective, interesting, and valuable, although they, too, do not give unmediated access to children's perspectives, and they generate their own biases.[9] A second point of access might be retrospective subjective sources, either written memoirs or, as in my case, oral histories or memory stories. Again, neither brings unmediated access to children's perspectives, but they are at least "from the inside out." Oral histories—recorded spoken autobiographical narratives about past experience, which I choose to call memory stories in order to emphasize both their remembered and their storied dimensions—always contain unknowable modifications layered over time. I wanted to explore the relation between the adult and child selves in terms of how memories are recounted, to recognize explicitly that the adult tells of a past that is distant in both time and person and simultaneously and unreservedly intimate and proximate to the teller. Here lies the potential for deeper reflection on the intersections between individual and collective memory. How, then, do these adult-told memory stories help us perceive children's experiences in the past? It is probably impossible to hear the voice of the child in these accounts, but is there another way in which they help us access the child's past?[10] What kinds of experience can they help us understand? What characterizes these kinds of memories and the ways they are narrated?[11]

On one level it is, of course, impossible to *know* what happened in the past, just as it is impossible to *know* another's experience "from the inside." Any response is an approximation. However, using these spoken autobiographical narratives as a source of knowledge provides insight into varieties of experience in the past and, importantly, the present too because of the nature of memory. What distinguishes history, typically, is that it deals with what is finished. It is told in the past tense. But oral history leads us toward the kind of history that "is concerned with the present as much as with the past and with mediating between these two."[12] In Hayden White's words, this poses a "historiological problem quite different from that stemming from an interest in 'what happened' in some local domain of the past."[13] Memory stymies the past-present divide as it is only ever partly about "what happened." Owain Jones writes of memory, indeed, that it is "not about the past." He describes it instead as "a fantastically complex entanglement . . . intimately entwined with space, affect, emotion, imagination and identity."[14] So instead of asking these memories to tell me what happened—because they are unsuited to responding—I am keener to ask of them, Which kinds of thing can you tell me? What do you do? What actions do you perform, as memories? What are you made of? What constitutes you? How do you form and change?[15] I answer not as a cognitive or cultural psychologist, a neuropsychologist, a psychoanalyst, or a sociologist but as a historian.

THIS BOOK IS MADE OF MEMORIES

The memory stories used to write this book are an explicitly heterogenous sample. They are drawn from archival collections recorded at different times, by different agencies, with different motivations. They have different emphases, different patterns of questioning, and different outcomes. They are, in scholarly terms, of wildly differing quality. What is the advantage of working with such a sample? Would it not facilitate rigorous, comparative analysis if some of the variables were removed? Perhaps. But from the perspective of what I seek to do, such restriction raises two concerns.

First, a restricted sample would be less likely to expose variety. Contingency and heterogeneity open possibilities.[16] When memory stories are poorly managed by the interviewer, recorded haphazardly, or archived without context, what new analytic opportunities emerge? What becomes visible that a tightly controlled interviewing and archiving process conceals? The testimonies of perspective, of political shaping, of cultural norms are there in the stories. An intricate dance between interviewee, interviewer, archive, listener, environment, moment, and so on produces *something* each time, generating story and context.[17] A heterogenous corpus is thus a rich source of knowledge about how remembering happens.

Second, imposing limitations on the sample by controlling its sources is an expedient act rather than a faithful one. Given the logical impossibility of hearing the memory story of every person who was a child in France during the Second World War, all choices to restrict the sample are arbitrary ones; they work to "impress [themselves] on a wiggling world like a snap-on grid of shape-setting interpretability."[18] To put it another way, as Kathleen Stewart asks, where do we start, and where do we stop? There is no end and no beginning of such a sample: we will always be in the middle of it.[19] As we are in the middle, we can scoop anywhere, pond-dipping for memories. The next scoop would reveal a different set of creatures, in a different configuration, going about the business of living; another scoop would be different again. But each scoop is a sample that is revelatory, varied, wriggling with life, and, in its way, part of a whole.

Such a heterogenous set of memory stories sheds light on the "complex ecologies of memory (and forgetting)" around the French wartime past.[20] Memories are created through interactions between people, events, institutions, discourses, objects, environments, temporalities, and more; as Maurice Halbwachs and many others show us, memories are inescapably social constructions. Shining a light into how and why they are constructed in this or that way, rather than directly at them, is one of the possibilities this sample opens. Another possibility is a response to Hirsch and Spitzer's call for a "broadened . . . archive of memory" in the face of exclusive and competitive memorial landscapes.[21] Their concerns relate specifically to the repurposing of memories of Holocaust suffering for nationalist ends through discourses of uniqueness and exceptionalism, rather than recognizing what is held in common among humans who suffer.[22]

I relate this to my work in two ways. First, it was my desire not to put trauma front and center of this study. Such an emphasis may suggest that only traumatized children have a history, which is simply not the case. At the same time, it both overvalues and devalues trauma. Time and again, these memory stories reveal functional adults who nonetheless experienced potentially traumatizing events—persecution, bereavement, violence, family separation, conflict, fear—in their childhoods but who do not see themselves as victims. They reveal individuals capable of relativizing their own sufferings in relation to those of others and capable of sharing sympathy and empathy.

Second, I did not want to separate Jewish experience. Jewish people were living and still live in French society as part of a broader population—some of which is and was hostile, much of which was and is not. Jewish children's experiences took place inside a complex web of interpersonal, family, and social interactions and are explicitly heterogenous.[23] Although Jewish narratives relate experiences that non-Jewish narratives do not, they also contain much that is shared, even if differently inflected. Taking inspiration from Spinoza, Gregg and Seigworth write that we should not attempt "the generic figuring of 'the body' (any body), but, much more singularly, [endeavor] to configure *a* body . . . , its ongoing affectual composition of *a* world, the *this-ness* of a world and a body."[24] So while any child mattered in terms of the sample, what emerged from the stories was the very *thisness* of each child's life, circumstances, struggles, responses, options, and ideas.

Putting Jewish children's experience alongside non-Jewish children's may run the risk of being seen to seek equivalence, relativize, or do away with difference. However, my purpose here is to lay experiences side by side, not directly to compare or to impose a hierarchy. It will be clear to the reader that Jewish children were persecuted by the French State and by individuals in specific ways because they were Jewish, and that they suffered shocking forms of maltreatment that shaped their lives thereafter. Experience and later knowledge of the scale of murder and brutality reflect back through the memory stories as they are told. I hope it will also be clear that there are intersections with non-Jewish children's experience, however—for example, living through certain national events (the invasion of 1940 or the liberation of 1944), becoming refugees, or being bereaved. These experiences need not be viewed as the same, but they forge points of connection rather than continuing to separate and, indeed, emphasize the unknowability of the other.

The corpus of interviews comprises 120 people and is detailed in the appendix. All interviews were recorded in French, and all translations are mine. Fifty-two of their stories were recorded by me. After writing to around two hundred municipal and departmental archives in France to inquire whether they had holdings of recorded interviews with people about their wartime childhoods, I identified an accessible route that would optimize my access to these. By no means did all two hundred archives respond, and the majority did not have oral history holdings of the kind I needed. Others put me in contact with regional and local museums, memory associations, and individuals who could help. The corpus comes, then, from the departmental archives of Seine-Saint-Denis, the Val-de-Marne, the Meuse, and Saône-et-Loire; the municipal archives of Beaune, Sète, and Dunkerque; Rails et Histoire (the Association pour l'histoire des chemins de fer, AHICF, the railway history association); the association Le Son des Choses, operating in the regions of Champagne and Ardennes; and the Centre d'Histoire de la Résistance et de la Déportation (CHRD) in Lyon.[25] Together, these interviews describe childhoods lived out in a wide range of geographical locations. Of the eighty-seven metropolitan French departments in 1939, nearly 40 percent are represented in the memory stories: Ain, Aisne, Alpes-Maritimes, Aube, Bouches-du-Rhône, Côte-d'Or, Côtes d'Armor, Cher, Creuse, Dordogne, Eure-et-Loir, Finistère, Gironde, Haute-Vienne, Hérault, Ile-et-Vilaine, Indre, Isère, Loiret, Marne, Mayenne, Meuse, Morbihan, Nord, Pas-de-Calais, Rhône, Saône-et-Loire, Sarthe, Seine (encompassing all of the Paris region), Seine-et-Oise, Somme, Yonne, and Vosges. Not well represented are the southwest of the country and the Normandy coast, a reflection of the practicalities of my collection process.[26] The motivations for which these archived oral histories were recorded are not always known or shared with visiting researchers, but they can sometimes be detected from the kind of institution, certain characteristics of the interviewees, or the type of questioning. All interviews used were archived with permission given by the interviewees at the time for their full names to be used, except in cases where I have used abbreviations or pseudonyms. Naming is a fundamental part of oral history practice, in contrast to other disciplines where anonymization is required. Many oral historians see anonymization as a form of erasure and problematic in terms of power, ownership, identity, and representation.[27]

My own interviews in 2009 were tightly focused on the Allied bombing of France, particularly around the city of Lille, the Paris suburb of Boulogne-Billancourt, and the Breton port of Brest.[28] Interviewees spoke, however, about far more than bombing; bombing was my focus, not theirs. One of the intentions behind this book has been to do justice to the wider shape of their wartime lives, which my 2016 book *French Children Under the Allied Bombs* could not. My 2009 interviews followed a semistructured set of questions, lasting between 45 and 120 minutes; they were recorded digitally in interviewees' homes, fully transcribed, and archived in France. My interviews in 2016–2018 were nominally about child evacuees from Paris to the Creuse department in central France. However, I ended up gathering far more than that, such as the stories of child refugees (not evacuees) and of rural children in whose homes the Parisian evacuees were billeted. These interviews were much more loosely structured, given that the stories were more heterogenous to begin with. I also wanted the interviewees to have more freedom to develop their narratives rather than following a structure imposed by my research requirements, as had been the case in 2009. Most were more than an hour long but not more than two hours; they were recorded in interviewees' homes or second homes, conversational, loose, and generally rather relaxed affairs. More of my own interview practice will emerge across the book, particularly in part 3, "Memories Told." Suffice to say here that I hesitate to ascribe any consistent or rigorous methodological technique to my interviewing. Such an attribution would only be a post hoc stance for the sake of form, as my lived experience of interviewing is highly variable and influenced by circumstance.

The archived interviews collected across France also varied widely in how they were structured. One of the freest groups of interviews—that is, those that seemed not to have a pointed agenda, save the recording of experiences of war in a particular region—came from Julien Rocipon's interviews for Le Son des Choses. His questions probe but do not direct, he is clearly interested in anything the interviewee can tell him, and there is a consistency to his practice. The interviews from the AHICF are similarly well structured, formed, and particularly well and comprehensively archived. Everyone interviewed by that association had or has a connection to the railways, either as a child of railway workers, a railway employee in later life, or someone with a particular railway story to relate. The stories recorded by, or simply archived by, the two Paris-region archives used here—Seine-Saint-Denis (these were video recordings) and Val-de-Marne (which has a comprehensive oral history collection and archiving practice)—included a lot of Jewish children, although the Val-de-Marne did not hold only Jewish stories. The collections of stories I encountered in Beaune and Saone-et-Loire were more motley: the archivists directed me toward anything they had that was within my scope of interest, which seemed to be the fruits of donations rather than of collecting campaigns. The set of materials I was given in the Meuse department was the result of a highly focused collection by a local historian about the working-class industrial community in the town of Sorcy. The VHS videos I was presented with at the CHRD concerned interviews with children of former resisters; however, the museum also held some others, notably a few related to the German massacre of Oradour-sur-Glane in June 1944. The Dordogne archives also has a collection of interviews with former resisters, which are very well contextualized and available online, but only two were relevant to me, the rest of the interviewees having been adults during the war. The town of Sète has also recorded some interviews and published them, edited but still useful, online. Sometimes, then, the interview contexts were very clear, and at other times they had to be inferred. This provides for a varied and diverse collection of memory stories.

The locations interviewees describe were urban and rural, coastal and inland, industrial and agricultural. Just over half of the sample were women. The oldest interviewee was born in 1924, being fourteen years old when the Second World War broke out. The youngest was born in 1941. Her memory story focuses on the continuing consequences of what she lived as a very small child after the war had ended. The birth years for the largest number of interviewees were 1930 (fourteen interviewees) and 1934 (thirteen), followed by 1928, 1929, and 1933 (each with ten). Members of the 1930 cohort were ten years old when France was defeated and fourteen (the end of their compulsory schooling) when France was liberated. In the 1934 cohort, children were six years old when France fell and ten years old at the liberation. The two groups correspond to an earlier childhood (the J1 group of Vichy's rationing system) and a middle childhood (the J2 ration group).[29] At least ten dates of birth were not recorded among the archived oral histories. The earliest interview was recorded in 1982 and the latest in 2017. Again, a number of interview dates were not stated in the archival records. However, the years in which the largest number of memory stories were recorded were 2009 (forty-five) and 2017 (seventeen). These were the main years of my own recording activity, but some other recordings swell the number in those two years. Otherwise, the recordings are scattered across the 2000s, with the 1990s and 1980s less well represented. Given that a number of birth dates and a number of interview dates are unknown, there is corresponding gap in knowing the age at which each person was interviewed. However, from what is known, the most common ages at which interviews were recorded were seventy-eight (thirteen people) and eighty (twelve people). The youngest person was fifty years old when her story was recorded. Twelve people were in their fifties or sixties, forty-seven were in their seventies, and thirty-seven were in their eighties.

AN AFFECTIVE METHODOLOGY

In 2018, Alistair Thomson noted that "oral historians have been doing histories of emotions for decades, though often without using that label."[30] His comment can be extended to encompass more than emotion. Indeed, while specific works in the field of affect studies are only rarely cited, the modern practice of oral history is saturated with affect. Alessandro Portelli's *The Death of Luigi Trastulli*, one of oral history's most influential works, is packed with ideas familiar to scholars of affect. Portelli wrote of inconclusiveness, fluidity, slippery subjectivities, power, performativity, and possibility.[31] The modern practice of oral history emerged in the late twentieth century out of the "hidden histories" imperative of the preceding couple of decades, imbued with a poststructuralist spirit that focused attention on discourse, interpretation, and meaning. These two drives, the revelatory and the hermeneutic, seem to have nudged affect aside. Yet, as I suggest in this book, there is a case to make for bringing it into better focus, not least because of the different questions it enables us to ask and answer.

The postwar generation of oral historians sought to make visible the people and practices that written archives obscure or omit. Theirs was a project of documenting social movements and exploring the lives of people marginalized by traditional historical practices. Oral history owes much to women's history. Feminist scholars and activists of the 1970s and '80s brought women's experiences into the light in ways that "empowered both us and our narrators."[32] Their revelatory aims and documentary practices aligned with those of gay and lesbian oral historians/activists, working-class and labor oral historians/activists, and historians/activists of Black and minoritized ethnic groups. This research was necessarily broadly positivistic, adapting social scientific methodologies, creating records—often collaboratively—to render people visible and voices heard, claiming for and with them the right to exist. Simultaneously, oral history claimed its own right to exist. Many of these earlier aims endure in the work of contemporary scholar/activists, as does their rigor.

Yet as a postpositivist practice of oral history emerged,[33] the scrupulous attention given to, say, women's words seemed to some to be compromised by the poststructuralist move away from documenting experience to thinking about, say, gender discourse as it filtered through oral history interviews. Marginalized subjects seemed, once again, to be written about rather than speaking on their own terms.[34] "Sharing authority" with interviewees over the interpretation of their words thus became a frequent goal.[35] Other scholars argued that discourse was fundamental in shaping how lives were lived and thus a necessary component of analysis.[36] It is in this sense telling that Sherna Berger Gluck and Daphne Patai's foundational text *Women's Words: The Feminist Practice of Oral History* has inspired, more recently, the volume *Beyond Women's Words*, echoing a shift in thinking that now reaches more explicitly beyond language and discourse to take in embodiment and, to a degree, affect.[37]

More recent scholarship takes things further in different ways. For queer oral history, for example, the stakes are different. As those earlier generations fought to make their methodology legitimate, the "renegade" quality of their work faded.[38] They built a canon and codes of practice, occupied positions of scholarly power, and even argued that oral history had "lost its radical edge."[39] But perhaps what is radical has changed. Normative oral history practices can and perhaps should be challenged, with a health warning: it may involve theory! Queer oral history needs to be renegade; it needs to be nonnormative and combative. It may be queer in content, in method, or both. It rejects canonical thinking and respectability. It circles back to earlier feminist epistemologies, questioning "knowability," subject-object relations, and disciplinary norms and "emphasizing epistemologies and performativities that are often ongoing and incomplete."[40] In fact, it may well be affect that makes queer oral history both radical and renegade. Affect is central to current, innovative, embodied oral history practices and necessitates deviant methodological practices because it cannot be recorded, archived, documented, or analyzed in conventional ways.[41] Much oral history still operates in the revelatory mode, and why not? Plenty of lives remain silenced by archives. But as affect is not *there* in a conventional, ontological sense, a hidden-histories approach may struggle to engage with it.

Despite interest in the "wider range of emotional evidence" offered by oral sources in comparison to written ones,[42] oral historians have tended to stick with what is "narratively structured and organized"; "emotion is," writes Jenny Harding, "more amenable to analysis" than affect.[43] The concern with finding meaning in discourse, narrative, and language endures in much oral history research—again, why not?—but often restricts the analysis of feeling in oral history to history-of-emotions territory: tracing representations or systems of emotion and evaluating emotional expression.[44] It may be that oral history has struggled to incorporate insights from affect studies because of the imperative to extrapolate meaning from language. Some scholars have certainly taken an interest in the extralinguistic dimensions of oral history practices,[45] and embodiment has come into the frame in more recent years.[46] But much discussion of feeling in interviews still belongs more properly in the realm of the linguistic and hermeneutic than the affective. I will use part 1, "Memories Felt," to elaborate the wider range of embodied, sensory, emotive, and affective territory—what I call the felt realm—that oral history can be used to explore.

Oral history has long placed intersubjectivity close to the heart of its methodological and interpretive endeavors. Once again, it is surprising that the literature of affect, then, has not had a more prominent place in oral historians' thinking. Affect is implicated in all oral history works dealing with the intersubjectivity of the interview encounter but is rarely tackled explicitly. Representational interpretive paradigms—including those that do not go "beyond [the] recitation of our positionalities and their epistemic limitations"[47]—may struggle to account for the fleeting, contingent, interaffective impulses emerging, dissipating, and affecting in unknowable ways the context and content of interviews. Across the four main parts of this book, and particularly part 3, "Memories Told," I suggest a complex set of interaffective drives surrounding the interviews of this corpus that may involve the subjectivities of those involved but are not determined by them; I sketch a larger web of affective impulses acting on those subjectivities but also alongside, around, and beyond them. Acknowledging interaffectivity, rather than just intersubjectivity, allows interviews recorded by me and those recorded by others to sit side by side and not be treated as different kinds of analytical objects.

Interest in issues surrounding the reuse of oral history interviews recorded by others has been growing over the past twenty or so years, and this book offers a contribution to this discussion.[48] Every set of interviews generates an archive that can be exploited as a resource—a resource for thinking about history, memory, local identity, folklore, language, social relations, and so on—later down the line. However, particular anxieties have been raised over the unknowability of the context in which the interviews were recorded. This precludes an examination of the intersubjective relationship that was at the heart of early oral historians' analyses and thus seems to limit their reuse. As far back as 1990, Ron Grele reflected on the reuse of some of his interviews by someone else and on that person's inability to know his motivations, his ideological positioning, or the intersubjective dynamics he was experiencing while interviewing.[49] Undoubtedly, there are epistemological blind spots, as indeed there are for historians with the vast majority of sources: it is all but impossible for a historian to know the exact circumstances in which a written source came into being. An informed inference can be made from the nature of the document and its content, but this is not the same as knowledge. A set of minutes may reflect the input and outcomes of a meeting and perhaps some of the contributions, but it may hide as much as it reveals. Even when the interviewer does know what those circumstances were, what his or her positioning was, or what his or her experience was before, during, and after the interview, how often does that kind of highly reflexive, highly personal material make it into published analysis? The oral historians Joanna Bornat and Graham Smith have both engaged with questions of reuse; both strongly counter the claim that only those involved in the initial collection can understand the context sufficiently to interpret it.[50] Indeed, Bornat speaks highly of the "rewards" of reuse, both of one's own interviews recorded at earlier moments for other purposes and of other people's interviews.[51] She remarks that while one trap is an overly critical perspective on another interviewer's practice, this itself is worth considering as a part of the cultural and social context around the interview. Jackson, Smith, and Olive agree, suggesting that some forms of analysis only become possible at a distance, in time and in person.[52] There is, they note, a "complex interplay" between interviewer, interviewee, and subsequent researchers, which is dialogical. Reading against the grain is common practice in text-based disciplines; it may well be that reuse of interviews activates a conscious listening against the grain and that this is where fruitful thinking can emerge.

Such listening against the grain forms part of the affective listening prac-tice central to my methodological engagement with these oral histories. Jodie Matthews found herself "leaning in" to passages of the gypsy and traveler oral histories she uses that make her feel ashamed.[53] She remarks that when her neck prickles, her skin flushes, and her discomfort becomes acute, she is forced to evaluate more carefully, and differently, the words of the interlocutors and, as a result, to reorient her research questions and conclusions. The researcher's feeling body is as much part of their interpretive toolkit as their thinking brain; indeed, the two are inseparable. My methodological approach to oral history interviews is likewise affective and subjective rather than quantitative or objective, relying on intensive and reflective listening practices. I must listen, sometimes I watch, but I cannot just read. Even when presented in an archive with an interview and its transcript, I make my own affective transcript. This differs from a transcript that might be archived with an interview because it is both incomplete—in terms of what was said—and subjectively overstocked with my thoughts, observations, feelings, and the interconnections between this interview and others I know. An affective transcript is not a record of the interview but a record of the listen-ing, specifically of *this* listening. By engaging intensively rather than extensively with oral history interviews, I learn from them. Part of the knowledge I gain is affective: it is not in the words or even in body language, vocal inflection, or ges-ture. The affective knowledge I gain emerges in an assemblage of past knowledge, encounters, experiences, people, places, discourses, moments, emotions, histo-ries, and interviews; and unfortunately for those who prefer to sport the emper-or's new clothes of scholarly objectivity, it can only be me who gains *this* affective knowledge; you would learn something else. While it is possible to engage with the affective landscape of an interview in all sorts of ways, I tend to avoid pro-cesses of coding and counting, probably influenced long ago by Portelli's remark that oral history reveals a "mosaic" that confounds the social scientist's prefig-ured "grid."[54] Such decisions are part of this affective methodology. They are dic-tated not by data but by preference.

Prior to embarking on this project, I had only worked with interviews I had recorded myself. However, I have found that using interviews conducted by others creates a new set of opportunities for thinking about how remembering happens, what is remembered, how memories are communicated, and how the listener engages with them. Listening to other people's interviews was as feeling laden as conducting my own: different feelings but by no means an objective, detached process. Reusing other people's interviews led me to understand my epistemological practice as both imaginative and affective. I engaged with the feelings that interviewees expressed in words and stories by imagining a person whose face I did not know; I heard street noises from open windows, bangles clanking, grandchildren playing in a nearby room. I heard the interviewer struggling to understand a complicated, disjointed story; I heard the interviewer getting it wrong, misunderstanding, as I have done. I heard microphones knocked about by flailing hands and emphatic gestures; I heard the chest thumped as a deeply felt point was made; I heard the gulps, the swallows, the quivers of emotion in voices that cracked and recovered themselves. In those situations, I also felt the uneasiness of the interviewer who had caused distress: I knew it because I had experienced it. I imagined people in rooms talking together; I was taken by their words into the past places they recounted, introduced to their friends and family, and I tried to understand their joy and pain. As an interviewer myself, I engaged with the other interviewer. Inevitably, at times I was frustrated by poorly formed questions and angered as children's perspectives were dismissed, but at other times I marveled at the patient drawing out of thoughts, at what was comprehensible to them but not to me, and at the subtle cues that encouraged speakers to develop their stories. Listening from the outside provides the opportunity to think about how and why interviewers stick to well-trodden ground in choosing interviewees or question strategies: it allows us to see how dominant versions of the past are constructed and preserved in sound archives and to listen for the ways that memories chime or clash with what interviewers seem to seek. The anxieties over the reuse of interviewing focus on what is lost by not being *there* but forget to look directly at what the listener gains by being, actively, *here*.[55]

My interpretation is my work as a historian. But in interpreting these stories, both against the grain and faced with all sorts of unknowns, I have to be comfortable not only with uncertainty and the recognition that I make only one interpretation among any number that are possible, but that my interpretation may not accord with one that the interviewee might make. I am not interested in whether the memory stories match up tidily with a past that actually happened because I know that the past that interests me has no trace against which I could verify the memory. Where would be the record of what a little boy's mother told him as he boarded the evacuee train so I could check whether the man told me the truth? I might find a record to say that he boarded the train, but that would be all. Where would I find the record of the awe felt by a little girl as the German troops passed her window? I might find a record to say that the German troops passed by, but that would be all. Where would I find a record of the dinner the family ate, the bed the child slept in, the shoes she wore? I might find records of other families' dinners described, other families' furniture, other children's shoes, but not these.

These are memories and these are stories, but that does not make them untrue. Truth, though, is the wrong standard by which to judge them. The interviewee Henri Buc said to me of his own memories, "I would not accept them from anyone else without archives, not for science. . . . I would want just the hard facts, so far as I could find them, and an ideology underneath which wasn't my own." A scientist, he recognized the paradox in what he was doing: he wanted hard, confident facts, and critical distance. His own subjectivity and the vagaries of his memory troubled him in his interpretation of his own past. Can we imagine a history without hard facts, where every statement is a possibility, an interpretation, one among many? Historians use all sorts of strong, rigorous, and creative methods to turn "this is what might have happened" into "this is what must have happened"; on certain matters they can assuredly get to "this is what happened," but not all. This study is not history in the realist mode; it is history in the impressionist mode, filtered through multiple subjectivities, suggestive, fleeting, and self-aware. The memory stories have allowed me to learn the things that 120 people sought, in very specific circumstances, to communicate about their childhoods. These things may or may not have happened in quite that way, but they have been told that way in good faith and represent a set of truths about how an individual remembers his or her past. They are the remembering of the past, not the past itself. And they are not just about the past. In the words of Owain Jones, they are "living landscapes seen obliquely from an always moving viewpoint of on-going life."[56] As such, establishing a static, fixed, whole truth is less interesting to me than tracing memories' movement, their configuration, and their relationality.

FOUR PARTS

The four parts of this book are structured thematically around aspects of remembering that have emerged from the oral narratives: "Memories Felt," "Memories Located," "Memories Told," and "Memories Lived." These were chosen for their flexibility and for their ability to cut across particularities of individual lives, to include all speakers, and to raise to prominence certain areas of stickiness, accretion, and intensity among the hundreds of singular incidents communicated by the rememberers. These categories enable me to respond to these questions: "What kinds of thing can you, memories, tell me?" "What do you do?" "What are you made of?" There are also ten moments of pause across the book. These provide an opportunity to focus on part of a particular person's memory and to explore a theme or idea in greater detail.

An initial chapter sets out the theoretical positioning that underpins the four main parts of the book. Readers who do not wish to begin with theory could skip this chapter and return to it later if desired. Indeed, as the book does not provide a chronological narrative, the chapters could feasibly be read in any order. The "Positioning" chapter lays out my thinking in relation to affect and its scholarship. Drawing on Sara Ahmed's ideas about feeling as a driver of action, I first remark on my turning away from conventional historical analysis and writing. I consider why and how work in memory studies, the history of memory, and the politics of commemoration seemed inadequate for my analysis of these memory stories and what I desired in constructing a different framework. I then indicate where I turned instead. First, I take a less conclusive, more open-ended position that recognizes the unknowability of the past and does not seek to master or dominate past people. Second, prompted by the affective qualities of the memory stories, I lay out my working usage of the terms *emotion*, *affect*, and *feeling* and argue for attention to be paid to the emotions of history. Third, I introduce the idea of assemblage thinking to conceptualize history and oral history. I suggest three temporal planes comprising the oral history event—the happening past, the memory story, and the listening encounter—and position them in a useful framework that holds in tension the commingling of diverse objects (people, memories, discourses, material objects, environments, emotions, ideas, events, and so on), the contingency of experience, the multitemporality of memory work, and a politics of affect that values and devalues certain versions of the past.

Part 1, "Memories Felt," establishes a central premise of this book: that memories are made of feeling. Things are remembered because they are felt, and conveying a memory is an attempt to convey a state of feeling. I argue that feeling sticks: it sticks to memories, it sticks memories together, and it sticks memories down. Chapter 1, "Articulated Feeling," analyzes the expression of feeling something in the memory narratives. It is divided into the sharing of past sensations and the sharing of emotions, including emotions in the past and emotions experienced later about the past, emotions embodied during the telling, and the pondering of absent emotions. Chapter 2, "Affects and Intensities," looks at the kinds of feeling that are not explicitly articulated through emotives but that can still be perceived: language is only part of the expressive toolkit here. This is achieved first by attending to the ways memories form, circulate, and disperse in the recounting of the event and what brings them to the point of utterance. I then look at the deepening intensities of feeling around particular kinds of experience that emerge as shocking, frightening, or shaming. These emotions are not articulated explicitly, but the form of their communication permits us to understand them as present. I pause on two memory stories in particular to explore aspects of "Memories Felt" in more detail. Daniel Berland's description of his family's participation in the civilian exodus of 1940 is a powerfully multi-sensory, mobile story of visual, haptic, and proprioceptive feeling, deeply underpinned by fear. These terms are specific and will be explained. Nicole Kahn's account of her imprisonment in Drancy internment camp (Paris) illustrates peaks of extraordinarily felt intensity that rise above her more generalized recollections of her life in the camp.

Part 2, "Memories Located," explores the interconnectedness of the spatial, the temporal, and the traumatic. Geographer Owain Jones has written that "memories are spatially and temporally complex, or even weird." He notes the "twisting of space time" in memory, which, I continue, results in processes of scrambling, stretching, and magnifying.[57] Chapter 3 pulls apart the weirdness of memory time within oral accounts of traumatic experience. It looks first at moments acting as pivots on which lives are made and unmade and at the way time freezes in memory stories at moments of particularly strong intensity. Then it explores nonlinear, nonchronological time inside memory stories, such as how time slows down and speeds up, how it can bounce or shuttle across temporal planes, and how it stretches out into futures as yet unlived. Chapter 4 considers place in relation to trauma and the affective intensity of the place where something (bad) happened; this might be narrated as the place of *my* trauma (the rememberer's), or the place of *their* trauma (someone else's suffering). Chapter 5 brings together ideas of space and trauma. I look first at the body's positioning in space and the tactile, haptic, and mobile qualities of being-in-space in traumatic circumstances. I then consider space as freedom and space as constraint, space occupied by others, and the ways in which safe spaces were understood and are remembered. There are two pauses. Nancette Blanchou's memories of happy people, happy places, happy times on her family farm before the arrest of her parents exist on one side of a pivot, weighed down on the other by memories of later violence. Hélène Zytnicki's harrowing account of her time in hellish places—the Vélodrome d'Hiver, Beaune-la-Rolande camp, and Drancy camp—demonstrates the corporality of anti-Semitic persecution bearing down on her body in space as pressure, confinement, and denial.

Part 3, "Memories Told," focuses on the realm of the transactive and the dialogical, examining the circulation of memory stories among people and across groups of people. It is well established that memories are situated socially and are shared, blended, shaped, resisted, and prohibited in dialogue with discourses, ideas, and other people.[58] Here I seek to broaden out from two knowable subjectivities in the interview space to encompass the wash of interaffectivity flowing across a mnemonic network. Chapter 6 considers memory stories in relation to the (vertical) regimes of memory in which they are told. Grossberg notes that "regimes of discourse" constitute the way we live our lives; they may or may not overtly direct what it is possible to think, say, or remember, but they establish the possibilities of expression in particular directions; they are affective regimes, or regimes of feeling. I look at the ways rememberers' stories resonate with regimes of memory and the more abundant ways in which they are dissonant. Chapter 7 looks at (horizontal) communities of memory (which are also affective communities, communities of feeling) and at how affective flows within them shape remembering. I consider here the transactive remembering between generational peers, as well as those considered peers, such as other child victims of war. I also look at the interaction across the divide between interviewer and interviewee and conclude with a discussion of distant transactive remembering beyond the interview space with audiences real and imagined. Part 3 includes two moments of pause: First, Jean and Édith Denhez illustrate the flexing and mirroring of memory as it is told between individuals who are generational peers and a married couple. Second, the formal and filmed interview with Marie-Madeleine Viguié-Moreau gives an example of an interviewer's agenda at odds with a story.

Part 4, "Memories Lived," deals directly with the realm of the everyday. It uses ordinary and extraordinary experiences to show how the world thrusts itself into people's lives and how they insert themselves into that world. Chapter 8 examines the materialities of children's everyday lives in relation to eating, wearing, playing, and learning, illustrating how and where memories stick to objects and activities, all of them saturated by the war. Chapter 9 considers affective others—mothers, fathers, Germans, and so on—in everyday life in relation to expressions of love and aversion. Finally, chapter 10 shows how memories accrete around particular events of national importance, usually because of their place in dominant regimes of memory. Thus, the big events of 1939/40 and 1944/45 are prominent but are characteristically remembered as little worlds of sensory and affective experience lived in the spaces and places of children's daily lives. Three pauses punctuate part 4: First, Henry Buc explores the evolution of the war games he and his friends played, conveying the boys' taste for adventure but also the dangers of an encroaching war. Second, Danièle Dubowsky reflects on her mother's enormous courage and presence of mind when conducting her three young children through arrest, internment, and a journey to Palestine; this strained mother's strength, however, had its limits. Finally, Robert Bernier's discussion of his father's clandestine slaughterhouse illustrates the contingency of moral meaning in the peculiar atmosphere of wartime France. Robert's story shows the ways in which the meanings of resistance and collaboration were and are continually defined and redefined.

PAUSE—ANNE-MARIE AND HER FATHER

Anne-Marie Laurens, whose account of her railway-worker father's resistance activity was recorded by the AHICF in 2012, is the first of the pauses that act as focused interludes across this book. Anne-Marie's memory story illustrates how the main themes of each of the four parts interlock: memories felt, memories located, memories told, and memories lived are not discrete categories. It gives insight into the sensations and emotions expressed by Anne-Marie about her father; it locates her memories of him in space and time, including their last goodbye; it illustrates how her memories are recounted in dialogue with a public regime of memory which she feels compelled to rebuff; and it feeds into our understanding of a child's contingent, wartime everyday life, shaped by material needs, affective ties, and the events of war.

Anne-Marie was born in 1935 and lived with her parents and older sister in Châlons-sur-Marne (today, Châlons-en-Champagne, Marne), where her father was deputy stationmaster. During the civilian exodus of 1940, when frightened civilians fled the advancing Wehrmacht, the family was bombed on the road. Her father was injured and hospitalized. Once the family was reunited after the June Armistice, Anne-Marie spoke of his dedication to his work and what she later learned to be his resistance activity. During every air raid, he would leave his family and rush to the station. Archival documents situate the start of his resistance activities in March 1941, as part of Résistance-Fer that disrupted and sabotaged German supply lines and later the military information network Uranus, under the S. R. Kléber umbrella of French military secret service operations.[59] In 1944, Anne Marie's parents evacuated her to relatives in the countryside. She recalls her father arriving by bicycle one evening in August. He stayed briefly to rest but would not remain. Anne-Marie said goodbye and never saw him again. His resistance activity had been denounced. He was seized by the Gestapo, imprisoned, tortured, and deported, dying in Dachau on March 2, 1945. His family learned of his death in August 1945. It was Anne-Marie, age ten, who stepped forward to receive his posthumous medals.

The telling of Anne-Marie's memory story took place in a specific context, which becomes evident from remarks made toward the end of the interview. In 2008, the French television journalist Françoise Laborde published a book, some phrases of which railed against the 2007 railway strikes in defense of state pensions and retirement ages. Laborde wrote: "But nobody dares to recall that the trains of death which took Jews and resisters to the extermination camps were never held up by strikes and were always on time, all accounts settled up front by the Nazis. Without French trains, how could deportation have taken place?"[60] Laborde also claimed that railway workers' resistance activity had been exaggerated into myth by the French Communist Party.[61] The points are not unworthy of examination, but they wrongly castigate hundreds of people. There were strong objections to her caricatural invective and manipulation of the past to attack public-sector pensions. Her comments were part of a wider set of controversies touching the SNCF (the Société Nationale des Chemins de fer Français, the French national railway company) in the 2000s. In 2011, SNCF president Guillaume Pepy officially recognized his company's role in deporting Jews from France.[62] Laborde's words appear to have catalyzed Anne-Marie into action, so strong was her feeling that her father's life and resistance work were being discredited. She stated explicitly that she had agreed to be interviewed because of what had been said about the *cheminots* (railway workers) on television. She called Laborde's work "shameful" in its reduction of railway resistance to an instrument of communism and its characterization of resisters as "terrorists." She denounced these ideas as "lies" and as "scandalous." In indignation she cried: "Everything has been forgotten!" What, and by whom? Multitemporal connections, from the interview to Laborde to the communists to her father's resistance, intertwine and complicate what this story is about.

Anne-Marie's memory story is told from her perspective; it is her story and her childhood. From it, we learn plenty about children's everyday lives in wartime France. But a vertical regime of memory—public, authoritative, top-down—that acted to denigrate the railway resistance presses upon it at all times, squeezing and shaping its content. Feeling flows. Laborde and others were angry over protests to protect public-sector pensions; by invoking the Holocaust and the deportation of the Jews, she tapped into deep, wide, public feelings of shame, grief, and more anger; for descendants of railway resisters, proud of their parents, scarred by bereavement and the knowledge of torture, the response is also angry and indignant. Here I identify only a few obvious channels of affective circulation as they are suggested by the story; there are, of course, others. The motivation for telling a memory story publicly is not always known. But in this case it is, and this gives rise to certain strong emphases across the narrative.

The story is also dense with memories felt—with sensation and emotion. These reach particular intensity in relation to the suffering of the Jews and her father's compassion toward them. Anne-Marie uses these memories to counter the accusations that railway workers were complicit in deportation. She asserts her father's recognition of the injustice facing the Jews and describes a number of his actions to dissociate him from it, making her points with evidence. First, she describes the visual image of a vandalized synagogue: "the synagogue was in a terrible state. Everything that was glass had been smashed. The psalters were all over the floor." Her father had taken her there to teach her about injustice: "he explained to me what they were doing to the Jews." Second, she describes his emotional response to seeing trains of deportees: "I remember extremely clearly Dad, several times, he'd come home saying 'My God, if you could see those poor people,' I have a memory of it, the tears in his eyes." She repeated later: "he'd said to us 'those poor people, if you could see those poor people,' he had tears in his eyes as he spoke. That's an exact memory." She labels the memory not as general but as precise. Third, she presents the evidence that he collected letters dropped from the deportation trains and sent them onward to their destinations. She said "people replied to him. There, you see those documents, the two letters": proof is given to the interviewer. Finally, she gives the evidence that moves her to tears in the interview: the words of a former neighbor who telephoned her condolences when Anne-Marie's mother died. "You know, Annie," said the neighbor, "your dad was really someone quite extraordinary." She explained that Anne-Marie's father had alerted his neighbors to what he had seen but, she said, "people didn't believe it." Sensation and emotion are active inside the narrative, working to push blame away from her father.

We can also see the workings of space and time—memories located—inside the memory of her father's resistance work as seen from the perspective of the little girl, in two ways. The first is a time freeze on the moment Anne-Marie saw her father for the last time. The moment is remembered in detail; the telling of the story slows down, and she conveys, in tears, an active scene, people in places (the house, the table, the edge of the town), with important dialogue. She begins this part of the story in response to a question about whether she remembered the D-Day landings.

> But that, that was terrible, the American advance, the Allies, that was terrible; and there, I've told you the last memory I have of Dad, it was there, it was the summer, he came to see me, he came to see me at my uncle and aunt's, on his bike from Châlons. And he arrived exhausted, and I remember at the table, my uncle—this phrase has stayed with in my head, "Paul, you must stay. You mustn't leave. Paul, you mustn't leave," and Dad said "No, no, I have to go back." He left the same day, it was a hot day, that's certain, and he said to me, "Walk with me, come a little way," so I went with him, he was on his bike and I walked next to him. At the edge of the town, of Bar-sur-Seine, he kissed me, and he cried, and said to me "Goodbye." [She is in tears.] And, there you have it, I never saw him again.

As time freezes on this moment, the words "You mustn't leave" act as a window to other parts of her story. The narrative fabric is rubbed thin and links across time and place to other parts of story in which her father was called upon by his wife not to leave his family.

I suggest, then, that the second manifestation of space and time in her story comes through the repeated motif of her father's movement *away*. His presence—whether he was or was not there—is central in the memory story. Anne-Marie's memory of the declaration of war is characteristic: "we were on holiday together,

Dad was there, he must have also been holiday with us." Her memory of the 1940 civilian exodus too: "everyone fled onto the roads, my parents from Châlons, Dad was with us, my sister, Mum, we went to meet up with my uncle and aunt and my maternal grandmother in Bar-sur-Seine." But during the exodus, something changed. Anne-Marie recalled: "I have a very clear memory of a terrible air raid on the station in Bar-sur-Seine, where everyone was screaming. Mum covered me with her body [on the ground], my sister next to us, and Dad left us. I still have a very clear memory of Mum screaming: 'Paul, Paul, stay with us,' but he ran to help. . . . That was his first act of resistance." She immediately links this departure to his resistance: it must be justified. Later in the story, perhaps after 1943, as the Allies' bombers came down over Châlons: "As soon as we heard the planes coming—and this is a memory which I can never get out of my memory, out of my head—Dad would jump up, leave us. He'd say 'Quick, quick, get out,' and we'd leave the house, running to the fields away from our house. . . . And he'd get on his bike, he'd go to the station . . ., he'd say 'I have to get to my work.'" She describes another moment, her mother crying, calling, "But Paul, stay with us, stay with us." It is difficult for Anne-Marie to talk about this, despite the justification of his resistance work. She said: "Straight away he'd, he would always, straight away—, he'd leave straight away. He'd leave us frequently, yes, and that, perhaps, the atmosphere was a little bit bitter because Mum thought that he left us very often. There weren't any serious arguments. But [she is very hesitant], that, that, yes. He did often leave us." The story is wound around this movement away, a pattern of behavior that bore down on the family's life until one day he went away and did not come back.

Finally, the story is instructive in terms of how a child, *this* child, lived her everyday life in wartime France. Yet every part of this, too, is filtered through the memory of her father. Food shortages are at the heart of the French wartime experience. In Anne-Marie's story, described in some detail, her father, alongside his railway and resistance work, actively sought provisions. He grew vegetables, raised rabbits, cycled far and wide to get eggs and butter, made new soles for their shoes from old tires. A sensitive man, he struggled to kill the rabbits when he needed to. He would fall asleep at the table, and when he was arrested, his daughter said, "he was exhausted from having done so much." But his resistance took priority. Anne-Marie's relation with an affective other—the enemy German—is also recounted through this lens. She recalls seeing soldiers marching through the streets of her town: "I used to like to—, when I heard the singing I'd run to the window to look at them, but Dad made me stand back quickly." His prohibition suggested dangers; she read these too in his face when, at his workplace, a German railway worker approached her: "I remember the look of fury on Dad's face behind the German's back." This memory is recounted twice in the story: a look of fury that stuck. She also recounts an episode in which her father intervened when a German soldier was beating up a man in the street: "I begged him, I begged him, 'Dad, stop, stop!' Well, the German stopped too. Dad said to me afterwards, 'Don't tell your mother, don't tell your mother.'" Bound up in the anecdote are the chance happenings of everyday life in occupied France that a child, *any child*, might encounter—violence, unpredictability, victimization—as well as the consistency of her vision of her father and their father-daughter complicity. Anne-Marie mentions school a little. At her Catholic school the nuns told the girls "that we had to make sacrifices," a point mentioned, perhaps, because of the great sacrifice that her family (among others) had made but that Laborde (among others) was demeaning. The other memory of her schoolfriends she gives also relates directly to fathers: "There were lots of girls whose dads were prisoners [of war, in Germany]. That I remember, and particularly one girl, Thérèse D—, I really remember her because I remember that her father came back. Her joy. They came to find her at school to say her dad had just got home." A schoolroom scene: a little girl filled with happiness because her father had come home. It is no surprise that this event, among so many others that must have happened at school, is the sticky one.

The affective drives that animate Anne-Marie's story cannot be ignored. By tracing their routes through her words, we gain access to particular kinds of knowledge. Her father's work in the resistance and his death color every event and every activity she narrates. They lead her to talk about everyday life, the Germans, the 1940 exodus, the liberation, and the end of the war; they give us insight into how the Allied bombing and the French resistance interacted on the ground and how this was experienced inside a family. The story, then, serves as a way into understanding "public feelings that begin and end in broad circulation"—about nation, freedom, war, heroism, the Holocaust, guilt, pride, anger—but that "are also the stuff that seemingly intimate lives are made of."[63] Affect is an integral part of memory. Kaitlin Murphy writes that "although affects, and the structures of feeling that forge and feed them, are impalpable and operate 'beneath' and 'alongside' conscious knowing, they can nonetheless be impactful and enduring, shaping the way people experience their lives."[64] We do not need to know specifically what these affects are, and often we simply cannot. But our knowledge comes from spotting their ripples spreading on the surface or the foamy shape of their agitated wake. This book is made of memories. But it understands those memories not as static objects that wait, transparent and knowable, to be put to use, but as flowing and agential, suggestive of many things but always inconclusive.

POSITIONING

To be affected by something is to evaluate that thing. Evaluations are expressed in how bodies turn towards things. To give value to things is to shape what is near us. . . . To be more or less open to new things is to be more or less open to the incorporation of things into our near sphere. Incorporation may be conditional on liking what we encounter. Those things we do not like we move away from.[1]

Sara Ahmed's words refer here to our everyday practices and to the objects of our research interest if we study the everyday; but they can also refer to our research practices. In writing this book, I found myself drawing away from the vast body of research on the memory of the Second World War (in France), written by historians, historians of memory, and memory studies scholars, and toward an interdisciplinary set of writing that chimed better with my thinking as it arose from the memory stories I was working with. This reorientation was affective. I did not want to write top-down analyses of collective memory, cultural memory, political memory, social memory, where ordinary—mundane, everyday— memories rarely got a look and even the idea of "ordinary" was frowned upon; where hierarchies of value in relation to victimhood were critiqued but implicitly upheld by analysis; and where authoritative voices sought to master unruly historical subjects by flattening difference, categorizing things, and pulling them into conclusive patterns.

Interdisciplinary contacts opened my near sphere to a set of ideas from cultural studies, cultural geography, anthropology, film studies, archaeology, museum studies, and less structural forms of sociology that I found myself liking. This redefined my relation to the interviews, their content, and the potential for this research. Instead of being problems of historical method that risked being crushed by the weight of disciplinary norms, the interviews became "happy objects."[2] I found the tools to seek what I knew existed but did not feel I had the permission, or the language, as a historian to express: both the powerful and chimeric emotional charge that linked the past, the present, the story, the teller, and the listener and the exciting potentiality of contingent, unstable, and fleeting memories. One of the outcomes of this book is the emergence of a kind of affective historiography. This chapter outlines how that came about.

DISSATISFACTIONS

Paralyzing Doxas

The bibliography on history, memory, collective memory, and the Second World War, in France and elsewhere, is enormous. Yet notable is the near absence of work on French children's lives during this period.[3] This absence speaks of long-standing interpretive restrictions on analysis of the Vichy period and a tendency toward canonical thinking.[4] In 2011, the Australian historian Colin Nettelbeck wrote a sharp critique of "existing accounts [of the Vichy years which] have virtually excised" school-age children. Jewish children have received a certain amount of scholarly attention and form a part of wartime public historical representation and commemoration.[5] Yet this approach ignores the majority of school-age children. Restoring children to the nation's historical past "*must be done*," Nettelbeck urged, "if our understanding of the Vichy period is to have lasting credibility";[6] without them, our understanding will remain incomplete.

Much historical writing on wartime France operates through a "conflictual model," that is, "a narrative dominated by heroes, victims and perpetrators." Nettelbeck states that children's experiences are ignored because they are a "bad fit" with this model.[7] More recently, Pierre Laborie has written of the need to escape the dominant markers or indicators (*marqueurs*) that govern the recounting of this past, whether by historians or others. Such *marqueurs*—resistance, collaboration, persecution, deportation—have a preponderant weight in how the period is (re)constructed. They affect how we view historical protagonists (heroes, victims, perpetrators) and characterize the broader population as passive, *attentiste*, and therefore culpable. Work on the period, Laborie contends, is defined by where the historian positions him- or herself in relation to these *marqueurs*. He suggests the existence of a "paralysing doxa" created by historians and propagated more widely.[8] Michael Rothberg's recent work on "implicated subjects" allows for thinking outside the categories of victim/perpetrator; it begins a complex process of reconceptualizing how power is inhabited by wider populations who "play crucial, but indirect, roles in systems of domination and histories of harm."[9] Thinking about non-Jewish people, even children, in a perpetrator state such as Vichy France as implicated subjects further complicates notions of guilt and innocence, knowledge and ignorance. Rothberg recognizes variable "lines of connection" between victim and perpetrator groups. "No one is essentially an implicated subject," he writes; because events, people, and power are intertwined in complex ways, a person may be both implicated subject and victim.[10] To work alongside established frameworks is to ignore neither the importance of their content nor the erudition of their scholarship. As Elizabeth Adams St. Pierre notes, this is not a question of rejection but of "displac[ing] a structure to make room for something different."[11] It enables new holes to be bored into the past through which to glimpse action and meaning.

There is a continual return to certain orthodoxies in memory studies. The same names, like numbers on a bingo card, are called again and again; exemplary is the comment from the introduction of *Images et comportements sous l'Occupation* that references "the conceptual frameworks sketched out by Maurice Halbwachs, Pierre Nora, Paul Ricoeur, and, for the Second World War itself, by Henry Rousso."[12] Bingo. It is broadly understood, drawing on Henry Rousso's *Vichy Syndrome* schema, that war memory in France has passed through various stages. Using a psychoanalytic metaphor, Rousso describes them as an initial period of mourning following the compound traumas of defeat, occupation, and conflict, then repressions and "re-writing" the past as a history of heroic resistance, then a "broken mirror" in the early 1970s when France confronted its collaboration with the Nazis, followed by an "obsession" with French culpability for participation in the persecution and deportation of Jews.[13] This hegemonic process of memory building at a national level, with a counterhegemonic attack and then the disintegration of any "national" narrative into a multiplicity of claims to commemoration from various "identity groups," follows the dynamics of popular memory theory.[14] Such processes are "discovered," maintained, and reinforced by a historical scholarship that takes collective memory and its attendant commemorative practices and problems as being most worthy of study.[15] Insistence on the social, political, and thus collective character of memory binds scholarship to a focus on structure, institution, and transmission. Robert Gildea noted that for many years in France there was "no interest in the oral testimony of the individual, which is deemed partial and partisan" because historians have tended to "see themselves as constructing a universal and objective history."[16] Within this process, millions of personal experiences of ordinary historical actors are ignored; those in subaltern social positions, including children, are more at risk of disappearing.

Michael Roper writes that much scholarship has valued so highly the way that memories—national, local, or personal—are constructed and reconstructed that they become dissociated from the "underlay" of events, emotions, and experiences that generated them.[17] Interest is structural not phenomenological. Memories that fall outside of accepted constructions of the past are "held to the level of private remembrance," as Graham Dawson has it;[18] indeed, they go "not only unrecorded, but [are] actually silenced."[19] Memorial practices do not emerge ready formed; a process of negotiated construction takes place over many years.[20] As a new memorial paradigm emerges, some aspects of the past drop out of sight. Others never make it into the system. Ruth Kitchen points to a "narrative economy" inside public discourse, where value accrues around certain ways of telling the past.[21] It seems important to focus on this flow of value *as a flow* and not just on the structures it flows around.

Structures, Fixings, Objects

In her critique of the way the social sciences, through methods and rules, seek to "get their representation [of the world] 'right,'" the anthropologist Kathleen Stewart comments that "models of thinking that glide over the surface of modes of attention and attachment in search of the determinants of big systems located somewhere else are more and more like road blocks to proprioception than tunnels that yield."[22] Her words contribute to critiques not only of structural models as artificial representations projected a posteriori onto data but of the fixing of versions of reality, past or present, by authoritative assertions that distance observers from the object of their gaze. Reading Stewart's work brought my corpus of memory stories of French wartime childhoods into focus as emergent, vital, and performative, precariously contingent, and alive with affect.

John Dewsbury and colleagues have remarked on the "curious vampirism" of scholarly convention, including historians', that "drains" the world of life in order to lay bare the "orders, mechanisms, structures and processes" of the world.[23] In this framework, historical evidence—whether written, visual, or auditory—derives value only through its capacity to reveal and represent underlying social structures hidden from historical protagonists but not from external analysts. In the words of Stuart Hall, structural thinking was "the 'scientific' break from where things appear, where people speak and live, where they tell a hundred stories. It is the rejection of E. P. Thompson's efforts to recover the consciousness of real people and Raymond Williams's attempt to recover the structure of feeling of life as it was lived in particular periods."[24] We could see structuralism as belonging to a particular historiographical moment, but its influence endures in the humanities and social sciences. Much historical research seeks to reveal the underlying structures (of motivation, mood, behavior, institution, ideology, class, gender, and so on) that provide convincing explanations for a teleological unfurling of past into present. In terms of the French wartime past, those structures might be the ideological continuities feeding into mechanisms of Vichy policy or the networks of social relations underpinning, say, resistance activity: both are perfectly sensible ways of understanding the past. Yet in this quest to generalize and categorize, something of the phenomenological experience of living in the past can get lost. As Dewsbury and colleagues write, "the world is more excessive than we can theorise."[25] The consciousnesses of real people, "structures of feeling," the "provisional, immaterial" dimensions of social worlds, and the "lived complexity" of life must all be "downplay[ed] and deaden[ed]."[26] To construct an historical account that is narratively logical, structurally analytical, authoritatively assertive, and thus validated by their peers, historians need (and tend) to lose the "hot mess" of life that seethes at the edges of their gazes.[27] Anita Kumar shows that while cultural scripts—the culturally shaped strategies of self-narrative—structure discourse on the self, to view them as the exclusive influence on autobiographical narrativity is to ignore the "lived history and singularity" of each individual.[28] If we apply similar thinking to memory, Harald Welzer draws a distinction between "cultural memory"–type analyses that see individual memory attaching itself to fixed, abstract points in fateful and determined ways and "communicative memory"–type analyses that are situated inside the messiness of everyday communication of and about the past.[29] Structural ways of thinking seemed inadequate to get at what was bubbling out of the corpus of memory stories.

Raymond Williams wrote that the problem of most social analysis, including history, is that it uses "the habitual past tense": it makes everything it studies finished.[30] It may seem counterintuitive to understand "the study of the past" as unfixed, but without a shift away from the diachronic temptation to fix *then* from the position of *now*, we remain "locked into nineteenth-century modes of description, representation, and explanation."[31] Here, characteristically, Hayden White's position is sharply drawn. But I agree that history of the past *as passed* is interested not in the potential *becoming* of the past but only in its teleological march toward *now*; as such, it has little interest in the unfolding present either. So, following Kathleen Stewart, "getting the representation right" is a block to understanding the value of the past in the present. The "last word" of closure with which the historian's interpretation must be sealed in order to be conclusive and thus "right" as a faithful representation of past realities creates barriers to allowing the past to flow freely out over time along unruly and inconclusive channels. Instead, I suggest, a less determinate position on the past might account better for the unarticulated, unfinished way life unfolds in the everyday.

Work in the history of emotions provides a good example of how representational modes of knowing that rely on what is fixed and framed produce restricted kinds of knowledge. Work here defines itself as unwilling or unable to analyze the "embodied, sensate" world of past emotions, only their material traces—that is, the "discursive representation of emotions" in text or perhaps image, and their evolution over time. So when Stephanie Trigg writes that historians of emotions study how people in the past "experience, narrate and perform" emotion or how emotions are "processed [and] described," she is a little incautious: research that focuses solely on the discursive representation of emotion, in texts or maybe images, can never tell us what was "experienced" or, indeed, what was "processed" by a sensate body in time and space. Texts can only *represent* experience; in doing so via language, they affix meaning and tempt analysts into fixing still further an interpretation of past feeling authoritatively as *this* or *that*. This is very much the "history of emotions" rather than the "emotions of history." The latter might explore but also admit the never-knowable nature of past affective states that fall outside what is represented in words: what Jenkins describes as the haunting excess of the past.[32] How to manage this overflow, which always escapes what gets fixed and framed by representational history? Kathleen Stewart has deployed in her work what she calls different "modes of attunement and attachment."[33] Perhaps what is knowable through representative means—texts, images, words—is the exposed tip of an epistemological iceberg that extends also to what is feelable and what is imaginable, that is, what is perceivable and what is conceivable.

In attempting to fix the past as *this* or *that*, historians and other social scientists must "judge the value of their analytical objects," writes Stewart.[34] Fixing is an evaluative task and a suasive one; it seeks to convince audiences of the scholar's interpretive mastery of the object of his or her analysis. Yet the politics of this object mastery sit badly with my corpus: the memory stories resist examination at arm's length. Not only was my own involvement in generating them important, and not only were these objects also subjects, with their own agendas, agency, and trajectories, but the powerful affective dimension of the memory stories called for another kind of analysis. Together, they acted as an "archive of feeling" that I experienced rather than observed; I was in it rather than outside of it.[35] Hayden Lorimer notes that "affect presses against generally accepted versions of disciplinary politics, ethics and methods."[36] That is particularly the case in history, where the authoritative observation (mastery) of past objects (people) represented by their material traces usually goes unquestioned. Kathleen Stewart has called for greater exploration of "the potential modes of knowing, relating, and attending to things" and Luisa Passerini for "new ways of listening," referencing feminist and subaltern studies, where the distinction between subject and object collapses and new tools become available.[37] The "viewer" is no longer outside of the observable phenomena; she is situated inside the affective throng; she has jumped off the riverbank and into the water and, in so doing, becomes part of the water's flow.[38] Following Lorraine Code, Andrea Doucet promotes research practices rooted less in "information, findings, data, and representation" and more in "engagement, intervention, knowing/being/doing, and participating." Knowledge is not sucked from a static object that only awaits the observer's attention in order to reveal itself but is instead derived from the researcher's direct material engagement with the world.[39] Code vigorously advocates ways of knowing that are not controlled by a "spectator epistemology"—observation by spectators who supposedly bring "no affective, personal, historical, or idiosyncratic baggage"—nor by an "epistemology of mastery," which "presumes a unity of the subject to multiple spectator viewpoints."[40] Data, says Doucet, is a relationship, not an "object to be mined."[41] Ben Highmore has noted that part of the research task should be to "generate a form that [can] be adequate to the ideas we [want] to articulate."[42] The key, then, is an exploration of ideas and form, which has given this study its distinctive shape and focus.

METHODS AND MEMORIES

Memory as a source for history has achieved a certain amount of recognition, but this is by no means universal and particular obstructions still exist. Plucking one example, Matthieu Devigne's 2018 monograph about primary schools during the Vichy period evidences a certain attitude toward personal memories. During his doctoral research, Devigne had collected the written memories of about twenty older people who had been primary school teachers in the early 1940s; none featured in the published book. The problem with these narratives was, he wrote, that they were "in disjointed pieces, imprecise and incomplete, which, once read, show no kind of logic except the diversity of lived experiences."[43] He is not wrong: memories are imprecise, incomplete, and unlikely, particularly when taken collectively, to be "logical" in relation to outside criteria against which they are judged. Yet Devigne situates his interpretive problems with the memories themselves and not inside his own practice.

Some scholars argue for the term *oral sources* rather than oral history. History, after all, is what you *do to* sources, so oral sources are just another variety of source to be practiced on in the same way as written or visual ones.[44] Even if we were to accept—which I do not—that there is only one way of practicing history, the distinction between oral history and oral sources is not one of method but of ideology. Oral history is not about doing things to sources; it is an active, creative, and dialogic process of speaking and listening with other people. To understand memory stories as "oral sources" misunderstands their epistemological status. Rarely will an analysis that treats memory in the traditional historical mode— as a representation, as evidence of the really-out-there world—be satisfactory. However, this attitude is rooted in wider anxieties about the authoritative role of the historian, popular participation in history making, and disciplinary conventions around conclusive, complete narratives.

Paul Thompson stated that oral history allows for the re-creation of "the original multiplicity of standpoints"; while recognizing commonalities, it foregrounds the heterogeneity of experience.[45] Yet the promotion of individual over collective or universal versions of the past is not always welcomed. Olivier Wieviorka has written that "the heterogeneity of conditions [in wartime France] has thwarted the emergence of a common memory" of the past; such a multiplicity of perspectives impedes, he argues, the "coherence of the national narrative."[46]

Henry Rousso has further pathologized French memory of the Second World War as "a public problem" because of "individual identities" forever, it seems, at odds with each other.[47] Yet why should there be a common narrative of the past? Is diversity a public problem? Is identity dangerous? Sometimes, maybe, but not necessarily. Rousso expresses concern at the proliferation of singularities hindering the construction of a national past.[48] A teacher, he writes, could invite all the eyewitnesses they wanted to speak to their pupils, to express differing, "often conflicting," perspectives, "but, at the end of the day, it is down to the teacher to give the history lesson, that is, to produce a narrative which can be accepted by the greatest number."[49] Rousso is wary of motivations; with agenda-driven subjectivities, eyewitnesses are unlikely to contribute usefully to the construction of history. Wieviorka expresses something similar: "[While] research can separate out these different levels of analysis [war, occupation, and Vichy], the French people themselves ["les Français, eux"], subjected to roundups, air raids, shortages, authoritarianism, spare themselves such subtleties, melting into one the memories of their days." The inability to practice history as an objective sport may have "hazardous" consequences, as boundaries blur and insistences are misplaced: "it has generated—and still generates—competition between victims, groups experiencing their relationship with the past as rivalry rather than complementarity."[50]

These assertions exclude laypeople from contributing to the construction of the past, in particular because of their reliance on their own memories which, Rousso has written, cannot be part of an "approach to knowledge." He continues: "Memory falls within the register of identity; it carries affect along with it. It tends either to idealize or demonize the pasts which it reconstructs. It can compress or stretch time, and ignores any form of chronology, at least any rational form."[51] I agree, but positively. Memory is a source of epistemological interest and, indeed, knowledge about the past. Rousso hits the nail on the head: what is remembered and what is recounted depend a great deal, perhaps entirely, on affect—on feeling and on feelings. But the goals of a widely accepted interpretation and a national shared memory allude to a project that is not mine. I am not looking for the general or the national or to fix the past into an authoritative interpretation. This book seeks its history in the people who inhabited the past, in their heterogenous multiplicity, and in the endless possibilities of their existences.

Memory building and scholarly history making are not the same thing, but both feed into public discourse about the past. The scholars whose knowledge is solicited for documentary and feature films, museum exhibitions, television debates, newspapers, magazines, blogs, peer reviews of scholarly publications, funding applications, or judicial processes are the generators of the value that accrues around aspects of the past, shaping what is deemed worthy of discursive investment. To date, that has very rarely included school-age children, messy personal memories, or the felt realm of experience. In order, then, to contribute to the "more refined appreciation of behaviors"[52] called for by Laurent Douzou in relation to war history and war memory, I have turned toward a set of inter-disciplinary tools less commonly used by historians.

DESIRES

The more I listened to the memory stories in my corpus, the clearer it became that what was remembered was what was felt. Feeling was not always expressed as emotion, but it was there; it saturated my listening. It was there in relation to the events the child experienced in the past, the people she or he knew or encountered, and the adult's attempts to express, explain, and come to terms with them, both in the interview and over time. There were moments when the intensity of this feeling seemed to deepen, perhaps around the suffering of others or around emotions such as fear, shock, and shame. While I did not want to lose sight of a past that had happened and that was of historical interest, it seemed that these sources did not tend toward the construction of a narrative account of a past that had passed. It was still live, being made and remade in words, feeling, encounter, and transmission, each of them unstable and changeable. I wanted to explore these stories in ways that did not depend on the structures of childhood (such as biological development or schooling), chronological staging (a year-by-year account), or linear progress (leading to a particular point). These sources pulled toward an account of experience that reflected the embodied, performed, and ever-emergent nature of the world.

I wanted to try to value the affective intensity of doing this kind of memory work for the historian, the interviewer, the rememberer, and the listener. Michael Roper has written of the "unconscious work" of history, particularly in relation to "the emotional force of testimony, and the historian's struggle to respond to it."[53] Affective labor went into the recording of, listening to, and interpretation of the stories, as well as the process of remembering as rememberers worked across complex emotional territory, finding ways of communicating to me and to wider or imagined audiences. Writing about their words and their memories as though they were a fairly straightforward representation of the past would ignore this encumbered affective terrain. Furthermore, the tension between public versions of the past and private memories seemed irreducible to an opposition between the individual and the collective. Owain Jones writes that "in the end [collective memories] are lived out in individualised contexts of everyday lives in bodies moving through timespace."[54] I wanted to find a way to pick apart the intertwining of macro-level and micro-level remembering, not because I believe the (weaker) latter is determined by the (stronger) former but to suggest that while the frame of this remembering is unconditionally social, it is, as a frame, unfixed, flexible, and somewhat heterogenous. There was something here about individuation that I struggled to put my finger on, but the collective/individual dichotomy that is so frequently referenced and that I had used in my book *French Children Under the Allied Bombs* seemed inadequate. I had proposed another opposition in that book. I asked, "Children or adults?," noting that "memories laid down in childhood now belong to adults . . ., the experiences, however, belong to children."[55] Clear, but again inadequate. Memories are not so easy to separate from experiences. I sought new ways of thinking about all of these issues: about emotions and feeling, about expression, about time, about experience, about dichotomies, and about a kind of writing that respected the sources, attended to the voices, and was purposeful in its aims.

ATTRACTIONS

Toward Open-Ended Histories

Certain aspects of Hayden White's thinking are alluring in relation to the analysis of the memory stories in this corpus. Of particular relevance here is what he calls a "progressive history" that is "concerned with the present as much as with the past and with mediating between these two." White posits progressive history making as a force for positive change in the present as it aspires to something more than a disconnected "interest in 'what happened' in some local domain of the past."[56] It wants to undermine the supposed mastery of present over past, pulling the past through into the present to shake the power of knowledge as exclusive, proprietorial, and transactional. In a similar mold, Keith

Jenkins makes the case for "radical history" that, "discarding the desire for clo-sure, builds uncertainty on uncertainty," refuses to fix some kind of past or pres-ent reality, and explicitly recognizes the "interminable openness" of the past and present. For Jenkins, this hope is "empowering and uncompromisingly eman-cipating for those people needing these things: most of us."[57] These ideas rarely make it into empirical historical investigations. Perhaps it is too risky, or even impossible, to hold back the desire to conclude, the desire to appear to be right. Yet cultural geographers and scholars of affect have aimed to shake off some of what Lorraine Code calls the "instituted" social imaginary of knowledge mak-ing: that of hegemonic disciplinary mandates that separate the spectator-knower from the object-known.[58] For the nonrepresentational theorist and cultural geog-rapher Nigel Thrift, the aim has been to "inject a note of wonder back into a social science which, too often, assumes that it must explain everything."[59] For Jonathan Flatley, the function of what he calls "affective mapping" is not creating "stable representation[s]" or "establish[ing] a territory," that is, owning and fix-ing, but instead "providing a feeling of orientation and facilitating mobility."[60] If cultural geographers can rethink their discipline, drawing on cultural and affect studies, to move beyond the representational and deterritorialize the epistemo-logical terrain they tread, if they can find ways to "privilege . . . the fluid over the fixed,"[61] why can't historians? Of course, being open to the new is risky: incon-clusive and nonauthoritative interpretations are prone to conflict and may even be reinterpreted in ways we see as "monstrous."[62] But surely the risks are part of the stake and the reward.

Recognizing the past's resistance to clear historicization—that it is never closed, never certain, and never fixed—requires a shift. The anthropologist Kath-leen Stewart's writing on "ordinary affects" seeks to evoke "forms of living" in their "textures and rhythms, trajectories, and modes of attunement, attachment and composition." Stewart's work called for an epistemological shift in order to generate new ways of gaining knowledge away from the "structured seduc-tions" and "static plane[s] of analysis" of traditional scholarly epistemologies.[63] For geographer Hayden Lorimer, these modes of "attunement" might allow us to perceive "how life takes shape and gains expression in shared experiences, every-day routines, fleeting encounters, embodied movements, precognitive triggers, practical skills, affective intensities, enduring urges, unexceptional interactions and sensuous dispositions . . . [which] escape from the established academic habit of striving to uncover meanings and values that apparently await our discovery, interpretation, judgement and ultimate representation."[64] Reading these possibilities of nonrepresentational study—or more-than-representational study, as Lorimer terms it—is invigorating. Here, scholars seek the dynamic, performative, embodied dimensions of life in ways that are rarely considered for the past; these reflect back into the corpus of memory stories in fruitful ways, which the four parts of this book will explore. As Stewart notes, this is not a question of "getting it right," measuring our representation of life, of the past and present, against an "out there" reality that we can perceive if only we have the right methodology. Referencing Eve Kosofsky Sedgwick, she propounds an idea of "weak theory" rather than the more standard scholarly "paranoid" or "strong" theory, which needs continually to "defend . . . itself against the puncturing of its dream of a perfect parallelism between the analytic subject" (in the case of this book, me), "her concept" (the nature of wartime childhood memories), "and the world" (where those real children lived and those real adults remember).[65] The relational ontologies of these thinkers twinkled as I considered the hundreds of thousands of words, experiences, and meanings I was juggling, the shifting affective landscape, and the overflowing nature of these sources.

The ideas I borrow are not new in their respective domains, but they are rarely invoked in history writing. In that sense, they are experimental. History, inherently conservative, has been resistant to making its methods "dance a little."[66] Gilles Deleuze in particular and, often, Félix Guattari are inescapable presences in the scholarship of affect. Deleuzian ontology is relational; it can be used to take a "social frameworks of memory" approach into an extra dimension.[67] Deleuze's relational ontology considers "bodies, things, ideas, social institutions or—for that matter—emotions as existing or having integrity only through their relationship to other, similarly contingent and ephemeral, bodies, things, ideas or social institutions."[68] That memories are always social because humans are always social does not get us very far. But that memories must be more than social—as ideas flowing, gaining substance, mutating between bodies of all kinds, about things within social contexts inside a "sheer mangle of ontological relatedness"[69]—is not only exciting, it accounts more satisfactorily for the "hot mess" of life oozing, slopping, swirling, and bubbling around the memory stories I collected. Second, in proposing a rhizomatic (free-sprouting) model over, or alongside, an arboreal (hierarchical) one, Deleuzian thinking makes it easier to glimpse and grasp the singular, emergent nature of a contingent social world that calls out from the memory stories. These ideas are present across all four parts of the book, but are particularly salient in relation to the telling of the memory stories in part 3, "Memories Told," and part 4, "Memories Lived," in which the unfolding, contingent present of the past is discussed. Renold and Mellor evoke in Deleuze's thought a "wild empiricism that can capture the unstableness of everyday life."[70] The corpus of memory stories did seem wildly empirical—so multiple, so unreliably comparable, so patchy in its qualities, so unknowably subjective, so affectively suggestive—and it pulsed with instability at every level. Deleuze's work, the sociologist Nick Fox writes, conceives knowledge, past and present, as "fleeting, emerging in unpredictable ways around actions and events."[71] Little seemed better to describe how and what I was learning from the stories. As Brent Adkins explains, Deleuze and Guattari's rhizome allows us to value the "heterogeneity of wildly diverse things"; to look multiplicity directly in the eye and not separate artificially the one and the many, the individual and the collective; to draw the map ourselves, exploring where it leads us, and not simply trace our thoughts atop preexisting outlines; and to plunge our knife where we see fit, recognizing the assumptions inherent in carving along seemingly "natural" joints.[72] In making methods "dance a little," there is a risk. As Deleuze and Guattari point out, who knows how the new creation will turn out?[73]

Toward Affects

Oral sources, oral history: regardless of which term is preferable, "oral" suggests by the mouth, through the spoken word. Working with more than a hundred memory stories of wartime childhoods, I had a growing awareness that what was by the mouth was only part of what this source was, compounding my view that "oral sources" inadequately describes the complexity of the communicative encounter. So much of what I was experiencing was feeling. What was being remembered was what had been and what was being felt. Feeling is not a by-product of speech but a core element of communication and intersubjectivity. The remembering process was saturated with feeling, and to ignore it was to ignore an affective kind of knowledge: what they knew because they felt; what I knew because I felt. Not the history of emotions, then, but the emotions of history. Stephanie Trigg wryly quotes an unnamed "expert historian" responding to a question about how she felt about the destruction of certain artifacts during the English Reformation: "I'm a historian," Trigg says she replied, "it's not my job to feel."[74] Yet how could I account for the fact that what they (the rememberers, the interviewers) knew and what I knew came not only through words, by the mouth, but through attempts to convey sensation, to share emotion, and to affect things—ideas, people, objects, and events? Part 1, "Memories Felt," lays out an elaboration of the felt realm of remembering, which is picked up continuously across the rest of the book.

Sara Ahmed's work on emotion and affect is influential. The so-called affective turn of the 2000s continues to inform thinking around the importance of feeling, past and present. Affect is a wide-ranging and sometimes contested term. Donovan Schaefer has described affect theory as "being about how systems of forces circulating within bodies—forces not necessarily subsumable or describable by language—interface with histories. It is about how discourses form ligatures with pulsing flesh-and-blood creatures."[75] Yet discussion of affect has less frequently entered historical research. This is partly because of disciplinary boundaries erected around the history of emotions, partly because of the injunction for historians to leave their emotions at the door, partly because of a reluctance to engage with theory, and partly because certain parts of the arts-in-the-humanities (literature, art, music, film, performance) have always been about feeling.[76] Rarely, though, have I come across work like Ahmed's—a "phenomenology of the political",[77] or the livedness of discourse, power, and self—for explicitly historical topics. Ben Highmore's book *Cultural Feelings* looks directly, indeed stares, at feeling—in his case, as "mood"—which flows *between* the objects that are more usually located in the center of the gaze. But his work is not history, despite its attention to certain parts of the past.[78] Reluctance to get involved in the affective turn may also stem from the debates over terminology, particularly affect and emotion. Of affect and emotion, Ahmed writes, not without frustration, that like egg white and egg yolk, "just because we *can* separate them does not mean that they *are* separate"; she later comments that she "hope[s] for an intellectual horizon in which emotion and affect are not taken as choices that lead us down separate paths."[79] Perhaps Highmore's attention to feeling and mood takes us closer to that horizon. He emphasizes the valuable vagueness of *feeling* as an analytical category, in opposition to the more theoretically defined terms *emotions* or *affect*, and, like Ahmed, sees the interdisciplinary wrangling around definitions as a bind.[80]

In this study, I take emotions and affects as different but intertwined aspects of the felt realm. Like Fox and Ahmed, I take emotion neither "as something escaping from the interior of a body" (we do not "give off" emotions) nor "the product of exterior forces seeping in" (emotion is not a contagion we catch from others).[81] Emotions and affects shape our orientations toward or away from the objects of our interest. The distinction I will make in this study is that emotions are those affective orientations toward or away from things we are aware of and can name, label, or communicate in words or even gestures to others, who are likely to recognize them. Affects are those orientations toward or away from things that we may not register but that modify action, thought, ideas, or feelings and shift orientations. Grossberg suggests that the difference between the two might be the "gap between what can be rendered meaningful and knowable, and what is nevertheless knowable."[82] I will also use the word *feeling* to express, more collectively, the realm of what is felt, whether individually or collectively, as emotion or affect. Highmore writes that "sensitivity to the liveness and lived-ness of affective life" should open the way to identifying historical or cultural instances "within patterns of feeling": "If a general concern with feeling tends to be attentive to moods and atmospheres of optimism or hostility, say, then affect theory is useful for staying alert to the peculiar arising and diminution of energy that accompanies such feeling." Studying affect is a question of tuning in to the "interests, sensations, pulsions, energies, senses and so on that take definite shape, color, tone and texture in our social and cultural life."[83] It is about looking for knowledge between, around, or alongside objects, not just in them. It can be known and felt by an imprint or by "the way that something picks up density and texture as it moves through bodies, dramas, and scenes": *something*.[84] Why should such ideas not hold for historical as well as contemporary analysis? They need a historian who is interested in the "ongoingness" of the world, however, rather than its fixity.[85]

Roy Huijsmans describes emotion as "knowledge that moves."[86] Quite aside from his plea that emotion be recognized as "knowledge in its own right" (akin to what I call affective knowledge) and central to how we know what we know, the quality of motion can be seen in three ways. First, emotions move us; that is, they make us feel. They have the capacity to affect us. Second, Ahmed emphasizes that they make us move: they make us orient ourselves toward and away from the objects of those emotions. Third, they are on the move. A central tenet of Ahmed's work, and indeed much work in affect studies, is that "emotions circulate between bodies"—people, objects, institutions, ideas, and so on.[87] From this idea, she builds thinking around the "stickiness" of emotions: What objects do they cling to? Are the objects sticky, or are the emotions? Where do emotions cohere and accrete? With what consequences? Patricia Clough has written of an economy of affect, again promoting the idea that affects circulate and may gain or decrease in value.[88] The scaling of affects is theorized by Brian Massumi, who qualifies affect as the "collaps[ing] of structured distinction into intensity."[89] Intensity can be thought of as a thrumming, as the volume and or vibration of affect, which can be more or less dampened, more or less vibrant. In Massumi's analysis, the naming of affects as emotions is one of the ways in which their intensity is dampened.[90] Thus, when considering affects in this relational way, we are less interested in classifying, categorizing, naming, or labeling particular emotions. However, in order to establish working differences between sensation, emotion, and affect in memory, chapter 1 will deal with emotion head on. With affect, as Seigworth and Gregg put it, the interest lies "not [in] what something is, but how it is—or more precisely, how it affects and how it is affected by other things."[91] The stickiness of affect, its accretion, and the increase or diminution of its intensity are illustrated in chapter 2 and deployed thereafter.

Toward Assemblage Thinking

In the writing around relational ontologies, affect, and nonrepresentational theory across disciplines, it is difficult not to bump into assemblages. Historians can be wary of the specialized terminologies theorists elaborate, and I too wondered whether the past needs assemblages to be comprehensible. It does not. But concepts should be treated as tools to help us think. Assemblages struck a chord. They too derive from Deleuzian thinking. As dynamic kinds of "hodgepodges"[92] that conceptualize the relational nature of reality, they seemed just the thing to help revisualize the memory stories, whose complex articulations of people, ideas, objects, memories, affects, emotions, feelings, space, time, movement, and more overflowed diachronic, representational, knower-known, and dichotomous kinds of analysis (adult-child, then-now, life-story, memory-history, me-them). Assemblages allowed me to think about these elements as a connected, unstable, temporary whole, brought together in a moment but constantly shifting. They gave me a way to evoke the sense that the past, the narration, and the interview were always on the brink of being, having been, or becoming something else. Assemblages enabled me to think about the relational materiality of moments in the past that were recounted; they enabled me to think about the contingent singularity of the story as narrated in a particular instance; they enabled me to think about my encounter with the interviewee and/or with their story as a moment on the move. And they permit all of this: open-endedness, inconclusiveness, messiness, are understood as the way of things. In short, assemblages delineate a "thicket of connections" around remembering the wartime past that positioned the memory stories as contingencies, singularities, and relational multiplicities.[93]

Deleuze states that "in assemblages you find states of things, bodies, various combinations of bodies, hodgepodges. . . . [H]odgepodges are combinations of interpenetrating bodies."[94] "Bodies" here relates in a large sense to the various objects that can be allied to the assemblage. These can be anything: people, parts of people, memories, ideas, emotions, stories, animals, objects, images, discourses, buildings, spaces, places, times, and so on. Assemblages are ubiquitous: "every aspect of life," writes Nick Fox, "can be understood as an assemblage, at sub-personal, interactional or macro-social levels."[95] The capacity of the assemblage to bring into relation such heterogenous objects and to recognize that they interpenetrate—that is, they are impossible to prize apart and may indeed not have any quality of separateness from one another—was particularly exciting in relation to the memory stories. The bodies in an assemblage are not linked by well-defined threads; they are allied, usually temporarily and fleetingly, by affect. Assemblages are permeated by "affective relations [that] create desires and capacities."[96] Affect provides a kind of sticky force that flows, blows, trickles, or runs around the assemblage. Fox writes that in an assemblage, "there is no 'subject' and no 'object', only a confluence of elements in affective relationships to each other which changes their states, and their ability to act—what they can do."[97] Thus "desires and capacities" and the "ability to act" are the product of affective shifts around the assemblage, and between assemblages, that cause things to happen. A set of entwined, heterogenous, material and nonmaterial objects including people (including me), objects, times, places, feelings, events; an affective flow driving shape, emphasis, direction; the intervention of social actors: this, to me, described the memory stories that came into focus as assemblages on three interpenetrating temporal planes.

The first plane is the assemblage of the happening past. It comprises the events, experiences, objects, thoughts, or feelings that existed somewhere in the unfolding past that the interviewee narrated. The second plane, the memory story assemblage, was the narrated story, narrated by someone, somewhere, sometime, of memories, discourses, feelings, or other people's thoughts and actions, being multitemporal, multivocal, multilocational, and so on. The third is the listening encounter, during which the memory story about the happening past was heard by someone. The second and third planes might include the interviewer(s) and interviewee(s), the instigation/motivation of each, other audiences (present and imagined), the room and environment, the materiality of recording equipment and the staging of the research, language and transcription, the performativity of all parties, the affective charges of face-to-face communication (expressed, understood, groping, missed), and so on. Researchers working with oral history have always been conscious of the complex relation between the past as lived, the narrated past expressed through (personal/social/cultural) memory, and the intersubjectivity of the narrating present. Assemblages provided extra ways of thinking about the inherent instability of each of those planes; the role of affect in generating, maintaining, or dissipating the goings-on in each plane; and, importantly, the connectedness all three. Separating them into categories (even these three schematic planes), allocating memories to one or another genre, and bisecting individual/collective relations, past/present relations, or subject/object relations no longer seemed necessary or desirable. Not only can they not be pulled apart; they do not need to be.

The second valuable characteristic of assemblages is their sheer contingency. Grove and Pugh write that "assemblages are never stable . . . because they embody virtual potentialities: they are effects of force relations [which we can read as affects] brought into relation with one another in particular ways, which can always potentially be reconfigured in different ways."[98] The listening encounter, the memory story, and indeed the life as lived could always have happened in different ways. The task of the person examining these sources, then, is as much about finding the "actual" as about the "virtual in the actual."[99] The virtual can be understood as the thing or the moment that is "there in potential . . . waiting to happen in disparate and incommensurate objects, registers, circulations, and publics."[100] The way things come together to make that event or this moment is just one of a potentially infinite variety, but it has its own thisness, which we can also call its haecceity (derived from Latin, meaning "thisness").[101] At any point, there are multiple and unknowable courses that could follow; the one taken, a telos that leads to now, is "thrown together," the "hap" of happening, as Sara Ahmed has it.[102] And at the crest of an unfolding present, those lines of possibility still leave everything in play. The present, then, is a continuously generative and emergent advance. In the throes of happening, no course of action was predetermined. The traces of immanence are evident in the narration of those pasts that never happened, the "shared possibilities" and "uchronic dreams" that Alessandro Portelli discerned in the what-might-have-beens of futures imagined, told, but never lived.[103] This idea is particularly valuable when, in part 2, "Memories Located," the weirdness of memory time is discussed. In each memory story, structure, content, and shape emerge out of presently situated concerns, interactions, and possibilities. As part 3, "Memories Told," shows, the words used to describe *this* event are those available to the narrator at *this* moment; what is forgotten might have been remembered tomorrow. Each utterance is improvised, produced on the spot, drawing on cultural resources or repertoire, but always potentially something else.[104]

The interview encounter epitomizes the "hap" of happening. Performative, unstable, and frequently unruly, the meeting between interviewer and rememberer is a threshold of uncertainty. While experience may help an interviewer ride this unruliness, the fact that almost anything can happen in the interview means that the performances of all parties involved are always subject to the contingency of the unfolding present. Logging trucks roar past so loudly that the words cannot be heard; an unexpected person at the table interrupts continuously; flies buzz around the room, landing on your arms and face; roasting a turkey proves a distraction; you don't connect, they seem suspicious, you feel defensive; friendly guests arrive and settle down to listen; the accent is so strong; it's terribly hot; it's snowing outside; they've made you lunch but your flight is waiting; you arrive late, lost en route; tears flow, you pause and comfort; your questions are irrelevant; they have a bad cold; you didn't sleep well; you become entangled in an accidental disagreement; the recorder was off and the interview must be rerun. Each assemblage produces the affective forces shaping the capacities, desires, and reticences of interviewers and interviewees in unknowable but endlessly productive ways. The outcome of the interview encounter—a recorded memory story about the past—could always have been different.

Third, the assemblage provides the capacity to understand time better than diachronic or linear models, which emphasize both the distinction between then and now and the structured progression from then towards now. Then and now collapse as distinct entities inside the assemblage, making those fears over rational chronologies redundant. Yannis Hamilakis explains the value of this for archaeology, but it works for history too. He writes that the Bergsonian model of durational time "does not imply continuity, but rather co-presence." He continues: "Past, present, and future are not dots on the line of time, but rather inter-penetrating and commingled planes. In that sense, every given present carries with it all pasts, but, of course through the selective process of memory, only specific pasts are conjured up at any specific moment."[105] Once more, this idea of interpenetration between elements of the assemblage and between assemblages resurfaces—in this case, and usefully with regard to memory and the narrated past, through temporality. For although I have outlined three assemblages—a happening past, a memory story, a listening encounter—that may appear to inhabit specific points on a linear trajectory (and certainly, the happening past precedes the other two), all three are intractably commingled in memory. We might think of them instead as existing on three temporal planes that are intertwined. The immanence of unfolding presents is multitemporal: all previous time *could* be mobilized to drive a trajectory toward this particular present; all presents *could* unfold in multiple ways. Thus, the present always contains within it various pasts and various futures. This happens in "condensed and virtual forms,"[106] which are perceptible as the memory is narrated. For example, interviewees mobilize older layers of family or national history to explain events unfolding. As chapter 3 explores in depth, their stories shuttle or leap between narrated pasts, more distant pasts, past presents, and possible futures; all of this happens from the point of an unfolding present, which may be at the moment the story is told (which itself can be articulated multitemporally) or the point at which that story is listened to later on (likewise). What is characterized by the detractors of memory as illogical, not chronological, meandering, or just plain wrong is in fact a function of time inside and across the assemblages and a rich source for understanding not only the connections between past and present but also decision making, agency, and the value attached to actions, events, and feelings.

The conjuring of specific pasts brings us to the final feature of assemblage thinking that resonated in relation to the memory stories. Hamilakis posits that the way only certain pasts get conjured, or "actualized" in his words, is political. "Territorialization" is the name Deleuze and Guattari give to the process of colonization, or activation, of specific pathways through the past, which create a "politics of affect" that, Fox states, "permeates life at every level. This micropolitics is played out upon . . . daily actions, desires, feelings."[107] It is this process that assembles or disassembles assemblages, that builds affective "intensity and weight" around certain elements of the assemblage. Territorialization occurs when certain "voices" or "temporal instances" become "sensorially and affectively dominant" as a result of the deliberate intervention of the "power and ability of a social agent, [with] certain social and political consequences."[108] This produces a dynamic, politicized landscape where certain versions of reality (the past, the present), certain pathways through the past to the present, voiced by certain agents and not by others, acquire dominance and become "stickier," more attractive, more intense, and weightier.

Two examples of this process may be cited, although the following chapters will illustrate it further. First, during my research on the Allied bombing of France, when I interviewed someone about being bombed as a child, their bombing narrative was activated as a pathway through all the possible aspects of that past that could have been narrated. My prerogative to instigate and guide an interview, derived from my power as a scholar, had the consequence of shaping what got told and archived for posterity. My work was then published as a book, creating what was valued. The scientific field of interest around child war trauma also activated some of the narratives I recorded over others, giving the traumatic more value. It acquired greater affective weight and intensity and thus became "stickier": more accreted around it—more research, more conference presentations, more publications, more value, more interest, more elements in the new trauma-bombing assemblage. The activation of traumatic narratives over nontraumatic ones established a politics that highly valued trauma and implicitly devalued, and even excluded, the nontraumatic. Consciousness of my participation in that process of hierarchization underpins the present study. A second example, which appeared plainly from my collection of these memory stories, was the territorialization enacted by the powerful resistance-collaboration diptych that has dominated and still dominates discussion of the French wartime past. Interest in these aspects of the period, propagated widely through authoritative scholarly, media, and heritage discourse, has shaped the collection practices around oral narratives of the wartime past, the archiving practices, and of course their content. It also generates unarticulated affective imprints (defensiveness, guilt, sorrow, pride) inside the stories.

This chapter has illustrated a process of affective reorientation that guides the following four parts and their component chapters. What can I see when I see with affect? What can I know, think, and feel if differently attuned to memories as being made of feeling? And what do such affects do to the creation and sharing of knowledge about the past? I use assemblage thinking to illustrate and power my analysis of multiplicity and singularity. I use open-endedness both as an ethics of nonmastery and to describe something of the contingent nature of reality.

My starting questions—what was it like for children in Second World War France, and how can we know this from the inside out—seem already to have lost some feasibility. The book thus proceeds as an experiment in pulling away from and returning to these original ideas. Trying to represent "what it was like" has been interrupted by the impossibility of representing *it* in its fullness and instability; so what can be done instead? And knowing "from the inside" is less achievable if I am inside too; so what can be known instead? While open-endedness, affects, and assemblages are consistent presences across the what follows, certain emphases exist at different moments. Part 1 explores the felt realm, illustrating distinctions between sensations, emotions, and affects. Parts 2 and 3 concern assemblages and their affects in relation to space, place, time, discourse, and performance. Part 4 tends to focus on the contingent unfolding of reality. Through this reorientation there emerges a form—I hope one of many that are possible—of affective historiography.

PART 1

MEMORIES FELT

In her study of remembering and forgetting, Naomi Norquay writes that the "memory of the event is precipitated by the memory of the feeling."[1] Feeling sticks things down; strong feelings glue the memory of an event, mundane or dramatic, into the mind. Feeling is therefore central to the remembering of past events. Indeed, sometimes only feeling remains. When I interviewed Henri Buc about his wartime childhood, he began with an anecdote "which," he said, "at a first glance, has nothing to do with it." He spoke of an incident in his adult life, working in a laboratory in Germany in the 1970s:

> I was one of the last in the lab, around midday, one o'clock, and I needed to have my lunch, and instead of leaving by the front door, I went out the back to go and buy some sandwiches. And when I came out of the backdoor, my legs suddenly started to shake. I nearly fell over, and I wondered what was happening to me, and I looked, and there were some German workmen digging trenches [nearby], and they were dressed just like the soldiers I saw when I was a little boy. So things happen which get embodied, which go so much *further* [he emphasizes the word] than you can remember.

Henri's body appeared to remember something that his mind could not. Megan Watkins draws attention to the Spinozan distinction between *affectus* (the force of an affecting body) and *affectio* (the impact it leaves on the body affected). She writes that "*affectio* may be fleeting but it may also leave a residue."[2] Henri had witnessed some acts of violence as a boy (an air raid, a violent arrest), which he later recounted to me, and had certainly lived the war years in an atmosphere of anxiety. Here was the residue. The shock he felt at this visceral experience thirty or more years later prompted him to begin his interview with this story. We ponder the past using reason and evidence, we question our memories, and we may think we know all there is to know about our own past, but sometimes feeling catches us out and makes us reconsider.

Scholars interested in affect suggest that we look at the impressions that bodies make on bodies—the stone dropped in water or the impact of events on memories—by attending to the shape and size of the ripples. These tell us something of the bodies themselves.[3] Henri's anecdote does not tell us about specific events in his wartime childhood, but it does tell us about how those events left ripples of feeling down the years. Feeling and memory are shown as mutually constitutive, codependent, and entangled. Feeling must be recognized as a central "way of knowing" about human experience.[4] I contend that memories are made of feeling. Feeling is fundamental to the encoding, storage, and retrieval of memories; feeling underpins why people remember what they do, how, when, and where. It implicates the autobiographical work of remembering one's past, the present identity of the narrator, and the broader sociocultural setting in which living and remembering are taking place. Feeling is a form of knowledge—affective knowledge—for historical actors and historians alike. It can be personal (receptive, experiential, phenomenological), social (expressive, communicative), and cultural (taking place inside broader structures or patterns of feeling).[5] Feeling encompasses perception and sensations, articulated emotions, and the unarticulated affective impulses that move us to act in one way or another.

Across part 1, "Memories Felt," I examine feeling memories explicitly. I analyze aspects of sensation, emotion, and affect in the memory stories to respond to the questions "What are you (memories) made of?" and "What do you (memories) do?" The sociologist Eduardo Bericat states that "as human beings we can only experience life emotionally: *I feel, therefore I am.*"[6] If that is the case, then memories of experiences must be memories of feeling. Psychologists recognize that memories of feeling are the "basic building block of the stories individuals, groups, and even societies construct and reconstruct about themselves."[7] But as Henri Buc's story suggests, memory and feeling are bound together in complicated ways. We might speak of memories of feeling something directly or feeling something *about* something; we might speak of remembering feelings experienced in the past, having feelings about our memories or the process of remembering, or feeling something in the here and now through our memories.

Re-remembering, to borrow Michael Roper's term, generates new layers of feel-ings.[8] And of course the feelings we remember may not be the feelings we had. Nor are they only our own: it is quite common for the (perceived or real) feelings of others to permeate our memories. Part 1 contains two chapters. The first deals with types of feeling that are consciously articulated in the memory stories, the second with feeling as affective flow and intensity. The two categories overlap, but dividing part 1 thus teases apart certain strands of remembered experience for examination.

Broadly, "Memories Felt" understands feeling as both a quality of body (embodied sensation, phenomenological experience) and of mind (cognitive, affective, relational). Thus, one aspect of feeling relates to the body's response to sensory input: the human-material interaction that structures our phe-nomenological experience of life. Brian Massumi argues for the separation of what is bodily, precognitive, and identifiable only by its intensity, which he calls affect, and the cognitive "socio-linguistic fixing of the quality of an expe-rience," which he calls emotion, into something that becomes "conventional, consensual . . . [and] narrativizable."[9] He argues for a kind of feeling that pre-cedes the recognition and identification of an emotion state. That process of recognition and identification, he says, decreases the feeling's intensity. But, as Ben Highmore notes, "the interlocking of sensual, physical experiences . . . with the passionate intensities of love, say, or bitterness, makes it hard to imagine untangling them."[10] What is experienced bodily can be identified in language and spoken about, but the body is never divorced from the mind's processing of that experience. Desjarlais and Throop remark that "the body is not only a corpse- or text-like entity that can be examined, measured, inspected, inter-preted, and evaluated in moral, epistemological, or aesthetic terms; it is a living entity by which, and through which, we actively experience the world."[11] The body's encounter with the world produces a "shifting stream of experience . . . compounded of feeling and thought," making the embodied, ongoing experience of feeling simultaneously a cognitive one.[12]

Massumi's precision is useful. There is something of his distinction in Henri Buc's experience in Germany, when intense feeling became narrativizable emo-tion as Henri remarked his experience, pondered it, and then recounted it. But we can equally take the embodied, phenomenological, and cognitive as being entangled inside the memory stories. To pull them apart too roughly risks desta-bilizing the whole. Sara Ahmed posits that affect and emotion do not relate to "different aspects of experience . . . [comprising] separate spheres between consciousness and intentionality, on the one hand, and physiological or bodily reactions on the other." Two valuable points, she writes, are '[not to] assume we always know how we feel" and "that feelings do not belong or even originate with an 'I', and only then move out towards others."[13] Feeling exists relationally in the coming into contact, inside an assemblage, of bodies—things, people, events, places, ideas—that affect and are affected by one another.

CHAPTER 1

ARTICULATED FEELING

SENSORY MEMORIES

Childhood memories often recount sensory experience. Describing what was seen and heard in the past was extremely common in the interviews. Feeling stuck to the visual and the auditory in communicable ways, but smell and taste were less common. This could appear surprising given the powerful connections between smell, taste, and memory.[1] Yet while smells and tastes evoke feelings, they seem to be less communicable. This may be either because they are internal to the smeller or taster and thus never truly shareable or because they rely on immediacy: it is *re*-smelling or *re*-tasting in the present that triggers the memory. The realm of touch, also called the haptic realm, is better represented in the oral narratives; more precisely, the tactile (sensing through touch), proprioceptive (the sense of location, movement, action), and thermoceptic (perceiving heat) emerge in memories of positioned bodies and feeling skin. While one sense may dominate a story, the senses "work in unison, not in an individualistic manner"; Hamilakis adds that "sensorial modalities are . . . inherently synesthetic."[2] Inside each sensory experience is another and another; what is felt may also be smelled, what is seen may have been heard, what is tasted may evoke past feeling, and sights recalled may be revisualized in the present. Hamilakis calls this a sensorial assemblage: a "flow of substances, memories, affects through bodies."[3] This chapter examines sensorial assemblages of sights and sounds and then moves on to tastes, smells, and the haptic realm to see what this kind of sensorial remembering might reveal of past childhood experience from a dimension of the "inside out" that has to do with the feeling body.

Certain visual memories were quite effectively described in the interview as speakers drew on their linguistic resources to transmit an approximate representation of the remembered scene. Max Potter, in La Chapelle (Paris), opened his curtains after an air raid in 1944 "and I saw the apocalypse! The sky was like the scenery of a theatre set, orange, the mouth of a blast furnace, everything was aglow!" He uses a metaphor to indicate the scale of destruction and a simile for detail. Color indicators—orange, phosphorescent—are easily communicable. We cannot see what Max saw, and he does not speak of streets or buildings. But the visual memory conjures affects that are more than visual for the listener too: fear, shock, awe.[4] Robert Belleuvre, in Boulogne-Billancourt, describes what he saw when the town was bombed in March 1942: "Curious, but not panicking, I went to the window, where I could see a great mass coming towards me, by rue Gallieni, about fifty meters from our block of flats. Well, a mass, it was a plane, of course, coming in from the Seine, and you got the impression that it was going slowly, that it was a heavy flight, like a raptor hunting its prey." He alerts us to aspects of his emotional state as he looked, combining detail with precise figurative imagery. Whether or not Robert was afraid, he had time to take this strange sight in. Psychological research might suggest that at this moment of stress, hyperarousal activated his capacity to encode detail.[5] Robert uses a retrospective commonsense meta-statement to comment on the unidentifiable object—"it was a plane, of course"—which intensifies its strangeness to him in the past.[6] The visual description builds meaning, interweaving sights, feeling, and knowledge, both emergent and retrospective. This communication provides strong verbal clues about what was most shocking or most strange; these appear as "peaks of intensity" in this memory.[7]

Peaks of intensity also arose from the known or imagined futures that flowed out of revisualized past experiences. The sensorial assemblage is inherently multitemporal. Speakers oscillate between their visual memories and knowledge of later outcomes. This is particularly clear with those who were very young. For example, again speaking of the air raid on Boulogne-Billancourt in 1942 when she was nearly three years old, Danielle Durville said of her only memory: "it's always just a flash, just seeing all these ruins, smoking, people screaming, and Mum holding me." She marked its meaning by recounting its later impact on her: "It seems that I was traumatized all the same, I stopped eating. . . . As soon as the siren sounded, afterwards, I was very frightened. . . . I was a bit traumatized. I could only think of one thing, getting to shelter, going down to the cellar."

The behavioral consequences for little Danielle were recounted secondhand ("it seems"); only the visual memory was her own: "I've still got this image of the ruins which were smoking and smoking. Even now when I think of it, I can see that scene again." Raymond Frugier was four years old when he escaped the vicious massacre in the village of Oradour-sur-Glane, which was burned down by the German Waffen-SS Das Reich Division on June 10, 1944, and 643 of its inhabitants murdered. He said that he had only two memories from that early part of his life: "I have a very clear memory of flames in the distance, reaching high up in the air. And that affected me. That, there, is a very precise image which has stayed with me, and which I hold in my memory. The other memory is when my father decided to take us—my mother, my sister, and me—into the woods. . . . We stayed there for nearly three weeks." The only memory recounted directly is the visual one. The second is less clear: is it a memory, or is it retrospective knowledge of the unfolding future? Does he remember the decision being made, or being taken to the woods, or staying there for three weeks? It is not recounted as any of these, just as the knowledge that it happened. In both Danielle's and Raymond's cases, the visual memory is made sticky by what came afterward.

Like many others, Maurice Goldring said he had very few memories of being five or six years old, but those that stuck were visual. The first: "I have a memory of being at school . . . and seeing my father, who I'd not seen for some months, arriving in his uniform. I was so proud to see my father in uniform. . . . It's quite a nationalistic image." A Polish Jewish immigrant, his father had volunteered to fight for France against the Germans in 1939. The memory is visual, but it is also a "nationalistic image"; its stickiness is created not just by what the boy saw but by a feeling of pride and also by the later betrayal of Jews by the French nation. Maurice's parents both survived the Holocaust but not without complications that diminished his pride in his father, who had a (near or actual) extramarital liaison while the rest of his family were in hiding. One of Maurice's later memories, from around 1942, of being arrested as the family tried to cross the demarcation line between the northern Occupied Zone and the southern Free Zone, is likewise strikingly visual but equally multitemporal: "I was struggling to keep going . . . and the German soldier put me on the saddle of his bike. And I can remember the nape of his neck, it was shaved really, really close, well, like a soldier's neck, really." The memory of the soldier's neck is a memory of proximity to potential futures. The family managed to get out of the prison where they were held—Maurice does not know how—but the story could have turned differently at any point from their arrest onward. Maurice-the-boy's attention to the soldier's neck—such proximity to danger—stuck in part because of what Maurice-the-man knew of their future escape.

Sound memories projected futures in similar ways to visual ones. Bernard Lemaire's large family was unable to leave Lille during the civilian exodus of 1940. Instead, they hid in their cellar. He says: "We heard the Germans going past. Because the cellars had vents, you know, and you could hear them going past. . . . And I can still hear them, eh." At ten years old, he said, "children, well, they don't really understand," but added, "it was the collapse of everything, of the country." There must have been all sorts of sounds, but these stuck because of what these marching men represented for the nation's future. Speaking of her daily life in Villeurbanne, just outside Lyon, probably in or after 1943 when she was about eight, Denise Algret said: "I believe that everyone's memories are—, there were roundups, there was the blackout, black curtains, all the window panes painted blue, there were air raid sirens—." She provided a list of sights and sounds that boded something but were quite generic. She then focused on a more personal memory: "This sound of the boots, there, where I was, where I lived, perhaps six times a day, columns of German soldiers marching, and the song 'Heili Heilo,' which was a popular German song." As with Henri Buc, the sound memory resurfaced later in her life, bringing with it a set of feelings from her childhood. Living in Germany in the 1950s, she heard some children singing the song: "I really thought I was going to cry out, because for me, this 'Heili Heilo,' it was linked to the sound of the boots, the sound of that permanent strain." The sensorial assemblage throws together, in and for a moment, her presents and her pasts (1940s, 1950s, 1990s), Germany and France, German popular culture and Nazi occupation, boots marching and children playing, wound around with anger, fear, repression, and freedom.

Sounds, then, have a powerful affective capacity and can conjure and trans-mit memories of deep distress. Paul Maubourg's father was a resistance activist who was captured, tortured, and killed in France by the Nazis in brutal circum-stances that were extremely painful for Paul to relate. He was not present during his father's torture but recounted it in distress in his filmed interview. Yet the sound memory he associated with this devastating knowledge was his own: an incongruous memory burning with pain, pity, and loss. He said: "And the mem-ory that I also have, is that my father didn't have a proper burial, no funeral. It was the refuse lorry from Oyannax that took the bodies from Dortan to the cemetery.

I can still hear the sound of that truck, I saw it go past, it made a very particular noise. . . . Yes, I can still hear that refuse truck, I can still see it there, going
into the cemetery." The sound of the refuse truck evokes his father's mutilated
body, his resistance activity, and his son's bereavement; there is no talk of
heroism here.

   Hélène Zytnicki's filmed narrative of another kind of childhood trauma is
filled with the sounds of human distress. Hélène was arrested, age ten, with her
mother, and together they were held, like thousands of other Jews, in the hellish
Vélodrome d'Hiver (Paris's indoor cycling stadium) in the hot summer of 1942.
On the night of July 16–17, 1942, 13,152 Jews, including more than four thousand children, were rounded up by the French police and held in the Vel d'Hiv
for several days in terrible conditions. Mother and daughter were then trans-
ported to the French internment camp at Beaune-la-Rolande. Hélène's mother
was soon deported, and Hélène, with the other leftover children, was moved to
Drancy internment camp in Paris, from which her father managed to free her.
Her memories of the Vel d'Hiv are synesthetic, but sound has an overbearing
presence:

> The children were screaming, there were a lot of them, I remember people
> fainting, I think it was because of the heat. It was terribly hot. . . . It was abso-
> lutely packed, eh. Absolutely, completely jam-packed—. Women were calling
> for their children, children were calling for their mothers, it didn't stop, they
> were screaming, babies were crying. There were so many babies, they were
> thirsty. How on earth we lived through those five days, I don't know. . . . Well,
> it was atrocious, those five days in there. . . . And my mother never left me,
> and I never left her, we clung onto each other.

The memory is visual and thermoceptic (sensing heat) but is dominated by a
cacophonous sound-image of others' distress. She clung to her mother, whether
agitated or stunned we do not know. Later, at Beaune-la-Rolande, the terrible
day arrived when her mother was wrenched from her. Her memories fix on the
sounds of human distress, including her own and her mother's: "Like all the
other children. Screams, cries, I clung on to my mother, and then—, I don't
know who, who separated us, my mother was screaming, she spoke French
very badly, my mother, she was speaking Yiddish, she called out to me, then
[Hélène is crying]—the wrenching apart—[she wipes her tears from behind her

glasses and looks directly into the camera]." Paul's sound memory was an associative memory—the sound of the truck evoked suffering and grief—whereas Hélène's is immediate. Sound and movement—proprioceptive memory, toward and away from her mother—intertwine: the sound is of the separation and the separation is made of sound. Remembering these sounds is an intense, embodied experience of distress for Hélène. Affect circulates across the temporal planes: the listening encounter is also deeply felt, not with the same feeling as Hélène, or indeed as Paul, but deep sorrow nonetheless, feeling alongside. Such sensory evocations facilitate sympathetic engagement with other lives in concrete ways.[8]

Sound can do something that vision cannot. We use language to share simulacra of sights, deploying words with shared meanings, similes, and metaphors. But sound can be vocally simulated. Interviewees frequently perform sound memories to communicate something of their childhood experience. Such vocalizations lose something in transcription; on the page, they depend on my hearing of them, my rendering of the consonant or vowel sounds I hear, and how I choose to write those in English. Abstract vocalization was used in a descriptive way to convey strange noises to an uninitiated listener. Jean Caniot, for example, in Lille said: "We'd hear, I can still hear it ringing in my ears, the whistling of the bombs, 'Fsssssssssshhhhhhhhh,' or you could say, 'sssssssshhh-hhh,' a whistling." He also described the crashing noise of a lump of shrapnel falling on his house: "There was a dreadful racket, 'Rrraaaaaaaaaaaaaaahh!'" Serge Aubrée in Brest used sound to emulate the noise of the mobile antiaircraft guns shooting at Allied planes: "There was a truck there, passing up and down with DCA machine guns on it, following the planes 'Taran ta ta ta, taran ta ta ta.'" This performative dimension of the memory story is more than descriptive, however. Sounds had precise meanings, which children learned to understand. Simone Fauron explained that the sound made by the planes alerted her to danger or safety. She said: "They were laden, because we knew when the planes were laden, it went 'Voooo, voooo, voooo' [slowly articulated in a low-pitched voice], and when they were coming back, 'vooovooovooo' [faster and more high-pitched]." If the planes were heavy, they were frightening, menacing, and dangerous. If they were light, they were not: they had already dropped their bombs elsewhere. Bernard Bauwens used this kind of emulation to evoke the perceived qualitative difference in the British and American bombing of French targets.[9]

The Americans largely bombed from a higher altitude for technological reasons relating to their bombsights. Bernard said: "The English, you'd hear them come down 'whoooooooo, rrum, whoooooooooo, rrum!' The others, we never heard that—, it was as if, quickly falling in a string, you see, 'dr-dr-dr-dr-drrrrng,' finished. What people said, they said that they're bastards, the Americans, you see, because they don't bother to aim. The English, they aimed." The different sound representations not only evoked a difference in practice but an affective difference in how Americans and British were (and, in many cases, still are) perceived. These sounds held a set of moral, political, and affective meanings that went beyond direct representation.

Bombing provides numerous examples of tactile, proprioceptive, and thermoceptic memories, which combine with pulmonary or respiratory feeling and smell in a synaesthetic mash that can also include sound and sight. Sensory memories show the *affectio* in terms of movement and space, heat and suffocation in relation to the *affectus* of the bombs. Sonia Agache did not recall sounds but said that "all I remember is the blast of air, which pushed us all back." The sensation of the body in space, rocked by the blast, overrode other memories. Childhood friends Henri Le Turquais and Yves Le Roy in Brest, interviewed together, enacted the side-to-side motion of their gaze, like spectators at a tennis match, to replicate the tracer bullets in the sky. For André Dutilleul, the proprioceptive memory was one of contraction, the body diminished in a dangerous and agitated space, teeth clenched, enacted physically in the interview: "We were in a cellar, we'd feel the cellar doing this [gesturing a movement up and down with shoulders and hands]. Oh yes. And there, we were like that [mimes whole body hunched over], a handkerchief in the hand, gripped like that [makes a clenched fist]. You don't say anything, you grit your teeth." There were more invasive sensations too. Michel Floch described the bombing of the oil reserves in the port of Brest: "It made a terrible black smoke. You could even feel the heat of it from here." The smoke created a visual memory and the heat a thermoceptic one. For Lucienne Rémeur, living in a bomb shelter in Brest in 1944, danger also crept in via the lungs.[10] A German munitions store, illegally housed in the bomb shelter, had caught fire: "There wasn't any smoke. But there was, you know, like a smell of—, which got you in your nose and your throat." The chemicals from the burning ammunition alerted her to danger. In Fives, an industrial suburb of Lille, André Dutilleul and his wife Josette recounted their bombing experiences—they were not together at the time, but the memory is shared—in a sequence of synesthetic intensity in which odor played a part:

> ANDRÉ: And after that, there were the whistles of the bombs—
> JOSETTE: —that we'd hear—
> ANDRÉ: —and after that, more than anything, the thuds in the ground.
>   The detonation, and then the ground moving, and everything. All of that,
>   it made a noise which traumatized me. That's for sure.
> JOSETTE: A noise, and then the smell, because plaster when it falls, when
>   it's crushed, it smells, it smells, there's a particular smell—when you
>   knock a house down, today, well, it smells, the house does, when you
>   knock it down—, and well, it smelled like that. If possible, you'd have a
>   hanky so as not swallow all the dust—

Across these memories, sensations are strongly remembered not only because of the way they affected the body, but because of their strong association with danger and fear.

Bombing accounts for many but not all of the smell memories recounted. Léa Duclos, whose family found refuge in the rural Creuse department twice during the war, recalled the smell of ripe pears in the garden of the house where they were staying. For Léa, this smell mattered because it fixed the moment of their arrival as late summer. But this unsettled her memory story. As she spoke, Léa struggled to recall the years in which her family went to the Creuse. She assumed it was September 1939 when war broke out, and she believed they returned in 1944. But elements of her story suggested to me and to her that it may have been in 1940 that they first went there, during the civilian exodus, because there were German bombs and a demarcation line. The smell of pears provided a marker on which she hung the memory but confounds the possibility that it was 1940 (when refugees were likely to have arrived in early summer). The memory of the smell, then, is far stronger than a memory for time or date. Jacques Kermen also recounted his arrival in the Creuse, with his brother and young sister, as evacuees in 1943. His memories are quite fleeting. A woman collected the children from where the coach deposited them: "The lady with her bike—, she was walking with it. And what I remember really well is the smell of the hay, because there was—, we were bathed in that fragrance. And so, we arrived in the first village, where my sister was going to stay." Smell is central to the memory of the journey. The children walked several kilometers with the woman. Jacques's sister was to be left with another family in the hamlet next to where he was staying. Perhaps the smell memory is so strong because of the feeling that accompanied it. Jacques had been instructed by his parents that under no circumstances should he allow his little sister to be separated from him. The walk, with its surprising rural smells, was also permeated by his anxiety over his responsibility for her.

Two interviewees recounted having deliberately invoked smell or taste later in their lives in an attempt to retrieve happy memories. Colette Streicher was happily evacuated to a loving family in La Cellette, a village in the Creuse. Together with the son of that family, in adulthood she had revisited certain smells:

> We loved to go back, the two of us, to the [blacksmith's] forge. There's the same smell. There, all those odors, oh yes, I really like them. It's like, when I go to La Cellette, when I visit, I like to go into the sacristy, to get the smell. All those smells have stayed with me from my childhood . . ., and sometimes I need to find them again, I need to. The forge, it's the same thing, and well, I tell you, I breathe it in, I breathe it all in—.

Retrieving the smells seemed something of a compulsion. It acted as a gateway into a past world, to the happy memories of freedom and kindness associated with this past. Nancette Blanchou's wartime childhood was tainted by the arrest of her parents for their resistance activities. Her father was deported and died; her mother was released from prison but seriously ill. Yet Nancette also tried deliberately to evoke the past, this time through taste.

> Last week . . . there was a man on the market selling cornbread, and I bought some—, but I can tell you, I didn't find it had the same taste. Because I think that the cornbread people used to make, perhaps had a little bit of wheat in it too—, and I was, it actually quite disappointed me, because I couldn't eat this cornbread that I'd bought [laughing]. I wanted to make myself a Proust's madeleine with it, to re-taste that bread—

Perhaps Nancette's desire to relocate herself in this past was with the intention of retrieving the happy memories of life before her parents' arrest. Both women recognized the affective power of smell and taste memories to conjure the past.

Smell and taste are internal senses difficult to convey in words, but they remain powerful triggers of past feeling.

EMOTIONAL MEMORIES

Recounted emotional states, past and present, are another variety of memories that articulate a dimension of the felt realm explicitly. Sometimes this was through the mutually comprehensible language of emotives ("I was afraid," "she was happy"), sometimes through descriptions of emotional situations, and sometimes through emotional behavior in the interview. Very many of the emotional memories recounted were negative or stressed. Some psychologists might judge these as more accurate in their relation to past experiences.[11] However, I am just as interested in how people *say* they felt in the past. In the naming and communicating of emotion, there is a cognitive process that, Massumi and others suggest, diminishes intensity.[12] Yet communicating emotion in language is an efficient means of seeking and gaining recognition from a listener.

Emotions Identified

Returning to the memory stories of Nancette Blanchou and Colette Streicher, I begin with memories identified as happy ones. It is important to note in the first cases, and that of Denise Algret which follows, that there is no specified object of happiness. Happiness is bound up in a time and a place rather than directed toward, or experienced as, an affect of a specific object. This contrasts with the more frequently recounted negative emotional memories analyzed across the rest of this chapter. Of her life on the family farm before her parents' arrest, Nancette Blanchou said: "Ah, ah! Marvelous memories. First, because I was a little girl who loved working in the fields. I loved the farm, I loved the animals." Happy memories here are not linked to a particular event. Her happy feelings are created through an idealization of the time before tragedy struck, which I will explore further in part 2, "Memories Located."[13] Evacuee Colette Streicher recalls the celebratory events of harvest time but does so rather generically; the memory is not of a specific incident or moment. "It was, oh! What a joy threshing day was, eh. I'm nostalgic for those times, eh. I won't ever forget them. . . . Let's just say, when you're a kid, and you see the threshing machine coming, well . . ., it's just so wonderful. We'd all be there, kids arriving from everywhere, whenever the thresher arrived." Colette was sad to leave the Creuse and her foster family after the war and experienced the same loss of freedom as other happily evacuated children when they returned to their home cities. Colette labels her memory as nostalgia, perhaps idealized, certainly longing, but the memory itself is broad and general. Denise Algret's happy memories were also linked to her evacuation, where she found herself in a lively, youthful home that contrasted with her older parents' mode of life. She said, "I loved it, oh I loved it! That's also part of my really, really good memories!" She mentioned in passing country walks, that the man was a plasterer and the woman a seamstress, and that she had "some really good memories" of school there. No more detail was given; no particular incident or object created happiness. Although less common, happy memories could be more specific. Brothers Michel and Claude Thomas had been evacuated from Boulogne-Billancourt to their grandparents' house, and through the summer of 1944 during the chaotic period of the liberation, they had no news of their parents. Michel says that one day, "we were dumbstruck to see them arrive, I can just remember my father coming through the little garden gate." Claude added that they could not believe their eyes. Michel continued: "We were surprised and happy to see them arrive!" Nonetheless, more generalized memories of happiness, often implicitly contrasted with other, less happy, memories, were more common than specific ones.

The majority of emotional memories recounted were more negative. One set is those of generalized anxiety. These were not usually attached to specific objects and were often associated, in the telling, with children's ignorance. Rachel Jedinak spoke of the time before the war when her parents and their Jewish friends discussed developments in Germany. She said: "When you're very young, when you're three or four years old, you don't understand what's going on. But nevertheless, you feel things. And I felt—, I saw their serious faces, I felt this anxiety heavy around me, but without really understanding what was happening." Rachel emphasized that children do not need to understand in order to feel and that those feelings are storable and retrievable as memories. Anxiety flowed around the outbreak of war. When asked how she experienced the war, although she was older than Rachel—eleven in 1939—Georgette Transler's abiding memory was: "Fear. I was afraid. But I didn't understand much. You couldn't understand. You heard the planes, Mum saying to me 'Get down!,' all of that. 'Don't say anything' . . . I was afraid, that's all. Well, I was young, eh. I didn't understand very well, I was just frightened." Across her interview, Georgette's memories of the period were rather muddled. Fear was generalized and the memory of airplanes not situated in place or time. Statements about not understanding often occurred when a rememberer could not recall specific incidents but an affective residue remained. Genevieve Giraud, far away from trouble in the rural Creuse (a native, not an evacuee), also spoke about anxiety in broad terms. Even though they were isolated, she said, "my parents, they were afraid as well, they—, we were really living in a state of fear, all the same. I think—I remember, my uncle, he brought his truck, to hide his truck at the house, and afterwards, my dad, he couldn't rest easy. He was always wondering what was going to happen to him—, there was lots of anxiety even so—, there was always a worry." Genevieve suggests an object of anxiety, which she does not develop (perhaps she never knew): the truck. But by and large, the story is one of fearfulness rather than fear. Such memories throb dully and evoke a vague haze of feeling, a mood perhaps, rather than the piercing impact of traumatic ones.

Frequently in memory, though, general anxiety or fearfulness became fear when a clearly threatening object, was present. Attacks from the air, whether from the Germans who bombed and strafed during the invasion of France in 1940 or the Allies, were one such object. Yet as Pierre Haigneré remarks, that object was not always comprehensible to a small child, although its *affectio* remained. Of being machine-gunned during the 1940 invasion and its consequent refugee exodus when he was five, Pierre said: "My memories of it, it's simply fear, panic, the surprise of seeing people lying on the ground. The memory of seeing a toy a bit further away on the ground—because there were other children. . . . But, well, it's just fear, that's all. I—how can I put this?—could I identify what caused that fear? No." Thérèse Leclercq was only four when she experienced an Allied bombing in January 1943 in Hellemmes (Lille). She links her emotional state directly to the event, which had a lasting impact on her:

> It's an image . . ., you could say that, I feel like I can see it again. . . . The fear, I have a memory of—, of shaking, of—, it's an intense fear, you know, a fear, I don't know how to explain it. . . . The nuns, I can see them taking off their, they wore these aprons, and they threw their aprons over us because the window panes were smashing, flying. . . . Well, I lived in a state of fear right up to the end of the war.

Both Pierre's and Thérèse's memory stories described an embodied response and are saturated by the bewildered children's fear.

Another specific object of children's fear was the Germans. Many had been taught to fear them. Pierre Tainturier stated that as the Germans advanced in 1940, "everyone was scared because of the German: the German scared you. That's just how it was."[14] At another moment of his story, however, he personalizes the fear: "Me, well, I was a little bit—perhaps because I wasn't very brave, I don't know—but I was a little bit terrified." Madame Gaultier also described her fear of the Germans: "I was convinced that the Germans were lions who were going to kill us when we arrived at the [demarcation line]. Such a terrible dread, I can still feel it, I was afraid to pass the line, we were all so afraid, but me, I was terrified." In other cases, fear was linked to a specific incident. Ginette Renaud recounted seeing the occupying Germans parading in Paris. A young woman on a bicycle refused to stop. She continued to ride, barely disturbing the parade, when a young officer "knocked her off her bike, and threw her onto the pavement": a small act of violence compared to many, but a shock for a child to witness. Ginette continued, describing a caricatural Nazi: "They really frightened me, with their black leather boots, their helmets, the monocle, that really frightened me." Cécile Bramé compounded her own fear of the Germans through an act of proud resistance—a very sticky memory, alluded to repeatedly in her interview—at the age of eleven or twelve, in Brest:

> I got on the [bus] and I saw an empty seat, and sat down, and the German, he'd come forward too to sit down, and well, because I was already sitting down, I didn't get up, and he came towards me and he shook his fist in my face. When I got home, I started to cry, and my mother said, "But he didn't do anything else to you, did he?" She said, "Don't cry, you're still here." But the fear, at that moment, for me, exploded. I had been very, very frightened, but I didn't want to cry in front of the German. So I didn't cry, but when I got home I burst into floods of tears. That's how scared I'd been.

Stifled in the moment, emotion exploded as soon as she felt safe. Such examples show us not only the dangers that had crept into the children's everyday lives, and thus something of what life had become like for them, but also the communicability of certain memories of fear, particularly fear that has an object.

Jewish children experienced particular kinds of fear associated with the increasingly high stakes of their persecution. Germans were an important object of fear, but that fear was intensified by future projections of what their presence in France might, and later did, mean. Charles Baron was fourteen when the war broke out. He said that his fear began "I think, when I saw my first German" while separated from his parents during the 1940 civilian exodus. He said: "From that year onwards, I believe that right up to the end, I was always afraid. It was fear, because when you heard what had happened before the war, when you're a kid you read a lot, well, you give yourself ideas. . . . But fear, I was always— . . . fear, yes, it was a permanent fixture for me." Charles's parents, arrested in 1942, were killed in Auschwitz. Charles remained with his uncle; they were taken to Drancy, from where his uncle was deported. The fear triggered by that first German permeated the whole period, during which he was actively hunted, watched close relatives be taken, and narrowly escaped death himself. Maurice Goldring recounted a specific incident of anti-Semitic persecution that may seem small-scale compared to Charles's experiences, but the intense fear felt by the child was powerful. One day he boarded a Paris metro alone and realized too late that he would break the curfew imposed on Jews. "I remember," he said, "this kind of panicky fear, of not being able to get back home in time." Fear is heightened in the memory story by the adult Maurice's knowledge of virtual futures: what might also have been. Guy Lazard also pinpointed the beginning of his growing fear. The Germans arrived in his hometown of Mâcon in late 1942. The following year his aunt and cousin, coming from Toulon to visit, were arrested en route: "We never saw each other again," said Guy. Until Guy's family left Mâcon in mid-1943, he said, "we were living in fear." The feeling of fear, Sara Ahmed writes, "presses us into [the] future"; fear always relates to the future as "anticipated pain."[15] That impression is doubled in memory stories. Events in the happening past anticipate future pain, creating fear in the child's unfolding present; at the same time, the adult-told memory story is impressed with the pain of the known future, of the genocide that did indeed unfold.

The multitemporality of fear in memory is clear in Hélène Zytnicki's account of her and her mother's arrest in Paris on July 16, 1942. Her father and brother had gone into hiding, but none of them believed that women and children would be targeted. Hélène recalled a knock at the door, her mother answering it, and two men telling them to pack their cases. Responding to the interviewer's question as to whether the knock had awoken her, she described—sometimes through her own memories, sometimes through her father's—the bodily impact of fear:

> The noise woke me up. . . . But I must have been so—, I don't really know what happened to me that night, but I must have been so afraid that—, my father told me this later, he came back to the apartment the next day, there was nobody there, and I was ten years old, and for the first time, at least since I was a baby, I'd wet the bed, it seems. From fear, I suppose. He told me afterwards, you'd wet the bed. I think that I'd been paralyzed by fear. I remember that my mother had to dress me as I was paralyzed by fear. The noises had woken me up, and, well, I'd wet the bed. [She struggles to control her speech. Closing her eyes, she breathes in. She smiles, opens them, and looks away.] My father told me that.

In the face of this overwhelming fear, she lost control. The horrors to come, in the Vel d'Hiv, Beaune-la-Rolande, and Drancy and losing her mother, are all anticipated inside this fear. She recounts not an imagined future, but a known one. The assemblage of this memory story is multitemporal, multispatial, and multivocal; it is emotional, embodied, and intensely affective in both its content and its narration. The named emotion—fear, a child's abject fear—works to imprint upon any listener the searing cruelty of these crimes.

Emotions Transferred

Part of memory's social dimension is the incorporation into the recollection of the happening past of other people's perspectives, particularly those of people with whom we live in proximity. Yet there is no way to know how somebody else feels or felt, not least because the quality of feeling is so fluid. Neuropsychologists observe regions of cognitive activity in the brain and measure hormonal levels; psychologists use self-reporting on various scales that rely on language and a priori shared meanings. Both methods separate individuals from their longer life histories and restrict their phenomenological encounters in order to optimize experimental conditions.[16] They must turn memory's multidirectional flow into a coagulated solid: discrete, analyzable, categorizable.[17] In daily life, we depend on more or less reliable forms of imaginative empathy, particularly projected assumptions about what someone must or should be feeling. Other people's emotions as well as feelings about other people's emotions are core parts of the relationality of feeling and the sociality of memory. It is "not about one person's feelings becoming another's" but about bodies—people, things, events, places, and so on—"literally affecting each other and generating intensities," which circulate.[18] In memory stories of childhood, relations with parents, siblings, and other protectors are important, and reflections on their emotions frequently have explanatory power. Children learned about the world through flows of feeling between themselves and others. Through such examples, we see what emotions *do* as they circulate between bodies and how they work to constitute not just children's worlds but the broader communities of feeling that are the focus of chapter 7.

Interviewees frequently remarked on how they were affected by their parents' emotional states. The parents in question were often mothers, usually because they were more present than fathers.[19] As with emotions identified as one's own, anxiety (without a definite object) and fear were common. When I asked Léa Duclos whether she understood, as a little girl of six or seven, that there was a war going on, she replied, "For me, I could see it through Mum's fear, because she was terrified as anything. She was really, really scared." Léa posits her mother's fear as fundamental to her knowledge of the world at that time. She does not articulate an object of fear, so war becomes a feeling rather than a set of events. In other cases, interviewees knew the objects of their parents' fear. Again, fear of Germans was widespread. The sociologist Ian Burkitt criticizes cultural theories of affect that see it as a "mystical force or charge akin to an electrical current."[20] But in these memory stories, affect—as mood, feeling, emotion—flows, and not mystically, around the invasion in relation to the Germans, derived materially from a combination of heterogenous elements (family histories, regional histories, past wars, injuries, pain, bereavements, politics, popular culture, national discourses, and so on) brought together in particular moments. Édith Denhez from Cambrai noted that when war broke out, "my mother was terrified, my parents were terrified. That's why, straight away, it was a question of getting away, because in the other war, they'd been hungry, people were killed." For Sonia Agache in Hellemmes, her father's past experience generated both his fear and her own. Witnessing the Germans arrive, "my father went as white as a sheet, eh. Well, I used to listen to my dad, and being a war veteran, he used to speak about it. . . . My father had been gassed in the 1914–18 war, so it's true, it was a really dreadful fear, eh." Parental fears translated into concrete behaviors. Rémy Ménigault had a clear memory of his mother throwing sweets given to him by a German soldier into the stove: it was, he said, "the terror of the Prussian German, that's for sure. We weren't allowed to eat the sweets because they'd have poisoned them." The little boy objected: to recognize the fear was not necessarily to share it.

Françoise Yessad, born in 1937, recalled her parents' anxiety and pondered its transferal. She spoke of the mischief she and her siblings made but then added a counterpoint:

> FRANÇOISE: Oh, for us, it was a really happy time! Although, all the
> same, we knew, we felt the anxiety. We could feel our parents' anxiety—,
> we felt it.
> LINDSEY: And how did you feel it?
> FRANÇOISE: I couldn't tell you. They didn't say anything to us. But we
> could feel it, feel it. We soaked it up, like sponges. Perhaps my mother
> and father spoke about it at the table. Not that we were allowed to speak
> at the dinner table, of course.

Françoise positions the children passively but absorbently. But children's responses were not only passive. Marie-Rolande Cornuéjols remembered her response to her mother's anxiety on their journey into the countryside in 1940: "It's a flash memory that has really stayed with me. I was sitting next to Mum, and Mum was looking out at the countryside as night was falling, and she said to me, 'Do you think we'll get used to it? Do you think it will be alright?' And I remember thinking to myself, 'How can an adult ask advice from a child of ten?' It really shocked me." The flow here is not just from adult to child. Marie-Rolande resisted her mother's emotions. Rémy Ménigault, age four or five, resisted his mother's fear because his goal was the sweets and he did not understand the threat the German represented. Marie-Rolande, on the other hand, questioned her mother's anxieties because she recognized the loss of protection the circumstances were generating. Her indignation and disappointment made this memory sticky and worth recounting.

Interviewees noted instances when their parents' emotions did not transfer to them. Michel Jean-Bart saw it as a conscious effort on his parents' part. He said "they didn't want to go on at us about the wars from before. They'd rather keep [it] to themselves. They didn't want to tell us about the sadness of war." Sam Krouck was interned in Douadic camp with his mother. He recalled her response: "It was atrocious, it was awful there. My mother, she was sobbing when we arrived, it was—, well, it was a camp. There was barbed wire, watchtowers, all of that." His mother's distress was not recounted as transferred, though. He said that they were not treated too badly, although rations were scarce, but, like Rémy above, his priorities, knowledge, and comprehension differed from his mother's: "I was happy enough. I played, that was about it. It was quite good, I had mates of my own age . . . and as we were kids, we could pretend we were in a holiday camp! [He laughs a lot.]" Known and virtual futures project back, perhaps: Sam's family survived, and his later knowledge of what a concentration camp or even a death camp could be affects how these memories were told.

Absent Memories, Absent Feelings

Several interviewees noted an absence of memories about emotional experiences, which surprised them. Theories of trauma differ in psychology and psychoanalysis, the former suggesting that traumatic memories provide an impediment to working memory and so are stored in less accessible parts of the mind, the latter positing the idea of repression into "darker" zones of the mind.[21] Some neuropsychologists suggest that memories of stressful (if not traumatic) situations are likely to be better remembered. In the memory stories, we also encounter "ideal affect."[22] People believe they *should* have memories of aspects of their childhoods that were striking in one way or another. The *should* derives from what moves them now, as adults. They want themselves to have been emotionally affected in the past in ways they now believe are appropriate to the situation.

Brothers Claude and Michel Thomas did not recall feeling scared during the war, in spite of the air raids on their town. They emphasized that for them, the war was not characterized by fear:

CLAUDE: What's surprising is the feeling that at no moment did we really feel very afraid—

MICHEL: No, no—

LINDSEY: No fear—

CLAUDE: I don't have—, in any case, that's not that kind of memory I have from that period—

MICHEL: Not at all, not at all, no.

LINDSEY: You didn't feel in danger—?

MICHEL: No, no.

The continuing flow of daily life and their active interest in following the events of war provided the central core of their joint narrative. They speak in conscious contrast to wider national narratives about this period and seek actively to counter assumptions about children's experiences of war. Michel returned to his perspective on the heavy RAF air raid of March 3, 1942, on Boulogne-Billancourt as he sheltered in the cellar: "Well, it lasted, it lasted a long time. And even so, I can recall the idea that I had in my mind—I wasn't terrified! But I said 'For Heaven's sake, please let the building not fall down on us.' . . . It would be really hard to get out, I said to myself. But I didn't think we'd be killed—, just that we might be buried." The air raid was the first he had experienced. He recognized some of the dangers in a practical sense but not the mortal threat it posed. His memory is of thoughts and feelings related to potential outcomes, but as death (or injury) seemed not to have entered his mind, the feelings were not explicitly fearful.

Serge Holand's absence of emotion around the circumstances in which his family found themselves after the roundups of Jews in Paris in July 1942 surprises him. With his parents, he moved to a tiny flat, sealed and apparently abandoned from the outside, with food delivered via the window of the internal courtyard by a neighbor. His parents packaged him off with "someone." He said:

> I—, I have—, I am shocked, but I don't have any dramatic memories, at all, at all, at all. It's as though all of that was almost normal. I was, in '42, eight years old. So then, I passed—, someone came to get me. To take me over the demarcation line. Without my parents. And I just accepted it, no problem— or at least as far as I remember. I've always said that during this whole period, I don't have any memories of anything particularly dramatic for me, as a child. I accepted everything, rationalized it—, and I'm still shocked even now. . . . A child of eight years old, you can tell him whatever you like. . . . To be shut up in an apartment, totally sealed, lights only on for a bare minimum, no noise, all that, it's going to affect a child—, no. Yes, to have memories, that would be because it affected me, but I don't have any memories. . . . I can't even say I have a bad memory of it.

Serge has searched his memory. He puts it down to his age, to his character, to his parents' reassurances, which he can no longer remember. He wants to know what he felt. He cannot recall fear or even a negative set of feelings linked to these dramatic events, and he is puzzled by the relation between the memory and what he believes he could or should have felt. His family ultimately survived. As one pathway—of luck, judgment, options—was activated through a multiplicity of virtual bleak futures, certain emotional experiences seem to have dropped out of recountable memory.

It was around the issue of separation from parents that interviewees expressed the most surprise at the absence of emotion. Most were parents, grandparents, and even great-grandparents themselves. The idea that children might not experience a wrench as they separate from their parents is a difficult one for parents to accept. This generated puzzlement and speculation. For example, Christian Le Goff, evacuated from Paris to the Creuse at age six, remembered, with a warning: "You know, all of that—, the separation from my parents and everything, I don't remember that. Because often, I hear people say 'Can you imagine, for a child—!' No, you get used to it quickly! You should be careful about that, eh." What "people" thought might be a child's experience of separation was not his. Christian was very happily assimilated into a loving foster family: this important consideration must accompany his warning to me. Roger Davre, whose evacuation was similarly positive, simulated what he might have felt but did not: "I didn't shed a tear for the whole journey [acting the sad child], 'Oh, Mummy, Oh Daddy, I won't see you again!' No, no!" The supposed words of a distressed child were put forward in contrast to his own remembered feelings. Michèle Martin recognized that her absence of anxiety for her parents' safety could be viewed badly: "I don't have the feeling that I was worried about my parents. Perhaps once or twice, but no, not really. It's not left an impression. It's not very nice to say that, but still!" She was conscious of how an absence of emotion might be construed, but her memory did not register a strong feeling. Again, a positive outcome led to some parts of experience sticking and not others. When Serge Holand arrived in the Creuse, via Lyon, after the roundups of July 1942, he was reunited with his parents. Asked whether he felt happy or relieved to see them again, he said, in surprise: "I don't have the slightest memory of that. But I definitely was. Because I was very close to my parents. But, no, not the slightest memory!" What he remembered, he said, was that it was cold. The declarative memory of emotions comprises, then, not just what was felt and what others felt but also what was not felt, or not remembered to have been felt. This was shaped both by future trajectories, real and imagined, and by ideal affects around what could, should, and must have been felt. These derived from present-situated cultural and social norms about children, family, and feeling.

Emotion Into the Present

As Henri Buc's anecdote showed at the beginning of part 1, and Denise Algret's later on, the emotion of the past does not just stay in the past. It plays out in the individual's unfolding future, both across time and in the interview itself. Emotion about the past experienced in the present was not recounted as the same emotion that had been experienced as a child. The interviewees do not claim to relive their emotional pasts. Emotion resurfaces differently. For example, Yvette Chapalain was about fourteen years old when the bombing of Brest formed part of her daily life. She recounted only one frightening incident, when an air raid happened while she was looking after her baby brother. Yet she recalled a moment, years later, unexpectedly seeing the beams of a lighthouse in the night sky. The sight brought back the past "brutally." She began to tremble: "And then and there, I was very scared. Why? Well, probably even as a child, I had nonetheless absorbed that anxiety, and it didn't show itself until fifty years later." The residue of fear was somewhere in her implicit memory, she supposed. But the adult's fear did not accord with the remembered experience of the child.

The emotions of the past also manifested in the present as health problems experienced by adults and attributed, accurately or not, to traumatic childhoods. Such a phenomenon was mooted by Simone Courant's widower Eugène and their daughter Yolande, whom I interviewed together. Simone had passed away some years previously. As an eight-year-old girl, Simone had been evacuated from a loving but very poor and rather chaotic family in Paris to the Creuse, where she was housed by a single woman in her forties, Lucienne, who unofficially adopted her after the war. Lucienne provided for her and evidently cared for her, although the two did not have an affectionate relationship. Simone suffered emotionally all her life, Eugène and Yolande suggested, as a consequence of this complicated childhood, particularly in relation to feelings of shame, belonging, and indebtedness. But, said Yolande, it went further than feeling. Her mother had suffered from a complicated heart condition, and Yolande said: "There was always this buried sorrow. And so if she had cardiac problems, of course, right from the start she had been storing a lot of things up." Attributing her heart condition to the past may not have been medically sound, but it had an explanatory power for her family. Another woman, Mme S, who chose not to be interviewed but who wrote to me about her multiple evacuations across the war, many of them unhappy and some abusive, attributed her lifelong struggle with depression and anxiety to these experiences. Hélene Zytnicki, whose traumatic persecution as a Jewish child included the wrenching separation from her mother in Beaune-la-Rolande, was physically afflicted in the immediate aftermath and far beyond: "As soon as I came out of the camp, I started to have the tremors, my heart racing, nonstop, which gave me—, at least, you could say, from that period, I started having nervous tension. . . . I had nightmares, every night, I saw my mother every night, really, for years and years, I'd dream of my mother. I dreamed of her every night, every single night . . . for years and years." She suffered illness across her life and sought psychological treatment. Interviewed in her fifties, she said that she was now a little better, but for many years she would tremble uncontrollably if she saw the police. Such responses are understood as part of posttraumatic stress, from which many child Holocaust survivors suffered for many years without medical support.[23]

Emotion in the Interview

Emotion also emerges in physical, embodied ways in the interview encounter. Hirsch and Spitzer have critiqued understandings of trauma in testimony that overly depend on visible embodied emotion. Breakdown—the loss of language, tears, fainting—they say has become the "ultimate" expression of trauma, to the detriment of what can be expressed in words.[24] Such thinking seems to underpin some preferences for filmed oral history: observable emotion is seen as somehow more valid or more valuable (to law, to science); it is *there*, it can be counted, it seems readily comprehensible. Yet across part 1, I have suggested a wider range of ways that past emotional experiences are communicated. Emotion present in the interview encounter is only one of these, although it is worth remarking nonetheless. Sometimes that emotion is conveyed by explanation, and sometimes it overflows linguistic capacities. The mistake, however, is to think that embodied emotions speak for themselves. They still depend on understanding and interpretation by the interlocutor(s), also emotionally present in the exchange of the listening encounter.[25]

Several interviewees commented on how speaking about their childhood made them feel during the interview. Simone Fauron laughed when she said to her interviewer, "with all of this you're making me stir up things I'd almost forgotten." Laughter is difficult to interpret. Simone laughed a lot, but it was unclear whether stirring things up was a good or bad experience for her. Other interviewees were more precise. Arnaud Saunier told his interviewer that "speaking about this, with you, has been a relief for me." The comment is ambiguous because the interview was quite muddled. Arnaud struggled to remember things, but from what he said, his family seemed to get along with neighbors, avoided the Germans, and coped with restrictions. This underscores the difficulty of knowing what people feel and why. Serge Holand, who recounted his family's flight from Paris, showed me photos of the people he befriended in the village where they found refuge. He said: "I'm really happy to look at these photos again." The interview provided an opportunity not just to remember persecution but also to emphasize the importance of cherished friends. Madame Ghisolfo's memories of childhood and adolescence in Sète were recorded by the local archives. Her narrative contained stories about interactions with Germans, fear, adolescent resistance, allusions to shame or guilt, and a discussion of the suffering poverty wrought on her family. She said: "Thinking about all of this, it does something to me." The interviewer invited her to explain. "It makes me shiver. It's a pleasure to talk to you, but [there is a pause], it's the past." Again, the comments are ambiguous. Thérèse Allglas-Cymmerman described being a hidden Jewish child. Sent away as a baby, she was taken in by a family who raised her as their own. She said: "Each time I tell this story, it does me a lot of good." Although the context is the genocidal destruction of the Jews, as in Serge's case, the interview provided an opportunity to recognize kindness, solidarity, and love. Shedding tears for lost friends and family, these people also witnessed human goodness, which affected them positively into the present.

Embodied emotions are evidently more available to observe in filmed interviews or in those where I was present. But even visible emotions do not speak for themselves. At times, body language seemed comprehensible. Across his filmed interview, Paul Maubourg, whose father was arrested for resistance work and tortured to death, looked very sad. His shoulders drooped, his hands were tightly clasped, and he was not at all animated. He looked away from the camera very frequently. Watching the interview is uncomfortable; the camera stares unblinkingly while the interviewee struggles to know where to look. Despite the extra layer of information future researchers may gain, the camera brings its own dynamic. Its impassive gaze is unresponsive, unequal. It is not an engaged, compassionate interlocutor. Nicole Kahn's interview was also filmed. But even without an image, we can hear the smile and the lightness in her voice as she described being reunited with her father and brothers after being imprisoned away from them in Les Baumettes in Marseille. The awful experience of the prison gave way to something equally terrible, so it might seem: "When the train was leaving to take us from Marseille to Drancy, we were reunited with my father and my brothers, everyone was in chains [she is smiling broadly], with handcuffs, we were reunited on the platform in Marseille." Why does she smile to see her family handcuffed, in chains? While transferal to Drancy was hardly a cause for celebration, being reunited was. Nicole's voice brightened with the emotion of the memory, as did her face. Drancy was faced by the family together, and that mattered in her memories.

It was often when speaking of close family members that emotion became evident. Sylvette Leclerc recounted her father arriving home from a prisoner-of-war camp, where he had been since 1940, only to leave straight away to visit his mother. She died suddenly, though, before he got there. Sylvette said that "it was such a dreadful sorrow for us all, because he never got to see his mother alive again." The statement was followed by a long pause as she recovered her composure. Anxieties around her father's imprisonment permeated her narrative. The anticipated joy of his return cannot have materialized in the sorrowful atmosphere of his bereavement. Sylvette's distress comes from imagining his grief as well as mastering her own. At the end of his interview, Christian Gaillard asked to be excused for his "emotional moments." He said that was his nature. His voice cracked, he gulped, and he spoke through tears at seven or eight points across his narrative. Each one of these points related to his father, who was also taken prisoner of war in 1940. Christian's first emotional moment predated that, though, as he recounted his grandfather's death when his father was nine years old. Later on, he only just held back his tears when describing the advice his father sent to his mother about Christian's schooling from the prisoner-of-war camp in Germany. He was moved, he said, by his father's "strength to have thought about it, in the middle of the war." His emotion was audible when he spoke of not receiving news from his father, and he broke into tears when speaking of other children's fathers being released and not his: "It was quite hard to swallow." The intensity of feeling around his father, created by his wartime absence and by more general recollections of a now-deceased parent, was clear. Eugène, the widower of Simone Courant (the Parisian evacuee taken in by foster-mother Lucienne) was also tearful when imagining the pitiful figure of his wife as a little girl, initially unwanted by any of the villagers. He said "she was completely lost" and wept as he articulated the words (maybe) spoken by Lucienne: "I want that little girl, there, standing all alone in the square." It pained him to imagine the little girl he later loved as his wife, but he was also perhaps moved to relive Lucienne's gesture of friendship, which ultimately brought Simone into his life.

When I interviewed Michel Jean-Bart about the Allied bombing he experienced at his home in the railway workers' housing estate next to Lille-Délivrance station, his wife was also present. She had not been bombed and remained silent for much of the interview. But at one point, her feelings overflowed:

> Look here, I mean to say, I didn't get bombed. Oh, this is going to be hard for me to say [she is clearly distressed] because—, I had a brother, he was a first-aider. He was part of a group of five first-aiders. They weren't soldiers. They went to help clear up at Lille-Délivrance. . . . And one day, just like that, they were arrested by the Germans. And they were shot. [She struggles to control her tears.] That was my brother. He was seventeen.

Taken by surprise, I encouraged her to tell me more about what happened. Although she was very young at the time, she had a lot to say, and she showed me the order of service card for a commemorative ceremony held in memory of the young men. She cried and told me "it still hurts a bit. . . . You know, all of that, it's not forgotten. You can't forget."

Two very strong moments of embodied emotion came in relation to life saving and its opposite, life taking. Jean-Pierre Becherel was not quite four years old when he, his mother, and his baby brother set out from Normandy, in fear and disarray, during the civilian exodus of 1940. He said that as soon as his mother felt safe, "she stopped. She stopped somewhere where people wanted to take her in. [He becomes choked up and tearful.] That's the magnificent act." I interviewed him in the home of, and alongside, Denis Graveron, son of the couple who took in the family, who were strangers to them at the time. Of their welcome, Jean-Pierre said, tearfully: "Well [a pause; he gathers himself to speak], it's very [pause; tearfully], very important." He mimed the life-saving action of eating the fresh bread that the Graveron family offered them, saying "Every time I eat bread [silence full of emotion]—". It was difficult for him to articulate his gratitude for this generosity, and he was visibly overwhelmed. In the case of Rémy Ménigault, the railway history archivists who recorded his interview noted in the accompanying meta-data form that they had decided to cut part of his account out of respect for the interviewee. They recognized that this was an erasure of important nonverbal communication but had chosen, nonetheless, not to archive the full extent of his emotional breakdown. It was, and this was their hope, still very clear how he felt. He vividly described being a little boy of around six years standing on a rural train platform where his parents were stationmasters:

> I'm on the platform with my mother, and a train is coming, it's slowing down, it's not going to stop, but we hear children screaming, crying, they were throwing things from—, and so I asked my mother, "Why are those children crying?" And she said, "Well, what can you expect, they're just little children and they've been taken from their parents, and they're sending them to Germany." That was it. Just, they're little children—she didn't say Jewish children—just little children, they've taken them from their parents. Who had taken them? We didn't know—in fact, it was French people, not Germans—and they were taking them to Germany. To do what? That was it. And me . . . well, I was barely six years old, I asked her questions anyway, lots of questions. But that, the story of those children left such a mark on me. Why? Well first, because it was children, they were in cattle wagons, do you understand, and you couldn't see their faces, but you could hear the screams, screams . . .

Here, the interview is cut, jumping to a more solid-voiced Rémy on another topic. His words are important, and the cut was made with a sensitive explanation on the archival record. I have thought a great deal about Rémy's tears. Perhaps Rémy cries in frustration: his six-year-old self's frustration in the face of inadequate explanations and his adult's frustration at a powerless past self. Perhaps he cries in deep sympathy for the children whose fate he now knows. Perhaps he cries in sorrow or shame for these barbarous acts carried out by his fellow countrymen, implicated in their crimes.[26]

Feelings as emotional states consciously articulated, declared, and communicated are at the heart of these childhood memories. They are there in the happening past of childhood, in unfolding lives narrated in the memory stories, in explicitly emotive language, in the pondering of emotion's absence, and in the behaviors that make emotion visible and audible in the interview.

PAUSE—DANIEL—FEAR ON THE ROAD

Daniel Berland's memory story, held by the Archives départementales du Val-de-Marne, appears to have been filmed in his study. It is a twenty-five-minute account of his family's experience of the civilian exodus in early June 1940. He seems to speak from fairly copious notes, showing great care for precisely locating places on the route. At the time, things were confused and confusing, but now the story has stabilized. At one level, it is plainly descriptive. It resembles many other exodus narratives. The destination was relatives in the Limousin region of central France. The small family—parents, Daniel, and his older brother—traveled mostly on foot, piled with their belongings, receiving some assistance later from the French army. They walked along crowded roads, experiencing fatigue and the danger of German machine-gunning. Daniel's reliance on his notes makes for the kind of memory story that lacks spontaneity and could be seen as disappointing or inauthentic. Yet listening attentively to the peaks of sensory and emotional intensity reveals something of what this experience was like for a child. He recalled that they left in the afternoon and spent the first night at Morangis:

> I remember having slept in the hay. My father was pulling a handcart, my mother carried the suitcases, my older brother wheeled the bike which was overloaded, and I had my satchel. I was eleven years old at the time. Morangis, the hay. Then the next day, still fleeing in the midst of a considerable crowd, the next day we went round Tour de Montlhéry, and it took us forty-eight hours, if not more, to get to Bouray-sur-Juine, to a place where the people let us stay in a little house in their garden, which had a tiled floor. I remember, there was nothing to lie down on . . . and the tiles were really cold.

The stopping-off points are recalled through sensory memories of where he slept: Morangis is the hay, and Bouray-sur-Juine is the cold tiles. These details are qualitatively different from the narration of place, which drives the story onward. Sleeping in the hay on the first night was perhaps exciting, the start of an adventure, but strange, itchy, perhaps, in the dark night. Trying to sleep on cold, hard tiles sounded less pleasant. Daniel does not attribute emotions, but these details pull the listener into a lived experience rather than an external account. The hay and the tiles made the memory sticky. The exodus is shown to be an evolving, increasingly hostile, encounter with the material world.

Soon, though, the encounter was not material but human, and hostility became intentional. Daniel's memory moves beyond the sensory:

> We arrived near to Orléans. And there, what I remember is, not far from Orléans, all of a sudden a cry rang out from the crowd, screams, it took me a moment to understand: "Planes, planes!" And yes, the planes were coming, we heard it, the throbbing of the engines, the noise of the machine guns, because they were shooting up the roads. We scrambled over a ditch, I remember it was difficult because it was quite deep, and threw ourselves onto the ground in the fields beyond. And I was lying flat on my stomach on the ground, my face in the soil, and suddenly, the noise of machine guns was getting closer and I saw in front of me [here, he swallows], the earth spitting, a few meters away—, was it the bullets, I think, was it the cartridge cases, it didn't last long, the planes went on their way and the screams, of course, cries of injured people, cries of fear—. We were sort of grouped by family, and the first thing for me was to look around me, my parents were moving, my brother, no one had been injured. That was the first trial we faced. But it was [he stammers a little, and looks directly into the camera, holding the viewer's gaze for a moment]—it was truly death flying over us. Euh—, I was eleven, I hadn't understood that you can, just like that, want to kill people.

Auditory signs construct the memory temporally, building Daniel's knowledge and corresponding to shifts in feeling. Warning cries from the crowd, initially unclear, revealed the oncoming danger; airplane motors approached menacingly; machine-gun fire made the threat real. The moment death came so close was sensed by the boy on the ground. Flat on his stomach, he felt the earth spitting or crackling (he uses the verb *crépiter*, both visual and auditory). Human cries followed, of pain and fear. The memory is full of movement—planes, people—and describes the proprioceptive experience of clambering, throwing himself down, face in the earth. His immediate instinct to check his family tells of a known fear that flashed across his mind, and he suggests his relief at seeing them move. In the last words of the story, Daniel narrates a shift in his understanding of the world: people were trying to kill them.

Daniel continued, recalling a field kitchen, the smoke rising from it, where they were given food. A military lorry offered them a lift; he recalls the babble of refugees' voices on the road outside. He remembers the crush of refugees pushing and shoving to get across the bridge at Orléans amid rumors that it would be imminently blown up. He recalls running across the bridge as the dynamite was put in place. Once more on foot, the family experienced three more airborne attacks. Just beyond Orléans, sleeping in a haystack, the sky was ablaze as Orléans burned, and ominous planes approached. As in other memory stories of bombing, recalling the words of a loved one in the moment of terror generated intense emotion.[27] Speaking of his brother, he said: "And I remember that Serge—, because we were both flat on the ground, of course, lying on the ground—, he said to me 'Daniel, say your prayers—' [he stops talking, and looks down. He swallows several times to master himself. He looks up.] A difficult moment [he looks down again]—." This was the most visibly emotional moment for Daniel in the memory story. He halted and recomposed himself. That moment contains so much: the terrifying materiality of the situation, the now-known threat repeating, burning skies, sounds of fear, the murderous intention, and brotherly love and despair. Numerous virtual and real futures are held in the moment, of potential loss and pain, and the known future (known to him, not us) of his relationship with his brother.

The final two attacks on the road were narrated with less emotional intensity but were sensory and sticky. Other memories were attached to them. Near La Ferté Saint Aubin, the cry "planes, planes" went up again from the refugees, but this time Daniel does not recall the noise of the approaching planes. Instead, "I saw the bombs coming out of the planes. And the strings of bombs—, I think they were Stukas, the German planes, which had sirens on the bombs, I'm not sure, but as the bombs fell, they whistled, whistled—, and that created fear and panic among those who were underneath. At that moment, we ran into a side-street, leaving all our things in the road, on the sidewalk." The sights and sounds of falling bombs must have been accompanied by the thuds and booms of detonation. He recalled entering a barn and his mother shouting "my things, my things" in fear for their belongings. The final attack happened before Vierzon. Hearing the approach of the planes, refugees on the road leaped into a ditch on top of one another. After the machine guns passed over, they clambered out except one. A bullet had struck a Belgian soldier in the knee. Daniel's memory here may be his own or a family memory: his mother stood in front of a passing army vehicle, refusing to move until they took the Belgian soldier for medical attention.

Exhausted after ten or eleven days on the road, they arrived at his grandparents' farm. He was, he said, so happy to see them, the farm, and the animals. The interview ends with Daniel stating that in the autumn they returned to Paris, but that was another story. Most noticeably, the first two experiences of attack have the greatest affective intensity. They are near misses and represent a mortal threat. One provides primacy—the first experience—and the second is intensified by knowledge. They reveal the nature of war, the will to kill, and a new depth of emotion around terror and relief. Fear is created by the future possibility of pain and death. Daniel's story, then, is excellent example of an assemblage, comprising interpenetrating temporal planes (the happening past with its real and virtual futures, the memory story as constructed in the filmed interview, with notes, and my encounter with his interview in the archives), people of all kinds, human-material-spatial interactions, buildings, movement, places, sensorial intensities, emotions, circulating affects, and the war unfolding in 1940, its outcomes known to the man but not to the boy.

CHAPTER 2

AFFECTS AND INTENSITIES

Following Kathleen's Stewart's recommendation to try seeking different "modes of knowing, relating, and attending to things,[1] I am not just interested in the communication of feeling through sensory and emotional declarations or visible emotion. Cultural theorists of affect often write of "in-betweenness."[2] As I listened to this diverse range of narratives, I thought about what was in between the articulated anecdotes and what was in between the stories as they called to, and called upon, each other. Part of some historians' frustration with memory sources is their disorderly nature. Memory lurches from the absurdly minute to the blandly generalized; it jumps irrationally from subject to subject, moment to moment; it meanders and exaggerates; the irrelevant eats into the relevant. Its ability to tell us something, the validity of its claims, and the reliability of the witnesses' words may seem doubtful.

I will argue, first, that the morsels of memory in a story are linked by affective lines—unarticulated lines—which, if discerned, might lead somewhere. Like the Pleiades in the night sky, such lines are a hazy kind of presence, glimpsed from the corner of the eye while attention is elsewhere and hard to keep in focus. Second, I shift the demand and expectation that memories should *tell* us something and instead try to learn by feeling, imaginatively and empathetically, for and with what lies beyond language. My feeling is not the same as another's; my interpretation is contingent on me, as yours is on you; that is what I seek to expose. My analysis is suggestive, open-ended, and inconclusive; it leaves the past unmastered.[3] Yet these anecdotes exist to share something that cannot be articulated directly. Why tell the long story if an emotive declaration would have done the job just as well? Why retain such minute detail if there was not something at stake? An engaged listener cannot stand watching from the riverbank but must jump into the flow.[4] Meanings come into existence under my gaze, or yours; they are not an out-there reality for anyone, or everyone, to seize. To understand more of what it was like to be a child in war, it is worth trying to pull some of those affective lines into focus.

STICKINESS, THREADS, AND VECTORS

Memories are not just about feeling; they are made of feeling. They are glued into place, and to each other, by feeling. The threads that bind clusters of memory or link chains of memories are affective ones. And the vectors that carry memories can also be made of feeling. Léa Duclos described the house where her family lived as refugees in the Creuse. Her memory seemed precise: "It was a little house, it wasn't very big [looking for paper to draw on], this little house, it must have had a little window there, here there was a bank, sloping down to the road. And there was a walnut tree there, in front of the door." As she continued it became clear that something had stuck this memory in place. She said: "I know that there was this slope down to the road because one time, I ran down it, toward the road, and my uncle . . . really told me off, and he made me stand there, not moving, under the walnut tree, and there were lots of ants there. . . . He was so afraid that I'd run out into the road . . . and so he was very, very cross, and punished me like that." The house, the slope, and the walnut tree exist in her memory because she was punished, perhaps upset, perhaps ashamed, perhaps afraid of or disgusted by the ants. In another example, a description of material practice seemed glued into memory and glued to feeling. Danièle Dubowsky, age eight, interned with her two younger brothers and mother in Drancy internment camp, helped some Jewish women:

> I remember very, very clearly, my Mum saying to me "there are some ladies who want to write letters home—, you will go—" not *do you want* to go! "— you will go and write their letters for them because they don't know how to write." And I remember this little material detail, that perhaps you've never known, the carbon pencil, a pencil that you had to lick a little bit so that it would become inky. So I had this little carbon pencil, and I went to see one or other of these ladies, and I remember very clearly, the corner of a wooden plank—I don't know whether it was a table or not— . . . and one lady dictated

to me, and I wrote "My dear husband"—and there, I asked myself the question, I said to myself "Why are these grown-ups lying?" Because they were writing letters like a child in a holiday camp: "My dear husband, I am well, I'm eating well, I'm sleeping well, don't worry, everything's fine, the children are behaving well, I hope to see you very soon," things like that. I obeyed. I wrote what they told me to write, but I couldn't understand why they asked me to write that.

Alongside the details of her mother's instructions, the pencil, the wooden plank, the women, is the strong feeling of disbelief and of something out of place in the world. The feeling of out-of-placeness, as I will explore below, has intensity in a lot of memories. Here we see its role in gluing material objects and practices into memory.

Memories can appear to leap erratically from one thing to another. Instead, I see a connecting line: a thread of feeling along which memories tend. Luce Terrier, whose memories were recorded because of her family's important resistance activity, said: "We had dug trenches in the garden. We spent our childhood playing marbles in the trenches. Sometimes there wasn't time to even get there—we'd lie flat on our bellies among the potatoes. With the Colorado beetles. The potatoes were infested with Colorado beetles." Her memory moves along a line, from trenches, to marbles, to air raids, to potatoes, and the Colorado beetles, the *doryphores*. This is a strongly connoted word, used in wartime France as a euphemism for the German occupiers. The thread I see connecting these memories is the feeling of things awry: the incongruity of playing marbles in trenches, of potatoes and mud, and of disgust at an infestation. Colette Streicher's description of her journey as an evacuee to the Creuse also leaps around:

On the train, I can remember the black smoke, you see. . . . I remember, now that I'm talking about that black smoke, we also had black bread, because we were given black bread, and there were some teachers with us . . . and when they saw it, they couldn't understand how anyone could eat such a thing. And then I remember something else too, it's—, I mustn't forget to say that, when I was leaving home, my Mum had said to me: "When you get there, you should say to the lady that she should change your dress, because you'll be dir—, you won't be clean, your dress will be all dirty."

The memory of the smoke immediately conjures the black bread—surprise, disgust—then the thread reels back in and throws out another line from the black smoke to the dirty dress. This memory is intense and must not be forgotten, she says: it links her mother and her foster mother and the first expression of care she received in her new home. For when she arrived: "The first thing I said to her [to her new foster mother] was that she had to change my dress. So she changed my dress, but she also said, 'if you like, you can have a bath, and then you'll be nice and clean,' so she gave me a bath." The little girl showed confidence and trust and was rewarded with kindness. This memory has a foundational quality in Colette's transition from one family to another. In the narrative, it sprang from the sooty smoke.

Feeling acts as a vector for memories. Some memories are carried on a wave of feeling, which underpins and propels. Jacques Prieur was evacuated by his mother to the Creuse when very young; Jacques cannot remember this, nor does he know the date. He remained with this foster family until he was nine years old, in 1947. One day, his mother, a stranger, arrived out of the blue and took him back to Paris with her. The story is deeply felt, as loss, anger, rejection, but Jacques insisted particularly on the happy memories with his foster parents. The memory of learning to read and write there kept recurring. Jacques said of his foster parents' house: "For me, that was my home, where I lived, it was there that I learned to read and write." Later, referring to his first school he said: "the primary school, the village school they called it, the village school. That's where I learned to read and write." And later, "I don't remember the school very well. I remember the building, the playground and that, as I said, that's where I learned to read and write, but I don't remember the classrooms, what they were like." Back in Paris, he said:

> And when I got back in '47, I already knew how to read, write, and count, because when I got back, I had to go into—I don't know what it was then, it must have been CM1 or CM2 [names of different primary school grades], and so I had a level of attainment that was completely normal. When I started class again in Paris, it went alright, eh. I can't say that I came back not knowing how to read and write.

This memory of a smooth scholastic transition from the Creuse to Paris creates an assumption that acts as a memory. He does not recount the process of learning or being taught but deduces that his learning was on track because he recalls no problems restarting school. The vector for this memory is the feeling that rolls along underneath it. Learning to read and write is foundational; he articulates its location as part of his origin story, linked to infancy, home, belonging, even identity, and to attentive adults. Learning to read and write in the Creuse fixes his belonging there; the memory rides atop his broader narrative of uprootedness.

DEEPENING INTENSITIES

The following discussion focuses on the quality of intensity, again in memories where specific emotions remain unarticulated. I focus on ideas of surprise/shock, fear, and shame, which are indirectly evoked very frequently and emerge from the corpus as widespread and intense.

Shock

Surprise and shock express the gap between expectations and realities, which is full of unarticulated affect. These gaps create sticky memories. Shock and surprise can be threatening when they interrupt the known and expected world and may generate relief when a return to normality ensures. Shock and surprise tell us about children's knowledge of the world and their expectations about norms, ordinariness, and authority because they mark the out-of-placeness of people and things. As such, they reveal something of what life was like for these children. Returning to Jacques Prieur's memories of his time in the Creuse, I have already stated that he recounted no specific memories of learning to read and write; in fact, he had very few specific memories of the Creuse at all. Those memories he did have were surprising or shocking; such occurrences made a strong impression because they were intensely felt. The unusual clarity of these memories suggests a little boy's gaze drawn to something strange, his attention held. One such memory related to his foster mother's mother:

> I can remember the grandmother, who must have been [her] mother. We used to go and see her. She was an old lady, we'd go and see her, we'd go on foot. . . .
> I remember this lady because she'd be wearing, like the country-women of the day, these big black garments, and I can always remember that woman

because she took snuff. You know, snuff, tobacco powder from a snuffbox [he mimes inhaling the snuff], it was quite a sight, and then she'd blow her nose. It had a really strong smell!

An old lady dressed in strange black clothes and taking snuff was an unusual sight that clearly captured Jacques's notice. Similarly, he described his foster father:

When he'd kill a rabbit—[he bangs the edge of the table abruptly, as though swinging the animal's head onto a hard surface], pretty impressive for a child to see that, killing a rabbit, eh! *Psshuut, boiiiing*, he'd pull down the skin, like that. Impressive! . . . In the basement of the house, he'd kill the rabbit, just like that, then he'd hang it on a hook, then he had to take off the rabbit skin [he mimes pulling the skin down across the hanging body] . . . [Smiling] I can remember that. You see? It's a childhood memory.

This slightly gory memory made Jacques smile as he mimed the actions; it was associated with a happy period of his childhood and a man he admired, and he was confident in it as a memory—one of few specific ones he recounted. It led to a further memory about the rabbit-skin dealer who would call to buy from them. These striking visual images were related in some detail, which can only have come from the boy's attentiveness to a scene that was out of the ordinary.

In other cases, children's shock or surprise came from encounters with a world thrown into disarray. The incongruousness of ordinary things out of place, damage, or even chaos attracted attention because it signaled danger. Such memories were formed under stress and are often detailed. Colette Streicher described her family's Paris apartment after a bomb had fallen nearby: "We went back up to the flat, and the window panes had all gone. None left. And I remember that my mum went to hang out the washing, and the lines were broken. I also remember that there was no heating." The detail of the washing line suggests an event, a small domestic drama, that surprised them, perhaps leading to discussion or concern; it was impractical and incongruous, a minute part of domestic normality disrupted by war. Colette remembers that she was distressed, she said "traumatized," after the air raid, which precipitated her evacuation to the Creuse. This future trajectory again helps to stick a memory down. Léa Duclos recounted the aftermath of the German air raid on the country town of Aiguerande in detail:

I know that we went into town, we were in some kind of transport, we weren't on foot, and when we went past the square—, I saw the main square of Aiguerande . . . there were suitcases that had burst open, with babies' bibs hanging out, linen, bibs, that really struck me, and a boot with flesh inside. So that was the bombing of Aiguerande. This square, the suitcases that had burst open, the bibs, which really stuck in my mind, and the boot, a boot—

Her attention focused on the most incongruous objects: bibs strewn on the ground and, more horrible still, a boot with the remains of a foot. The memory was vivid; it comprised the mundanity of everyday objects—bibs, cases, bedding, a boot—made shocking in their sudden and violent disarray.

Parents are central to childhood memories. They are the regulators of norms and represent authority and knowledge, connecting children to the world outside the home and establishing values, roles, and patterns of behavior. Parents who behave in out-of-place ways transgress expectations, creating intense feelings that stick occurrences into memory. Such feelings include surprise, deception, and disappointment. Guy Lazard reported his mother's crying during the Munich crisis when her husband, a First World War veteran, was remobilized. Rémy Ménigault also described one of his first memories, a flash, when he was about three years old in 1940: "a memory I can't shake from my mind: my mother on the platform, I was clutching at her apron, and she was crying." Rémy's mother was the stationmaster and needed to regulate arrivals and departures. Her tears were for her eldest daughter in a village a mile away that German fighter planes were machine-gunning. This explanation is not part of his memory; his memory is only of her tears. A parent's distress was distress out of place: it marked because it shocked. So too did parents' lies or their seeming lack of competence. Marie-Madeleine Viguié-Moreau described finding mattresses and blankets in a basement room of her home where the jams were stored and she was not supposed to go: "I asked my mother the question: 'Mum, there are people down below, why's that?' 'Oh, no, my girl, no, no,' and well, so it seemed, I wasn't allowed to know anything about it." Disappointment stemmed from her knowledge of the lie and her exclusion from her mother's confidence. For Marie-Rolande Cornuéjols, the out-of-placeness of her mother's behavior as they crossed the country during the 1940 exodus was both physical and emotional. It exposed a clear divide between how things were and how they should have been:

And so we left . . . and I will always see, but this is because I was so young, I will always see my mother, completely exhausted, sleeping *on the ground* [she emphasizes the words] in Limoges station. That's really stayed with me. Mum lying *on the ground*! [Again, she emphasizes the words.] Really, on the ground! In the station—. I wasn't asleep, I was next to my brother, looking after my brother, and I was cross. I said to myself "It's not possible to do such things." The shame of it!

Her anecdote names her emotions as annoyance and shame, but these stem from a sense of how out of place her world had become. Her recognition that her mother was exhausted justifies why she slept, but the young Marie-Rolande was astonished. Such behavior not only transgressed the norms and values of respectability but also left Marie-Rolande to look after her brother.

A frequently recounted shock was when the child himself or herself suddenly seemed out of place. A gap opened between expected treatment and the jarring realization of a reality that did not match. Refugee and evacuee children often experienced a kind of othering in the places where they were supposed to find a welcome. Yvette Cadiou and Yvette Chapalain, both evacuated from Brest in 1941, were subject to exclusion because of their status as refugees. Yvette Cadiou was with her family; they and other urban refugees were seen as competition for scarce resources. Yvette Chapalain and her young sister were evacuated to a Catholic boarding school in rural Finistère. The refugees ate black bread, and the local girls refused to share their better provisions with them. Bernard Bauwens was also sent from working-class Billancourt to a Catholic school (*école privée*) for a period at the declaration of war in 1939. He remarked that "we were seen as workers from Renault, eh. We were workers. They called us sewer rats. At the Catholic school, they called us that, the sewer rats. It was very difficult. Very, very difficult." He remarked that he and his fellows were educationally behind when they arrived, having lacked the opportunities of the private-school children. His word *difficile*, repeated, suggests shame and sorrow. Happily, he was not there for long, taking up an apprenticeship that suited him better. For Jacques Prieur, the return to his biological mother's world in Paris after having lived contentedly in the rural Creuse was alienating: other children mocked his "bizarre" accent. These children were treated differently as a result of being displaced. Displacement was just not a movement in space but a shift in the eyes of others: they were not just in a different place, they were out of place.

Strong evocations of feeling suddenly out of place came not just from those who had moved from place to place but also from those who stayed still while values moved around them. For Jewish children, the experience of suddenly being other was lived as a powerful intensity of feeling and vividly remembered. This is not simply a question of identifying and labeling emotions. Through the anecdotal narration of their singular experiences, people attempt to share something of what this past was like for them. By attending to feeling as it moves around inside the stories, the listener comes closer to feeling alongside the speaker, even though it is impossible to experience the same feelings. Stories are stark and sad, recalling moments of being left out, excluded, and feeling awkward, wrong, ashamed, and distressed.

Rachel Jedinak recalled being forbidden to enter public parks: "I remember hanging like a monkey off the railings of the public garden where I usually played with my friends. They were allowed to play there in that garden, but not me." Rachel was more explicit in describing her response to wearing the yellow star at age eight: "I wore it with a lot of difficulty. I hated being labeled like an animal, branded like an animal. Sometimes they teased me. You know, children are sometimes very mean. It was a horrible experience for me." Even as a young child, Rachel recognized this injustice and its effect on her; the memory involves her sadness and anger, as well as hinting at the dangerous future. It evokes the gaze of others, both the children who mocked and the listener whom she invited to comprehend. Hélène Zytnicki was ten years old when she started wearing the yellow star. She described her first walk to school with it:

The first day that my mother put the star on me . . . I went to school, and I didn't know what was happening to me. I couldn't understand it at all. All my schoolfriends, as we got closer to the school, they just dropped me. I ended up all alone walking into my school. I remember, I was crying, I was so sad, but I didn't understand that it was because I was Jewish and I had the star on [she speaks indignantly]. They dropped me, little by little, like that, as we got closer to the school, all my schoolfriends crossed the road. But me, well, I didn't know anything, that it was because of the star. I hadn't changed just because I was wearing the star.

The anecdote tells of distress and confusion. The world had shifted around her; attitudes had changed without her knowledge. Even the schoolteacher now spoke differently to the Jewish girls in the class. She said: "That really struck me, and it made me sad because I couldn't understand. Or rather, yes, I understood, but I didn't understand why. All of a sudden being Jewish, that could change something." Suddenly, Jews were out of place; they were to be placed outside—of parks, of friendship groups, of teachers' care. Hurt is clear in the phrasing of disbelief and incomprehension in her memory. Charles Baron was older than the two girls. Fifteen when he first wore the star, he said:

> Terrible. It's terrible to be on the outside. It's terrible to be branded like an—, and what's more terrible, it's seeing people, the people who won't look at you because they don't want to offend you. And the people who don't give a damn. . . . Then there are people who, from the moment that you're clearly labeled a Jew, at that moment, they've not got enough sarcasm to throw at you, enough dirty tricks to play on you. Yes, there was all of that. It's hard when you're not even sixteen. . . . It's hard. It's very, very, very, very hard.

Wearing the star was a moment of reflexive shock. Being watched, observed, seen, demeaned by others was, he says, painful and extremely difficult to bear. Nothing and everything had changed: out of place, the child was now in danger.

Wearing the star came as more of a shock when children had no prior sense of being different. Marcel Zaidner, for example, said: "I'd never really understood what it was—, what it might be to be a Jew, for example. It wasn't any kind of problem for me. I was one little kid among many in Belleville. It wasn't really part of our home culture at the time." In a district of immigrants, everyone was something. He did not feel any different. Serge Holand remarked on his primary school teacher's concerted effort to rebuff the anti-Semitism imposed upon his classroom. When the first boy arrived at school wearing a star, "the teacher, he said to the class 'The first one of you lot who makes any kind of remark, I'm throwing him straight out of the window.'" Lola Grynberg also recalled that she was not treated differently by her playmates because she was Jewish, and when the star had to be worn at school, "the day it was put on, our Headmistress said to us all 'there is absolutely no difference between the children wearing the star and those not wearing it.'" She told the Jewish girls to turn their jackets inside out when they went into town, so the stars were not visible. Danièle Dubowsky remembered her shock at the end of the war when, returning from a period in

Palestine and restarting school in Paris, a classmate expressed the opinion that Hitler had not finished what he started. She said:

> I was astounded, in the very strongest sense, although not really angr—, I was angry at her and her mother, but I just said to myself, she's just a stupid fool, full stop. But what really choked me, is that I believe that—and it's afterward that I've thought about it—but on the spot, I was absolutely staggered because [her words here are very emphatic], from one moment to the next, all of a sudden [it sounds as though she strikes herself on the chest], what had been a universal suffering became something that had happened to *me* [emphasizing the point; it sounds as though she is laying her hand on her chest], and to some of my people, but not to everybody. To *me*, because Danièle Dubowsky is Jewish. But by that point, and at the time I was eleven, I had a different level of reflection compared to when I was five or six.

The revelation was a shock. The war years were complicated and distressing for Danièle's immediate family, although they all survived. As a little girl she had not understood that all of that complexity, the persecution and camps, was only happening to part of the population: "Everyone was at war," she had felt. "It was a universal tragedy." Her sense of being other, of being out of place, came only when she returned to the city of her birth in 1947. The emotional force of her language seems underpinned by feelings around betrayal, shock, and disappointment.

Fear

Fear emerged in the memory stories as a consciously articulated emotion about the past, as we have seen, but also through anecdotes in which it remained unarticulated. Affective intensity is generated through imagination and empathetic communication, which is a two-way process involving the speaker's desire and effort to be understood and the listener's will and capacity to understand. Sometimes fear is recognized by the remembering adult in a recounted situation that was less well understood by the child. Sometimes it surfaces during the listening encounter as the listener apprehends the emotional intensity of a particular anecdote.

Colette Streicher's parents decided to evacuate her from Suresnes in the Paris suburbs after her anxiety about bombing became a serious concern. This was triggered by a particular situation: fear for someone else, her father: "My dad was part of the *Défense passive* [the municipal civil defense authority], so I always watched him leaving. He'd take us down to the cellar every night, there were air raid alerts every night. . . . So he'd leave us in the cellar, and then we'd watch him leave." While the region did not experience bombing regularly, air raid sirens sounded frequently as planes flew over. Colette's loose anxiety coagulated into fear after a particular incident: "I had a schoolfriend who lived in the apartment block next to mine. And her dad was killed because the block took a direct hit, and he'd gone upstairs to fetch her a jumper because she was cold." In Colette's telling, the friend bore an unintentional responsibility for her father's death. Colette does not explicitly make a causal link between the three points (her father leaving each night, the friend's father being killed, being evacuated), but the listener understands this as the tipping point when anxiety became fear for her father's life in a terrible imagined future. Colette had to be removed from the situation.

In his interview, Yves Richard was offered the opportunity to talk about whatever aspect of his wartime childhood he chose. The question was not well formulated, but the interviewer suggested some things he might consider: the Germans, food, daily life. Yves responded: "One thing that really made an impact, and that I remember—, in 1942, we came to Sorcy. And in '44, nearly at the liberation, we had a visit from—what d'you call 'em?—the Gestapo. They came to see my father—." Of all the memories he might have chosen, this was the one he recounted. In 1944, he was fourteen years old. Yves's father had lent his typewriter to a neighbor, who had been doing resistance work. Typed material had been intercepted, and the Germans were looking for the source. The idiosyncrasies of the keys that stuck and those that made lighter imprints on paper matched the document. He continued, "and everyone at home was crying, and I said 'That's it, they're taking him away,' and that's what happened. That's just what happened." Yves's father was taken for questioning, and although he promptly returned, this moment of domestic drama and accidental entanglement in the political events of the war marked Yves's memory as a standout moment. He does not speak of his own emotions, but we understand from his description that feelings of shock, fear, and anxious uncertainty have made the memory sticky. Neither Colette nor Yves uses emotives, but intense feeling—fear—is present, evidenced by what it does, how it affects the happening past and the telling of the story. In Colette's case, it reshaped her future; in Yves's, it gave him the desire to tell *this* story, thus shaping the narrative in *this* way.

In Sonia Agache's description of her family's eight-day exodus in early summer 1940 in the Nord department, a series of events unfolded out of fear, but the object of that fear is unarticulated. Sonia was only six at the time. She was traveling with her mother and older siblings, stopping at farmhouses for the night. One morning, the last of their short exodus, she said:

> I remember at the last farm, my sisters had gone to fetch some bread. While they were queuing up for it, the Germans arrived. The Germans arrived, full of high spirits, of course, because they were the conquerors, as you'd expect, and when my mother saw them, she was afraid, my sisters were young ladies, all of that, and the troops were looking to have some fun. So what did she do? She said, everyone said, "Harness the horses, we're off." But she said "We'll get the girls on our way, they mustn't come back here." So we left, we picked the girls up on the way, not just my sisters, but the daughters of some neighbors, and we left, and we came back home.

Fear of what the conquerors' high spirits might mean for adolescent girls and young women dominates the story. Did Sonia understand her mother's position at the time? Probably not. But she does now, and this creates the anecdote as one that marks and is retold. Fear, Ahmed writes, is an activation of past histories of fear as well as a projection into an imagined future of hurt or injury.[5] Like so many others, the memory story is multitemporal: from the present moment of telling and the rememberer's full knowledge of the past's unspoken implications to imagined futures, virtual realities in which the sisters were assaulted, and back to family experiences of German enemies in the First World War or even the Franco-Prussian War. Temporal layers build valency, increasing intensity and fixing it in memory.

A child's fear is signaled, then, not just through emotives but through anecdotes recounting singular and specific instances. Affect ebbs and flows around and between the words recorded; it is in the story as a whole, not just the language. Marcel Dumas was five years old, living in the Creuse. His father had escaped from a prisoner-of-war camp and was being hunted by the police. Marcel said there were regularly knocks at the door during the night, and he remembered one moment particularly: "And there was one night—, it was often at night that they'd come knocking, to see if he was there or not, when they were looking for him, and my mother took me down to the cellar, wrapped up in a quilt, and she held on to me so tightly that I was suffocating, I couldn't breathe, I was suffocating, to stop me crying, to stop me saying he was there." The story suggests a child's fear emerging in tears, his fear of the frightening people, fear for his father, fear of suffocating, as well as the mother's fear and even, perhaps, the adult narrator's. The last two stem from a virtual reality: an imagined future that could have unfolded had he not been silenced and accidentally betrayed his father.

Even small children were at risk of direct violence. Paul Maubourg was arrested with his mother and thirty others on suspicion of resistance activity: "Imagine what it's like to be a child of eight years old, having to walk two hundred meters with a gun pressing into his kidneys, his mother the same, walking in front with a soldier behind her, a gun in her back." He exhorts the listener "imagine," to try to connect with this nightmarish situation. Paul felt the physical threat on his own body and also feared for his mother. He said he fainted. Nancette Blanchou, nearly seven, was held with her siblings and their childminder in their farmyard while her parents were violently arrested in front of her: "We stayed at the bottom of the farmyard on the day of the arrest. And one of those young Miliciens [right-wing paramilitaries of the French State], he came and took me into the fields, because they needed to find all of our workers. So he took me out into the fields, he said to me 'You're the one who'll take me to them.' [Pause.] He put a revolver into my neck, and he said 'Go on.'" The experience was not just terrifying because of the gun. She was being forced to betray the farmworkers, who were friends. She started to sing as she walked along, hoping the noise might alert them; only one got away. The rest were rounded up. She says "I was so afraid that they'd kill them in front of us": fear is named at that point, with an object (witnessing the killing), but not specifically before.

Shame

Like fear and shock, shame flowed around the wartime memory stories. Shame, as Sara Ahmed notes, requires a witness: it needs someone to observe the failure to uphold shared values. Shame confirms failure. The witness need not be a third party; one can feel shame when alone, as one's own observer, knowing that a gap exists between expectations for oneself and enacted realities. Ahmed describes shame as "the affective cost of not following the script of normative existence."[6] In memory stories of wartime childhoods, norms and normativity are constructed in different ways. A person may recount a humiliating situation that exposes to the listener the cultural norms and values that were being violated. Or an interviewee may tell of past events or behaviors in a way that shows they feel some degree shame now, in the moment of the telling, as present-day norms are violated by what they or others did.

Some rememberers described situations in which modesty and poverty generated shameful feelings. The humiliation felt when gendered norms around modesty were violated shows how such values were internalized. Young girls felt exposed in ways that they understood as wrong, searing shame into memory. Simone Courant arrived as an impoverished, bomb-shocked, eight-year-old evacuee in the Creuse wearing a sailor suit, her hair cropped short. Not knowing whether she was a girl or a boy, the organizers of the evacuation looked in her underwear. Simone had recounted this detail to her daughter Yolande as a humiliation. Yolande understood this as an important factor contributing to the little girl's distress at this bewildering time. Aged fourteen, Lucienne Rémeur and her mother had survived the explosion in the Sadi-Carnot bomb shelter in Brest in September 1944 that killed hundreds of French civilians and German soldiers. In the confusion of the blast, wandering injured outside in their nightclothes, they were picked up by a German patrol and taken for medical treatment. Lucienne told me: "and no underwear on. It's that which made me—, for me, that was something terrible." Shame stuck the detail in place. Édith Denhez's family lost their possessions and their home in an air raid on Cambrai in 1944; this followed the devastating death of her brother also under the bombs. Édith's mother was ill with depression, did not claim any compensation, and with her three remaining children struggled in the aftermath of these calamities. Édith described her clothing: "We'd pull in our sleeves like this, to do that [tucking her sleeves around her elbows, and holding her arms close to her body to hide the imagined holes]. To go to school. To go to Communion. It's not much fun, when you've got holes in your shoes, to get down on your knees." The priest told her to have humility in the face of her suffering, and the nuns berated her sister (Édith left school as soon as she could) for the state of her clothing. Their poverty—and their mother's incapacity—was exposed to public view, and judgment was cast on their failure to live up to expectations of propriety and humility. Édith told the story with a smile; but why tell it at all unless it communicated something—about injustice, pain, shame—to the listener?

Some interviewees measured their child self's behavior as inappropriate according to present adult-held values. The telling of such anecdotes suggested shame for past attitudes. Certain transgressions seemed rather minor. Rémy Ménigault, his older siblings, and his mother arrived in the Landes of western France during the 1940 exodus. His brother and sister were allowed to cycle to the sea, a sight none had seen before, but Rémy was too young. He said, sheepishly, "so there, me, spoilt little kid that I was, I had a jealous tantrum, 'I want to go!' " His siblings brought him back some seashells, but what stuck was his tantrum, for which he chides himself. As the 1940 exodus goes, this incident is a scrap of nothingness, the tiniest of details in a little boy's life. But Rémy remembered it and told it; it had affected him. Ginette Renault tried to understand her child self's disgruntlement during celebrations at the liberation of France, when she and her sister had no pretty clothes to wear. Her childish jealousy tinged her story, and her memory of this momentous event, with shame. All of their clothes had been dyed black as the family was mourning Ginette's father, who had died in an accident. She assured the listener that they had "mourning in our hearts," fending off an imagined judgment. In both examples, the adult rememberer uses the story to illustrate a child's limited comprehension or misplaced attention but cannot help feeling a little ashamed of themselves. It is not clear, however, at what moment they became ashamed of their behavior. Would such memories have stuck and been recounted if they were not associated in the happening past, not just in later interpretation, with strong feeling? Perhaps both children were told off, upset, or shamed at the time for their attitudes.

Marie-Josèphe Devaux spoke in a fair amount of distress about her parents' involvement in black market activity. She said that they suffered a bad harvest the first year they arrived in the Dordogne from Belgium.

My father [her voice rises in volume, it sounds like it hardens. She exhales, almost panting, twice]—I can talk about the black market [she pants again, twice; it sounds anguished]—my father [her voice cracks], seeing that he used to be able to get across the town of Périgueux without being stopped, well, they had to live too [she is struggles to say these words] and seeing that my mother had worked so hard, like a drudge, she'd seen what had happened in the 1914 war, she knew [breathes deeply], she knew what you had to do to get by.

She described how her parents bought meat and took it secretly to a particular hotel. Her brother would accompany her father on the horse cart as they felt a young boy would make him appear less suspicious. She breathed heavily, speaking haltingly as she recounted that the local police, who benefited from the meat deliveries, warned her father of a letter denouncing him. I was surprised at the extent of her anguish. I wondered whether recounting this, near the beginning of the interview, was a relief for her but also a struggle. Unlike other interviewees, she did not say that "everyone" did a bit of this or that in order to survive. She did not normalize her parents' activities. We do not know how much she knew at the time, as a girl of ten or eleven. Her parents were newly arrived in the locality and were isolated from the community as incomers. Marie-Josèphe's strong feelings reflected the struggle and hostility they faced. Clearly there was ill feeling, as the denunciation illustrates. It seemed as though Marie-Josèphe was experiencing a compulsion to confess the story, which she knew reflected shamefully on her parents. She expressed no judgment on her parents' activity. The anxiety of shame came about through a presumed gaze that would find them morally wanting.

After the war, many Jewish children, and the adults they became, experienced shame very differently, not as an anticipated judgment but as a part of daily life. Anti-Semitic othering did not cease when the war ended. Maurice Goldring situated Jews' feelings of shame in the way that their suffering was characterized as passive, unheroic, and nationally worthless: "The noble deportees were the ones who'd done resistance work, and in some kind of way, anyone who'd been deported, this was never said outright, but it was kind of understood as such, anyone who'd been deported had been deported for their resistance work. To be deported just because you were a Jew, that really grated on people, if it was said at all. At the time, it was like that." To be deported for what you were, not for what you had done, compounded alienation.[7] The return of Jewish deportees was not publicly celebrated. Jewish families sought their survivors, retreated into silence, and sometimes fell into shame—the shame of survival, the shame of finding a loved one amid so much grief, the shame of still being out of place, still being wrong. Unlike Maurice, Hélène Zytnicki spoke not of a social phenomenon but of a strong personal feeling of shame entwined with fear:

I don't know if it was shame or fear, but for years and years, I didn't dare to say that I was Jewish. For years, even, I didn't even dare to say what had happened to me, as though I was ashamed of what had happened to me. I think maybe it was fear. . . . You felt so guilty for being Jewish. . . . You didn't have the right to be a Jew at that time. You shouldn't be a Jew. . . . That's how it was in my mind, even many years later. I never dared to say that I was Jewish.

Hélène lived for years in a state of tension around guilt, shame, and fear. Her psychological and psychosomatic problems stemmed from something she would not even discuss with her doctors. It can be hard to understand this attitude from the outside, particularly in the present day when Holocaust survivors are recognized so widely as having been victimized; why should she feel ashamed if she did nothing wrong? But, as Ahmed argued, shame is "the affective cost of not following the script of normative existence";[8] being Jewish remained beyond the bounds of the normal in postwar France. Hélène experienced time and again the lasting consequences of being out of place.

PAUSE—NICOLE—INSIDE DRANCY

Nicole Kahn was ten years old when she was arrested with her family in Marseille in 1944. The family originated from Alsace but had moved south for their safety once the Occupation began. Nicole said that her father, a doctor, decided not to take them to Switzerland or the United States when he had the chance. Very patriotic, his attitude was, she said: "I'm a French Jew, a French officer. Nothing will ever happen to me." After six weeks in the terrible conditions of Les Baumettes prison, where her father and brothers were separated from Nicole and her mother, the family were taken to Drancy internment camp. For very many Jews, Drancy was the point of departure for the death camps. On entering the camp, Nicole's mother lied: she was not Jewish, she said, but an *Alsacienne* from a village now destroyed, untraceable, and her three children were half-Jews. Although her story was greeted with skepticism, the family were not harassed further. Indeed, all survived the war, Nicole said, "thanks to Mum's bravery; she never put a foot wrong." She kept up the lie, used bleach to lighten her hair, and was released around June 1944 to collect the identity papers she had pretended were lost. These were new ones, fabricated by resistance contacts, that "proved" her false identity. She was released, her adolescent sons too; their father was paroled into a Paris hospital where his medical skill was needed. Nicole said "at that point,

I remained in the camp, like a hostage." A remarkable situation, perhaps, but survivors' stories are full of such strange happenstances: lies that worked, lucky breaks, inventive ruses, a chance meeting, gullible or compassionate bystanders, friends and acquaintances with the capacity to help, the real and the surreal, events unfolding in *this* way at *this* moment. Inside these conjunctures, survival happened. Nicole's memories of her time in Drancy are of interest because of the peaks of intensity that stand above the ordinary.

Nicole narrates her time at Drancy in contrast to the confinement of Les Baumettes prison, where SS guards mistreated the girl, her mother, and other prisoners, she said. At Drancy, she made friends and received schooling, remembering "we put on plays." She was given, she does not know by whom, two little cloth dolls made in a sewing workshop. She recalls "lots of friendship." However, this narrative does not simply overlay bad memories with nostalgic good ones. Anxiety permeates it. This anxiety generates peaks of intensity that rise above the more generalized memories of her life in the camp. Yet, she states, as a child she was unaware of what awaited camp inmates; she only knew that they were taken away and did not return. In the interview, she said she did not fear deportation because she did not know what it was. Instead, there was "rather, a fear of having your head shaved. To see it—, how, everyone had been shaved, it's really a memory, everyone had their head shaved before being deported." She asserts the inmates' shaven heads as a precise memory; why was this remembered? In memory, it prefigured separation, loss, and no doubt the distress of those left in the camp. She recalled that the young man who taught the children math had his head shaved, but "I particularly remember that we were so happy because he came back." In her optimistic narrative, the stronger memory is of him arriving to teach them when they feared him already gone. Another example of a head-shaving was recounted twice. A little girl from Nancy called Jeannine, with whom Nicole was friendly, "she too, she had her head shaved." The memory tailed off; she did not continue. Later in the narrative, she said: "I remember having made this little friend, she was called Jeannine, and she also had her head shaved, because after that, as well, she was deported." Was it the shaving of Jeannine's head that she recalled or the anxiety and anticipation that associated the shaving with loss?

Nicole recounted another incident that may have affected the anxiety around shaved heads and the mystery of what followed. She said: "I have a really clear memory that one day, just by chance, I saw a woman throw herself out of the window. Afterwards, they told us that she was dead. I think it might have been the night before a deportation, I'm not sure." Witnessing the woman's suicide was a shock and was accompanied by a struggle to understand. Using the indefinite pronoun *on* suggests Nicole was not simply speaking of herself as a ten- or eleven-year-old girl; the incomprehension was more widespread: "And I can remember that we [*on*] said 'But why? Why? When we're just going to a work camp?' I know, for example, that when my grandmother was deported, my uncles, aunts, and cousins, we were sure we'd see them again." Despite the doll, the school, the friends, and the plays, the underlying anxiety, fear, and suffering pervade her recollections of Drancy. A superficially and strangely cheerful account of a child's life inside the camp is riddled with pain. The narrated ignorance and lack of comprehension around the deportations exists in temporal tension with a known future in which these people did not return.

Nicole also recounted two memories of her release from Drancy. While being reunited with her family must have been a moment of great relief, that is not her anecdote. Nor does she recall how she came to be released. She knows that it was before the liberation of the whole camp. She recalls being on a bus, without her family, and an older boy of around fourteen boasting to her: "'D'you know what? I got myself some false papers made, you'd never believe it, I sorted it all out myself, and now I'm out.'" Her memory is of her response: "and I said, 'me too.'" Here, she smiled broadly in her filmed interview. Amused by her lie, perhaps pleased to have countered the boastful boy, this memory was the sticky part of her release from Drancy. The second memory of her release was one that she remembered, she said, with pride. While she and her mother were in the prison in Marseille, her mother unstitched the suspenders of Nicole's skirt, slid money inside, and sewed them back up. Nicole said "that money, it stayed for the whole of my time in Drancy, there in my suspenders." Whether the little girl was aware of it or not is unclear. She said, with another big smile, "and it was thanks to this money that we were able to get by at first in Paris, because we didn't know anyone there. We got out of the camp, and we didn't have any money except what was in my suspenders. So I was always very proud to have kept all that money in my suspenders! [Here, she smiles broadly.]" Nicole had been left as her family's "hostage" in Drancy so that her parents could work for their definitive release. Not only was this kind of abandonment viewed in somewhat heroic terms, but Nicole further contributed to rebuilding the family's future with the money she had kept hidden.

Stories of survival hinge on unpredictability and chance and emphasize agency rather than passivity. In Nicole's memory story, both she and her mother are cast in active roles, building the family's survival. Her recollections of quite happy times in Drancy and of friendships may seem unreal, even distasteful, but she recalls no physical harm befalling her and no personally directed acts of persecution. Her story of Drancy emerges from the worse conditions she remembers at Les Baumettes. It was Drancy that led, in Nicole's case, to the family's release, in very real contrast to so many Jews in France. These circumstances play back and forward across her memories. Affective intensity deepens around the shaving of heads, the loss of her friend, the tense possibilities that head-shaving suggested, and, of course, in the space between what she believed at the time and what she later came to know. The relief of release is boiled down to two sticky memories (the boy, the suspenders) that shape her as a participant in her own destiny.

PART 2

MEMORIES LOCATED

To be, wrote the philosopher Edward Casey, is to be in a place.[1] To be is also to be in time, at a time, and over time. To *almost not be*— to experience a mortal threat to oneself or one's close companions, the condition of trauma—must also be spatially and temporally located. Bodies and places "interanimate each other": the body is the "specific medium" through which place is experienced; thus any challenge to bodily existence and the place in which it occurs are codependent.[2] Traumatic experiences often create vivid memories. Some psychological research suggests that memories of emotion in traumatic experiences are likely to be more "accurate" and that stressed conditions produce the capacity for greater recording and retention of detail.[3] As I have said, I am less interested in judging the accuracy of memories than with the place of emotion, feeling, and the details of lived experience as "affective facts" in the memory story.[4] Graham Dawson writes that "psychic 'sites of trauma' are formed within the internal landscape, that are derived from—and completely related to—the material sites of violence within social environments, together with the meanings and the memorial markers that constitute cultural landscapes of violence, horror, and mourning. Memories of traumatic events commonly focus on, and return in imagination, to the sites where they 'took place.' "[5] Across part 2, "Memories Located," I will be asking, broadly, what does traumatic experience *do* to memories of places, spaces, and time? And conversely, how do place, space, and time when recounted in memory help constitute the traumatic experiences the child lived?

Place, space, and time are both phenomenologically experienced and imaginatively construed. As Lyytikäinen and Saarikangas write, we interact constantly with both lived and alternative (imagined) spaces onto and into which we project ourselves, our values, and our ideals.[6] This process is fundamental to identity formation and experience. Casey states that "the dialectic of perception and place (and of both with meaning) is as intricate as it is profound, and it is never-ending."[7] Our senses engage with spaces and places, making sense of them, giving rise to feelings, and generating the capacity for memories to cohere around them. Humans are attached to places, those they know and those they imagine, by affective lines "fuelled by sentiments of inclusion, belonging, and connected-ness to the past."[8] The geographer Yi-Fu Tuan describes place as a "concentration of value," suggesting a felt intensity rather than just a geographical coordinate.[9] Intensities of feeling are brighter or duller in imagination and memory as a result of the meaning of a particular place or spatial configuration in the construction of a person's identity, past and present. In Casey's conception, places emerge as a kind of assemblage, although he does not employ the term:

> *Places gather.* . . . [P]laces gather things in their midst—where "things" connote various animate and inanimate entities. Places also gather experiences and histories, even languages and thought. . . . By "gathering" I do not mean merely amassing. To gather placewise is to have a peculiar hold on what is presented as well as represented in a given place. . . . First, it is a holding *together* in a particular configuration. . . . Second, the hold is a holding *in* and a holding *out*.

He continues that the holding-in-place also reflects the contours of the local landscape; it is not divorced from a topographic reality. Finally, "places also keep such unbodylike entities as thoughts and memories."[10] As with all assemblages, heterogenous elements combine in a generative kind of tension. So places gather, hold, and keep memories, but it is also the case that memories gather, hold, and keep places.

What is the difference between space and place? Yi-Fu Tuan describes space as more abstract than place: "what begins as undifferentiated space becomes place as we get to know it better." Place, in the way I am using it, is a named and known locality. Place describes specific locations that may be imbued with a range of cultural and social meanings, layered over time, that bear down on people's experiences in the happening past and its remembering later on; or they may hold meaning solely because of what happened there to the rememberer or to those they know. Tuan says that space is "undifferentiated"; I do not quite follow that definition. I see space as the qualities of the environment in which a body exists that consist of many and varying features that are differentiated: earth from air, floor from ceiling, street from park. Tuan describes place "as a pause" and space as "that which allows movement"; he writes, "from the security and stability of place, we are aware of the openness, freedom and threat of space."[11] While place does, in my reading, evoke a quality of stability (a place is known, a place is located) even if the meanings and feelings attached to it may change, it may not bring security; nor is space necessarily open, free, or threatening. I will be using space to describe the locatedness of bodily experience in relation to its environment, encompassing movement in an environment, as well as the web of control, threat, and danger active across and inside that particular space. In this, I nod both to Michel Foucault, whose ideas around spatial order conceive of space as a set of relations that arrange and produce power, and to Henri Lefebvre, who was interested in the social production of space: that space produces social relations.[12] In both cases, the thinkers give space an active role in producing the social realm.

Bringing affect, feeling, space, and place together aligns some powerful meaning-making tools. Owain Jones has written that places and spaces are "as much as temporal processes as they are spatial entities."[13] Time is an inseparable component of this web of meaning making, but Jones also notes "the twisting of space time" in memory and describes time in memory as "weird."[14] Bergsonian ideas of time, usefully articulated by the archaeologist Yannis Hamilakis, have some bearing here. Hamilakis writes that for Henri Bergson, "all pasts co-exist virtually with the present, but only certain pasts are actualized at specific occasions."[15] Time is not a series of consequential dots on a line but a cone tending to the bottom point of "now" where all pasts are condensed. The present does not just coexist with all pasts but, "because every perception is full of memories," writes Hamilakis, "also with its own memory." Recognizing the virtual potential of all times contained in the present and activated voluntarily or involuntarily, Hamilakis says, makes for "a more complicated but perhaps more interesting temporality."[16] Thus chronology, like truth, may not be an appropriate measure for memory.[17] Instead, to examine the way memory contains in any utterance various pasts, presents, and futures, the way it shuttles between temporal planes, the way time accelerates and decelerates, is to be alive to the ways that memories signal their meanings. One intention of my research has been to seek out different ways of knowing, relating, and attending to things. Attending to the way traumatic memories mobilize time, place, and space in specific ways helps guide responses to some of my earlier questions: What are memories made of?

Feeling, we know, but what can memories tell us about time, space, and place? And what do traumatic memories of space and place do for those who speak and those who listen?

Part 2, "Memories Located," begins by pausing to look closely at Nancette Blanchou's memory of happy places and happy times before her parents' arrest. It provides an example of how later trauma (re)shapes earlier memories. Chapter 3 then focuses on time in memory. It reveals moments in time as pivots, tipping backward or forward. It explores the way time appears to freeze at certain moments and the varied nature of nonlinear time as speeding, slowing, leaping, shuttling, and stretching out into its own future. Chapter 4 discusses the function of places in traumatic memories, looking first at the places of *my* trauma (the rememberer's) and then at the places of *their* trauma (other people in the memory story). Chapter 5 considers space inside traumatic memories. I look at space as freedom and constraint, competition for space, and understandings of space and safety. A fifth pause examines the attribution of space as a core component of persecution in Hélène Zytnicki's experiences of imprisonment.

<hr />

PAUSE—NANCETTE—HAPPY PLACES, HAPPY TIMES

Nancette Blanchou's parents were arrested brutally and dramatically before her eyes at the family farm in the Dordogne in September 1943. Both were active in the resistance. Born in 1936, Nancette was not quite seven years old. As we will see, the place and moment of that arrest shape the internal landscape of Nancette's traumatic memory. But the farm, its yard, machinery, stables and stalls, the farmworkers, and all the animals predate the day that the Milice arrived and everything changed. Nancette's memories of the time before trauma lack precise detail, but they create a strong mood of a happy place and of happy times. As Carrie Hamilton has noted, while nostalgia is frequently dismissed as a rose-tinted fabrication of the past, it has an important agential function: for the rememberer, it matters that "the past [is not] defined exclusively by pain and suffering"; we need to pay attention to "what is gained" through the process of happy remembering.[18] First, Nancette's happy memories are highly populated. The farmworkers are characterized as good friends; her father's reputation for treating his workers well endured after his death and is a core part of Nancette's understanding of his integrity and honor. These qualities also account for his entry into resistance and his silence under torture. Nancette emphasized a collaborative spirit between farmers, situating it in the time before the arrests:

> Oh, we had a good life there, because, well, it was a big farm and there were lots of people there, at the time we called them servants [domestiques], really, they were agricultural workers, that's what you call them now—but it wasn't a bad word then, eh, it's just the word we used at the time. And they used to eat with us, so at the dinner table, it was always—, there were always so many people around the table, it was wonderful, a really lovely atmosphere, really nice. So we had a good life, you know. We had all the produce of the farm. It was joyful, really joyful. . . . Everyone used to work. . . . The farm-yard was swept every Sunday, I do remember that really, really well. And I remember the wonderful moments at threshing time, whole wonderful days spent at the threshing, there were lots and lots of people, such an atmosphere, everyone chipping in. People used to help each other out. It's not like that now, where everyone's got his own tractor. Back then, people helped each other out.

Her enthusiastic description, marked by emphatic repetitions, positive adjectives, and orderliness, re-creates this past time as a good time. She asserts the strong bond between the farmworkers and her family. This happy place is populated not only with people but also with memorable objects; these are remembered affectively through her interactions with them. She recalled collecting dropped ears of wheat and passing them through the combine harvester, as well as helping to plant potatoes. "Me, well, I was the little girl sitting up in the—, in the—, I'd load the potatoes in when there weren't enough, so that there wasn't a gap in the planting." She recalled the responsibility of her role with pride, but also her childishness, laughing "and once, I fell right into the potato hopper!" She also remembered that "we had horses" pulling the machinery—it was more common to use bullocks at the time—"and I loved getting up on the horses, and they let me do that, too." Nancette was very young, four, five, or six perhaps, but she anchors herself inside the farm community, integrated not just socially but materially with the plants, machines, and animals.

Nancette's mother was released from prison some months after her 1943 arrest but had suffered severely from the ordeal, which included being given electric shocks. Her despair grew when she discovered that her husband had died following his deportation. She became suicidal. Nancette recounted staying home from school to watch over her mother; still a child, she was forced to be responsible for a woman broken by mistreatment and grief. Nancette's mother died of tuberculosis in 1950. The idea of being a responsible, capable little girl is tightly bound to her memories of her father, in a happier place and a happier time:

> And they trusted me. They trusted me . . . and I remember that, a little bit before—, before my dad was arrested, I was absolutely set on learning how to scythe with a real scythe. And we had a field of alfalfa, you know, and alfalfa it's not that difficult to scythe—, and I learned to—, well, I say learned! Let's say, I tried, and my dad trusted me, and I tried to scythe the alfalfa, with a real scythe, a grown-up-sized scythe—, oh, yes, yes, indeed! I loved that. I really loved it.

She learned to scythe under her father's guidance, and the delight in her memory arises from their closeness: he gave her his attention, and he trusted her. Her joy in his trust is echoed later in more somber circumstances. On the day of his arrest, she was allowed to speak to him before he was taken away. His face was covered in blood, and he was washing it in the water trough:

> And there and then, he gave me all of his advice. And that's something which has shaped my whole life. All his advice, that I needed to be brave, that I be good, that I listen to my parents—, to my mum—, that I be kind to my brothers, that I was a little girl who was very, very brave and strong, etcetera, etcetera [she draws in a deep breath], and that promise determined the rest of my life.

Nancette's happy memories of happy times in happy places construct the world before the trauma and herself as rooted there. They enable her to create continuities from that period through the very difficult years that followed and out the other side. They form a reassuring thread that allows her to maintain her connection to her father and to a world that was orderly, cheerful, and honest.

Psychological research has suggested that positive memories are more likely to be reformulated and framed by "ideal affect": what the rememberer thinks they felt at that time and certainly what they would have liked to have felt.[19] Instead of seeing this as a source of inaccuracy in memory or dismissing nostalgia as a memory warp, I see in this process an illustration of Yi-Fu Tuan's "concentration of value."[20] Memories are multitemporal: they already contain within them what came later. The future events on Nancette's farm neither erase nor falsify the moments before, but they render the feelings attached to them—happiness, love, joy, warmth, comradeship—intensely felt: they concentrate their value. Yi-Fu Tuan coined the term *topophilia* to describe the "affective bond between people and places," which can be based on aesthetic appreciation, memory, pride of ownership, or dependence for livelihood or security. He writes that topophilia is not merely a response to a place but "actively produces places for people."[21] Nancette's love of this place in the past is actively created by the affective bonds that animate her memory of it. These are social and familial bonds: a searing pride in her father's work as a progressive, a humane farmer, and a good and brave man, and his later suffering and sacrifice. Her memory reconstructs a time and place in which she and her family were trusted and trusting, assured of their roles, with promising futures, and where responsibility was requested rather than imposed.

CHAPTER 3

THE WEIRDNESS OF MEMORY TIME

PIVOTING BACKWARD

Nancette Blanchou's memories of the family farm pivot on her parents' arrest. The pivot tips backward, and happy places filled with happy times are produced through the lens of later trauma. This kind of memory was not unique. For those children whose unfolding present was ruptured by some kind of trauma, the times before stand out as happier than later ones, and places become topophilic imaginaries, gathering past happiness. Happy evacuation memories contain something of this as well. Jacques Prieur recalled few details of his time as an evacuee in the Creuse, but the period evoked a happy feeling, in contrast to his return to Paris. In the photograph album he showed me in the interview, there were nine photographs of him at his foster home. He had written above "happy memories," telling me "it was the war. . . . No, but for me, it was a happy time, a happy childhood." Colette Streicher was also happily evacuated to the Creuse as a six-year-old. While her return to Paris was not the stark rupture it was for Jacques, she recalled crying a great deal and insisting she did not want to go with her parents. She wanted to stay, get a farm of her own, marry a local boy, have lots of animals, she said. Her memories of the place sketch an intricate map of interpersonal relations steeped in her happiness:

> So I was living in La Cellette, but sometimes they'd take me to Montfargeau, in Montfargeau, it's near to Genouillac, there's the family farm, and all that. And there, I was really happy, there were—, I had an uncle, an auntie, grandma, grandad, so lovely, and I had the nicest bedroom. . . . I also went with Jean [the son of her foster family] who was courting Marie-Louise B----- who lived at

la Grange du Pont, I was often at la Grange du Pont because Marie, she was young too, and I used to go there, and her mother was just great. We called her La N----, and she used to make for me—, she'd take me into the fields with her, and she'd make me a seat out of branches so I could sit down. There was a great big chestnut tree, and I'd take blankets into the garden, lots of books, and I'd spend—, I'd be there the whole afternoon, under the chestnut tree reading, eh. . . . And I'd also go to Les Combes, and at Les Combes lived another grandmother, Marie-Louise's grandmother. And that grandmother, it was the same thing, she treated me as her own too. . . . And I'd also go—, I had an auntie and an uncle who had no children, on the road to la Châtre, and there, it was goat cheese, all of that—, I'd spend a couple of days there. Everyone wanted me to visit, I'd be here, there, and everywhere. I was as happy as anything!

The little girl arrived inside a set of family relationships that did not simply accept her but actively sought her out. Like Nancette, she felt valued. They wanted her, she wanted them: affective desire flowed in both directions. The catalogue of places Colette visited are not just mapped locations, they are places full of people and full of welcoming, loving spaces and objects: the nicest bedroom, gardens and fields, gifts and goats.

Interviewees who lived through the devastating impact of air raids often constructed their memories of the time before the event as happy. Happiness was contained within the place and generated by the people in that place. For example, Andréa Cousteaux spoke of the town of Brest before the war:

Brest was such a happy town. There was the Navy there in Brest—, all those sailors, you know. It was great, and there was—, it was so joyful! There was the arsenal, with all the men working there, making warships. All of that. There were always people out and about, because there was no television, but it didn't matter, we were happy, so happy. And then we started hearing rumors that there was going to be a war.

She was thirteen years old when war was declared: old enough to remember the time before but perhaps too young to know much about the hardships of dock work. Her comment that there was no television at that time works to build the otherness of this public sociality for modern listeners. Her broad generalizations of a universal happiness do not necessarily correspond to a real-world experience, but they serve a function in magnifying change and loss. The ravages of aerial bombardment, particularly during the siege of Brest in 1944, destroyed the spaces of this sociality and thus, in her recollection, the happiness they had contained. Michel Jean-Bart and Pierre Haigneré had both lived in the railway workers' housing estate La Délivrance in a suburb of Lille. Constructed by the railway company, this garden city was bombed first in 1943, then more heavily in April 1944, destroying much of the estate and killing five hundred of its inhabitants and the same number in neighboring districts. Both men had happy memories of the garden city until the pivot of the air raid. Michel said: "We really had a very nice childhood on that estate, with our mates and everything. They called it the city in bloom, because everyone made an effort with their garden, and all that, and with the neighbors, close friendships, playing out together, and we'd say 'Ready, steady, go, hide! Hide over there!' It was really very, very, very nice. There were no problems there. That's it. Until the day when, sadly—[he trails off]." Michel's memories are, like Andréa's, of people in a place. The flowers and their gardens created the landscape, or playscape, of the children's world, which marked the *cité* as an unusual place to be for working-class urban children. Life there was, for these young children who knew little of their parents' daily struggles, happy, or, in Pierre's words, "simple . . . no real worries," until the bombs crushed gardens, houses, families, and more.

A pivot has two sides. When happiness gathers in a place as a result of a later traumatic event, the other side of the seesaw, the future stretching beyond the event, is also implicated. Feelings of sadness, sorrow, loss, and disappointment are attached affectively to the times that follow. In this way, memories of happy places and happy times show the coexistence of all time,—time's multitemporality,—in a recounted moment. The memory cannot help but contain everything that came before and everything that comes after. This is striking in Jewish narratives of wartime childhoods, where time afterward is marked by such devastating loss. Serge Holand's memory of the time before is populated with joy: the family's small flat in the Gobelins district of Paris overflowed with friends of all nationalities from their Bund connections:[1] "I grew up in an extremely joyful environment. The key was under the doormat, you could do that at the time, and when you got home, often there would be something there, already cooking—, [someone] who'd turned up with a bit of steak, and was making dinner. There were often gatherings at our place—." He described having been put to bed and longing to be part of the group "because in the main room of the flat, it wasn't big, but it would be full, in that room, I'd hear them singing. People sang a lot. I'd hear them all laughing." His world was full of Jewish friends, of bonds between nationalities, of laughter and singing. After the Vel d'Hiv raid in July 1942, returning from a first period of evacuation, he found his parents living elsewhere "in a flat that was completely sealed up, as if it were uninhabited." His parents did not leave the flat, Serge said, "they never opened the door." The time pivot could not be more unequally balanced: a door that was always open was now sealed shut. Such memories are intensified by the awareness of how many of those singing, laughing people never returned from deportation. Rachel Jedinak lost both parents. Her father was arrested in 1941, her mother in 1942. Born in 1934, Rachel was still young when the war broke out, but she said she had a "really warm memory of my parents" and added "that's what helped me stay strong later." She recalled her very first memory, attributing it to the electoral victory of the Popular Front government in 1936: "I'm up on my father's shoulders, and there's a huge crowd in front of me. . . . I've kept that memory of the huge crowd, me on his shoulders, very happy to be there." In Carrie Hamilton's terms, there is an important gain in these golden memories: her memory had the power to sustain her though the terrible years after the traumatic pivot of loss, fear, abuse, and suffering.

PIVOTING FORWARD

Time pivoted on traumatic moments, then, and sometimes the interviewee leaned backward into the past. Places *before* gathered affects—love, freedom, happiness—as well as people and objects; interviewees held those feelings in, acting as barriers to the encroaching sorrows of later times. The time pivot also worked in the other direction, pitching people forward into their futures. Beyond the pivot, the child was not the same. Hélène Zytnicki, arrested with her mother and taken to the Vel d'Hiv in July 1942, makes this point clearly: "My childhood stopped on 16 July 1942. It was over. Over." Like many Jewish children, Hélène suffered multiple traumas after the first arrest. The Holocaust had a unique power to shift life courses, but other children also experienced, in different ways, ruptures with past selves as a consequence of violent events. For example, Pierre Haigneré spoke of his life after the heavy air raid of 1944 destroyed the worker's garden city in La Délivrance: "It's as though I passed—, almost, not from childhood to adulthood, but, at least, I can say that my hap-py-go-luckiness was shattered, and there was a brutal confrontation with horror. Afterward, our outlook, our vision of things, the fact of having to leave a life behind—, life became something completely different." Pierre was not the same boy he had been before: he had new kinds of knowledge, new depths of experi-ence to pull into his day-to-day, and new ways of perceiving the world around him. Hélène's memories are of loss and finality. Her childhood ended, whereas Pierre's frightening but one-off experience tipped him into a new vision of life on the other side; a part of his childhood had gone, but only a part.

Both Marie-Madeleine Viguié-Moreau's and Nancette Blanchou's fathers were arrested, deported, and killed for their resistance activity. For both women, the moment of arrest acts as a pivot in time. As with Pierre Haigneré, Marie-Mad-eleine's memories are of self-transformation. She says of the arrest: "I think that then and there, I understood. Something abnormal was happening. Our quiet life—, I think that then and there, I grew up. In fact. Without anyone telling me what was going on. I saw. I understood." The pivot tips her forward into a more adult understanding. This is not so much a loss of innocence as an acquisition of knowledge that forces the world to make more sense. Nancette explained a similar kind of transformation:

> I'd been a carefree little girl. . . . I became a little adult. [She pauses.] There you go. Who, afterwards, could never be understood by grown-ups, because I had certain attitudes which weren't normal, you know. Not for a kid of that age. I wanted to do things like the grown-ups, I wanted to take the reins of the house, to replace my dad, to replace my mum, I'd be in charge of the budget, it's inconceivable, afterward, what I managed to do, and which wasn't understood at all because—, if it were now, there'd be a psychologist who'd tell you—, but at that time, there were no psychologists to help us. So you had to—, you had to face up to it, you had to take it on yourself, we were little adults, you know. But without a full understanding, perhaps. An understanding that we'd lost our parents, yes. An understanding of this huge drama, yes. But what we should do or be, no. The grown-ups still saw us as children. But we weren't children anymore. I wasn't a little girl anymore. Of that I'm sure. [She pauses.]

Nancette characterizes the changes as interaffective. While for Marie-Madeleine, growing up made sense of certain aspects of the world, in Nancette's memory, it was *she* who no longer made sense in the eyes of others. The little girl was old before her time, misunderstood, blocked, and confused, particularly after her mother returned from prison physically and mentally ill. The time pivot changed the paradigm of what the child was capable of knowing, doing, and feeling. Moods, as Ben Highmore describes, "enable us to focus our attention and orient ourselves" in the world; they are "a kind of state of readiness for some affects and not others."[2] Time pivots are moments of sharp rupture where mood shifts. Memories tip backward into a younger, happier past and forward into a darker and more adult future.

TIME FREEZES IN INTENSITY

Thinking of time as a pivot draws attention to what happens on either side. Yet an examination of the pivot itself can expose the clarity of memories formed and encoded in a flash (sometimes called flashbulb memories, characteristically formed under stress and particularly well remembered) but also inflated in significance because of later events. Even if not strongly encoded at the time, the details that remain may be rehearsed over and over to create a particular intensity of feeling. André Dutilleul's memories of being bombed on the outskirts of Lille in June 1941 freeze time on a few seconds' life-changing experience:

> And so I was at the end of the kitchen, on the first floor. I was reading my book, Arsène Lupin—I still remember what it was. I only had that much left to read [gestures with his fingers, very few pages]. My father was putting my sister to bed. My father had—, he'd had a leg amputated, and that's why he was still there. And my mother had gone off to try to find provisions near Saint-Omer, up that way. She didn't come back until later. And so, it was supposed to be bedtime. He called up to me "André, are you going to bed?" I said "Yes, Dad, I'm just finishing my chapter, then I'm coming." "You're coming *right now!*" I close the book, I cross the room, I go through the door, I see a bright flash, then I'm in the dark, on the ground, because all the ceilings fell in, all of that, we were in complete darkness. Completely stunned. I got up. There was no room next to me anymore. Where I'd been sitting, the bomb fell right there. Right where I'd been sitting reading. It's a miracle I'm still here!

Some of this detail may seem superfluous, but the long explanation matters: it was his father's authority that he ultimately obeyed, despite the gripping book. The exchange between father and son can only have taken seconds, but these movements and their timing were crucial; had he disobeyed, he wants the listener to understand, he would have been killed. Henri Buc recounts a moment in 1940 on which his future hinged, again with a stylized and acknowledged filmic freeze:

> We knew that France was very strong. And then all of a sudden, we heard the storm, and well, of course that bit's not true.[3] It was the beginning of May. . . . So, I'm in the kitchen, and there's a lady who's a friend of the family, and she's talking with my mother. She's saying that the Maginot Line has been breached. And I'm looking at the map of France, and in a corner there are some little soldiers digging holes in the ground. And I say to myself, "that's really bad, breaching the Maginot Line." And then, just like an Inspector Clouseau film, here's this lady all worked up, saying "No, you have to leave!," and the lamp shook, and then everything was moving, the noise of the storm had become the noise of the cannon.

Which parts reflect the happening past faithfully and which tumble from the conscious imaginary of disaster are unclear, but again time freezes in memory: the woman, the map, the words, the lamp, the noise clang simultaneously as "everything" started to move. The family departed, leaving behind Henri's father. A doctor, Henri's father worked in a sanitorium for tubercular patients and had contracted the disease: "My final image of my father," said Henri, was "a statue, at the second-floor window." Another frozen image: a man forever watching his family leave and knowing his own fate. It is partly the stress or strangeness of the moment that freezes images, feelings, and events in place and partly the later recognition of their significance. Once again, these examples highlight the coexistence of multiple pasts, presents, and futures inside these memories and the weirdness of time that ebbs and flows inside such accounts.

NONLINEAR TIME

Memory's multitemporality makes it achronological.[4] Time is not always linear in memory stories, nor does it proceed at a steady pace, although it can do both.

Instead, time drags in places and accelerates in others. It shuttles and bounces explicitly among pasts, presents, and futures in unusual ways that are particularly evident in traumatic memories. Marie-Madeleine Viguié-Moreau spoke of the time spent waiting for her father to come home after his arrest and deportation:

> We went back to school. It was very strange, actually, we felt—, for myself, at least, I felt a bit lonely. We couldn't really talk to everyone because those people hadn't been affected—, their lives continued as normal, it was—, see, this feeling of being a little bit apart, that, I kept that for a very, very long time, and particularly after the war, when the deportees came back. Because for us children of the people who didn't come back, we were almost—, I had the impression that we were pariahs. I didn't know what that meant at the time, to be a pariah. . . . And that was something that really, really affected me. I'm not talking about solidarity, because we weren't in need—, they gave us food—, no, it wasn't that. It was the fact of being—, we just weren't anything anymore, the children of the deportees. And that was humiliating. My mother barely went out any more. She had a lot to do because she still had five children, my brother died at around that time, almost around the birth of my youngest brother who was born in September 1944—, so we started thinking about the end of the war, of course, we'd had the Normandy landings and it was still—, we were still far from it, it wasn't the end of the war, we were a long way off coming out of it all. And so we waited, and I remember that too, across that whole period, we waited for our father to come back—, it was long, long, very long.

Her life was paused while her classmates' ran alongside at a different pace. In some stories, the Normandy landings, the liberation, and the end of the war concertina together; but here, time stretches. Her memories fragment around feeling abnormal; the narrative creates a time outside of chronological time, distorted by hopes and fears. The story reaches into those moments when prisoners started to return, into September 1944, back to June 1944, birth and death, false hope, the end of the war, and beyond; time both moves along and hangs suspended. The objective chronology of a war running its course was bent around time subjectively experienced through the absence and possible return of her father.

The opposite effect is created in Paul Termote's narrative. Born in 1935, Paul spent the war in Hellemmes, near Lille. His father had been mobilized in 1939

but was quite quickly demobilized as an essential railway worker. Paul participated in the 1940 exodus, albeit briefly; he had lived through air raids and various kinds of family separations, seemingly without any lasting effects. Indeed,
he played down the impact of the war on his life, radically condensing events,
collapsing the Second World War:

> The war was just a part of my life. At the very worst, I came into the world at
> a bad time. We came into the world at a bad time, but, well, that's how it was.
> We came into the world, our parents came to live here, and they worked, my
> father worked. Then one day, there was the declaration of war, which we chil-
> dren didn't see, we didn't know anything about it, and then one day "Boom,
> boom!" And then we arrive at the liberation, and there, we've got memories
> of the liberation, and after that we started to build our lives because, well,
> I started work at fourteen.... There were other children who definitely suffered
> far more than us, who lost their parents, other things, well, life! Eh? Anyway,
> that's war, that's war, that's war, eh. It's very—, so we had that, and then after-
> wards, we had the war in Algeria, eh, and that, well, that was something else!

It was the Algerian War of Independence (1954–1962), in which Paul fought, not
the Second World War, that was intensely felt. His memories skittered across
time, from his parents' arrival in the Lille region to his starting work at fourteen;
the Second World War was referenced through its declaration and the liberation.
Certain aspects of his childhood were later explained in more depth, but with
some reluctance. For Paul, the Second World War shrank and was dismissed as
not formative.

Nancette Blanchou's memories of her father shuttle back and forward, back
to a time before her own consciousness and forward across her adulthood. Given
that her memories of him are so few, she makes use of other people's words to
give him more substance. In her memory story, she shuttles back to his working
life, forward into her own, and then back to the war. Her father was a progressive, both politically and in the management of his farm:

> And truly, the people he employed really loved him, they loved him a lot.
> First of all because he knew how to lead. He wasn't at all harsh, he was under-
> standing. I'll tell you something. I'm a nurse. And when I do home visits, on
> some farms I've come across photos of my parents. And when I tell them I'm

Dolet Blanchou's daughter, people started crying, they showed me a photo of my father. I've *seen* [she emphasizes the word] his photo on sideboards in the countryside. . . . He put his principles into action . . . . [A man I knew who] had worked at our farm, he always said "Your father, he was really someone." And it's true, I've had other reports like that. I just can't understand how he came to be—[her voice cracks a little here, and she gives a sigh, seeming to recompose herself].

Nancette's present and recent-time experiences of encountering her father, in his photograph and in other people's memories, act as a kind of evidence for her. A reassuring necessity, building her sense of her father over time, creating and confirming her belief in his compassion, they also make the idea of his denunciation harder to comprehend. Inside that pivotal moment, alluded to in a few words heavy with feeling, pasts and futures both real and virtual vibrate around her father's memory, mingling her life with his in ways that extend far beyond his lifetime.

TIME STRETCHES INTO ITS OWN FUTURE

In *Ordinary Affects*, Kathleen Stewart writes that every moment "has tendrils stretching into things that I can barely, or not quite, imagine."[5] That stretching is particularly evident in traumatic memory stories, where possible, imagined, or barely thought futures coexist in virtual potential with real futures. What Portelli called "uchronic dreams"—which may also be euchronic dreams, ideal but unrealized futures (wistful what-might-have-beens)—rub shoulders with what we could call dyschronic dreams: fantasies of alternative futures in which things could have been so much worse. Dewsbury and colleagues write of the way that memories produce worlds "between potential and determination, between what has happened and what could."[6] Time stretches tendrils into its own futures. Yet the actual future, of course, is already present in the recounted past, which can lead to a heavy sense of inevitability. When Daniel Fevre spoke about the Germans arriving in 1940, he noted "they behaved themselves," but he immediately added "later on, it was something else entirely." Later atrocities are prefigured from the start. Édith Denhez's twelve-year-old brother Jacques was killed in Cambrai 1944 when a bomb shelter collapsed, burying him alive. Near the beginning of the narrative, Édith described her family at the start of the war, but the description reached into the future. In the interview, she wondered with her husband Jean about her youngest brother's date of birth:

> ÉDITH: Well, there were four of us at home. There was my eldest brother
> Jacques. After that, Claire, Édith, and then Henri, the littlest. . . . And
> Henri, was it 1940—, what year was Henri born?
> JEAN: In '39?
> ÉDITH: He was perhaps born during the war, or just before. He was
> younger, he was—
> JEAN: Yes, yes, he's the same age as Gérard [referring to his own brother]—
> ÉDITH: And after the bombing, we were only three children, because my
> eldest brother was killed. But we didn't know straight away that he was
> in that cellar that had collapsed. But before that, there were other things,
> eh. Because there was the evacuation [the 1940 civilian exodus], for us—
> [she goes on to describe the events of 1940].

She moves from a moment when there were three children—before Henri was born—to a moment when, again, there were three, after Jacques's death. Later in the interview, Jean Denhez was speaking of the means by which his family managed to feed itself:

> JEAN: —even if you had a ration card, we were in the country, so there
> were no problems for us—
> ÉDITH: Jacques might still be here if there hadn't been all those problems
> with rationing. My brother.

Our discussion was of other topics, but for Édith, memories of rationing formed a chain to her brother's death via her mother's obligation to leave her children unsupervised while she went to find food. She did not explain this here in the story; it came later, when she spoke at length about the air raid that killed him. But his future death is an inevitability, inescapable at all moments of the story.

It was not uncommon for imagined futures to be recounted as part of the narrative. Charles Baron's parents and his uncle, and certainly others not mentioned in his interview, were murdered in the Holocaust. He survived, but in precarious and traumatic circumstances. When, in the first few sentences of the interview, he described his family unit, he commented that he had no brothers or sisters: "luckily," he added, "because they would have been arrested with my parents and gassed." Such was the inevitability around the fate of the Jews that Charles did not permit his imagined siblings the possibility of escape. What could have been, in this instance, was only bad. When speaking of her father's mobilization in 1939, Rachel Jedinak imagined a different future for him, in which things might have turned out better. She describes the day his battalion left, wives and children crying: "And I was crying too," she said, "without really knowing what was happening . . . . And we went back home, and then the waiting began." For many children in this study, mobilized fathers became prisoners of war. For some, sorrow and distress ensued, and the emotional distance created in the years of separation could never be mended. In the case of Rachel's father, however, he was "demobilized, unfortunately. I regret that to this very day." Although she got her father back, his return stretched into a tragic future as in May 1941 he was summoned to the police station and never returned. Rachel said that she was sure that had he been taken as a prisoner of war, he would have survived. Her certainty about this euchronic future, in which her father was protected in a German prisoner-of-war camp, is wholly imagined. Yet it serves a function in her memory. Perhaps it was helpful to believe his fate was not inevitable.

A common trope of these stories is the near miss. As time froze on André Dutilleul's bedtime reading, above, the possibilities of what might have happened created a detailed, structured memory story. To account for survival, the story needed to be told with its possible futures exposed. In another anecdote, André's own cunning accounted for his survival. As he was going home one evening, the air raid siren sounded:

> *Oh là là.* I ran to find a shelter . . . towards my home . . . . There was this huge factory on the way—, I said to myself "I'm going to have a better quality shelter in the factory than if I carry on." So I turned right, went down rue de l'Église, and [the bombs] started to fall at that very moment, all the windows were smashing. I was still on the staircase, I remember. And they were falling just opposite! Well, that time there, if I'd carried straight on . . . there was a tobacconist's where all the people [sheltering] inside were killed—

He styles his decision to go to the factory as one that saved his life. Virtual futures demonstrate the knife-edge contingency on which all futures rest. Robert

Belleuvre described bumping into three of his schoolfriends on his way to the cinema, on April 4, 1943, in their hometown of Boulogne-Billancourt. They invited him to join them, to see a different film at a different cinema. He declined. They tried to persuade him: "I hesitated, but then I said 'No, I'm not going to come with you.'" He did not fancy the film that was showing there. On reaching his chosen cinema, the bombs began to fall. The air raid happened so quickly that the sirens did not sound in time. Robert sheltered safely. Later, though, he discovered that his three friends had been killed. He concluded: "If I'd listened to them, I'd have been the fourth death." His own death was projected into a virtual future that flowed from his friends' having convinced him to join them. All elements of this story—date and time, film programs at different cinemas, the route he walked, the decisions he made—were aligned so that Robert survived. But he was aware that at each point a different future could have unfolded.

Grégoire Guendjian also told a near-miss story in which he showed himself highly aware of a future unfolding in which he and others had perished. In May 1944, Grégoire, his brother, and around four hundred other children boarded a train at the Gare de Vaise in Lyon to be evacuated. The air raid siren sounded. An argument broke out between the stationmaster, who wanted the children off the train and into a bomb shelter, and the train driver. In the end, the driver disobeyed and drove the children to safety in the nick of time. The station was struck. Grégoire exclaimed: "Because, I tell you, it was certain death! The station was completely wiped out. . . . Everyone should know this! 500, 600 children [he exaggerates the number] that's 500, 600 families—that's enormous, that is." In this virtual future, it is not just the hundreds of children who ceased to exist. Thousands of their descendants owed their existence to the train driver as well. To recognize memory as multitemporal and time in memory as weird is not only to recognize the achronicity of memory and its pivots, leaps, and shuttles but also to recognize that a core dimension of memory is the virtual. Memory is full of alternative realities. Their presence is imprinted on the real and the spoken, orienting the story and impressing on the listener that things matter. Time reveals itself as an active dimension of memory.

CHAPTER 4

PLACES IN TRAUMATIC MEMORY

Traumatic childhood memories are strongly located in place. Where one was when something happened or where a loved one was when something happened to them is a core component of the event. Place pulls action and person together in such a way that without it there would have been no action, or no action of that kind. Place exists in memory not just as the located, material environment but also as an active agent; thus, places make things happen in the way that they do. As such, they loom large in the imaginative processes that conjuring and recounting traumatic moments entails. As Graham Dawson writes, drawing on Stewart and Strathern, place is a material environment comprised of human-material relations: bodies are emplaced relationally inside an assemblage that connects people, events, memories, things, feelings, practices, discourses, and so on.[1] Places are both intimate and cultural, saturated with creative and imaginative meanings and associations.

PLACES OF MY TRAUMA

Many of the bombing memories are strongly situated in place. Michèle Martin's account of the heavy, rapid USAAF air raid in Boulogne-Billancourt in April 1943 gives a sense of the topography of her traumatic experience. It matters very much where she was and why as specific places, whether deliberate destinations or happened-upon locations, make meaning in relation to fear, death, and survival:

MICHÈLE: So, we were, we were going to see my grandmother in Viroflay.
Everyone was on their bike, and we were going over the Pont de Sèvres.
And as we arrived at the level of the Pont de Sèvres metro station, the
siren went off. The police wanted us to go down into the metro station.
Mum wanted to, but my father wanted to carry on—, and we carried on,
luckily for us, because there was, all the people who'd taken shelter there
were killed. It was a very quick air raid, it was the Americans, and *vlannn!*
[She makes a dramatic whooshing sound of something falling.] That was
it. It was a very nice day, there were lots of people out and about, there
was a festival over in Saint-Cloud, or something, and everyone wanted
to be outdoors. There were such a lot of people about. And we carried
on, and we sheltered under a chestnut tree—as protection from bombs,
it was hardly ideal!—on the other side of the Pont de Sèvres. I was with
my sister, but we lost sight of our parents just for a moment, they were a
little way behind us. And there, we saw the bombs, we saw some things,
people flipped up in the air, and the like—

LINDSEY: You saw that?

MICHÈLE: Oh yes. And then our parents reached us, where we were
sheltering. There was this kind of, a little hill, and some cellars, and
we hid there, waiting for—, the siren—, there had been a siren, it had
sounded—, we waited for it to all finish, and when it was finished, we
couldn't get back the way we'd come. It was impossible. We had to go
back using the Pont de Saint-Cloud, that is [gesturing to a map], here.
So there, we—, me, I actually saw the wreckage.

Michèle experienced a near miss but also witnessed violence done to others. Place
shapes the memory because it accounts for why the family was in that exposed
place at that moment: it is part of the singular contingency of the event. They
happened to be on their way to Viroflay and were not far from a metro station.
Her parents' difference of opinion as to the safety of the metro station makes
the precise spot where they stood meaningful inside the traumatic knowledge of
the direct hit. Had they been in a different spot, things could have been different. The fine line between being a witness or becoming a casualty is illustrated
through the narration of places: the chestnut tree, recognized ironically as useless
protection, a hillock, and some cellars; the crossing of one bridge away from

danger and another, further north, where Michèle saw the extent of the destruction and realized what she had so narrowly escaped.

I have already noted the importance of the family farm to Nancette Blanchou's happy memories of the times before her parents' arrest. This happy place
is overlaid with the traumatic memory of the arrest. Nancette, her siblings, and
an older woman who acted as their childminder were marched from the house by
the Milice and held at the bottom of the farmyard. At this point, her father was
still hiding. Nancette's mother was dragged violently from the house. Nancette
repeats her own location at the bottom of the farmyard, situating herself as a witness to and participant in these events of great rupture. Her narrative is audibly
disrupted by distress at several points:

> They made us leave the house. Mum—, at some point, they put us down at the
> bottom [she pauses, and swallows], they put us down at the end of the farm-
> yard, with a lady who worked there, who was quite elderly, they put us down
> at the bottom of the farmyard in the full sun, and Mum . . . at some point, she
> tried to run away. And the Germans fired at her, and, well [she sighs], they
> didn't hit her, but after that they started to drag her away—, and because she
> didn't want to leave her children, she grabbed hold of the gate. She told us
> this afterwards, they slammed the gate on her fingers. Mum screamed, she
> was screaming that she wanted her children, she shouted, and I have to say
> that it's a cry that I'm unlikely ever to forget. [Her voice is quiet; she sounds
> resigned; her voice trembles a little and she swallows.] It was—[sighs], it was
> very hard. So Mum was gone. We stayed at the bottom of the farmyard, on
> the day of the arrest. . . . We stayed half the day there, that whole afternoon,
> at the bottom of the farmyard.

Happy pasts lay dormant where formerly productive workers had gone about
their business, animals lived, and children played; atrocities were enacted in their
place. Past memories did not disappear forever, though; they will be recounted
elsewhere, the same place, a different time. But here place gathers meaning into
its assemblage; it gathers everything that has been and will be; it gathers people's
pasts and their futures, a child's joyful games as well as her pain and her loss.

Marie-Madeleine Viguié-Moreau also had strongly located memories of her
father's arrest; she was ten years old. This was a similar kind of trauma, but

the memory had a different relationship to place. Nancette Blanchou's memory was retold from her perspective as an onlooker, fixed in place, drilling intensity into the landscape as events unfolded. Marie-Madeleine's memory was mobile, across the town of Cluny where her family lived. Like Nancette, who was used by the Milice to expose the whereabouts of the farmworkers and as bait to force her father from his hiding place, Marie-Madeleine was directly implicated. She recalled being in the kitchen at home when Germans and an Alsatian translator arrived:

> And they said to my mother "Tell us, where's your husband? You must tell us where your husband is." And my mother, she was crying, she didn't know, she was completely distraught, and then the policeman turned to me—because I was the eldest of all the children who were there—and he said "You! You are going to find your dad." He picked up a coat that was lying on a chair, he put it on my back, and "There, you're going to find your father." But where to find him? I was in a real panic, I didn't understand anything at all. So I left, and people had started to be up and about in Cluny, so I said to myself "I'll go to my uncle and aunt's house," so I got there, to the Champs de Foire, but at my uncle and aunt's there was a whole load of Germans, or police, I couldn't get in. So I got away, unseen, quickly. I was running across the whole of Cluny. My uncle and aunt lived at the Champs de Foire, at completely the other end of town to us, and so I came back running, completely terrified, and in front of the Café de Paris, I was nearly back home, I saw a black truck. There were people standing round, some wearing big black coats, hats, and the Germans too. I saw my father between two Germans, who put him into the truck. I wanted to shout out, but I was paralyzed. That's the last image I have of my father. And there, I'll always remember it, I said to myself "He's going to see me, he's going to see me, he's going to say something to me." He was wearing a sheepskin jacket, his hat—, that's the last time I saw my father [she pauses]—.

Her father's absence begins here and continues after his arrest, with the family not knowing where he was. Marie-Madeleine's own presence is scattered. The town she knew well became full of unexpected dangers. There would have been some kind of symmetry had her father seen her and signaled his last goodbye. But he did not. The world remained forever imbalanced: she was in the right place, but he did not see her.

PLACES OF THEIR TRAUMA

Trauma is not only about direct experience. Witnessing a mortal threat to someone else, particularly a loved one, is also traumatic, as is imagining what happened to a loved one in mortal danger. Memories often dwell on the places of
someone else's trauma. The empathetic imagining of a loved one's suffering scars
and imprints place on memory; memory, like trauma, is not only about direct
experience. Paul Maubourg's father was in the resistance. He was captured and
tortured to death. It seemed important to Paul to anchor his father's last suffering to a place. Places were often revisited, mapped, and topographically detailed
by traumatized children. Comprehending the place of suffering in some way
acted to witness for the loved one and to accompany them in their last breaths.
Paul emplaced the memory of his father's suffering in detail:

> During the night of the 20/21 July, my father was taken into the forest d'Echal-
> lon, to a place known as le Fouget, with thirteen of his comrades. . . . [They]
> were taken by the Germans, interrogated, and then taken, all fourteen of
> them, to the park of the Château Dortin, seven kilometers north of Oyannax.
> There [he takes a deep breath], there in the park of the *château*, the Germans
> tortured them, until death. . . . They used a tree, an acacia, as their torturers'
> stake. I even saw it afterwards. It was completely ripped to shreds. The men
> were buried in a ditch. The funeral director in Oyannax had the sorry task
> of collecting the bodies, he told us that my father had been—[he looks away
> for all this time], you could say that, the top of his head was missing [looking
> directly, sharply, at interviewer]. He'd been badly knocked around, and the
> top of his skull was gone. Some of the other men had the skin of their hands
> peeled back, like gloves, cut at the thumb and peeled. . . . We had to go to the
> police station to identify his belongings. Together, I was with my mother,
> we recognized a scrap of his velour trousers, a scrap of his woolen sweater, a
> scrap of his hunting jacket, his comb, a little notebook [looking away from
> the camera] and a knife that he'd had in his pocket. So we were sure that my
> father was one of these fourteen men.

Paul had been to the site. He had seen the torturers' stake, inscribing the place
of his father's pain into his own internal landscape. The place was already

significant: Dortan was also the place of his father's birth. Images of events he did not witness were seared into his mind. He looked directly at the camera as he spoke some of the worst atrocities aloud. Watching, it felt like a challenge to enter into his torment. Being able to situate this pain did not seem to bring Paul peace; instead, it kept his father's suffering vivid and raw. It became Paul's own suffering, which was viscerally evident in the whole interview, deeply affecting and uncomfortable to watch.

For Marie-Madeleine Viguié-Moreau and Nancette Blanchou, however, an active quest to know of their fathers' last experiences seemed to bring some kind of comfort. Knowing the places where they died gave greater access to their suffering. For both women, it also brought them closer to their fathers, whereas for Paul Maubourg, knowledge of his father's ordeal seemed alienating. (It is worth pointing out that the interviews were recorded at different moments in these people's lives, which likely affected the extent to which they had come to terms with events; Paul was in his mid-fifties, whereas the women were over seventy.) Nancette's family knew that her father had died at Mittelbau-Dora concentration camp in Germany, where prisoners dug vast underground factories and storage for V-weapons in appalling conditions. The family had received a document giving the date of her father's death as February 4, 1944, but a survivor, Monsieur M——, told them that he had arrived in the camp at a slightly earlier date "and [my father] wasn't there anymore, so I don't know exactly but, well, it doesn't matter. It doesn't matter." In her memory, knowing when he died is less meaningful, ultimately, than knowing where he had suffered:

> Eight days, two weeks, it's two weeks of suffering in any case, so, well, it's terrible. It was terrible. But when you *see how* [she emphasizes the words], when you can *see* [she emphasizes the word again], when you *visit* [with emphasis] and when you see, what it was like, how it *was* [with emphasis], because Monsieur M----- told me afterwards, the deportees, they slept inside the mountain that they were digging out to make the factory. They slept there, in the dust, in the damp, in the horror, you see. . . . It was sheer horror, *sheer horror* [with great emphasis], and they didn't get out alive.

Monsieur M----- had described the conditions to Nancette, but the key was to be in the place herself; to see and to visit was to understand. She went with Monsieur M----- and his family: "So I got to go to Germany, to visit Dora, with them. And that! That, for me, was really something extraordinary. *To be able* [she emphasizes the words] to go there. I can never thank them enough, *to be able to go there* [again, emphasis], because financially, all by myself, I just couldn't, and also, if I'd been alone, I just don't think I could have managed it." At the time the interview was recorded, Nancette had not visited Buchenwald, where her father had been cremated. She expressed a desire to do so. But her visit to Dora had enabled her to know the place and imagine the conditions of his final days: to be able to move on, mourners must acknowledge their loss.[2] Anchoring loss to a place that was known and not simply imagined helped that process.

Marie-Madeleine Viguié-Moreau described something similar. Her family was visited by a returned deportee who had known her father in Mauthausen camp. He looked, she said, "like an absolute scarecrow," and she recognized now the difficulty of his task: "This poor man, what do you say to a deportee's widow?" The man had no knowledge of the moment of her father's death. He recounted the story at the time to Marie-Madeleine's mother but, it seems, not to her young daughter. Marie-Madeleine learned more later on:

> He died in horrendous conditions. We can't find what happened across the last three days of his life, but now we know, with everything that we know—, we'll never know, but it was horrific, sheer horror. And I understood that for a returned deportee, to tell a widow that her husband was killed like the worst animal is slaughtered—. I don't even think animals are slaughtered in such a way—, but all of that, I found out later. . . .

In later life, she and her husband visited Mauthausen in Austria with their eldest granddaughter. She said, halting at the end of the phrase, "I understood better once I made my first pilgrimage to Mauthausen, when you see how it all happened." Being in the place enabled her to understand and assimilate her father's trauma and her own. She added:

> —but somewhere, my father exists there, if you like—, it's no longer—, well, when I walked for the first time on the grass at Mauthausen, I was practically on tiptoes, saying to myself "I might be walking on my father"! But, of course, that's not true—, and then, I think that that allowed me to—. My father's dead. I know that. But when I speak of him, I speak of someone living. I never

had a chance to get to know my father well either. And so now, I've met people who talk to me, who've told me about him, and people dare to speak of it
now. That's helped me enormously.

Being in the place was not just learning the conditions of his final days. It was
to walk where he walked, almost to resurrect him, to make him live in the place
and die in the place. Going to the place was both to know him better and to let
him go; that could only be accomplished, she thought, where he had been and, in
some ways, still was.

Among the Jewish people whose memories form part of the corpus used in
this study, there was less evidence of a desire to go back to the place of loved
ones' deaths. I do not take this as representative of wider memorial and mourning practices. What Marie-Madeleine described as a pilgrimage to the camps in
Germany, Poland, and Austria, experienced as a desire, urge, or need to be in the
place, has been widespread among Holocaust survivors and their descendants.[3]
Yet many factors may prevent or dissuade people from wanting to return to
a site of their own or someone else's trauma. When asked whether she knew
how her mother had died, Hélène Zytnicki responded "Absolutely not." As of
1983, when she was interviewed, she had never received any information, nor
had her family to her knowledge attempted to discover how she died. Instead,
Hélène shuttled back in time: "That was the last time I saw my mother, the
day of the roll call [at Beaune-la-Rolande camp]. I never saw my mother again
after that." As she spoke, she looked directly into the camera; again, it felt like
a challenge: how could I have done otherwise? Hélène's relation to her mother's
death stuck at the traumatic moment of rupture. It was bound to that place
and not to where her mother died. Places, as Edward Casey said, keep things
in and keep things out. Beaune-la-Rolande gathered and held all of the pain of
that traumatic separation; maybe remembering that place kept at arm's length
any recognition of what her mother had later suffered. There was no relief here.
Watching Hélène's interview, it seemed as though, at that point, this was as far
as her remembering could go.

Some of the Jewish interviewees who had found protection in France and
survived the Holocaust went back to the places of their wartime experiences.
Thérèse Allglas-Cymmerman spoke of the village southeast of Paris where she
had lived as the adopted child of an older couple from 1942 to 1948 or 1949.
Although she had returned numerous times for holidays after the war as a girl

and a young woman, she had not been in later life. In the interview in 2009, she described revisiting her primary school in Mandres-les-Roses: "I went back there two years ago. I found the same tree in the playground. I visited a class—, I rediscovered a lot of memories. . . . It felt like I'd never left that school." The tree and the place triggered the past and created another of memory time's weird effects, collapsing time as though she had never left. The place recounted here brought together the broader, transnational, commemorative landscape of those later recognized as Righteous Among the Nations (as the couple who protected Thérèse were) and the inner memory landscape of a little girl. The memory was simultaneously happy and sad, evoking her postwar separation from her foster family and her growing understanding of the devastating context of her childhood. Lola Grynberg also spoke of how painful it was to leave the woman in whose care she had ended up, in Nice. They had exchanged letters for a while but later lost touch. When she married, she said, "the first thing we did, we went down to Nice." She searched out the places where she had lived, the market stallholders who had known her godmother (*marraine*) and who still called her by her clandestine name, Marcelle. The woman had left for Algeria, they told her, "and so I lost all trace of her," she said. The meaning of those places was made and remade by the presence and absence of people: the stallholders were there, but Lola was not; in her place, Marcelle was there, but her *marraine* was not.

Places in memory are agential. They have the capacity to do things, to make things happen. Sometimes their powers were actively and consciously solicited, as in the cases of Marie-Madeleine and Nancette. A place revealed something of the past and enabled the future to continue with more composure. In other cases, the powers of places were involuntary and acted on the rememberers with ongoing violence. Paul Maubourg remained powerfully affected by the place of his father's torture and death. For Hélène, Beaune-la-Rolande, where she was ripped apart from her mother, was the place of her loss, not where her mother died. The involuntary nature of trauma in place was suggested by Bernard Bauwens. He told me that he had recently driven past a place where, in April 1943, he had witnessed the aftermath of the heavy USAAF air raid on Boulogne-Billancourt: "When I went past there the other day, in my car, there, I went past, and, well, instinctively my head turned and looked over—, eh, it was strange. And that, that shocked me, really badly. What I saw there—, but—the thing—, seeing someone smashed up against a wall, without a head, brains on the wall—, just awful." The urban landscape retained the traces of past suffering. An unknown person's mutilated body was capable of moving Bernard to shock sixty-five years later. Trauma anchored memories to the places of one's own or other people's trauma. It pushed people toward new places, in quests to understand, know, and feel; it sent people back to old places; it jumped out of the walls. Kathleen Stewart evocatively writes that "little worlds proliferate around everything and anything."[4] Constantly made and remade, little worlds of affective engagement in an unfolding present draw constantly on memory as "the leading edge . . . [of the] . . . invisible progress of the past gnawing into the future."[5]

CHAPTER 5

SPACES IN TRAUMATIC MEMORY

C hapter 4 considered specific places and their signal role in the formation and recollection of traumatic memories; this chapter looks at how such memories are spatially located. By that, I mean the ways a traumatic bodily experience is located in an enveloping material environment that is shaped not just by its physical qualities but also by the qualitative understandings thought into it by those experiencing it. The material environment may take on a malignant or benign character; such affective renderings are socially and intersubjectively constituted. These ideas are influenced by Yi-Fu Tuan's thinking around space as movement, stability, containment, and freedom and by Foucault's and others' notions of a spatial order in which space works to produce, arrange, and enact power relations.[1] Paying attention to space in memory is a little like drawing a map using the sea not the land as the main referent; like feeling, space is not *there*. It must be discerned through the relational positioning of objects in it.

A BODY IN SPACE

Bodies are always situated in space. It is from *this* position that a person experiences the world, generating the conditions for sensing and feeling. Colette Streicher describes her arrival on a farm in the Creuse as a six-year-old evacuee from the Paris suburb of Suresnes. Her foster mother was horrified at the child's joyful bounding:

> And the day after I got there, well, they were really shocked by me—, me, well, I'd never even seen a chicken, eh! Never seen an animal in my whole

life. And of course, I was running around everywhere, jumping all over the machines, the harvester—, worse than any boy! Mum [her foster mother] was in despair. She said "I thought it would be better to have a girl as I was afraid a boy would be too boisterous and too—." I was like that for two days!

Space was inhabited differently in the country than in town; it was more ample and was shared with nonhuman inhabitants. Its use was also gendered: girls and boys were expected to appropriate space in different ways. Colette transgressed the borders of girls' spatial situatedness, but she was permitted to continue to inhabit that space fully, which, she suggested, cemented her profound attachment to it. Gender is far from the only way that power shaped space in children's wartime lives. The kind of healthy physical space afforded to one child was denied to another as a result of ideological and political discrimination. Colette's body was deemed worth saving from malnutrition and from bombs; the space she was moved into gave her access to all the plentiful resources of that environment for the benefit of her health and well-being. Space was not just freedom, it was life-giving.

Other bodies were deemed less worthy of protection. This is one of the ways evacuated children must be seen, using Michael Rothberg's term, as implicated subjects.[2] For Jewish children, memories of restricted space underscore the discrimination they faced. Confined spaces were not only punitive but represented limited access to resources, which had physical and psychological impacts. I have already noted that restrictions on Jewish citizens' movements, including curfews and denial of access to public parks or shops, and the movement of others away from them were felt strongly as alienating; these spatial discriminations were lived socially and felt affectively. Trauma is a threat to the bodily integrity of the self or others.[3] Memories of physical confinement were experienced as threats to bodily integrity not only because of violence or abuse but because the space itself—its shape, confines, and features—had become threatening. Nicole Kahn describes her family's railway journey from Marseille to Drancy crammed into cattle wagons: "The journey [she pauses for a moment] was hard. Because I remember that they left us for a long time at Marseille station, [and] I have a really clear memory of being extremely thirsty, because the Red Cross had given us some tins of sardines for the journey, but they gave us nothing to drink. There was no drinking water in the wagons, there was no way to get out, the windows were all shut. . . ." Such spaces were not necessarily designed to kill, but they were allocated with no care to basic human needs and as such became traumatic spaces. They act as heterotopias, to take Foucault's conception, spaces that are simultaneously inside society and apart from it: apart because they are carved out by a dominant agent for a subordinate to inhabit; inside because they belong to, are created by, and reflect the values of a society back to itself.[4] Here, the cattle wagons show the dehumanization of a subordinate group with deadly consequences because of either negligence or the calculated denial of basic human needs.

Colette's and Nicole's experiences are generated not just by the endowment of space with specific social value but through their interaction with the materiality of the physical environment. One little girl leaped from machine to machine; the other found herself caught up in the assemblage of salty sardines, magnified heat, bodies crammed into wagons, and a parching thirst. Danièle Dubowsky described the place where she, her mother, and her younger brothers were quarantined with around fifty others from Drancy before being moved to Vittel internment camp. As a Palestinian, Danièle's mother had British protected status; Vittel was the camp for British internees in France, and moving there saved the family from deportation. The human-material interaction is strong in this memory:

> And in there, we were dreadfully thirsty . . . It was January, and there were a lot of us in this small room. The windows were painted blue, and there was condensation, from the body heat inside and the cold outside, and the condensation made water trickle down the windows. We queued up to go and lick the windows—, and that's—, perhaps that's why I don't drink much these days, I'm a real camel. There was that. And we slept on straw, on potato sacks, on the ground.

Even though they were being moved to a "better" kind of detention, these Jews were still being spatially dehumanized through the denial of their basic needs (light, water). Things improved when they reached Vittel, but until then the French authorities maintained a crushing spatial hierarchy of discrimination. In her story and memory, Danièle links her direct, physical interaction with the space—licking windows—to a lasting embodied impact: her disinclination in adulthood to drink much water.

Danièle's story provides a strong example of the encroachment of space onto and into the body. We witnessed this previously in relation to pulmonary and respiratory responses to bombing. In Thérèse Leclercq's memory of sheltering from bombs in Hellemmes (near Lille), everyday household objects were transformed into a spatial threat:

> And my father took us down [to the cellar], he'd prepared it all. You see, if you like, in those days at our house we used coal. We had coal heating. And the coal went in the cellar. [When] they brought the coal round, there was a little grill, and they'd lift the grill and tip the coal in, and that created a lot of coal dust. So every bomb that fell, left and right, made a blast, and that blast sent the dust flying. So my father would spend all his time dampening cloths and putting them over our eyes, so the coal didn't go in our eyes, and all that. I remember it well! I remember that we were shaking like dead leaves. Really shaking.

A place fit only for coal was thus transformed but posed its own dangers. Thérèse lived in the industrial Nord department with coalfields nearby; the terraced back-to-back houses of her distract all had coal chutes. The experience of sheltering in a coal cellar is distinctly urban and industrial. The bombs, the blast, the encroachment of coal dust into the bodies in the shelter—their mouths, noses, eyes, their respiration—come together with her father and his damp cloths. Humans interacted materially with this kind of space in very particular ways. Jean Pochart described walking from the Brest train station to his family farm five kilometers away, at the age of twelve, following an air raid:

> I come out of the [station] . . . all these smells of powder, or burning. After an air raid, there are all sorts of odors in the air. It smells. You can smell there's been an air raid, and that's not even including the smoke bombs, because the Germans set off smoke bombs so that the whole town was under a blanket of fog. And that, well, it sticks in your throat when you breathe it in. It's harsh. And so the ground's covered in debris, as you walk over it, it goes *kliing, kliing,* and there are no lights on, so, let's imagine it, no lights, it's completely black. So I leave the station and at first, some people are walking with me, in the same direction, so that's alright. I've got my little suitcase with me. I'm on the main street, which was called rue de Siam: "Halte!" A German patrol, they want to see my papers. After a bit, they let me go and I carry on . . . and when

I get above the lifting bridge, which at the time was a turning bridge, you can hear the water down below, in the blackness. It's strange, you feel there's life down there, but you can't see anything. It's dark, you just keep going. I get a little bit further—stopped again by another German patrol. This time, it's the Feldgendarmerie. So they check my papers again, I carry on, out of town and eventually reach our farm.

His body acted on the physical environment as his senses were engaged in the dark, and the objects of that environment imposed themselves on him. He felt for altered and familiar spaces, their threats and dangers. Bodies are not situated passively in space but continuously make and remake the spaces around them through sensory engagement and material interaction with the environment. Those bodies are also being made and remade by the spaces around them, as gendered, empowered, disempowered, marginalized, endangered people.

FREE AND OCCUPIED SPACE

The Armistice agreement signed between French and Germans in June 1940 used space as a weapon of subjugation.[5] As France was geographically divided by the Armistice, occupied partially and then fully by the Germans, sharing space was central to the politics of resistance and liberation. Across the interviews, the nature of free and occupied space was experienced differently from place to place and by different people. Several of the interviewees had German soldiers billeted in their homes when they were children. Through this reallocation of domestic space, children gained an understanding of French people's new, subordinate position. Christian Gaillard recounted his family's experience of billeted Germans in a village near Troyes:

On our farm, there were two dwellings—my parents' house and my grandmother's. In my grandmother's . . . there was quite a big kitchen, a big room next to it, and two smaller rooms at the back. The big room was requisitioned by the Germans, who housed—if I remember rightly—five or six men in there. So they were there. My parents' house had a different layout. There was a corridor with two or three rooms, with doors onto the corridor, and one of those rooms was given to a German—

Because that room connected via a corridor to the outside of the house, the German officer did not have to walk through the family's living quarters to come and go: "Sometimes we bumped into each other in the corridor, but that was all," he said. Sylvette Leclerc recalled that domestic space was appropriated in ways that reflected the progress of the war, the enforced sociality of occupation, and its affective dimensions:

> At first, I was really scared of these Germans, and then a bit later, they requisitioned a room at my parents' house. There were only two rooms: one downstairs, and one upstairs. It wasn't really even an upstairs, actually, it was more of a loft with a mansard window. . . . In winter, it was too difficult to heat that room, so we all slept downstairs in the same room. And they requisitioned the upstairs room. We had Germans billeted there for quite a while, eh. It wasn't always the same ones, because they got moved around. And well, some of them really frightened me, and made a big impression on me. But others were nicer. And as the years passed, they became younger and younger. They didn't have enough men for their troops, so they were really young. I remember the last one. He can only have been eighteen, that's all. You could see he really missed his family, because he was always with us, the children, my goodness [there is a pause, and a catch in her voice. She sighs audibly.]

Sylvette turned twelve in 1944.[6] Despite the fact that half of the family's living space was appropriated, she notes that in winter they all slept in the same room anyway because of the cold. These Germans did not get the best space. The encroachment of enemy men sensitized the young girl, and certainly moved the older woman when interviewed, to the human costs of Nazi aggression. These younger and more damaged men were closer to the French children in both space and age.

Outside space was also redefined through its appropriation by the occupier. In parts of the country, particularly rural areas, Germans were absent. And some urban spaces, even in occupied France, seemed relatively free of occupation. Pierre Haigneré commented that in Lille's Délivrance industrial railway district, Germans were very rarely seen, to the extent that he recalled living until the bombing of April 1944 with the occupation in the background. On the other hand, in the naval port of Brest space was highly contested, with German-imposed rules of constraint, such as curfews and restrictions on street gatherings, redefining how public spaces were inhabited. Similarly, within the medieval walls and narrows streets of the Burgundian town of Beaune, the German presence created a sense of space unequally controlled and unwillingly shared. Listening to these memory stories left me with a feeling of claustrophobia. Footfalls echoing on the cobblestones, the Germans seemed omnipresent, not because of large numbers but through surveillance and control. Jean-Claude Bourtourault, born in 1938, had a very early memory of looking from the window of his house and seeing German soldiers just there, a memorable, anxiety-inducing presence for the young child. The fragile barrier of the window also featured in Daniel Fevre's memory of 1944, during the liberation of Beaune. Ten years older than Jean-Claude, he also recalled the threat of the German presence: "I remember being at the window, watching them leave." They were still dangerous: "I recall seeing a truck pass in front of the house, and I recognized Henri D---'s brother-in-law." The young man would later be killed. The inhabitants of Beaune lived the occupation in competition for their own urban space. Pierre Tainturier recalled the fear generated by restrictions on movement: "The occupation, I was so afraid of it. I was afraid of the Germans, because, well, first there was the curfew, and you couldn't meet up with anyone. It didn't do to break the rules they imposed on you, it didn't do to provoke them." Pierre was about twelve years old when the occupation began, and he understood the nature of the rules and the consequences of disobedience. The memory chain that started when he introduced the occupation led him directly to the curfew and his anxieties around it. Madame Sauvonnat recalled her mother leaving one evening on foot for the maternity hospital to give birth. She was stopped and did not have a permit to break the curfew. Daniel Fevre and his friends, adolescent boys of around sixteen years in 1943, joined the Défense passive (civil defense) in order to gain some kind of freedom in the evenings. Wearing a Défense passive armband gave them permission to be out after curfew. Otherwise, he said, "if there was a German patrol on the sidewalk, you had to step into the road." The sidewalks, he recalled, were the spaces of his childhood games: "They were really wide sidewalks . . . and when we were young, that's where we'd played, they were our sidewalks"; the sidewalks were not just places children had chosen to play, they were, in Daniel's mind, *for* children. And now children stepped into the road in deference to those who threatened them. In this small town, tensions between occupier and occupied seem to simmer like a pressure cooker.

A highly unusual memory of freedom in an occupied space emerged from Nicole Kahn's account of her arrival in the internment camp at Drancy. Drancy symbolizes where collaboration had led. In protecting the rump sovereignty of Vichy, the French government put its own anti-Semitism into the service of the Germans' exterminatory policy. Run by the French authorities, this internment camp in an unfinished housing estate to the north of Paris was for many Jews their final living place on French soil. From Drancy, they were deported mainly to Auschwitz, but also to Majdanek, Sobibor, Buchenwald, Kaunas, and Reval. In most memories, Drancy was a site of extreme deprivation and distress. Like other places of incarceration, it developed a particular culture and sociability.[7] For Nicole Kahn, it had a specific spatial quality. She arrived in Drancy following six weeks' imprisonment with her mother and a female cousin in a tiny cell in Les Baumettes prison in Marseille and a journey crushed into a cattle wagon:

> In Drancy, well the first thing was—, it was completely different to the prison. I really think I'd suffered, living in that cell. I really suffered from it, and it was a very harsh regime. And so when we arrived at Drancy, there was, despite everything else, a big lawn, you could walk around, go out. We were in a dormitory, not in a tiny cell—that made a really big difference. . . . For a child, only being able to get out for half an hour a day, into a tiny courtyard that was so—. Now, I wonder if it's just because I was a child, but it seems to me that the walls were dreadfully high, and the courtyard was very, very narrow. Having begged to be let out of the cell . . . and the German soldier himself told me I couldn't, that I wasn't allowed to. . . . Oh, you know, Drancy, in the eyes of a little girl, after that terrible time in prison, the camp seemed like a kind of freedom.

Nicole's strange recollection of Drancy is constructed in direct contrast to what had gone before: confinement is contrasted with space, restriction with freedom. Drancy was a repressive, frightening place, but Nicole's memory shows very clearly how feelings of constraint and release play into conceptualizations of space, place, and trauma. By no means does this diminish the crimes of those who controlled the camp. The camp was no better, nicer, happier, freer, or easier because Nicole remembered her experiences this way. But if we want to know what memories are made of and what memories do—and therefore understand better how, as historians, we can use them—here is an example of relationality and functionality. In her memory story, going to Drancy reunited the family. Moving there generated the conditions for their release and brought back hope. Drancy was not without fear for Nicole, as we have seen. Inmates' heads were shaved, suicides were witnessed, friends disappeared. But this singular experience is indicative of the way that memories and experiences, people and places, and far more besides, combine in unique ways that may confound expectations.

SAFE SPACES

Spaces contributed actively to building fear and danger, but they also worked to map out safety and to create it. Space is socially produced by the knowledge people derive from being in it and the ways in which they inhabit it together. The memory stories provide insight into the progressive understandings children and their families developed of how and where safety could be sought.

Understanding developed in constant confrontation with an evolving threat. It also developed as a consequence of conditions contingent on the specific circumstances of each child inside a family, circumstances such as geographical location, family composition, or access to social networks. For example, Pierre Tainturier described how in Beaune in 1939 or 1940 he helped his father dig a trench in their garden—the experience was a common one and a government recommendation—to protect them from possible aerial attack. "I remember that they passed over our garden, machine-gunning, and we were in the trench, and one plane came down." The trench now seemed inadequate as a safe space, particularly as their house was situated near the railway line. The family decamped into the hills near the town, to an aunt's house deep in the countryside. Surely, they would be safe there. But the Germans arrived; their target had shifted from an attack on a particular strategic point to the occupation of the whole territory. Even a house lost in the hills was not safe. In these examples, as the object of fear shifts, so too does the way it constitutes safe and dangerous spaces.

Something similar occurs in other memory stories. Marie-Rolande Cornué-jols's family had decided to move from Paris to Antibes at the outbreak of war. On the coast in the far southeast corner of the country they hoped to be safe, as the enemy's goal was understood to be the capital. In the first instance, the object of fear was the enemy: the family moved geographically, and there "we felt, if you like, protected." But when the Italians declared war on France on June 10,

1940, things shifted. The category of enemy broadened, and when the town was machine-gunned from the air, she said: "I remember that we went down into the cellar, but it was ridiculous. The cellar was only half underground, and if there had been a bomb, we'd have all been killed. It didn't make any sense." We do not know whether this inadequacy was felt at the time, but she described how a new conception of safety was formed. This time, the family would travel to the interior of the country, to the Limousin. Her story oscillates between macro and micro threats: the war, the enemy, the bombs, the cellar, the machine guns. Each regenerates ideas of safe space. In the end, the wholesale movement of the family unit for the second time was recycled as the best option.

Sam Krouck's description of his and his mother's escape from Paris after the Vélodrome d'Hiver roundup of Jews in July 1942 also pulls place and space together. As the pair moved from location to location, places and spaces oscillated from safe to dangerous and back again as a function of people entering and leaving them. In themselves, places or spaces may not be dangerous; they acquire those qualities as a result of the ways they are inhabited at particular moments in time. On the eve of the roundup, Sam's father, warned by a police officer he knew, tried unsuccessfully to encourage his neighbors to leave their homes. Sam and his parents left and lay low at a relative's flat in another part of the city. At that point, the threat was unrealized for the family. The day after the raid, not having witnessed it directly, Sam's mother sent him back to their own flat "to see what had happened." Telling his story, Sam laughed at her "imprudence." The boy returned to his mother and told her that the district was safe, so they went home. But safety could quickly turn:

> All of a sudden, she said to me—it was the beginning of the afternoon—she said to me "Careful, don't say a word." And there, well, in fact the cops had turned up. The cops arrived, but we stayed inside. She cut the electricity, and we hid behind the door. There was a kind of window from the landing, and one of the cops leaned down, but a neighbor from the apartment across the way called out "It's not worth your while, they've gone, they left for the countryside ages ago." In the end, they didn't persist, they didn't touch anything, they didn't force the door.

Sam's father found a *passeur* (a people smuggler) who would take his wife and son south. The two climbed into the back of a truck with about thirty other

Jews and, under a tarpaulin and piles of empty sacks, began their journey. But the safety of their hiding place was precarious: at one point, the truck broke down; at another, they were followed by a German truck; and when crossing the demarcation line, a German soldier lifted—half-heartedly it seemed—the tarpaulin. They were later captured and spent a short period in Douadic camp but managed to get away. On the final leg of their journey, on a train to Limoges, Sam's mother was tense. The confined space of the train compartment suddenly became dangerous as some French *gardes mobiles* (a kind of police) joined them. Sam felt his mother's anxiety increase as she gripped his hand tightly. They got off at Limoges and quickly walked away, putting distance between themselves and the police, but again danger caught up with them. The heavy tread of police boots could be heard pursuing them. Once again, they survived: the policeman was pursuing them, but only to hand Sam's mother a bag that she had left on the train. Sam's story builds tension in the telling; it is a constant movement from danger to safety and back to danger as events unfolded in their contingent ways. At every juncture, things could have been different. Danger rippled across places and rushed into and out of spaces with the thrust and suck of the tide. Sam was lucky. They found themselves, he said, "in some kind of paradise" in a village in the Creuse where they could finally stop moving and be safe.

Movement from danger was common in bombing narratives. Families in districts near targets sometimes rented other places to sleep at night. Until the Americans began bombing France in early 1942, the British Royal Air Force tended to bomb at night. Josette Dutilleul's family moved away from their home in Fives (a railway suburb of Lille) at night, while Christian de la Bachellerie's family took rooms in the sixteenth arrondissement of Pairs, away from Renault's Billancourt factories. The movement of children to spaces deemed safer is a key element of children's wartime experience. Jewish children Serge Holand and Marcel Zaidner, for example, lived hidden in plain sight, not clandestinely, with their own parents in the French countryside. Lola Grynberg was sent to the Mediterranean coast and adopted a new identity. As a baby, Thérèse Allglass-Cymmerman was integrated into a new family just outside Paris. At a basic level, then, safety was derived from a movement away from danger. But movement itself brought new dangers and complications, as Sam Krouck's story showed.

Some movements away from danger seemed rational. However, Henri Buc wondered about choices (were they choices?) made by villagers in Gouzon following a German air raid in June 1940. Cautiously noting the slipperiness of memory, he described a dreamworld of confusion, an imagined space in which spaces themselves were reimagined across the community:

> Everything people did across those twenty-four hours seemed steeped in what was dreamlike, unreal, unexpected. Because there had been one air raid, we knew they were going to come back. One little boy said "I'm going to go in the bomb crater, because bombs never fall twice in the same place." It was a dreamlike world. But what was dreamlike and the most symbolic, the strongest, was that we left our home, which was over there, next to the church, and we went that way, into the fields behind. All the children were frightened, and all the women were there, with their rosary beads, saying their prayers, they were saying their prayers over their money-boxes. They were all on the riverbank—, I remember that extremely clearly, there was something—, it was as though you had to be by the water. Why did you have to be by the water? Because it was a place of safety, a mystical place of safety. We were there because we didn't know where else to go, and so for a time, we were there.

Something beyond the rational drew them to the water. There existed, Henri seemed to imply (and Henri was a scientist, a man of reason), a deeply affective connection between the women of the village and the space to which they led their children. Later, when the village was again under threat, the women returned once more to the riverbank.

I have noted how the confinement of Jews in railway wagons, prisons, internment camps, and insanitary rooms was socially constructed in an ideologically and politically framed relationship of dominance and subordination. But in other circumstances, confinement and restriction were experienced more positively. In Lucienne Rémeur's case, the spatiality of safety during the siege of Brest (August 7–September 18, 1944) was a formative memory. The majority of civilians had been evacuated from the city during a ceasefire agreed by the Germans. Only three thousand people remained, and the majority of them found shelter in the deep, purpose-built shelters constructed during 1942, one of which had an entry on Place Sadi-Carnot and was known as the Sadi-Carnot shelter. Here, fourteen-year-old Lucienne and her mother, who had permission to remain in the town with a leg injury, were living. In the world of the underground mass shelter, space was carved up in new and particular ways: "Well, Mum was allowed to have a space. . . . But as for me, I'd be by her side during the day, sitting on the side of her bed, Mum made a little space for me, and there, we'd look after each other. . . ." As her description continued, however, Lucienne revealed a world in which competition for space was intense: "It was jam-packed! It was full when more people came in from outside, big families, and space became more and more restricted, you know. What you had you held onto. But I didn't have an allocated space. So in the day, I'd be with Mum, and at night I'd sleep near some people who were kind enough to make a little room for me." The way spaces were allocated in the shelter depended on the social relations between the individuals inside: her mother had the right to a spot, which suggests there was some kind of management of space, yet Lucienne depended on others to find somewhere to sleep. Lucienne would climb up to the surface to receive food from the Défense passive but return to the safety of the shelter after a little fresh air. In the end, the safety of this space proved illusory. Deep and strong, the shelter did its job insofar as it protected the civilians from bombs, but those very qualities turned it into a death trap when armaments being stored there (illegally) by the Germans caught fire. Lucienne slept near the partition between the German and French sides of the shelter. From that position, she was woken by the sound of an altercation; smelling burning and fumes, she ran from her sleeping spot to haul her mother to safety. The people who had made space for her to sleep, however, "they didn't come after me." She added sadly "it's a shame." The shelter exploded, killing nearly four hundred French civilians and larger number of Germans. Safe spaces could be imagined only so far as the threat was known. As threats evolved, safe spaces became inadequate, and their most protective qualities could also be their most deadly.

PAUSE—HÉLÈNE—PERSECUTION AND SPACE

Hélène Zytnicki's experiences as a Jewish child at the Vélodrome d'Hiver in July 1942, at Beaune-la-Rolande internment camp, and then at Drancy illustrate vividly how space and access to space act as a means of control and attack. Restricting and constricting the body in space deny that body its own integrity. To be is to be in a place, but the quality of being in that place may be ideologically determined. In Hélène's story, confinement, separation, and oppression are all spatial forms of persecution. To be able to move or be restricted in movement, to be let alone or be harried from place to place, to know where one is going or be crushed by uncertainty, to breathe and think in a livable space or be dehumanized in an uninhabitable space, to share space in solidarity or overflow space with desperation: these means by which Jews were spatially persecuted are clear across Hélène's story. Agitated and struggling to hold back her tears, Hélène spoke of the Vélodrome d'Hiver:

> I can see myself in the Vel d'Hiv, with my mother, and everyone else too, high up in the seating [she is distressed]. And as it was July, a stifling heat, just stifling. We had nothing to drink. Sheer panic. We stayed there for maybe three days, I don't know, maybe four or five days, and nights too. With my mum and all the others, crammed into the high seats, we absolutely couldn't, absolutely couldn't move. We couldn't even go to the toilets, nothing—, people just did—, moving just wasn't possible. Children were crying, and there were a lot of them. I remember people fainting, I think because of the heat. It was just a dreadful heat . . . it was atrocious, those five days in there . . . and my mother, she didn't leave me, and I didn't leave her. We held onto each other.

Denied access to toilets and to water, suffering grew, Hélène said, into panic. This panic found its form in the crying of children, in the distress and discomfort of everyone. Central to the traumatic experience of the Vel d'Hiv was the impossibility of its space: a stadium built for bodies in motion, for speeding bicycles, cheering crowds, and the muscular prowess of sporting achievement had become a spatial actor in the diminution of the Jews of Paris. But Hélène remained with her mother, clinging together in the heat.

The pressure of too many people on an inappropriate space acted as a means of control, weakening and subduing those within it. Spaces not fit for humans were the means by which humans were dehumanized. This is particularly clear in Hélène's memory of the journey from Paris to Beaune-la-Rolande:

> One thing that I'm sure of is that we travelled in cattle wagons. And that was awful too. A dreadful heat, they crammed us in like animals, with straw on the ground. All the entrances were sealed. It was the same, people were fainting in there, screaming, crying. I remember, well, we were children, we were smaller than the adults, me, I was suffocating in there, you kept searching for somewhere to breathe some fresh air—, and well, it was impossible to move

in there either. . . . The memory I have is of the awful suffocation in there. . . .
It was a real nightmare, that cattle wagon, the heat, the crush.

The memories Hélène retains are linked to her body in this confined space and
its struggling interaction with the material environment of the wagon. She does
not state how she felt. We discern her feelings in her description of the physical
environment acting upon her body: the crush, the heat, desperation, distress, the
sense of suffocation.

At the Vel d'Hiv, Hélène describes how she and her mother clung to each
other. At Beaune-la-Rolande, her mother was brutally wrenched from her grip
one day and deported. Hélène and the other lone children were transferred back
to Drancy. Here, Hélène's memories construct a new spatial world, of children
once more treated like animals. With no adult care, the trauma of losing her
mother, and no sense of what was happening, Hélène's condition deteriorated
such that she was physically very ill when her father managed to rescue her. Her
memories convey a dreamlike, nightmarelike world of children's distress, her own
and others' merging, confined inside confinement. The image proves a strong
contrast with Nicole Kahn's memory of Drancy. Hélène begins her description
with the same words with which she spoke of the Vel d'Hiv: "I can see myself in
Drancy." Hélène, an adult in her early fifties when interviewed, looks in on her
child self, simultaneously distant and close. With the other lone children of the
camp, she was shut in some kind of building, "like a stable. They crammed us
in there." There were no beds, just straw on the ground. The youngest children,
some of whom were just toddlers, cried all day and night. Again, she recalled "this
terrible heat." She said of the guards, "they literally threw our food at us . . . like
animals." The children were tossed opened tin cans; they had no bowls, and she
does not recall spoons: "And still that same memory: I never washed, never, not at
all. I don't know if it's true or not, but I think that, in any case, there wasn't much
attention to hygiene." The children could go into the concrete yard, but they did
not play. All the time they were watched by soldiers with dogs: "we were just
children, but they watched over us like adults," she said. Her abiding memory of
this time, the crying, shifts from something externalized—looking in on herself,
on other children's tears—to the more inclusive pronoun *on* (in this case, we) in
the telling: "There was crying, there was crying. We were crying, we were calling
for our mothers, but we were so little. We didn't know what had happened to
them." The separation of the children from their mothers made a hole into which

everything else collapsed. Even without their mothers, food, hygiene, and play might have been possible given an appropriate (even if basic) space. Yet the physical restrictions placed on the children destroyed their capacity to behave like children. Instead, they were fed like animals and cried their distress like animals. This degraded living space was the means by which the power relations between the Jewish child and the French state were made concrete in lived experience.

PART 3

MEMORIES TOLD

Assemblage thinking is a dynamic way of understanding oral history as an open-ended, contingent process situated inside everyday realities. Assemblages are alliances of bodies of all kinds: people, memories, places, objects, feelings, discourses, and more. They come together fleetingly in *this* way, at *this* moment. Any thing that affects or is affected by another thing can enter into assemblage. Thus, the glue of the assemblage is affect. All the elements of the assemblage have the potential to affect and be affected by one another. This potential is not predetermined by hierarchization, structure, or subjectification, nor is the assemblage ever static. As "affects are becomings," forever in flux, affecting objects and being affected by them, the assemblage never just is; it is always shifting, becoming, evolving, mutating.[1] Yet recording an interview solidifies something that was fluid. It turns a rhizomatic flow of remembering ("and . . . and . . . and") into "is."[2] Making a record is of course incredibly valuable, but it shuts down the process of becoming, giving an impression of memories as fixed. Assemblage thinking is valuable when examining the relational dynamics inside oral history interviews. Oral history interviews are often theorized as intersubjective, with the subjectivities of participants (gender, class, and so on) seen as shaping content.[3] As assemblages do not permit object-subject relations and pull all bodies into a flatter relationship with each other, new ways of thinking about interaffectivity rather than intersubjectivity emerge.

The objects in the assemblage of the memory story and the listening encounter include a range of known and unknown humans (e.g., interviewees, interviewers, later listeners, imagined listeners, the people who populate the memory stories), memories, affective drives past and present, past and present events, discourses (e.g., national memorial tropes), institutions (e.g., archives), objects (in the memory stories but also in the telling or listening contexts, e.g., recording devices, cameras, listening supports), places (e.g., dwellings, locations, regions, rooms), and so on. These heterogenous elements come together in this particular way, often momentarily, and could always have been otherwise. The interview encounter is a site of potentiality and possibility. I emphasize its contingent dimension and, therefore, the virtual that coexists with the actual. *This* interview, no matter that it has been recorded and archived, tells only one version of what could have been, and what could be, told.[4]

As elicited performances, oral histories "bring forth particular stories and social worlds, to the exclusion of others."[5] When an institution or interviewer chooses a focus, seeks an interviewee, asks a particular question, or misses an emphasis in the story as told, they participate in the construction of certain pasts to the exclusion of others. Hamilakis writes that "the mnemonic selection of certain instances and the forgetting of others will produce political effects, as distinctive times can operate instrumentally to valorize events, ancestors and situations past and present, whereas the forgetting of others can erase difficult or inconvenient truths."[6] Yet power does not flow in only one direction. Processes of actualization during the interview are more disorderly, which makes it such a rich site of possibility. What Nick Fox describes as "a rhizomatic flow of affects" operates during the telling. That flow, he says, "may coerce, discipline, habituate, subjectify, provide meanings or otherwise territorialize bodies and the social world."[7] (The Deleuzian/Guattarian term *territorialization* can be seen here as the process of "actualization," that is, bringing into reality one story, utterance, or feeling and not another.) To describe the flow as rhizomatic signifies its unruly or unstructured nature; possibility springs across, through, and out of the telling of the memories in neither sequential nor consequential ways. As Hamilakis remarks, memories and their affects are "not easy to tame and subjugate entirely, due to the anarchic nature of the sensorial and the involuntary power of memory."[8] The questions that interest me, therefore, are: Why are these memory stories told as they are, so far as I can tell? What do the memory stories seek to accomplish? What affective forces operate inside the interview encounter to actualize certain memories? And what might this suggest (because we cannot know) about what was not told?

Part 3, "Memories Told" is divided between vertically operational regimes of memory, which are also regimes of feeling or affective regimes (because memories are made of feeling), and horizontally operational communities of memory, which are likewise affective communities.[9] Both set the tone for the telling of this or that story. The first, a regime, is akin to what Jan Assmann has called "cultural memory."[10] Cultural memory, in this sense, is the way a society constructs and remembers its past through memorial culture and traditions. This kind of remembering is organized and has fixed points of reference (perhaps called *lieux de mémoire*). These may change over time, but while they are active, they orient what it is acceptable, expected, or normal to say about a particular phenomenon.[11] Versions of the past in dominant memory culture are also regimes of affect. They govern and direct the way we feel about our pasts—what we see in our ancestors' actions as wrong or progressive, say—in normative ways.[12] Such regimes are generated by "machines of affect," which might be contemporary museum cultures, trends in academic research, or television programs. Feelings about the past are held in place by "structures of affect" such as systems of memorial practice—e.g., behavior toward monuments such as statues, rituals of commemorative practice such as poppy wearing in the UK, official public apologies—which actively pin feelings to the past, making deviance from memorial norms difficult to sustain.[13] Harald Welzer also refers to the "social practices of memory management," such as archiving particular kinds of records. What he calls "social memory" is that "which transports and communicates the past and interpretations of the past in a non-intentional manner."[14] These affective regimes of memory partially account for why certain parts of the past are activated in certain ways when memories are recounted. Consciously or not, rememberers strive to demonstrate their proximity to (resonance) or distance from (dissonance) normative ways of understanding the past.

Horizontally operational communities of memory interweave with vertical regimes of memory, providing a warp and a weft in the communication of past experience. They broadly correspond with what Welzer terms, after Assmann, "communicative memory": the "wilful agreement of the members of a group as to what they consider their own past to be, in interplay with the identity-specific grand narrative of the we-group, and what meaning they ascribe to this past."[15] He notes that the organizational structures of historical narratives, the presence of certain actors in individual memory stories, and the judgments made on this past exist in explicit or implicit dialogue between individual and culture. We can make a link here to Raymond Williams's much-used (but difficult to pin down) concept "structures of feeling."[16] Jonathan Flatley explains that "when certain objects produce a certain set of affects in certain contexts for certain groups of people—that is a structure of feeling."[17] So when people who were children in France during the Second World War speak about their childhoods in interviews, the set of affects produced binds the group together as a community of memory, which is therefore also an affective community. It is not that people feel the same way about things. Rather, the set of affects, or possible ways of feeling, is such that it connects the rememberers, who express a "practical consciousness" of the sharedness of their experience.[18] This comes about in assertions of what "we" experienced, what "everyone" from our times felt or thought, how "we" acted, what "nobody" wanted, what was normal for "us." Hall states: "The basis for a (cultural) community lies in the sharedness of those definitions of historical experience. People locate themselves as belonging to a community because within it, some experiences are common and some of the ways in which they have been defined and understood are shared. How are they shared? Through the interactive communication between members of that community."[19] I am interested in the way communities of memory are constituted and evidenced during the interview encounter. How people locate themselves in a community of memory occurs between peers, across the divide between a community member and an outsider, and beyond the interview in real and imagined interactions with nonpresent others.

Graham Smith has used theories of transactive memory to analyze memory talk in oral history interviews.[20] Memory talk is "situated social action" in which speakers perform identity by positioning themselves inside social relationships, claim entitlement to the significance of their lived experiences, and construct "moral and cultural orders" through remembering.[21] These processes are identified by analyzing dialogic exchanges between interview participants that impress upon each other, molding, rebounding, or cohering to create or inhibit the (co)production of meaning about the past. But any analysis of dialogic exchanges must look beyond language and recognize the interaffective dynamics of interviewing, the circulation of affects, and attempts to communicate and share affective states. Interaffectivity and transactive remembering involve "imagined others" who may be named or vague.[22] All of these contribute to the activation of certain versions of the past in the interview encounter. Again, the assemblage proves a useful model to pull together, for a moment, real and imagined participants, affective regimes and communities, ideological standpoints, and the "interactional business" of the communicative exchange.[23]

In many interview extracts used in this book, I have removed the interviewer's questions because the focus of my analysis has been elsewhere. This is an expedient measure common to much oral history writing. To exclude the interviewer reduces him or her to a "vessel through which information is conveyed," an instrument of science, and not an equally weighted object in the assemblage.[24] Yet, as Karen Barad might have it, "the instruments [are] inextricably snagged in the scenes of their experiments."[25] It seems important to bear in mind that in telling their memory stories, interviewees are rarely expecting "a detached assent to an indifferent truth." Speaking out is searching for a "second-person acknowledgement from and of (an)other(s)."[26] Again, this shapes how the narrative is formulated, which versions of the past are activated, and which go unsaid.

PAUSE—FILMING MARIE-MADELEINE

Using interviews conducted by other people can be frustrating. Questions go unasked, responses are ignored, and it is tempting to be critical. Listening again to my own interviews, I often feel the same. This post hoc recognition that the interview could have been different is evidence for how content is being continuously shaped during the encounter. Interviewer and interviewee press upon each other, driven by their own motivations and comprehension. Scholars are both pessimistic and optimistic about the reuse of oral history.[27] Some years ago, Ron Grele argued that it is impossible for someone who was not present to understand the interview fully: what led up to it, what were the prior expectations, how experienced was either party, what happened before and after the recorder was turned on and off. No outsider can claim to know the motivations of either party.[28] Yet must interpretation rest on knowing in this way? Any later interpretation belongs to its own assemblage; interpretation depends as much on the interpreter's encounter with the interview as with the interviewer's. Interpretation depends on listening practices. We can understand something of the river from the bank by measuring its length, depth, temperature, or speed. Or we can jump in, feel the water, and join the flow as another object in the assemblage, affecting the water and being affected by it.[29]

Grele posits an inherent, unspoken conflict at the heart of every interview.[30] The interviewer wants to collect a memory that can be analyzed and archived.

S/he is likely to want to pin things down, such as places and dates, and keeps pulling a fluid discussion back to her/his own research interests. In Deleuzian/ Guattarian terms, this can be seen as a process of stratification: "mak[ing] the world by organizing forms and substances, codes and milieus."[31] This creates an unresolved tension, given that the interviewee's impetus is to tell his or her story, which, as we have seen, is likely to be composed of episodes generated by, and linked by, affect and feeling: a fluid narrative, a "heterogenous smooth space," where time is weird and much is vague.[32] This fairly common dynamic, which can be more or less pronounced, works to shape content, blocking certain avenues for narration and even hindering the development of the narrative as the interviewee may have hoped. Yet without the interviewer's invitation and prompts, the narrative might never have come into being at all. Something of this tension exists in the interview recorded with Marie-Madeleine Viguié-Moreau and archived at the Archives départementales de Saône-et-Loire.

I was given the interview to listen to in the reading room on a computer with no broader context as to why it had been recorded. The identities of the two interviewers were not stated. For a day, I worked intensively on this audio file, listening, relistening, and transcribing affectively (not all the words, but more than the words). I sometimes felt the main interviewer was a little insensitive, interrupting Marie-Madeleine and asking her to restart what she said. The interviewer had a list of questions and was clearly sticking to them regardless of where Marie-Madeleine wanted to go. On my second day at the archives, I was assigned a different computer to work on. All of a sudden, it became apparent that this was a filmed interview. The movie file had not opened on the first computer, and nothing else had suggested to me that it existed. Realizing that the interviewers were filming made a number of things clear. If the narrative was interrupted or Marie-Madeleine was not concise, the filmmakers did another take. I did not see the final cut. But I left the archives struck by how the conditions of a filmed interview had prevented Marie-Madeleine from developing a line of narrative that for my research was extremely valuable. Listening and then watching affected me differently. Until I saw the film footage, my mind dwelled on the child Marie-Madeleine. After I saw the film, my abiding memory is of the older Marie-Madeleine, poised and elegant on her sofa, waiting patiently as the filmmakers fiddled with lighting and microphones and trying to chat as they focused on their tasks.

The rigidity of the interview structure is clear from the start. An early question asked Marie-Madeleine if she remembered the declaration of war in 1939. She responded with some personal memories. The interviewer then made a surprising leap, requiring Marie-Madeleine to cover several years of her childhood at once, asking "Had you ever seen a German in Cluny before 1944?" It seemed that this question asked her to do too much. She responded: "Of course. Germans, even [emphasizing the plural]." This short but suggestive answer shows that she could have said (and maybe wanted to say) more about those Germans but was not encouraged to do so. Instead, the interviewer asked whether the Germans she had seen corresponded with ideas of Germans she had held before 1939. Marie-Madeleine was only five years old in 1939. She responded with a short anecdote that did not really answer the question but that finished: "and I asked Mum, 'What's a Jew?' And she replied the same thing again: 'We'll tell you when you're older.' And I said to myself, 'Oh no, that's not fair.' " Here she introduced a key motif of her story: she was always being told she was too young to know more. After this response, the interviewer asked her the same question again: did the Germans correspond with the image she had been given of them beforehand? She said "Yes. They were the baddies, if you like. I can't say the enemy, really. The German was the baddy. Now, about that word 'Jew'—", but she was interrupted. She did not have more to add about the Germans but wanted to develop the point about Jews, which seemed to matter to her narrative. At this point, the woman behind the camera broke in: "If you can, if it's not too difficult, if you could just try to pick up on the questions S----- asks you, that way, we can try and cut the questions out afterwards." Marie-Madeleine was asked to contain and reformulate her memories. She seemed abashed. She criticized herself, saying "one thing makes me think of another. I know that's one of my faults, yes, it is." The fluid nature of remembering, hardly a fault in other contexts, became one here. There followed a pause and some kind of confusion. Marie-Madeleine had lost her train of thought. So for a third time she was asked whether she had seen any Germans in Cluny before 1944. "Yes, I'd seen quite a few of them," she replied. She was told to develop her answer in line with the question.

MARIE-MADELEINE: Yes, I'd seen quite a few of them, because the
   Germans had come to Cluny [after November 1942], so we used to see
   them in the streets. Seeing these people dressed in khaki, with their

boots, they made a lot of noise, and so for a little girl, it was very strange—

INTERVIEWER: Did you understand that the German was the enemy?

MARIE-MADELEINE: Not the enemy. More someone who was disrupting our daily lives.

The point that Marie-Madeleine had wished to make—about not knowing what Jews were and her knowledge growing as events unfolded—was deactivated, even devalued. The response she gave to please her interviewers was noncommittal, yet it bears the trace of the coherence she wished to give to her story: she was only a little girl, her knowledge was limited, but the violent events of war would change that.

Across the narrative she kept returning to her child self's perspective on events. She moved into sad and emotional territory when discussing the realization of what her father's deportation actually meant. Her voice softened, lowered, and became hesitant: "so in the end, we had to acknowledge that our father would not be coming back. And that was the beginning of a dreadful time. Really dreadful." I sensed that she would have continued. But the interviewer followed this immediately with the question "So during that time, were you still going to school?" This could have been an interesting line, given that her daily life as a schoolgirl must have been impacted by her sorrow. However, this did not seem to be the interviewer's intention, as he added: "Did you get the feeling that your primary school teacher had Pétainist sympathies?" Perhaps he changed the subject because he found her sadness uncomfortable; perhaps he was not listening deeply and felt that with a point made succinctly, he could move on to the next. Across the interview Marie-Madeleine makes clear that as a child she was ignorant but that she can only speak from that child's point of view. She seems frequently blocked in developing more expressive and affective lines. She was later asked: "In those days, how did you learn about what was happening in the war, given that the press was censored?" At this point, it seems as though Marie-Madeleine gently fought back. She refused to apologize for her point of view or to generalize about what she did not know. She responded: "We just had one thing on our mind, in our family, and that was that our father would come home. *Bon*." The *bon* is final: this and only this was what mattered and what she recalled. How the war was going on elsewhere and how news was passed on were far from her preoccupations. I am not trying to make an unfair critique of a very moving filmed interview. The filmmakers have created a valuable record of a child's wartime life. But I was left wondering about the memories that were not actualized here: the virtual in the actual. What else could Marie-Madeleine have said? Given free rein to develop her own narrative, what would have been different? The material conditions of the interview encounter—a camera, microphones, lighting, two interviewers, the need to cut and edit, the requirement of narrative coherence, being concise, the unblinking gaze of the camera's lens, and the consciousness of being looked at—all affect the content. In turn, they affect me as I listen and interpret this encounter, affect flowing not just between the people present in the interview, in ways I can imagine but not know, but to me, years later, plugged into a computer in a room in Mâcon, and beyond.

CHAPTER 6

REGIMES OF MEMORY, REGIMES OF FEELING

The French wartime past is typically told as a story of heroes (the resistance, those who rescued Jews), villains (collaborators, Vichy, Germans), and victims (Jews, other deportees, bombed and hungry French civilians). Children have a place in this narrative only if they suffered as victims; otherwise they are excluded. Pierre Laborie sees a more reductive vision at work. He describes the "screens" of the "memorio-media" landscape onto which is projected a binary narrative of heroism and victimization. Such screens, in the other sense, also obscure various parts of French guilt: the villains are glossed over. In a binary vision of heroes and victims, Laborie continues, the rest of the population is reduced to "an amorphous mass, *attentiste* and even complicit in collaboration."[1] As he sees it, dominant versions of the past portray the resistance and the persecuted Jews as beacons in a murky historical landscape. Only these two categories can inspire imaginative engagement with the period across various public platforms and thus structure the regime of memory (top-down, often state-managed) for this period.[2] While international scholarship over the past thirty years has examined a wide range of experiences in France during the Occupation, a tendency to establish analytical frameworks based on the poles of collaboration, resistance, or suffering (of Jews or others)—whether to defend, attack, judge, categorize, or enumerate—endures.

RESONANCE

How do the memory stories of wartime childhoods used across this book resonate with a regime of memory that heroizes the resistance, deplores Jewish persecution, and either chastises or commiserates with the rest of the French population? How does feeling cohere around certain memorial tropes, actualizing particular lines (this story, this anecdote) or particular affective states (moods, atmospheres) and not others? Do the stories dwell on suffering in order to generate or alleviate guilt? And how does the dominant regime of memory delegitimize the child's perspective? Chapter 6 illustrates how a recognizable form of this dominant regime of memory surfaces in the narratives, either as a presence or as an impression in counter-relief.

In memories of childhood, little narrated scenes, anecdotes, and flashes may well be disregarded as interviewers seek responses to questions derived from the dominant regime of memory that are weighted with greater value. This is one of the ways in which the voices of subordinate parts of the population such as children are delegitimized and a certain version of the past is actualized. This happens across the interview with Jean-Claude Bourtourault. The interviewer asked questions that fit the grid of the national regime of memory (the good, the bad, the poor French): his impression of the Germans, Marshal Pétain, rationing, restrictions, the radio, resistance, and liberation. The questions prevented Jean-Claude from developing his own lines of memory. At one point, Jean-Claude described the impact of gasoline restrictions, the family's use of a horse and cart, and mentioned the "*gazogènes*," vehicles powered by wood-fired mobile gas generators that fascinated him as a boy. The interviewer cut in, asking "and did your parents listen to the radio?" She asked not for Jean-Claude's own experience but that of his parents. Later on, she asked whether his parents were surprised to see French soldiers arriving to liberate Beaune. Jean-Claude sticks to his own perspective. He gives an insight into his child self's mindset, which may also reflect how he wants to be perceived in the present:

Well, you could say that, me, I'm really patriotic. And so all that time, I'd been drawing French flags everywhere. I wanted—, so, you've got it in your imagination, in your fantasies, that surely the French will win, that—well that's for certain. All the more so because, what with all the movements of the troops that my father would plot on our map [with pins, in the kitchen], well, naturally, I wanted it to be France that won.

His response is the opposite of surprise. His answer gives far more than the question asks. Jean-Claude remembers being deeply invested as a boy in the kind of patriotism concomitant with the *maréchaliste* cult that never admitted the defeat was final. In this rendering, there was no chance that such patriots would become pro-German: always the aim was liberation. Such a positioning distances Jean-Claude from the "bad" French. His understanding derived from his "fantasies," but it was also performed in the movement of colored pins on a map. Jean-Claude was skilled at describing the details of everyday life but was frequently cut off. Did he see resistance fighters arrested in Beaune? He had already stated that his family had by then moved away from the town. "To his knowledge" was there any other resistance activity in Beaune? His personal experience is not solicited. Was he present for the liberation in Beaune? He was not. Did he witness the postliberation ceremony with General De Lattre de Tassigny? He did not. Instead of focusing on what he *could* talk about, the interviewer generated a negative imprint of her own preoccupations, which followed the major events of national and local history.

The child's perspective was sometimes devalued even in interviews that produced sensitive accounts of past experience. Memories are made of feelings that do not necessarily chime with understandings guiding the interviewer's questions. As Nicole Kahn, in her filmed interview, recounted her time in Drancy internment camp, her childhood memories jarred with the interviewer's expectations. Her anecdotes juxtapose the insouciance of a child's perception with the gravity of persecution and deprivation. The latter resonates with the dominant regime of memory, but the former confounds it. Nicole remembered two wealthier Jewish women arriving in Drancy. Seeing that Nicole had nothing but the clothes she stood in, they gave her a white nightdress embroidered with green flowers. Nicole was delighted and stood on the bed to show it off, managing in the process to rip it from top to bottom. Telling this memory, her face was alight with bright smiles, laughing at herself and perhaps the absurdity of the situation. The interviewer simply responded "Mmm," flatly. Nicole's face fell instantly, and the interviewer moved on to a question about food. Later, another childish experience garnered no response. Nicole's face grew animated as again she described an item of clothing: "I think that someone must have had some tea-towels, ones like we had before the war, really big ones, and so with two tea-towels, they made me a summer dress [she smiles broadly]. But the tea-towels weren't the same color. The skirt had red checks, the top had blue ones. Well, it didn't matter that much!" She looked directly at the interviewer, smiling, pleased with this memory for whatever reason; again, her face fell. She shrugged, looked away from him and down, and added "Yes, well, these are really only a little girl's memories."

Like Marie-Madeleine Viguié-Moreau, she apologized for her remembering. She appeared to attribute the interviewer's seeming lack of interest in stories of solidarity, everyday life, and emotion to the fact that they were a child's memories: unimportant, frivolous, and maybe gendered, with their focus on clothing. Had the interviewer probed or encouraged, what else might have been actualized in the telling? The dominant regime of memory imprints on the story in counter-relief, denying a victim any glimmers of hope in her suffering.

The devaluing of children's perspectives occurs in stories of heroes too, sometimes by the interviewer, sometimes by the interviewee. A filmed interview in the Archive départementales de Seine-Saint-Denis was recorded in the early 1980s with the leftist French film director and activist Jacqueline Meppiel. Meppiel was born in 1928 and might be expected to have had quite clear memories given that she was twelve when France fell in 1940. Yet she barely features in her own childhood memories. The youngest in a family of at least four children, Jacqueline said that her father spent the war in Switzerland, her brother was mobilized, called up to the STO, and then escaped to Switzerland, and her mother ran a boardinghouse in Châteauroux. Here, it seems from her narrative, they housed a young Trotskyist journalist whom Jacqueline found quite inspiring and two maquis agents. Her older sisters joined the Red Cross. One got involved in resistance work and helping Jewish children across the border; she was caught and put into a camp, where she contracted tuberculosis. Her other sister worked, she thinks, in Gurs internment camp, which interned Spanish Republicans, Jews, and gypsies. If this was a political awakening for Jacqueline, I might have expected to hear more about it. But in her account, only the active, activist, and heroic counted. This resonates with versions of resistance history that privilege action over attitudes. It also imprints on Jacqueline's story the values that mattered to her when she told it. Jacqueline's story revolved around the resistance work of others. As she, an adolescent girl, *did* nothing, she is not worth talking about.

Surprisingly, Nancette Blanchou's narrative of her parents' arrest and her father's deportation also devalues the child's perspective. Nancette provides a moving and sensitive exposition of her experiences. Yet the framing of this interview reveals the memory regime in action. The recording was made by the Archives départementales de la Dordogne and disseminated via the Mémoires de Résistances (Memories of Resistances) website. Interviews conducted mostly with former resisters are shared on the website, contextualized with factual information and searchable keywords. These archival practices facilitate the use of this interview by wider publics, but the process is not neutral. The interview is titled "Jean Dolet Blanchou—Résistant déporté [deported resister]—Nancette Blanchou." Nancette's father, his resistance and his deportation, come first. There is a photograph of him, not her. The keywords given are "arrest, social insurance, occupying authority, bombing, expression of protest, the Milice, political militant, mobilization, pacifist movement, Communist Party, rural population, propaganda, radio, French Section of the Workers' International (SFIO)."[3] Nothing here relates to Nancette as the child of resisters, bereaved and orphaned. In the interview, she refers to her father's politics but not at length in comparison to how she speaks of the impact of his death and her mother's imprisonment on her as a girl and a woman. In the interview track labeled "mechanization and social progress," Nancette describes her father's humanity as a boss, the cheerful farm atmosphere, and his workers' appreciation toward him. The content is more than factual, reflecting back the later loss of a good man. Furthermore, men, men's resistance, and death in deportation seem highly valued. Nancette comments: "I'm . . . the grand-daughter of peasants, militants, and my parents were communist militants." A few seconds later, "parents" become "father" as the interviewer reformulates her comment: "Your father was a communist militant, that's right, isn't it?" Later on, the interviewer probes: "That event, the arrest of your father was an event, you said earlier, that shaped the rest of your life. . . .?" Yet Nancette is the daughter of two parents. She had just described her mother screaming for her children, her hand crushed in the farm gate as she was dragged away. Her father's arrest was of course significant too. Nancette responded: "Yes. Or, at any rate, I believe so. I wanted to take care of other people. . . . Even though I received a lot of love, when you've lost your dad and your mum, you're missing something." On the day of his arrest, Nancette also lost her mother. Although she returned from prison, Nancette's mother's mental and physical illnesses profoundly affected her daughter. She died in 1950. The interview filters through the memory regime in which adult resistance mattered, and the martyred male deportee fits the heroic bill better than the imprisoned female resister, released but incapacitated as a mother.[4]

Conversely, other stories present a version of resistance in which even a child can resist too, resonating with a different aspect of an active memory regime. They reflect the idea of "la France résistante": the "resistancialiste myth" of consensual, national resistance against the Germans. This Gaullist trope sought to reconstruct damaged national identity in the postwar years. Young Cecilé Bramé refused to give up her seat to a German on the bus in Brest, despite his threat of violence. She said "that was *my* resistance." As such she claimed a stake, knowingly small, in the national story. Andréa Cousteaux, also in Brest, elaborated further, describing her resistance joyously. Born in 1927, Andréa was a young teenager in the war, and her antics reflect this. She does not claim particular significance for them, but she weaves them into a tapestry of anti-German activity. Sometimes this is us/we (*nous*), sometimes "all of us" (*nous tous*), sometimes a more generic us/we/they (*on*), and sometimes they/them (*ils*): not her, but her people nonetheless.

> The priest, every Sunday, he got us to do a procession. The Germans had forbidden it elsewhere, but this was around the church itself. We had banners, and we sang Ave Maria. The Blessed Virgin protects us in Brest. So every Sunday there was a procession. And us young folk, we'd be at the back of the procession, and so when the parishioners were all singing "Ave ave Maria," we'd be singing "Hail General de Gaulle, our idol art thou, amongst we believers." We'd all do that. . . . The Germans would stare at us, laughing, saying "look at those fanatics, going round the church like that". . . . They got some tracts made, down at the Arsenal, they did some tracts: born in Germany, salted in France, eaten in England. They drew a pig on it, standing guard, wearing a German helmet. Underneath it said born in Germany, fattened up in France, salted in the Channel and eaten in England [laughing a lot]. They stuck that up everywhere! *Oh là*, that made them mad!

Participation in these church processions allied her to other, more concrete acts of resistance that were identifiably part of the bigger movement. She claimed neither importance nor suffering for herself, but through her anecdotes she indicates that she—we, us, *on*, them-but-still-us—was part of a steady campaign of attrition. Her stories demonstrate French wit, creativity, and sangfroid against German bafflement, humiliation, and anger. Such small gestures align her with the France that liberated itself.

DISSONANCE

Across the corpus, however, many memory stories seemed dissonant rather than resonant. Interviewees seemed keen to demonstrate that their childhood experiences did not chime with what they considered to be popular, common, or dominant versions of the French wartime past. Memory stories pull individuals and groups into their assemblages, structuring group identities. But the generational identity of these war children is not internally consistent. The "us" and the "*on*" are not the same from person to person. But this does not stop them having a sense of a generational identity, which they often assert by correcting what they see as misapprehensions about the past, crystallized and transmitted through the regime of memory as they understand it.

The ordinary French population is often characterized as suffering through the hardships brought about by the Occupation, its violence, and restrictions. Hunger, deprivation, and family separation were realities for many, but have also served ideologically to counter accusations of opportunistic *attentisme*, greed, or disregard for the regime's victims. But various interviewees emphasized that they did not suffer in wartime. This clashes not only with a national regime of memory that flags penury as a defining feature of the Occupation but also with a transnational, transtemporal understanding of children as the inevitable victims of war.[5] However, memories of an absence of suffering may well exist in this form only because the rememberers were children and bore no (or very little) direct responsibility for events unfolding around them. Léa Duclos remarked that, apart from the frightening experience of seeing maimed flesh in a boot, "For us—, I didn't really experience it as suffering"; war, for the "*nous*" ("we") and "*je*" ("I") in her story, was "a period of my life that went by like any other." This kind of comment was not uncommon among those who were not bereaved, persecuted, or traumatized. On the face of things, Sylvette Leclerc refused to accept that war had altered schoolchildren's everyday lives: "At school?" she exclaimed, "it didn't really change anything for us." She immediately added: "although, actually it did! Here's a little anecdote—, that retired teacher we had, he had a really long cane . . . because he, at that period, he didn't hesitate to slap a child or cane them, eh, it wasn't like today, eh. Well, he called his cane Adolf! 'You're going to see Adolf!' That's what he'd say to us! [Pause] But otherwise, at school we had normal lessons." Manifestly, then, war had introduced new elements to her classroom, not least the retired teacher himself. But this was not the kind of dramatic change that war was expected to have made.

Other interviewees developed their absence of suffering in more purposeful ways. For example, Henri Buc noted:

> The war was an extraordinary moment because, as time went by, you could do things you wouldn't normally be able to do. By that I mean . . ., businesses weren't running normally, so to get hold of some wine, you had to get in touch with some friends you had in Montpellier, and they'd send you some wine, and you'd send them some potatoes. It was barter, and through that, the resurgence of a whole other way of life, which had been dying out. So you have to see that hospitality, that generosity of people, all of that, as a kind of return—a return to a regressive economic system.

Although Henri recognized that this existence was regressive, he also implied that people were forced into a better kind of sociality. Henri said this with full awareness that he had not been persecuted. But he seems to ask us to think twice before characterizing French society as simply *attentiste*. He emphasizes not opportunism and self-interest, but the principles of exchange and generosity. Henri's point counters a reductive version of the past which simplistically pits passive suffering against active profiteering.

Grégoire Guendjian's memories also contradicted the idea of wartime suffering, particularly in relation to food. He came from a poor family of Armenian immigrants, living in a slum suburb of Lyon. His memory story is steeped in pride. Poor, maybe, but the family had skills and knowledge:

> We weren't affected by anything, I can tell you, we were self-sufficient! Goats, we had goats. We ate loads of yoghurt, my mother made a lot of yoghurt. There was a farm nearby, and we'd buy cow's milk, and my mother made yoghurt a lot. People were disgusted—it didn't exist in France. . . . We all had our ration tickets, but there wasn't much to get on them. But us, we ate really well. Vegetables, all of that, we did it all ourselves. We ate bulgur wheat, corn, that's really fashionable today, and we also ate Jerusalem artichokes—now, you pay a lot for them, they're really expensive [laughing], turnips, we ate them too. There's nothing better than turnips. It's true!

Know-how derived from an ethnic food culture that could make the most out of meager resources: in the story, it raised them above French citizens who did not make nutritious yoghurt and were dependent on their ration cards, that is, above neighbors who usually looked down on them. (The commercial fabrication of yoghurt in France did already exist at this time, but the product did not become popular until the postwar era.) In common with several other interviewees, Grégoire took delight in the contradictory nature of his story. Jerusalem artichokes (topinambours) and rutabagas sound like gongs across wartime childhood memories; they symbolize the nation's food shortages. Often they are evoked with disgust, resonating with a discourse of wartime suffering. But here they are symbols of survival. Ron Grele advises listening for the "deep structures" in oral histories. Citing Eva MacMahon, he states that "the act of interpretation must always be concerned not with the intended meaning but what that intended meaning is about."[6] Grégoire's words are about more than wartime food. They contrast pampered modern folks with his hardier generation and celebrate Armenian resilience.

Grégoire's and Henri's memories are bold in their contrariness and rejection of victimhood. Refusing to be characterized as a victim may have different motivations, including a recognition of others' greater suffering.[7] In these cases, the way the memories are told acts as a corrective to the version of the past thought by the speaker to be operationally dominant in society. Brothers Claude and Michel Thomas were vociferous in their insistence that certain widely held views denied their lived experience:

MICHEL: What it's important to tell you is that it [the war, the Occupation] didn't prevent us from living. No. It didn't trouble us much. Perhaps it even allowed us, when things got a bit better and we could afford a few nicer things, to appreciate them better—

CLAUDE: —yes, yes, it's not—

MICHEL: —it's not only negative!—

CLAUDE: —exactly. Not everything's negative—

Claude and Michel do not claim universality for their view of the period, but they suggest that perspectives on the past that are too categorical miss the messy variety of lived experience. More emphatically, and with evident contrary delight, Roger Davre begins his interview: "So, well for me, let me tell you, [the war] was a period of freedom like never before. Because—are you recording this?" That the point was recorded mattered. He went on to explain that parental authority diminished and he had more autonomy:

ROGER: I lived it like it was one long playtime. Up until 1943, I had no paternal restrictions, because he was a prisoner of war. There was just my mother, and she was doing what she could to earn a living . . . and me and my sister, we went to school, and Mum came home when she came home, and if she didn't, she didn't. We just got on with it.

LINDSEY: Were there any shortages? Did you ever go hungry?

ROGER: No, we didn't suffer much at all. . . . Suffering from not being able to eat a chocolate bar, yes. From not having any sweets, yes.

Roger was later evacuated to the Creuse, an experience that again emerged as "freedom." He adapted to country life, making friends with, even outdaring, the village children. Notwithstanding their chores, country children were free to run, free from the dangers of traffic or pollution. Roger's friend Marcel added "we're going back to an extraordinary era." The way the memories are told kicks back against self-pity, accusation, and guilt to build childhoods, wartime or not, as places of growth and development.

Jewish children's memories also measure themselves against perceived expectations. When Nicole Kahn was recorded speaking with smiles about her "happy" moments in Drancy, it was the early 1980s. How did she understand her position in a wider national narrative and memorial culture at that time? Hélène Zytnicki's harrowing story and Charles Baron's distressing one form part of the same collection: some Jews were speaking out about the horrors they had lived through at this point. But in her interview, Nicole does not question why she remembers what she does, as interviews recorded later might do. Recorded in the 2000s, for example, Danièle Dubowsky emphasized that across the period of her family's persecution she had no sense of being treated worse than others. The negative impacts of anti-Semitic persecution only became clear to her after the war. Serge Holand, who found refuge in the Creuse with his family, likewise struggled to locate the sad or frightened memories he expected he should have. Maurice Goldring noted that despite his father's absence and despite internment in Douadic, "for me, the war years aren't a sad period. It's a period of playing games. Games with the maquis, games with my mates. There were barely any cars on the roads, so—, we'd hang around in the woods, we'd be off for the afternoon." In his story, Maurice does not build a Jewish "we" or "on" who did not suffer. His memories are recounted as specific to him and his family. But, like Danièle Dubowsky, Nicole Kahn, and Serge Holand, he nonetheless recalls a past that clashes with notions of Jewish suffering. Jacques Sémelin's research has examined how it came to be that 75 percent of Jews in France managed to survive the Holocaust.

He argues that survival depended on networks, agency, geography, support, and luck. The novelty of Sémelin's work is its focus on survival rather than death, but to do so remains unusual and controversial.[8] The top-down regime of memory around French participation in the Holocaust must and does research and commemorate those who were persecuted and killed. Stories that offer variations are often striking and, for the rememberers, even puzzling. Sometimes, then, regimes of memory control the way that a memory story unfolds, sometimes they are visible in gaps and silences, and sometimes we glimpse them in emphases and contradictions.

JUDGMENT

Regimes of memory act as more or less direct forces shaping interview content. Sometimes, though, interviewees challenge them explicitly. In establishing a defensive generational solidarity, interviewees make claims on behalf of a "we" group: an affective community imagined through an assumption of shared historical experience. They make a specific claim for knowledge that can only come from having been there. In doing so, they show their awareness of an audience beyond the interview encounter whence they assume judgment will emanate. Often this emerges in line with what they see as a distinctive wartime morality. Listening, I frequently felt that interviewees believed that present-day interpretations can never fully understand that their experiences occurred within a distinctive historical framework of values. A strong critique was made by Marie-Rolande Cornuéjols: "I get angry when I hear people who didn't live through that period, particularly young historians, who explain to me what I am, what I was, what I thought—bah! It's just not true! Who explain to me what I lived through—it's not true, it's not true. It's not what I saw, it's not what I thought, it's not what I experienced—, well, it annoys me a bit." In indignation, she rejects a representation of the past that presumes to understand her. Her words reveal a generational solidarity:

> Everyone you talk to who lived through that period is pretty annoyed to hear that we were all either collaborating bastards—yes, seriously!—or worthy resisters. Both are completely unreal. There were worthy resisters, of course, but most of them are dead now. . . . And there were also people who,

sadly, were just trying to survive, that's all. And then there's all of the dead, because we forget all of those killed by the bombs. And we're not allowed to speak about that because it was the English and the Americans who killed them.

She criticizes what she sees as a simplistic dichotomy that, she believes, places too much emphasis on the fact of collaboration (which she later qualifies as "survival"; she does not, here, allow for active or ideological collaboration) and obliterates the civilian suffering of the Allied bombing.[9]

Interviewees could be defensive about family members who did not join the resistance, reflecting an assumed judgment from a dominant regime of memory that highly values resistance. Jacqueline Béné was asked whether the family had discussed her brother's options when the call came for him to go to Germany in the Service de Travail Obligatoire (STO, the forced labor service drafting men to work in Germany). She said: "Well, no—but what do you expect? He could either go there or join the resistance." She suggested that hiding out in the maquis would have got him killed, whereas in Germany he survived. In this framing, those who "chose" the STO might be judged as passive, even cowardly, but Jacqueline defends her brother's actions. Yves Richard was also asked whether his father did any kind of resistance work. He responded: "What do you expect him to have done? He had five kids at home!" Yves feels compelled to defend his father, whom he characterizes as putting his family first. As we have seen, being a *bon père de famille* did not prevent other men doing risky resistance work. But as with Jacqueline, Yves's rebuttal of an implied criticism makes clear the moral stakes of the time and its memory.

The French resistance tugs at the narratives in other ways. What Henry Rousso terms the "broken mirror" phase of the so-called Vichy syndrome, in the late 1960s/early 1970s, represented a shift in the regime of memory: according to Rousso's schema, a "nation of resisters" became suddenly, shamefully tarnished as a "nation of collaborators."[10] In scholarship and culture, the French started to see reflected back not the heroic freedom fighters of myth but cowards, traitors, and perpetrators. But many interviewees refused to write the resistance out of the story. Recorded in the 2000s, Anne-Marie Laurens exclaimed angrily: "Everything's being forgotten!" She believed that a set of truths, in relation to her father involved in the railway resistance but by implication beyond him, were being falsified by a contemporary perspective on the

past that misrepresented his work and her sacrifice. Interviewees are sometimes aware they cross a line when they defend the resistance, so entrenched
has the skeptical view become.[11] When Madame Gaulthier remarked that her
family resisted from the start, she is aware of the now dominant revision-
ist view about 1940: that barely anyone heard de Gaulle's June 18 speech on
the BBC, Pétain was popular, the Armistice was a welcome relief, and most
resisters were "last minute." But she says nonetheless, "we always resisted,
completely…, eh, well I'm sorry, I'm very sorry, but—you can't please everyone—
but we never supported Marshal Pétain, sorry." The comments are laced with
apologies as she performs the transgression of what she sees as the operational
regime of memory. Michel Thomas also sought to assert what he saw as the
truth of his lived experience:

> Well, there was the Vichy government's propaganda, or, not really from
> Vichy, it came out of collaborationist circles, which tried to get the popu-
> lation worked up, to incite them against the English in particular and the
> Anglo-Saxons in general. That, well, that never took off. We never took any
> notice of it. None of it translated into anything anti-English for us. Not at
> all. We have to re-establish things as they were, because there's a lot of daft
> things that have been written, a lot of false things. The French people never
> collaborated with the Germans. We didn't like the Germans! If a German
> approached, we looked the other way. When they paraded down the rue de
> la Pompe, where I was at high school, we turned our backs on them. We
> wouldn't for anything in the world have spoken to a German.

Michel makes a clear distinction between collaborationist circles and the general population, which was, he said, anti-German through and through. His is a
voice that can "re-establish" things as they were, he asserts, because he was there.
The examples he draws from his experience serve as demonstrations of the "we"
group's attitudes and values more broadly. Plenty of other examples, in this book
and elsewhere, show that the Germans were greeted and treated in a variety of
ways. But Michel's vehemence is a defense of his generation, of ordinary people,
and of everyday forms of resistance.

Insisting on the complexity of wartime morality in the face of assumed
present-day judgments was also evident in relation to the *femmes tondues* (the
"shorn" or "shaved women"): those accused of sleeping with Germans, who had

their heads shaved in violent acts of mob justice in 1944 and 1945. Madame Puech calls attention to ideas of collaboration that, she thinks, have been unfairly applied to everyday struggles:

> You know that women were the ones who really suffered in all of that, eh. Be careful, eh. They shaved their heads, the imbeciles. They only did it because they had to, eh. You have to be very careful, because there are people who'll say to you "Oh, well, you know women . . .," but I'm telling you, women, sometimes they did that to put food on the table for their kids, you see. And some, they'd had children because of that. And if a German came and told you to—, what were you going to do, eh? You do it for your folks, for your kids. That's what I have to say about it, that's what I have to say. I'm not judging anyone. Because you can't ever know what was going on. And so that, I can forgive it. But that a French person should hurt a French person! That, well, it's—, I can't abide it. But, like I said, there were some Germans who were decent. I'll tell you that. Because they're like us. There are decent ones and bad ones, eh.

Again, she challenges a too-broad definition of collaboration, as well as characterizations of either French or Germans that generalize. She exhorts her listeners to rethink preconceptions. Her condemnation is reserved for those who judge without knowing. Those who shaved the women's heads were ignorant of their options. Those who were not there, in that bedroom or simply in the past, should not judge. Her indignation responds to a position that holds that the men who shaved the women's heads were right to do so. Most public and scholarly representations of this kind of mob justice are critical. But Madame Puech is clearly speaking in response to a discourse she believes exists about their validity.

Bernard Lemaire also spoke of the *femmes tondues*: "And the other thing that made an impact on me was the shorn women. The women who'd been with Germans. But, well, I've read some things about the shorn women, and you can say that it's really shameful. But there's another thing that's shameful, and that's that the women were shaved, and the men who'd gone with—you know—with Germans, nothing happened to them. But the women had their heads shaved." Bernard speaks of the gendered inequality of the punishment. Although he calls the shaving shameful, there is a certain ambiguity here, drawn from his own lived experience:

BERNARD: . . . when we walked past a lady who used to go out with
Germans, one kid who thought he was cleverer than everyone else, he
called this lady, "a dirty *bochesse*." So she said to him, "Come here and say
that. You know I could put your father in prison." So. Well, this woman,
in 1944 or 1945, she was shaved by the folks in the neighborhood.

LINDSEY: In front of everyone—

BERNARD: Yes, it's pretty bad. But, well, they did bring it on themselves a
bit—, there were three or four in our neighborhood. I'm not saying it was
right, though.

Bernard's attitude is complicated by the fact that the woman he encountered had
threatened the children. He strays into a gray moral area: by seeking out German
lovers, by using sexual influence to attack personal enemies, he says, did they not
go looking for trouble? He refuses to condone the punishment, however.

Some interviewees were more explicitly critical of how they saw the historical and memorial professions to be upholding a regime of memory that ignores
the realities of their lived experiences. Grégoire Guendjian's interview told the
story of his quest to name and publicly celebrate the train drivers who disobeyed
orders as an air raid siren sounded in Lyon in May 1944 and drove their train of
evacuee children to safety. Grégoire felt frustrated by the historical establish-
ment, museums, and archives. His memories were ignored and discredited, his
story (his survival, his life) devalued. He said of his local archives: "I'm telling you
that no one wanted to believe my history, no one! Even the historians! I've done
all the archives, the departmental archives, other—, I've been twenty times!"
Of the important local museum, the Centre d'Histoire de la Résistance et de la
Déportation: "We've got a Museum of the Resistance in Lyon—nothing, nothing,
nothing, nothing at all, you know. Do you understand?" All along, he criticized
"the historians": "Well, I telephoned the historians, those historians, they ask
you to leave a message but they don't respond. They don't give a damn. There's
nothing in it for them." How many people owed their lives to the train drivers'
bravery, yet professional historians seemed not to care! So Grégoire leaped at the
chance to tell his story to the local newspaper and as part of the railway history
association's oral history project. Other interviewees recognized the scope for
nuance and complexity that oral history interviews could bring to present-day
understandings of the past. Henri Girardon commented that "everything I'm
telling you, for example, it's from my point of view, but that's not to say that

someone who lived next door wouldn't say the same thing." Bernard Leclercq also commented that recording interviews was very important: "History, but *for real* [emphasis]—, we can still hear what people lived through, real people's lives—, it's not historians, it's not novelists, it's—, it's important to really know." He implied that memory stories were a more authentic form of history. Many historians would disagree, of course, and Bernard is conscious that his point crosses a line; otherwise he would not have placed his emphasis where he did. What these interviewees seem to value, though, is the possibility of revealing not all of the past but the complex interplay of parts of the past. When interviewees assert their own perspective as that of a "we" group, many of their generational cohort would surely disagree. But many of the same people recognize the heterogeneity of human experience; they value the oral history because they see that multiple versions of past events exist simultaneously and that much—about motivation, choice, agency—must remain unknown.

Interviewees recount their pasts in dialogue, explicitly or implicitly, with other versions of the past; these are part of the affective wash around the narrating of the past. They may cite vectors of the regime of memory—articles or books they have read, museums, archives, professional historians—inside their narratives, which are shaped by their understanding of how this or that version of the past resonates with their own experiences. The affective forces of feeling wronged, forgotten, or discredited, or feeling that others have been maligned or misrepresented, or feeling moved to assert a particular perspective thus impress themselves on the memory story. These are, in many ways, the emotions of history and an object of scholarly interest in their own right.

CHAPTER 7

COMMUNITIES OF MEMORY, COMMUNITIES OF FEELING

Acommunity of memory is an affective community bound together by feelings about the past. A set of interactions takes place between the individuals involved in the interview encounter: across the divide between the interviewee who was there in the past and the people who were not and, beyond those present in the interview, toward imagined audiences. The community of memory operates horizontally in dynamic ways. As an assemblage, the interview encounter fleetingly allies participants and imagined audiences, spoken utterances, articulated emotion and unspoken feeling, temporalities of recounted and imagined pasts, narrating presents and imagined futures, and so on. The interview is an unfolding moment of everyday dialogue, always on the verge of being something different. Attending to the interaffective dynamics of a community of memory reveals more of how and why one version of the past and not another is actualized in the interview.

BETWEEN PEERS

Transactive remembering between generational peers is clear in interviews with married couples and pairs of friends or relatives. André Jossent and Michel Pauty are cousins. They were evacuated from their respective homes during the war to stay with a mutual aunt in the rural Creuse department. When I arrived at Michel's home in the Creuse, where he had later settled, to interview the two men, both of their wives initially joined the conversation. Only Madame Pauty,

Michel's wife, was a native of the Creuse. Their conversation was difficult for me to follow. All four often spoke at the same time, making reference to people and places known to them but not to me. They often remembered as a group, and it seemed as though their memories had been frequently recounted together. These parts of the interview contained few personal memories, sliding instead between interpenetrating communities of memory: the cousins who had shared their wartime childhoods, the couple Madame and Monsieur Pauty, the quartet that incorporated the cousins and their wives, Madame Pauty's own family, and wider local and generational communities. I asked them whether they had seen the Germans arriving during the 1940 invasion. I mainly addressed the two men (the focus of my interview was their evacuation), but I included all four around the table in my gaze. Michel replied:

MICHEL PAUTY: No, no, no. I remember that my mother said that when she saw her first German, it made quite an impression on her.
MADAME PAUTY: They came past here when they did Oradour. [i.e., the SS Das Reich Division in June 1944]
LINDSEY: They came past here? Royère? [where we were conducting the interview]
MADAME PAUTY: Yes, yes. And I saw them.
MICHEL: (to his wife) How d'you mean? La M------ [referring to his wife's mother or another older female household member unclear to me], she took you, where was it—?
MADAME PAUTY: Yes, she took us to hide in the woods—
LINDSEY: Oh yes—
ANDRÉ JOSSENT: Me, well, I was—
MADAME PAUTY: Because, what you have to—[to the group, perhaps to André] hold on a second—there was the maquis, they had a house over at G-----, so they were hiding out there. They must have been denounced, because [the Germans] came to our village, they were looking to go to where—
MICHEL: —in the village, they set fire to the farm where the maquis was—
MADAME PAUTY: —they found it later, they set fire to it, but the maquis had been warned, they'd already left—
LINDSEY: And can you remember having seen those Germans?

MADAME PAUTY: Yes, yes, but it's vague.

MICHEL: Even her father, he took them some food, a sheep, to the maquis—

MADAME PAUTY: —because that was a big group, up there in G---, it was.

The exchange initially took place between Michel Pauty and his wife. Michel had no response for me and fell back on his mother's memory. Nor, it seemed, did Madame Pauty, but she refocused the discussion on a related sighting in 1944. She was determined to tell her story, which connected her personally, via a vague visual memory, to the celebrated maquis of the Limousin. André's attempt to contribute was actively postponed. Madame Pauty's memory connects her both to local heroes and to the national tragedy of Oradour-sur-Glane. For listeners in the know (her immediate audience, me, various future audiences), that these were the Germans who massacred Oradour heightens the danger they posed. André Jossent's wife, who was not a local woman, then chipped in: were they discussing the maquis site that they had later visited together? She drew on the quartet's long-standing shared commemorative and/or touristic practices. André asked his wife whether she meant a monument they had once visited. Michel explained that that particular site was a memorial to the first Creusois maquis, his wife adding that there was no memorial for the events she had described as that particular maquis had survived. The transactive dynamic pulled in diverse individual and group memories and actively built and expressed a community of memory whose stories resonated with dominant understandings of French heroism and suffering.

Couples often engaged in collaborative remembering, pooling personal, family, local, and national memories. This model understands memory not as belonging to an individual and emanating outward but as a kind of accretion and circulation of ideas, knowledge, and feeling. This echoes Sara Ahmed's model of what emotion is and does.[1] These expressions of memory are highly unstable and contingent on the moment of their telling. This instability also implicates the listener, who is likewise part of the assemblage, bringing ideas, knowledge, and feeling to bear upon the memory story.[2] When I interviewed Sonia and Lucien Agache, they spoke in concert about the experience of bombing, striving emphatically to communicate this unique sensory and emotional experience which I have never known. Their utterances sparked one from the next, pulling centrifugally from a core of generalized experience out toward subtly different personal experiences, and collided in shared expressions of their affective community:

LUCIEN: . . . I've got this memory, and I was starting to get worried because I seemed to be the only one—I've spoken about it to people since—sometimes it happened that after an air raid, the day after, in the streets, these piles of little silver papers, and we wondered what they were. Well, since then, there's an explanation: in fact, the Allied planes dropped them as a decoy, because the Germans already had radar—

LINDSEY: —ah yes, to block the radios—

LUCIEN: —it was really amazing for us children to go and pick up those bits of paper, because we wondered—

LINDSEY: —children collected them as curious things—

LUCIEN: —we wondered what they were, eh.

SONIA: But, well, it was terrible, and when you'd hear them—

LUCIEN: —but it wasn't the Allied planes that you'd hear as much as the German DCA [*Défense contre avions*, antiaircraft fire]—

SONIA: —yes, they'd be firing—

LUCIEN: —and that was, it was because—, really often, waves of planes would fly overhead—

SONIA: —it wasn't for us—

LUCIEN: —over our head, but it wasn't for us at all, but what we heard, on the contrary, was the DCA which—

SONIA: —they'd be going over, we'd hear them, they were bombers—ahh! And when it was bombers, you'd hear them, it sounded heavy, you know, it was a heavy noise—

Lucien doubted his initial memory and had asked around as his wife seemed not to share it. Illustrating the ongoing sharing of memory inside this generational community, he reported having had it confirmed and explained. I had also heard of these silver papers being dropped, known as chaff, and chimed in with a generic comment that children collected curious objects. I knew that bomb and shell shards were prized possessions, but I did not mention them now. Lucien appeared to agree, but his story went no further. It was either the limit of the memory or my intervention that derailed him. Sonia then took up the thread, turning the conversation toward sound. In her first comment, it is not clear which "them" she was referring to. Lucien pulled away from what he understood as her meaning, emphasizing German antiaircraft fire. To explain its presence, he described the relatively frequent occurrence of bombers flying over to Germany. Both speakers repeat the phrase it "wasn't for us," which often accompanied memories of falling bombs or passing planes: an expression of survival that many interviewees reported people saying as bombs were falling ("*ce n'est pas pour nous!*"). Several communities of memory intertwine. Lucien verified his memory with generational peers, the couple emphasized sound, but each person pulled toward their own meaning. My interjections were based on other interviews I had conducted; this drew my attention to a noticeable phrase, "it wasn't for us," which resonated because of the frequency with which I had heard it. It built an affective bridge across those memory stories, gathering intense feelings of relief, of dodging death, of luck and fate.

Monsieur and Madame Jean-Bart showed a constructive form of collaborative remembering in relation to a wife's concern for her husband's bombing trauma. Through her intervention in his memory narrative, it is possible to understand more about the impact of bombing on him. She echoes him, affirms his words, acts as his witness, and thus bolsters the possibility of his saying more:

LINDSEY: Do you recall there being a lot of air raid alerts? Were they frequent?

MADAME JEAN-BART: Oh, yes, yes there were. A kind of dread, when you're just a littl'un, when you're a kiddy. As soon as you hear the siren, when it goes off—, pfffffffsssh! You stay traumatized by it—

MICHEL JEAN-BART: —yes, you do—

MADAME JEAN-BART: —and for a good while, too. Oh yes indeed. For that reason, that's why we'll never forget the war. You can't forget it—

MICHEL JEAN-BART: —no, it's imprinted. It's imprinted. I'll even tell you, very seriously, that for me, for a very, very long time afterwards, I was afraid of thunderstorms—

MADAME JEAN-BART: —oh, yes he was—

MICHEL JEAN-BART: —I was. Until what age, I can't remember—, but we were already married, weren't we?

MADAME JEAN-BART: —we were already married—

MICHEL JEAN-BART: —d'you see what I mean? Thunderstorms. I'd see the flashes of light, the noise—! It brought back the window smashing to pieces. . . . It was so scary, we were really scared, I was telling you, afraid of thunderstorms, afraid of thunderstorms. Because, I'm telling you, it reminded us of the flashes of the incendiary bombs, the noise of the bombs. You see. Even after we were married, there were moments, eh.

MADAME JEAN-BART: Oh, yes, thunderstorms, they really frightened him. Yes, as soon as there was a thunderstorm, he'd be petrified. Yes, yes. Now he's back to normal, it's got better over time, but at first, it really was, as soon as you'd hear the thunder—

MICHEL JEAN-BART: —we got married in '58, you see, 1958, 1960, I still had the fear, let's say, the fear of thunderstorms—

LINDSEY: —and you think that that came from—?

MICHEL JEAN-BART: —yes—

MADAME JEAN-BART: —yes. For him, storms were air raids.

MICHEL JEAN-BART: —because—, we were opposite the window, my brothers were over there, Mum was over there with my sister, and we saw everything explode, and the bombs—, they were ones that lit everything up, or incendiaries, we had no idea—, but you could see the fire—

In the earlier parts of the exchange, Madame Jean-Bart uses the pronoun *on* (a kind of impersonal, informal "we") to connect them both into shared local and generational experiences. They, the war children, can never forget. The perspective then shifts, with Monsieur Jean-Bart personalizing his experience. His wife corroborates his truth and thus facilitates the elaboration that follows. By stating that the storm *was* the bombardment, collapsing temporally distinct episodes, she opens the way for his evocation of sights, sounds, and emotions of being bombed.

Communities of memory did not just consist of generational peers. Across the memory stories, a strong sense of identification with victims of war elsewhere emerged. The interviewees imagine themselves as part of a wider, transtemporal, and transnational affective community. Jean-Pierre Becherel, who, with his mother and baby brother, arrived in the Creuse as refugees in 1940, cited a moment in later adulthood that catalyzed him to act upon his silenced past. His mother felt ashamed to have fled Normandy in 1940 with her children:

In our family, we couldn't really talk about it. So it was a shock for me to see, it was at the time of the Iraq war, when the Americans attacked Baghdad

[2003], there was a journalist who took a beautiful photograph—, a woman, fleeing, she had one little boy here [he mimes carrying a baby in his arms] and the other there [mimes holding a child by the hand]: my mother! [He is silenced by his emotion.]

This photograph built an affective bridge between his mother and the Iraqi woman and inspired him to help his now elderly mother turn her shame into acceptance, even celebration, of their past. Our interview took place in 2017, in the wake of the 2015–2016 refugee crisis in Europe during which more than a million refugees struggled across the Mediterranean.[3] Jean-Pierre saw his mother there too: "All of the problems we've got today, it's so complicated, I don't know how we're going to come through it, all these refugees coming—my mother! It was like that!" This identification had a powerful affective intensity in the interview. It moved him to tears and, he believed, had shaped events across his life. He described how he had tried unsuccessfully to get the generosity of the Creuse, as he saw it, toward wartime refugees publicly recognized.[4] More successfully, he had reunited his mother with the Graveron family who had welcomed her in 1940.

Other interviewees also felt connected to other children in war zones. Experiences unconnected in time or space were seen as sufficiently similar to build an affective bridge, and a community of feeling derived from knowledge, imagination, and empathy. Bernard Lemaire asserted that "when I see everything that's going on in those countries, in Iraq and Afghanistan, when they show you all those poor people, well, definitely, it's terrible. But we knew that too, we did. Eh?" Likewise, Michel Floch said:

Today, when I see—, I can put myself in the shoes of those people who're being bombed now, when I see everything that's happening in the world, I say to myself, "good God!" We knew that, we did, we knew it too. We'd be asking ourselves every night if it was going to come again, boom! Boom! We didn't have any shelter, we only got shelters in 1942, 1943, we'd just be at home. As I said to you before, if it fell on you, it fell on you, that's all there is to it.

Shifts in technology, geopolitics, people, and places may seem to make these experiences incomparable. Yet Michel's assessment does not focus on circumstance but on affect. What builds the connection between victims of bombing is an affective stacking of extreme emotions which, to his mind, is shared: the inevitability of repeat attack, the uncertainty of survival, the precarity of protection, the knowledge of fatal outcomes.

Thérèse Leclercq added a further point derived from her knowledge of where childhood trauma led: "For me, when they show us the fighting in Gaza at the moment, when they show us everyone that war has—, when I see kids pulled out of the rubble, all of that, it still really affects me, eh. I say to myself 'Those poor kiddies, they'll be scarred for life.'" Thérèse had a sense of the longevity of their trauma through her own experiences. Serge Aubrée expressed the same concern for the future mental health of present-day war children, which gave way to impotent frustration: "My first thought is for the children. They're seeing terrible, terrible, terrible things. And for us, well, we were lucky to end up pretty balanced, if you like, in our heads, but for them—. It's such an evident truth that I'm completely outraged that *still* today—, I thought—, after the liberation, my father said to me, 'We're getting there, peace is here.' But peace! Where is it now?" Michèle Martin's sense of a connection to this affective community also led her to anger, both at the cyclical perpetration of violence and at herself: "There are dreadful things happening at the moment, in Gaza, all of that, oh! It makes me furious! For the people who are suffering now, and who'll make others suffer in turn. I can't stand it. Although I didn't really do anything to—, I didn't protest or anything." For these older French interviewees, memories encoded years ago are still vivid and communicable. For present-day children in war-torn regions, memories are still being encoded. Interviewees project those memories forward into as yet unlived futures. A community of memory need not be tangible to exist. Inside the assemblage created by the interview, people distant in time and space, real and imagined, are brought together as affective peers through sympathy, solidarity, and concern.

PAUSE—ÉDITH AND JEAN COMPETE

Memories between generational peers may compete for prominence, typicality, or emotional importance. This process can be difficult to manage in an interview. But it also reveals something of how the "social action" of memory talk is "situated."[5] Interviewees in dialogical exchange position themselves in relation to each other, to their pasts, and to the community of memory more broadly. When I met married couple Édith and Jean Denhez near to Lille in 2009, I felt that some kind of struggle was taking place. Édith's family had suffered terribly in both world wars; among other tragedies, her grandmother was killed by the Germans in the First World War, and her twelve-year-old brother was killed by the Allies' bombs in 1944. Jean's family, on the other hand, was not exposed to such traumas. Nonetheless, Jean wanted to share his memories of his wartime childhood with me as well, and I was happy to listen. Yet only so much of their experience overlapped, and what did not, particularly intense feelings, created an edge of conflict. That conflict, in moral claim if not in content, echoes conflicts over recognition of suffering at a national level that have been characterized as damaging the "coherence" of a national version of the French wartime past.

This conflict emerged as the couple spoke about the 1940 civilian exodus. Édith's father was employed by a wealthy man who asked him to oversee the transportation of his most precious possessions away from danger to a family property in Normandy. Édith's father was permitted to take his own family. He set out with his wife and three of his four children; the eldest boy, Jacques, had respiratory problems and was in living in a sanitorium further south. In the Somme department, not far from home, the Germans bombed the refugee column on the road. Édith explained: "My father got shrapnel in his leg, and he ended up with such a high fever that he had to go to hospital." In fear and anxiety, having been attacked, anxious about her eldest son, and now deprived of her husband's support and the car, Édith's mother deteriorated:

> So my mother found herself with only three of her children—the other one was on the other side of the demarcation line—and her husband in hospital, and she didn't know what would become of her. We were staying in a room that someone had kindly lent us, with a beaten earth floor. I don't know—, well, here's another little anecdote, I don't know if it's any use telling it—but my mother was in absolute, total despair. She made us say our prayers, with holy icons, our Our Fathers and our Hail Marys. Well, I couldn't remember how to say Hail Mary, and she flew into a terrible rage with me. She shut me outside, and I was screaming—my sister told me later, she was a bit older than me—and I was outside, I was banging on the door, screaming, it was dark, and I wanted to come inside. And she was inside, weeping with my little brother because they were terrified. And after that, my mother was never really well

again. After the war, she was always depressive. But—, it was a very difficult time. She went to see the mayor, and word for word, she said "Mr. Mayor, it's not a difficult choice. If you don't give me what I need, food for my children, there's a reservoir there, and I'll jump in, I'll jump with my children." It was a pretty awful life.

Édith questioned whether it was worth telling me, and future listeners, of her mother's condition. Yet her anecdotes reveal the traumatic consequences of 1940 that were often silenced in the postwar years.[6]

A few minutes later, I asked Jean, Édith's husband, whether his family had also evacuated from the region around Cambrai where they also lived in 1940. Jean was the eldest of seven siblings. He said that all the children, their parents, and their grandparents squeezed into his grandfather's car, but before they had got far, again in the Somme, the driveshaft broke and the car was abandoned. Jean told his story, remarking on the similarities with his wife's experience: "We left the car there, and carried on on foot. So we got as far as—, from there we went to Amiens, so it's the same, it's a bit like it was for you [to Édith]. I think that this is a memory: one day, my mother went into a farm and no one was home. But there were some pots of milk standing there, so she took some! So then she could give us something to drink." Like Édith's family, Jean's continued their journey on foot. However, unlike in Édith's story, Jean's mother was adept at managing a complicated situation. He continued:

JEAN: So then, after Amiens, we must have taken the train and gone to
     stay with my mother's cousins, who lived near to Poitiers. And there . . .
     we were in the countryside—. . . . It's the same too! We lived like savages!
ÉDITH: But you were with your family—!
JEAN: Yes, we were with family—
ÉDITH: You were welcomed by your family. It's not the same at all—

Édith took issue with Jean's claim that his experience was "the same" as hers. His initial assertion of similarity, that they found themselves on foot around Amiens, is only similar in this degree. The family were not bombed, the group stayed intact, and his mother coped. His second assertion of similarity, that of living wild, was strongly rejected by Édith. Her family lived in rough conditions, but there was no excitement of living like "savages." Édith's family unit was depleted and among strangers; Jean's grew as they joined their relatives. The dissimilarity grew, and Édith continued to dissent:

ÉDITH: But in Poitiers, were you happy? There weren't any Germans there—

JEAN: Oh yes—, we'd eat grapes all day long—

LINDSEY: And you said you were living like savages—, for you as a little boy, was that a bit of an adventure—?

JEAN: Yes, we'd chase after rabbits—

ÉDITH: —that's just it, that's happiness—

JEAN: —and because they had horses, sometimes we'd have a ride on them—

LINDSEY: —it is *quite* different—

ÉDITH: It *is* different! You didn't have the same—

LINDSEY: —and your family was all together—

JEAN: Well, my father did get lost. When we took the train, I think. Men weren't allowed to take it. So we were without him—. Even so, my mother was an extremely capable woman—

ÉDITH: —why yes!—

JEAN: —it was her cousin, so she took us down there. And then my father brought the rest of the gang, and we settled in town there. And you know, he wasn't one to stand idle, and I remember he must've planted leeks, stuff like that—

ÉDITH: —so that you all had enough to eat—

JEAN: —yes! And that cousin we were staying with, he was a pretty resourceful bloke, he'd go round collecting eggs, cheeses, from the local farms, and he'd sell them on afterwards. So, like you've said, we weren't miserable there—

ÉDITH: —plus you were all together—

Jean identified the places where he thought their stories chimed, which provided him with access points to enter the conversation. But for Édith, there was no parity on the affective level: happiness, togetherness, even joy and freedom were the opposites of misery, separation, distress, and confinement.

Édith spoke with great self-control and a fair amount of humor. She did not flinch from describing her family's suffering or from recognizing her mother's inability to cope. But she asserted two different orders of experience: the community of Édith's and Jean's memories can only go so far. Jean sought to bring them together, but Édith rebuffed his attempt. The impact of the 1940 exodus on Édith's family's future—her father's injury was lifelong, as was her mother's depression—endowed it with a deep resonance and an affective intensity that Jean's could not have. As the past unfolds into its future, more (and different) meanings and more (and different) feelings may cohere around particular memories. When people tell their stories side by side, each appealing to a listener, each asserting a claim to validity, a kind of competitive remembering may emerge and, depending on what is at stake in being heard, conflict may ensue. In this oral history interview, the stakes were perhaps not high and I gave time to both stories, which I see as complementary. In other contexts, however, victims or tragedies are privileged, light-heartedness or survival are discounted, and dissatisfaction with versions of the past that are valued more may grow into resentments.[7]

ACROSS THE INTERVIEW SPACE

Communities of memory, real and imagined, form among those who share, or believe they share, a common past experience. However, the interview encounter also gives rise to a different kind of dynamic interaction between interviewer and interviewee. Ron Grele has written that the interview is "an occasion for the struggle for meaning and the control of interpretation"; these are "deeply embedded in ideologies" that may "exist in conflict with each other," no matter how respectful and cooperative each party is.[8] Social scientists have long understood that the interview is not a neutral space. It is an arena in which identities come into question, knowledge is negotiated, assumptions are made, and, in oral history, particular versions of the past are actualized.[9] For the interviews I conducted, I can draw on my memories and feelings of how these dynamics affected me or seemed to affect the context and content. For those interviews I listened to but did not conduct, I could still discern relational dynamics in action as they appeared to me as an active listener.[10]

It was not unusual for interviewees to seem anxious about what they were expected to say. In some cases, the interviewer was called upon to make judgments about what was interesting or valuable. Interviewers sometimes worked hard to convince interviewees that their lives were of interest, while interviewees hesitated over what, and whether, to tell. Madame Th tried to recall the bombing of the Billancourt factories on March 3, 1942, by the RAF:

> MADAME TH: I would like it very much if you could tell me if what I say is wrong compared to what other people have told you, or if it matches up.
>
> LINDSEY: It matches up; other people have told me that too. Yes, yes. But I'm interested in *your* [emphasis] memories—
>
> MADAME TH: It's just to know if I've got an accurate memory for what happened, it's just for that.

In a reversal of Grele's supposition that the interviewer would be concerned for accuracy and the interviewee keen to narrate without impediment, I wanted her to relax and tell me whatever she remembered. But Madame Th knew she was going on record; she was anxious to get things right and curious to test the veracity of her recollections. She was watching herself remember, conscious of her place in a larger community of memory and the judgment she might draw from an imagined audience of peers or others. In some of his interviews in Troyes, Julien Rocipon, a skilled and genial interviewer, also encountered his interviewees' self-doubt, which he was called upon to ease. Simone Fauron asked him: "do you think this is interesting to you, what I'm telling you?" He responded emphatically, "Definitely!" Madame Th and Simone both hesitated and looked for reassurance across the interview space to an interviewer with the power to validate their contribution.

It was not unusual for interviewees to arm themselves with prepared notes. Édouard Magnin, interviewed by Julien Rocipon, told him: "I've written a few notes on this paper. I'll speak from that, about myself only, I'll speak from those notes, from this thingummy here—, and it's only my own perspective, only about me—". Julien reassured him with a cheerful "that's even better, because that's what I want—for you to talk about you!" Édouard continued: "I can only tell you what I did, me, myself. And I didn't do very much. Or rather, I only did a few things." He began to read from his paper, sometimes humming through his notes. The story was stilted. In the end, Julien told him, kindly, to fold up his paper and that he would ask questions. They would come back to his notes at the end so

Édouard could add anything he had forgotten. The energy changed and Édouard began to speak more fluently and less self-consciously. In another good interview, between former evacuee Colette Streicher and experienced journalist Philippe Béquia, there was an initial tension over what would be told. Colette wanted to begin her evacuation story with her arrival in the village of La Cellette in the Creuse on her seventh birthday. Philippe interrupted and asked if she could start with what led to her departure from Paris. She complied, but told him "I was going to come to that anyway." Later on, he asked her to describe what the *batteuse*—both the threshing day festivities and the threshing machine—was like. To her it seemed self-evident, but he urged her: "the people who'll be listening to this one day, they won't know what it was, threshing, so you need to give us all the details! Tell us!" He invoked an imagined future audience, bringing it explicitly into the interview space.

Other interviewees spoke in ways that suggested that they thought the interviewer needed teaching about the past. Either because of age or simply because they had not been there, the interviewer was assumed to be ignorant. These kinds of interviews can be frustrating. The narrative can be generic and impersonal as the interviewee explains to the interviewer how things were rather than how things were *for me*. I remember such interviews as slightly uncomfortable. I recognize my own irritation at being "taught" things I already knoew, although I know it is unfair to be irritated. Interviewees may have had little interest from younger people in their stories before, so beginning with the basics is standard behavior. And why should they not try to teach me what I cannot know in the way they do? When I interviewed a married couple Sonia and Lucien Agache, we spoke about how they responded to nightly air raid sirens:

> SONIA: Ah, no no. For me, it was instinctive. It's true. I'd be off. With my older brother and my sister-in-law, yes—
> LINDSEY: And you'd go on foot, where to?
> LUCIEN: Oh, well, we didn't have anything else in those days—
> SONIA: —there was nothing else—
> LUCIEN: —there weren't any cars—!
> LINDSEY: Yes, I know—
> SONIA: —really, it was only people who were well off who—, and even then—
> LUCIEN: —they couldn't get any petrol—
> LINDSEY: —and so where did you go to?

In my first question, I wanted to know where they went. I assumed they went on foot; that comment was a statement rather than a question. But unexpectedly for me, they both picked up on the issue of locomotion. Their emphatic response seeks to teach me something they assume that I, having grown up in the era of the ubiquitous car, am less aware of. Their perception of my ignorance draws further details from them that might not otherwise have come to light. But the genuine knowledge gap across the divide was not the same as the perceived knowledge gap. In affective terms, the interview has a resonance with me because of the discomfort I felt about how I was perceived. It affected what they told me, what I asked, and how I asked it.

This kind of dynamic is not uncommon in oral history interviewing. Interviewed by Julien Rocipon, Christian Gaillard wanted to clarify their relative positions from the beginning. When speaking of his grandfather's death, he said: "it must have been what in those days we called the miserere colic [la colique de miserere]—do you know what that is? Aha! I'm teaching you a thing or two, I am! Well, it's quite simply a case of appendicitis." Across the interview, Julien's questions were greeted with chuckles, and emphatic responses suggested they were viewed as rather naive. Julien asked Christian if he had gone to school "here," the village where he grew up and where the interview was taking place. He replied, laughing: "Yes, of course! There weren't any school buses in those days." Had Julien been properly in the know, he would not have asked this question, the laugh suggested. Christian also felt he could see through Julien's questions. When Julien commented that the summers were long in the 1930s and 1940s, Christian jibed back: "Aha, how did I fill my time, is that what you're trying to get me to say?" On another occasion, following a statement Christian made that the arrival of war "changed our lives a little bit," Julien asked: "how was that?" Again, Christian burst into laughter, causing Julien to inquire "what's making you laugh?" Listening, I sensed a tension, friendly though things were. As with Sonia and Lucien Agache, a small-scale struggle bubbles out of the exchange. Interviewees claim the upper hand through their access to experiential knowledge while the interviewer tussles to encourage explanation. Sometimes a misunderstanding or a misplaced emphasis derails or bends the story. These dynamics are an integral but unpredictable part of the way the memory emerges in the interview. They constitute their community of memory by marking the boundaries of belonging.

While the interviewees' perceptions of their interviewers affect the way memories emerge, so too does the way the interviewer presents his or her knowledge.

An interviewer who seems to know too little cannot elicit certain memories while an interviewer who knows too much may stifle memories. Jacqueline Béné, who was interviewed by a relative, expressed a small frustration as her interviewer tried to move her along too quickly. To me, it seemed that the interviewer seemed to want to stay within the borders of her own prior understanding. Yet Jacqueline had an important stock of memories around 1940 and the civilian exodus and wanted to dwell on them. She started by mentioning other people's movements, coming into her town and leaving it, and then moved on to her own family's experience, beginning: "Mum wanted to leave at all costs, and my father didn't. And he was right not to." To my ears, this was the beginning of a story: Jacqueline was about to explain why her father was right. But her interviewer's next question asked her to speak about the Armistice. Jacqueline exclaimed: "we haven't got there yet!" She went on to say a great deal more about what happened to the family during May and June 1940. Other interviewers seemed to have missed important parts of the story; this is easy to do, for various reasons, but nonetheless has an impact on what gets told and how. At the beginning of her interview, Danièle Dubowsky spoke at length to establish her unusual family circumstances, which boiled down to her mother having Palestinian nationality and her father being a U.S. citizen as well as being Jewish. She also remarked quite early in the interview that he was arrested just after Pearl Harbor was attacked. There was surprise in Danièle's voice later on in the interview when the interviewer asked her to describe the reason for her father's arrest. She said: "Well, the reason was because he was American."

Just as it is easy to miss a detail, which can destabilize the dynamic, a similar impact can occur with an interviewer who knows too much. In my interview with Madame Th, there was an early sticking point. Madame Th drew a strict boundary, geographical and social, between the districts of Boulogne and Billancourt:

MME TH: I always lived in Boulogne. And the air raids were at Billancourt, where the factories were. They're two different towns.

LINDSEY: Yes, I know—

MME TH: They were only joined together well after the war—

LINDSEY: Oh, that's not what I've seen. It was André Morizet who got them joined together—

MME TH: —after the war!

LINDSEY: Morizet died 1942. But that's another story—!

MME TH: You'll need to check that, because for me, well I think it was after—

LINDSEY: —it doesn't really matter—

MME TH: It should be checked. But that's why I'm always speaking about Boulogne, for my part, and the bombs, they were at Billancourt—

Although I was correct and the towns were linked and renamed in 1924, I desperately tried to backtrack. I had been studying the history of Boulogne-Billancourt prior to my interview trip. I knew that the former mayor, André Morizet, had raised the status of Billancourt in this way and was celebrated for his work. Because of the archival records I had been reading, I knew he had died in 1942 and a new mayor, Robert Colmar, presided over the town afterward. The double-barreled name Boulogne-Billancourt was all over the archival correspondence from the 1940s I had been working with. But for Madame Th, the distinction mattered differently. This was both an issue of identity (Boulogne was the bourgeois and commercial district, Billancourt was industrial and working class) and a rationale for the nature of her childhood experience. She had only vague memories of air raids, which targeted the industrial zones, and was never evacuated to rural relatives as she had none. Place was agential here; it created the story. The conflict across the divide fizzed into existence and fizzled out, but with what trace across the memory story?

BEYOND TO AUDIENCES REAL AND IMAGINED

A distant form of transactive remembering takes place in many interviews as nonpresent real and imagined others press upon the remembering processes. Grele has written that the existence of an audience outside the interview is "critical . . . because it raises the level of ideological discourse beyond the immediate situation of the interview." He makes reference to "hidden conversations" projecting into "the social world in which the interview takes place."[11] That social world encompasses regimes of memory operational at national or transnational levels. It also gathers in members of a specified or unspecified "younger generation." Interviewees sometimes have a sense of the posterity in their words and of the generational division that separates them from their children and grandchildren. Interviewees frequently desire that younger people try to understand their pasts, sometimes acknowledging the impossibility of their doing so.

The idea of a *devoir de mémoire*, a duty of memory or a duty to remember, developed in France across the 1990s, with specific reference to the Holocaust.[12] The phrase has become controversial, not least because it has been politicized in empty, or even dangerous, gestures.[13] Whom we are enjoined to remember depends very much on who is chosen by whom, and when, to be a victim deserving of compassion. Some dispute the use of the term *duty*; duty implies an imposition, rather than a human gesture toward another. Duty also anticipates recompense: we perform our duties in order to gain something, such as acceptance, rights, permissions, and so on. The interviewees who lived through the Second World War as children did not always see duty as a driving force for sharing their lives. Marie-Madeleine Viguié-Moreau stated categorically in her interview that the day would come when all firsthand witnesses were gone. She told the interviewers that "you" must take up the mantle. She endowed them with her trust: "I think that your generation, you've had enough encounters with people"; it was down to them, she said, to pass on the story. Her advice was: "Above all, learn history. Children need to really love history." The way to inculcate a love of history, she felt, was through personal encounters with the past, whether direct or filmed. It is difficult to love the parts of history that are painful or shameful, but Marie-Madeleine implied that loving the encounter with the past, any past, was of real value. Turning love into duty would damage this aspiration and the greater project of human understanding, compassion, and peace beyond that.

Those who lived through the Second World War as children recognize the importance of communicating their experiences, particularly to children. Although they are not the only people to tell their war stories, Jewish Holocaust survivors have led the way in educational contexts. The strong compulsion to pass on their experiences may stem from a sense of duty, but it is more frequently articulated through a more universal incentive: to help shape futures away from racism, anti-Semitism, and hatred. These eyewitnesses strive to build a compassionate connection. Rachel Jedinak's memories were recorded by the Archives départementales du Val de Marne in 2008. Rachel had been telling her story for some years before that and has continued to do so. As a little girl in Paris, Rachel and her sister were arrested during the Vel d'Hiv roundup of July 1942 with their mother and again in February 1943 with their grandmother. Both times they escaped. Rachel later found herself in the care of a woman who threatened to denounce her once she realized that the child she thought was from Brittany was actually Jewish. Rachel's father had been arrested in 1941. During the mass round-ups of Paris Jews in July 1942, the sisters and their mother were held in a theater before being taken to the Vélodrome d'Hiver. In that theater, Rachel's mother saw the chance to save her daughters: she told them to run for it. They escaped, but she did not. In later life, Rachel was instrumental in getting plaques mounted on the walls of Parisian schools to commemorate the Jewish pupils deported from each one. From the 1990s, inspired by her grandson's injunction to tell her story, she began going into schools to speak. A skilled narrator, her memories have featured in documentaries and books, and in 2018 she published her own memoir.[14] Rachel peppered her interview with meta-comments about speaking to children in schools, the questions they asked, and their responses.

The Archives départementales de Saone-et-Loire held a film made in the 2000s of Guy Lazard speaking to a class of children aged about eleven. This was the first time Guy had given a public talk about his wartime childhood in Mâcon. He spoke enthusiastically, including many interesting details, even adventures, about his childhood and the dangers he and his immediate family escaped. His memories lacked the structure that Rachel Jedinak's had acquired through years of telling, however. For my research, Guy's wide-ranging account was valuable, but I wondered whether the teacher might have expected something that focused more on the specifically Jewish dimensions of his experience. At the end of his narrative, the children's questions pushed Guy to explain better his emotions. They asked whether it had been difficult to flee his home, whether he had lost members of his family, if he had been afraid, what shocked him most, how he felt to come back to Mâcon, and what his worst memory of the war was. The children also asked for factual information, perhaps because they had to write up his story later. They wanted to know his age at the beginning of the war, what year he returned to Mâcon, and so on. In response to a question, he said that his "worst" memory of the war was hearing bullets fly as a battle raged between the Germans and the maquis around the isolated hamlet where his family were living in 1944. Fear is articulated through the proximity of violence, not the prospect of capture. He said "when you hear the bullets going by, hear the bullets whistle past, and you hear that, well that's something that's really stayed with me, which was still with me even when I was in Algeria." His talk here was not necessarily adapted to his young audience; would they understand his connection with Algeria?[15] His other "worst" memory, he said, was of 1940 when he and his mother were bombed during the German invasion and separated from his father, who had been mobilized. He was twelve years old. His response to the question of what shocked him most did not dwell on his experience as a French Jew either: "what really shocked me, in my child's mind, was all those people who were anti-German at first and then, all of a sudden, they became pro-German. That really shocked me. I couldn't understand how you could feel one thing and then switch to completely the opposite thing a few months later." The memory relates to his dawning sense of adults' inconsistency. He explicitly positions it in his "child's mind." Again, the comment might have been difficult for children to interpret, given that it related not to a specific event but to a shifting vision in his childhood in relation to the growth of French collaboration, which did not otherwise form a part of his narrative.

My archival research unearthed other filmed interactions with schoolchildren about young lives in the Second World War. The Archives départementales de Seine-Saint-Denis allowed me to watch the "rushes" of a video made (as part of a school project) by local teenagers in the 1990s about their town of Romainville in the northeastern Paris suburbs. The final film was not available to me. It seemed that the research focus had been on the political divisions in France and daily life during the 1930s (sometimes into the 1940s), when Romainville was still rural. The interviews were stilted; speakers were asked to perform over and over again to ensure that lighting, sound, questions, and answers worked for the film. As with Guy Lazard's classroom appearance, it seemed that the children engaged with the speakers through the lens of the pedagogical task assigned to them. There was little scope for spontaneity. A little rapport did develop on occasion, particularly when the children asked for more than just a description. The Archives départementales de Saône-et-Loire also held a film made by teenagers from the village of Saint-Martin-en-Bresse. The film *J'avais 15 ans sous l'Occupation* ["I was fifteen under the Occupation"] gives plenty of insight into the conditions of daily life in a village remote from conflict. The speakers tell of the hard conditions on family farms, restrictions in food supply, the peculiarities of their wartime diets, and some of the entertainments and pastimes they enjoyed. As in the Romainville film, the children asked questions mostly seeking factual description, acting as *enquêteurs* [investigators] rather than oral historians. There were chuckles of pleasure as past youthfulness was recalled and some more serious moments, but by and large the questions remained very safe. Neither personal nor national emotional experience was sought. No mention was made of Jews, deportation, or collaboration, and the resistance was referenced only via the maquis.

In more typical interviews, the rememberers frequently report having spoken to their own families (children, grandchildren) about their wartime childhoods. Rémy Ménigault remarked that although he had spoken very little to his parents about what the family had lived through together, he had shared far more of his childhood memories with his wife and children. Sisters Marie-Louise Linder and Suzanne Gobert, whose family had been refugees near Oradour-sur-Glane but who had escaped the massacre there in June 1944, remarked that because their parents were no longer alive, they felt a responsibility to "keep the memory alive": the passing of their parents had both liberated the speech of the child generation and added a duty to their lives. But, they said, apropos of their own children, "for the moment, it's very difficult to motivate them." Along with her mother, Lucienne Rémeur narrowly escaped the explosion in the Sadi-Carnot bomb shelter in Brest in September 1944 that killed hundreds of French civilians and German soldiers. She described the familial transmission of this experience as an affective engagement: "it's something that I can never forget. And I tell the children, 'I hope you never experience what I went through.' It's because of that that I'm very family-orientated, very close to my children." She implied that her children understood the resonance of their mother's past into their present. In other traumatic cases, though, transmission was blocked. Nicole Kahn said of her experiences of arrest and imprisonment in Marseille and in Drancy: "I spoke a little bit about it to my children, mostly when they were younger. I tried to explain to them what the war had been like," but before that her immediate family (mother, father, brothers) had never spoken of it. For Marie-Madeleine Viguié-Moreau and Anne-Marie Laurens, both of whose fathers were deported and killed for their resistance activities, there was a self-imposed taboo. Recalling the last time she saw her father, Anne-Marie said in tears:

> I never saw him again. And there, it's the same, I didn't speak about it again for a very long time, never. I never asked my uncle and aunt about it, never. Never. I should have asked them what he said—he came to tell them something, my uncle must have been in the resistance too, but, well, we never brought it up. I never ever spoke about it again, and that was—, never, ever, ever. That was over, it was over. Never to Mum, never—after that, it was a complete "block out" [she says the words in English].

The story was too painful for family members to share. Marie-Madeleine recounted the day the floodgates of her memory burst open. After retirement, she enrolled in a creative writing class. The theme in one session was childhood. She wrote solidly for ninety minutes, she said, but was too embarrassed to share her writing with her neighbor. The words "overflowed a bit, things I'd never told anyone." She had avoided speaking of it to her own children, but her grandchildren asked the questions their parents did not dare to. As with Rachel Jedinak, who spoke to her grandson's class for the first time following the desecration of a Jewish cemetery in France in 1990, once the constriction had shifted, these women continued to speak out. These accounts show blockages and struggles inside the memory communities of families and extended families. Silence grew from their own distress; they feared hurting others trapped in their own pain or upsetting their children and grandchildren.

Some of the former child evacuees I interviewed wanted to pass on their positive memories to their children in concrete ways. Roger Davre wanted to transmit more than memories; he wanted to make his past part of his children's present and their future: "the Creuse is my native land! When you're born in Paris, Paris, in the sixth arrondissement, with cobbles on the roads, asphalt on the pavements, trees trying to grow inside cages, you can't really say you've got roots. Yes, well, my roots, they're *there* [emphasizing the last word; in the Creuse]." He bought the house where we held the interview in 1966, not long after his children were born, saying "Well, that gave them a *terroir* [a local region, a rural belonging]! His own adopted roots became their real roots. There was no restriction or constriction in recounting this past, it seemed, nor in pulling his children into a little part of his own wartime childhood. Christian Le Goff similarly bought a house in the Creuse later in life. His daughter settled nearby, his grandchildren grew up there, and his wife now lived there permanently. Remembering the past for these men went beyond an act of transmission in storytelling (the interview, the classroom); it was a lived, daily experience, so quotidian that the wartime origin of their located lives probably went unsaid most of the time.

In other cases, the desire to pass on a positive wartime childhood memory was rebuffed. Jean-Pierre Becherel, who with his mother and baby brother arrived in the Creuse in 1940, made an effort to pass on his past to his children, but the results seemed ambivalent. He too had bought a house in the same hamlet where in 1940 they had been welcomed as refugees:

I thought that for my children, it was important. But no. Perhaps that's just as well. For them, the war with the Germans—it's just impossible. It's just stories they're told. Even despite—, no, it's not for them—, it's not an interesting topic. Although perhaps one of my daughters is starting to understand. She's nearly fifty, but she's just starting to get it. She'll probably come to the little house that I've bought here.

For Jacques Prieur, however, the block remained. He showed me a photograph album with nine black-and-white photographs of a little boy in a rural garden, holding a rabbit, on a scooter. Jacques had been evacuated to the Creuse by his mother sometime after her husband was killed in combat; he spent his youngest years with foster parents there. In 1947, his mother came to collect him and thereafter forbade him contact with his foster parents. Jacques remembered his rural childhood fondly. The words "My childhood in the Creuse—happy memories" were written above the photographs. He said:

> So, well, I've made this album here, with a few photos. It's for my descendants, to show my son how I lived. So that, those people who were down there—, there they are! [pointing at a photograph of him as a little boy with his foster parents]. . . . I thought to myself that perhaps there will come a day when my son or my grandsons will say, "Well, what about it, let's have a look at what Grandad did" [laughs]. But for the moment, they're not interested. Their lives are elsewhere.

Like Jean-Pierre, Jacques seemed to find it understandable that his son and grandchildren were not interested in his past. The photograph album existed for a day in an imagined future, perhaps after Jacques was gone, when they were. Jacques and Jean-Pierre struggled to build an affective community around their memories of war in the way that others had done. These attempts to constitute communities of memory are outside of, or beyond, the interview encounter, but they surface in the interview nonetheless. Remembering happens in continuous dialogue with all the remembering that has gone before, and such lines of memory as are activated are entwined with affects generated during previous acts of remembering.

For others, disinterest was one thing, but a singular impossibility to comprehend the past was another thing entirely. This stymies the hope of the *devoir de mémoire.* The rememberers expressing this view tended not to be Jewish; Jewish interviewees were more hopeful about the impact their memories might have. However, there was a feeling of pessimism in some interviews that spoke perhaps of the increasing marginalization older people may feel, of personal experiences of blocking or rebuff, or of the limits of empathy or communication.

Bombing seemed particularly hard to communicate. Of course, many tried and did well. But others wondered whether it was possible. Michel Floch said quite categorically that "young people today, they can't understand what it was like." He did not elaborate, but there was a sense that the complexity of the war was too great for description to be sufficient. Édith Denhez was more explicit. She indicated that the phenomenological quality of experience was for her husband, who had only witnessed air raids from afar, and by extension others, impossible to know: "I experienced real bombing. There you are, that's not the same either. When you're under the bombs and when you've never been, I don't believe it's the same thing at all. I *heard* [with emphasis] the bombs whistling." To know the bombs was not just to know what they looked and sounded like; it was to know a feeling; it was to know what they could do and what they had done. Christian de la Bachellerie had a different perspective. He said, laughing: "young people today don't give a damn! It doesn't interest them at all, it all goes over their heads, they don't know—no. There are only a few people left, like me, who remember. But I remember without any hatred, no hatred toward the bombers. No, that was part of the game. Sadly." The knowledge he describes is of a different kind to Édith's, but this is still a quality of affect. Because he had been there, he understood the complexity that Michel Floch alluded to, the subtleties of emotional and ideological engagement with this aspect of conflict.

A second element of wartime childhoods that interviewees believe is incomprehensible to a contemporary audience living in a world of consumerist abundance is the restrictions they faced. The audience to whom they speak—younger people, whether known or imagined—could never understand wartime penuries. Marie-Rolande Cornuéjols expressed strong reprimands about the younger generation's assumptions. Speaking of the creeping impact of the Occupation on her family, she said: "it took a little bit of time, but then we started to—and this too, for certain, those people who didn't live through that period will never understand it—we started to get hungry. Shortages." Brothers Claude and Michel Thomas spoke positively about their children's and grandchildren's interest in the war years but said that there were limits:

MICHEL: I believe that there is one thing that you really can't convey. There are some things that, if someone's not lived through them, you just can't convey them. And nevertheless, I'm sure there are people who can't speak of it at all, who'd just get told, "oh, those are old stories about the past, old Grandad telling his war stories," or what have you—, but with our own children, it was never like that. They're very attentive—

CLAUDE: —open to listening—

MICHEL: —but I just think there's something that can't be passed on—

LINDSEY: And what thing is that—?

MICHEL: Having really *known* [emphasizes the word] the war. Having known what war was like, the precariousness. And other aspects—, deprivations—

CLAUDE: —yes in all senses—

MICHEL: —and the things that it's difficult to make understood, for example, that we suffered—and even so, we weren't among the most unfortunate, there were many who were far worse off than us . . .—but that isn't transmissible. And another thing that can't be passed on, it's that, despite all the deprivation we had, the cold, the bad food, the few entertainments, the lack of money, no pocket money at all, you can't really say we were unhappy.

He and Claude had lived their wartime childhoods relatively contentedly, interested in current affairs, negotiating the obstacles the Occupation threw across their paths. But they too reiterated the deceptively simple fact: war is unknowable to those who have not lived inside it. Andréa Cousteaux in Brest remarked on the lasting impact of wartime shortages. Like Lucienne Rémeur, she attributed a behavioral trait to the period:

My daughters laugh at me because I'm always afraid to run out of things. When I bring a packet of sugar to the table, I always say, I really must get another to replace it, because I'm afraid—. And they say to me "It's not the war any more, Mum! You can hang on!" No, no, I must have my supplies, coffee, sugar, oil, anything you can't do without. And the minute I've used one up, off I go to buy another!

Andréa laughed at her daughters' gentle mockery, but her story speaks of the gap that interviewees felt separated them from their closest relatives. With these examples, we return to a community of memory that is generational and exclusive.

These interactions, taking place beyond the interview space, are both real and imagined and reveal two stances. One perspective exhorts the younger generations never to forget the horror of the war and hopes that explanation, discussion, emotional exchange, and communication will be enough to ward off a repeat of the suffering and degradation of their childhoods. The second perspective is more pessimistic. The stakes for those holding the former perspective are often higher: they experienced persecution, violence, and even genocide. Arguably, for the latter, they are lower. These perspectives create affective communities that can envelop and include or exclude and rebuff. Real or imagined interactions, distant in time, space, generation, comprehension, and experience, press the memory into the shape it takes in the telling. These are forged in a ceaseless, ongoing, and contingent way, in the "rhizomatic flow of affects," by participants' engagement with broader regimes of memory.[16] As such, the ways memories are told must be seen as patted, kneaded, rolled, and battered by a shifting set of forces beyond the interview itself. Some of these are identifiable, but most will remain forever unknown.

These examples demonstrate some of the ways that regimes and communities of memory are active inside the oral history assemblage. They affect why people tell the stories they do and what they hope to achieve by telling them, and they account for why certain versions of the past and not others are actualized both in the interview and beyond it. The dynamics of transactive communication within and beyond the interview space are too complex and contingent to be explained by an interaction between stable, known subjectivities. Those subjectivities are less stable, less knowable, and less predictable because of their positioning inside a multiplicitous interview assemblage.

PART 4

MEMORIES LIVED

T he cultural studies scholar Ben Highmore has pondered the "odd predicament" of the use of the word *aesthetics*. Going back to its older definition is useful for studying the lived experience of humans in their environments, past and present. Highmore references the German philosopher Alexander Baumgarten, whose mid-eighteenth-century writing on aesthetics was concerned with the study of "material experiences, with the way the world greets the sensate body, and with the affective forces that are generated in such meetings." Aesthetics was not, as it became, a scholarly discourse about fine art, beauty, and the sublime but was instead "an ambitious curiosity about affects, the body, and the senses."[1] Something similar could be said about investigating the unfolding, happening past in this corpus of memory stories. Here too we find, as Terry Eagleton describes it, "the whole of our sensate lives together—the business of affections and aversions, of how the world strikes the body on its sensory surfaces, of that which takes root in the gaze and the guts and all that arises from our most banal, biological insertion into the world."[2] It is to these "social aesthetics," as Highmore calls them, that part 4, "Memories Lived," turns. In the assemblage(s) of the happening past are innumerable "present moments of practice." These are, in Owain Jones's words, "the frontier[s], or the living space[s], of becoming"; they can be seen as the perpetual unrolling of time into the present, which is central to a Bergsonian understanding of durational time. Jones writes that present moments of practice are "complex time-space 'events' where meanings and values are constructed, [and] they are rich with ontological, political and ethical potentials": the present moment of practice is "where life happens."[3] One of my original research questions was to ask what life was like for children in the French wartime past. Examining where life happened for them, then, is imperative. Being ontological, political, and ethical, how life happened does not just reflect what matters in life to individuals and to collectivities; it creates what matters.

The present moment of practice is related to the idea of a "conjuncture," to use Stuart Hall's term, where "things come together"—political things, national and international things, personal things, family things, spatial things, sensory things, affective things, thought things, and more. The conjuncture and the present moment of practice are the same kind of assemblage: in a "thicket of simultaneity," where quotidian mundanity meets the historically significant, living is done, and memory is made.[4] Owain Jones is critical of the way nonrepresentational theory loads so much into the present moment of practice as *present*. He asks us to reconsider the importance of memory in carving channels through to the unfolding present.[5] Every moment, present and past, is (was) a becoming, and it is (was) always on the brink of potentially becoming something else. Little reveals this contingency of life more than when memories of things, people, and events are fanned out like a deck of cards, each holding something in common with its neighbor but necessarily differing in which, when, and how "things came together" for *this* person at *this* moment. Nothing is inevitable about a conjuncture, and the memory stories reveal the way that a "new moment" is created in a person's unfolding present when an "accumulation of different things" forms itself into singular, fleeting entanglements: assemblages.[6]

Part 4, "Memories Lived," is concerned with the unfolding present in the happening past. There, the events of war and occupation were happening to everyone. The French nation went to war in 1939, it was defeated and occupied in 1940, the Vichy regime collaborated with the Nazis, supplies ran short, violence and persecution were widespread, liberation happened mostly across 1944, and war ended in 1945. This chronology is common to all. But the contingent possibilities of the unfolding present give an emergent quality to experience: it could go in any direction and be disrupted anywhere, in any way, by anything. Each facet of memory that has been elaborated across parts 1, 2, and 3 of this book is present here: the sensory and the emotional, affective intensities and stickiness, temporal weirdness, agential places and spaces, and memories that chime or clash with others and that are shared, negotiated, and contested. Part 4, however, will focus less on what memories are made of and how they are told and more on their content. It covers aspects of children's everyday lives common to many accounts of wartime France—food, shortages, leisure, home, school, encounters with the enemy, events—but it does so with the relational dynamics of the assemblage (affective, multitemporal, contingent, political) in mind. Things are remembered because they are and were felt; unpicking the felt quality of these memories sheds light back onto the first three parts as we note the ubiquity of the felt realm, entanglements of place, space, and time, and the dialogic and discursive terri- torializaton that brings forth these utterances and not others. It is divided into three chapters. Chapter 8 looks at the materialities of children's everyday lives (things that matter/ed), chapter 9 considers affective others in the children's lives (people that matter/ed), and chapter 10 examines the accretion of memories around particular moments (events that matter/ed). My concern is with how things came together at certain moments of a person's past and how that made things—those that came together and others—matter enough to be remembered and recounted.

CHAPTER 8

MATERIALITIES OF THE EVERYDAY

Human-material interactions are, as the literary theorist Terry Eagleton has remarked, a two-way process: "the world strikes the body" and the body is "inserted" into the world.[1] Sylvette Leclerc's memories of the arrival of the Germans reflect this process. Her family sought shelter during the 1940 civilian exodus:

> We'd been living in this house for a few days, and that's where we saw the Germans arrive. We stayed inside, behind the shutters, watching them go past. And what I'll always remember, is that we didn't have much to eat, and my brother, the eldest boy, and our maid's daughter, they were always starving, and they'd found this jar of cherries in *eau de vie*, and they ate the lot, and slept for twenty-four hours, eh! They were completely knocked out!

The world strikes these bodies. France is invaded, so the family takes to the road. Hitler seeks to pacify France, so German soldiers spread out across villages. Another family left their house empty, so this family enters. Someone preserved fruit in alcohol, so the children get drunk. But these bodies also insert themselves into the world. Sylvette watches the Germans pass by; Sylvette's brother and the maid's daughter are hungry and gobble the cherries. Why do the cherries stick and not, say, her awe at the soldiers' arrival? Sylvette's brother missed a major moment in French history. Maybe Sylvette and her siblings taunted him about this afterward. Maybe the kerfuffle of the incident caused the whole family to miss what happened next. Perhaps he was vigorously reprimanded. Her parents must have been worried. And how they must have laughed about it later. The things that come together in this story—war, people, cherries, feelings—come together in a singular way. There were other children who missed the arrival of the Germans and other children who have accidentally eaten alcoholic fruit. But this conjuncture was specifically Sylvette's as the moment of invasion unrolled, with all its ordinary, extraordinary, material, and immaterial interactions.

EATING

Food is ubiquitous in the memory stories. Food shortages shape understandings of civilian life in wartime France. In parts of the country, shortages were dire and hunger and malnutrition common.[2] Discussions of wartime daily life seem often to be synonymous with food shortages, and two foodstuffs in particular act as a kind of *lieu de mémoire* for this community of memory: rutabagas and *topinambours* (Jerusalem artichokes). Edmond Magnin and his wife Ginette recounted, with much laughter:

> EDMOND: At that time, everyone just ate any old thing, rutabagas [laughing]—
> GINETTE: —Jerusalem artichokes—
> EDMOND: —and Jerusalem artichokes—

More commonly fed to livestock, rutabagas and Jerusalem artichokes were filling and grew easily.[3] Edmond developed the theme. He described how, for his family in rural Clairvaux (Aube), the first year of occupation was hardest as they could not rely on their usual suppliers: "Well, a year later, it started getting a bit better, because we could make do by ourselves. We planted potatoes—we'd not had any potatoes in Clairvaux, not at the beginning. That year was the hardest. Later on, everyone found a way to get by, I'm telling you, everyone had rabbits, chickens, everyone, eh. Pigs, everyone had a pig, oh yes, everyone." With land available for cultivation, the inadequacies of the ration system were less acute. Hunger continued to affect city dwellers, though, and Edmond's "everyone" exaggerates the extent of grow-your-own. Simone Fauron remarked emphatically: "If you only know how imaginative we became when we had nothing!" She said: "We had cheeses that were made with completely skimmed milk, and my father, he'd roll them in ashes, and after about a fortnight they were pretty good." Securing adequate food was not just a question of space and supply; it required creative cooking and preparation, some of which harked back to older times.

Although rutabagas and Jerusalem artichokes have come to epitomize war-time diets, in the memory stories carrots were mentioned just as often. Edmond Magnin added: "And carrots! Well, alright, carrots aren't that bad. But I used to eat beetroot leaves for example. I'd eat beetroot leaves just as though they were spinach." He ate carrots, he said, where previously he might have had potatoes. Jean-Claude Bourtourault also mentioned carrot-based cookery: "I remember we'd have semolina, not with milk, but with water—, we'd get some crusts of bread, when we had them, and put them in it. And we'd make jam out of car-rots, because they're sweet, but also beetroots and green tomatoes because they sweeten up as well. We just had things like that, not that pleasant." Jean-Claude was still hungry, though: "I didn't really care that it wasn't that good, never mind that, I'd eat it. But I had a sister who was a bit delicate, and often she'd not eat at all." Madame Jean-Bart grew up in Lille. Her mother too relied on carrots and other root vegetables: "My mother would make stews for the morning—carrots, turnips, whatever she had—so that we'd go to school with something in our tum-mies. We had this disgusting, gluey bread, and we wouldn't eat it, so my mother made us vegetable stew, and because of that we'd go to school having eaten some-thing at least." Eating soup in the mornings was an older rural French habit.[4] Other traditional forms of cooking were dredged up. Robert Potiquet from Saint-Martin-en-Bresse (Saône-et-Loire) described his family's morning routine. His mother got up, put the *gaudes* on to cook, milked the cows, then came back to give the children breakfast: "So, for breakfast, for me it was a flat *gaude*, with milk poured on top. I loved those *gaudes*. My sister wouldn't eat them, eh [laughing], so she'd go to school with an empty belly." Flat *gaudes* were a kind of pancake cooked on a griddle, made from a flour of roasted corn and milk. Once a staple peasant-food of the Bresse region (eastern Burgundy), *gaudes* had fallen out of fashion in the nineteenth century and were an oddity of folklore by the 1920s.[5] It is not clear whether Robert's mother revived this old custom because of wartime shortages, but Robert certainly associates it with this era. Again, shortages fell harder on fussier eaters.

Conflict over receiving one's fair share created sticky memories. Feelings of injustice built memories around patterns of sharing. Rachel Jedinak commented that obtaining rations in Paris was harder for Jews because of the curfew. She recalled her attention to food attribution at home: "I remember that sometimes

I'd count the pieces of potato, when we had potato, which were going onto each plate, for fear that I'd have less." In non-Jewish households too, restrictions generated new systems of sharing. Bread gathered memories. In a vivid haptic memory, Jacques Kermen mimed pressing his thumb into the table to pick up any tiny crumbs. Bernard Lemaire commented on sharing bread:

> Well, my brothers were entitled to a bigger bread ration than the rest of us, but of course, we shared everything with each other. So this bread, we'd cut it—, of course, when you cut slices it dries out quickly. So the morning after, the first slice would be [rapping his knuckles on the table] dry as a—, well. Now we give that to the birds. But I remember at home, that first slice, we all took turns to have the first slice, alongside the two slices we'd usually get. And you had to be careful not to forget your turn, you had to claim your dry slice—

Sharing the bread was both collaborative (older siblings shared their rations with younger ones) and competitive. Pierre Tainturier recalled the division of the loaf in his household: "We were entitled to 150 grams of bread, and I'll remember this for a long time, that was seven and a half centimeters. Because in a family of five or six, the bread rations were cut up like that. Mum would give it to us, and we'd eat what we were given." In Sonia Agache's house in the suburbs of Lille, bread was removed from the menu of the younger children and replaced with a porridge-like mush of flour and milk. "In the mornings Mum would say to us, 'You can't have any bread, it's for the adults, they're working hard.' . . . And when you're a kid of ten or eleven, 'Oh, no, leave that bread alone, that's for your dad, it's for your sisters, they've got to work.' Ah! That's another one of those little moments which you remember, eh." A little moment of feeling insignificant, or hard-done-by, of longing and hunger, perhaps tinged with shame at a childish jealousy: this memory sticks because of how the restriction made her feel in relation to other family members.

The micropolitics of food distribution was also clear in cases where children were sent away from their families to protect them from danger. The way food was shared or not shared had a strong affective intensity around pleasure, generosity, gratitude, and injustice. Roger Davre was billeted with a rural family in the Creuse as an evacuee from Paris in 1944: "I have a good memory, of coming here, of eating white bread with crème fraiche and with lard; it's good, lard spread on bread, you know!" Restricted Parisian diets were replaced, in memory, with a cornucopia of fatty local treats. Christian Le Goff also described the range and quality of food he encountered as an evacuee on a well-run farm: "We had good *fromage blanc*, with cream, and sugar, and even jam on top. They made cakes, apple tarts—that was the cake we always had there—and lovely chicken with good mashed potatoes, with buttery sauce, and everything." This experience of generosity was not universal for evacuated children, however. In Finistère, Yvette Cadiou spoke of the village to which she, her mother, and her sister were evacuated:

> YVETTE: They thought that the refugees would take their food. So they didn't really like having refugees there. They thought that it was—, that we were a bit—
>
> LINDSEY: Weren't the refugees very well integrated into the town—?
>
> YVETTE: Not really, no. Because they thought, yes, they thought that we'd take their—, they didn't have much to eat either. And so they were afraid we'd take their food.

Scarce resources here created tension toward outsiders. Yvette's mother resorted to selling items stolen from the Germans by her husband at the arsenal in Brest, at great risk. Yvette Chapalain, also from Brest, was evacuated with her younger sister to a boarding school away from the coast. Without her parents, she had to manage the upsetting experience by herself: "In a Catholic school, no less, eh. There was us, the refugees, and there were the children who lived there with their parents, lots of them were farmers. And those children were really spoiled. They had good bread, pancakes, things like that. And we had disgusting bread. We'd see them, we'd see them eating their good white bread, and us next to them—ah no. *Oh là là là.* There was no sharing." An affective resonance kept some of her anger present, and she remained critical that the local children, their parents, and particularly the nuns treated refugee children in this way.

Ginette Renard commented on the experience of queuing, which is another commonly expressed trope in the representation of daily life: "Hours and hours in the queue, we'd spend. My sister would go, and after a while I'd go out and take over from her, and, well, later my mother would come along, and she'd spend another half hour queuing just to get to the front and then, all gone! No milk left, no more this, no more that—, oh, it was dreadful, we were hungry." Other children contributed a more vigorous kind of labor. In the Meuse, Elvina Falchetto describes lifting potatoes as soon as she was old enough; she was born in 1937.

The laborers, adults and children, were fed by the farmer's wife after their work was done which, she said, meant fewer hungry mouths at home. The work was hard, lifting and rinsing potatoes, and unpaid. The sole recompense was the "evening soup," which hung in the chimney in a big cauldron.

The memory stories speak more of tackling hunger than of hunger itself. Whether one ate or not was a spatial matter: occupied France suffered more than unoccupied France, town more than country, city more than town, apartment more than house. Access to a garden or land was crucial. Marie-Madeleine Viguié-Moreau explained: "One day our father said to us, 'Right, kids, all the flowers, the lawn . . . we're taking it all out because we've got to eat.' And so the garden became a vegetable garden, and down at bottom there were cages with rabbits, and then there were hens, and we liked that, us children. And so no, we never went hungry, ever." Together, they transformed their garden into their means of subsistence. Léa Duclos was also among the many whose gardens made a difference to their diets. She described her father's remarkable efforts to support their health:

> My father used to go to Seine-et-Marne, fifty or sixty kilometers there and back in the same day, on his bike—and it was a really heavy bike. He went to get butter, eggs, he'd come back with other provisions, with bacon. And in the evening when he'd get back, his calves would be so hard, I'd rub them with camphor oil. Poor man. I don't know how he did it, I don't know how he used to do it. He'd bring back provisions, and afterwards we'd take a bit to our cousins, to share it—

When fathers were present, they were often recalled as managing household provisioning alongside their professional work. Léa said that if her father had been to the countryside, instead of bread dipped in vinaigrette, the children would have fatty bacon or lard on bread at teatime. Nancette Blanchou's family's connections allowed them to procure something out of the wartime ordinary. Her family gave the baker extra grain to supplement his baking, and he rewarded them with one white loaf a week which, she said, was reserved for the children. This precious loaf had its own rituals: "Mum would keep it in her bedroom, wrapped in a sheet. We were allowed to have a little piece of white bread."

Sweets, chocolate, and other treats surfaced regularly in memory; like sharing with siblings, this is, perhaps, a memory specific to children. Jean-Claude

Bourtourault and his siblings were permitted each one lick per day of a shared piece of hard licorice. Sylvette Leclerc, among others, spoke of "chocolate with a kind of white cream inside, very sweet, and not pleasant to eat." But tastes are personal. Denise Algret remembered the same product but said, smiling, "another good food memory, those bars of chocolate that I thought were nice, or rather, it wasn't really chocolate, it was a kind of chocolate coating with cream inside, but well, I used to like them." Children took treats where they could find them, and as Danièle Dubowsky commented, scarcity made them memorable:

> On Sundays—this is a memory—my grandfather, in a fitted coat, would come to bring us a little packet of treats. Well, it could have been frustrating for us, as it was such a little packet for the three of us, but we'd never known anything else. . . . So it was still a special occasion! He'd arrive, he was very serious, he looked a little bit like Freud, with his goatee beard and his little glasses, and he'd give them to us. . . . They were only these little apricot cakes, as I remember, you'd bite into them and they were soft inside, but because he'd told us it was a gift, well, it was one!

We only learn of the little cakes through the memory of the man, who acts as a vector here. When goods are scarce, an alternative economy might develop. For adults, there was the black market and all its variations.[6] Nicole Boscariol remarked upon how vitamin biscuits allocated at school were traded: "The bigger children used to say to the little ones 'If you give us your vitamin biscuits, you can play with us'. . . . They were real mercenaries, eh! That was at school. Our headmistress would hand them out—. But I never gave my biscuits away." Nicole's memory tells us something of the way these biscuits were coveted but also the playground stakes involved. Perhaps the memory sticks because she never gave her biscuits away and was thus excluded from certain games. Perhaps she was proud not to have given in.

Often, the denial of a sweet treat made it prominent in memory. Sonia Agache recounted a story saying "it's nothing much, just a kid's memory," yet something must have mattered:

> We had this sugar syrup, it was a kind of molasses, we'd get it once a month. Because there were six of us at home, we had a really big pot. And one time, my brother, one evening, he came back home—, he'd been out somewhere

nearby, with his mates and that, I don't know. And when he came home, what did he do? He got the big pot of molasses and took it to the kitchen table. There were these old ends of leftover bread, and he started eating it. Well. And he didn't put it away, did he. But then in the night there was an air raid. All the windows smashed in, and the table was right next to the window. It all went into the pot of molasses!. . . . And so we couldn't have our molasses because there was glass in it.

Sonia did not describe the bombardment; she described the loss of the syrup. The world strikes the body, and the body is inserted into the world. Bombs flown across the English Channel etched a jar of molasses syrup into her memory; the geopolitics of the Second World War splintered on the kitchen table.

Fruit was also a scarce treat. Édith Denhez described the house in which her family lived when they returned after the exodus of 1940. She said it had a large fireplace, "and from time to time, there would be an orange on the corner of the mantelpiece. We weren't allowed to touch it. It was for Jacques. It was incredible— an orange, or a banana, it seemed so extravagant. But it was for Jacques." The memory of the fruit sat, like the orange, on the mantelpiece. Delicate, with a lung condition, Jacques was to die tragically in an air raid in 1944. Édith's memories of Jacques were always emotionally complex, given the way that bereavement, guilt, and a touch of resentment were intertwined. Fruit was also at the heart of what Danièle Dubowsky described as her worst memory of the war, bound into the disappointment of freedom. Having survived the Shoah, the family left France for Palestine. As the train rolled across Bulgaria, Danièle exchanged the last vestige of her Paris life, a gray-blue scarf decorated with images of the Eiffel Tower, Sacré Coeur, Notre Dame, and the Arc de Triomphe, for a basket of fruit from a trackside seller. She recalled bananas, peaches, and cherries. And just as she took a wonderful bite of the peach, someone nearby remarked that there was malaria in Bulgaria. Her mother grabbed the fruit from her daughter's mouth and threw the basket out of the window. This memory presaged the start of very difficult period.

Chronic hunger is absent from many of these wartime childhood memories. Many of these children were adequately nourished, although that was not the case for the juvenile population as a whole, as the pediatrician Robert Debré wrote in 1945. He noted that children's vitamin and mineral intakes were depleted, protein was scarce, growth was stunted, and children lost weight across the country but particularly in the south; many suffered digestive ailments and general debility, which had caused worrying rates of tuberculosis and increased child mortality.[7] But the children in this study got by. This must be seen as the result of exertion, ingenuity, the exploitation of networks, willingness to break the law, geography, risk, luck, skill, and judgment on the part of the children's carers. We must note too that the vast majority of the rememberers here were not placed in internment camps such as Drancy, Rivesaltes, or Gurs, where starvation-level hunger and diseases of malnutrition were commonplace. Yet these seemingly mundane memories are affectively intense because they exist in a web of connected things that matter/ed. Memories of food are not just memories of edible objects but pull into play a wide cast of people, places, happenings, feelings, and singular occurrences that imbricate the materiality of lives as they are lived.

WEARING

There are comparatively few memories of clothing in the memory stories. The procurement and making of clothing may have been less visible to children. Clothing seemed not to have generated strong feelings of desire or abhorrence, as food did. Robert Bernier said: "My grandmother was a seamstress by trade and she was used to making new clothes out of old, let's say, and my mother, she was the same. . . . But I don't have any particular memories, if you like, of how they did all of that." Skilled women in the family took care of things, and there was nothing surprising enough here to stick memories down. Sylvette Leclerc's mother had to buy in the skill and labor to manage the family's clothing needs:

> Because she wasn't very good at sewing, we'd get a woman to come for the whole day, from time to time, once every two of three months, sometimes even more. She'd make us our little clothes, from bits of cloth, or from clothes that were too big that she'd remake in our size, or—, we were dressed in all sorts of odds and ends, really! And then of course we had these great big shoes with articulated wooden soles—, well, they weren't particularly solid, and from time to time, the sole would just fly off . . . [laughing].

Françoise Yessad too commented on her mother making do "with what we had. We'd undo it and redo it, unpick it and re-stitch it. Oh, well, we weren't very elegant, eh. But that was fine, we didn't care anyway." These children were more interested in eating and playing.

However, on occasion clothing could carry memory in meaningful ways when allied to more intensive affective experiences. For evacuee Colette Streicher, the clothes made by her foster mother, Madame Gadeix, provide yet more evidence of the affection that was heaped on the little girl and are thus affectively charged: "She made me these blue pinafores, she had some blue sheets and made pinafores out of them for me. And she knitted me woolen suits, and she had dresses made for me out of her own." Christian Gaillard was nine when war broke out in 1939. He was, he said, "in the middle of a growth spurt" across the years that followed:

> For me, clothes and shoes, oh well, it was really awful. I went from a 39 in shoes to a 42 in a year, and so, well, you're going to have moments when you're in pain because your shoes just don't fit on your feet, eh. I can remember that, I can. Same thing for clothes, you see, because as you grow, the sleeves get shorter—. I can remember having that kind of problem. It hurt me physically, but I felt down about it too, because I always looked a right old mess, badly dressed. If the kids could see what I looked like at that time, they'd burst out laughing, eh.

The memory sticks not only through feelings of discomfort but also because in his adolescent awkwardness he knows he cut a laughable figure, and a twinge of shame fixes the memory in place.

Clothing could take center stage in a memory story. Marie-Madeleine Viguié-Moreau's father was arrested for his resistance activity in February 1944. Her mother was pregnant and gave birth in September 1944. While she was still in the maternity hospital, her eldest son, Marie-Madeleine's brother, was accidentally killed with a live pistol he and a friend had been playing with. She described the bewildering aftermath:

> I started to really understand [what had happened] when my grandmother came to get us, my sister and me, she came to pick up our red clothes—we each had a nice little suit in red—and we went with my grandmother to the dyers, and my grandmother got our clothes dyed navy blue. She bought us each a hat, my grandmother, she came to kit us out, and little white socks and patent shoes, but we didn't understand, just absolutely nothing at all.

And anyway, then came the day of the funeral, and my grandmother said to us "Right, you're going to have to be very brave, I'm going to—, you're going to see your brother, but your brother—," I'm not quite sure how she said it to me, she said, "Your brother, you're going to see him sleeping, but he's won't wake up any more, not ever, he's not going to wake up." I think she didn't want to use the word dead.

Dyeing the clothes was a pivot, at which point when Marie-Madeleine realized something was very wrong. A recurrent motif of her narrative, Marie-Madeleine notes her shift from ignorance to knowledge. It was the beginning of a period of "total despair in our family," she said.

PLAYING

Advocates of Vichy's National Revolution put considerable effort into its propaganda for children, and ideological toys and games were available in shops and catalogues.[8] However, in this corpus of memory stories, people very rarely made references to any bought or manufactured toys and games; nor were books or comics recalled. Sometimes toys entered memory stories fleetingly as part of an anecdote and evidence for a point being made. Christian Solet said "because my parents were shopkeepers, I didn't really lack any material things. . . . I was lucky enough to have a bike, roller skates." Christian uses the evidence of these objects to show that the wartime penury we might expect was not inevitable. Colette Streicher mentioned the toys she received as an evacuee: "I can remember my first Christmas—it was wonderful! I got a little box made out of red cardboard, which I still have—a little sewing box. And I got a box of dominoes from the uncle and auntie, and I still have them." The listener is to understand how meaningful these objects were through the assertion that she has kept them. Perhaps this also testifies to the fact that they were objects of reasonably high quality. Their continued existence may also be the reason that the memory exists. Like Christian, however, she gives no sense of how she used or played with these objects. Instead, they communicate affection and integration. Thérèse Allglas-Cymmermann described the couple who took her in as a hidden Jewish child for the whole period of the war as "marvelous people." She said: "I was very lucky to have lots of toys because Monsieur M------ was very good at making things, he could make anything. There was a public tip nearby where people got rid of things they didn't want, and he could make something wonderful out of nothing." As with Colette, toys exist in memory as evidence of care and affection.

Michel Pauty recalled the immediate postwar period. Michel had been living in the countryside with his aunt, his cousin, and other evacuee children since the early years of the war. The return to Paris was difficult: "I was completely shocked, I was, when I went back to Paris. My parents had good jobs, we were alright, and when we got back, there were no toys, nothing at all. The only toy I had was a knife. That was the only toy we had." The memory cannot tell us in what circumstances his shock arose. I asked him what he made with the knife: he said the children carved sailing boats. Christian Le Goff, evacuated in the Creuse, recounted something similar: "We made our toys ourselves. Out of sticks, out of—, we all had a knife. The knife was the first step towards being a man. A knife gave you power—because you could cut things, you could make little things. So the knife is the first thing you'd give a child in the country, in order to eat, to cut his bread—." The knife was a gendered object, and an object of the countryside. Perhaps that accounted, in some way, for Michel Pauty's shock when he returned to Paris with a rural child's knife as his only plaything.

Toys and children's objects acquired particular significance for Jewish children. Danièle Dubowsky recounted the night of January 23, 1944. There was a knock at the apartment door. Her mother opened it. There was a policeman and, she thinks, a couple of Germans. Her mother was told to pack a suitcase:

"Bring some blankets, Madame, you're going to need them." Another German said to us children, "You can bring one thing each. Take one thing for yourself." Well, Sylvain didn't take anything—a little boy of five years old, woken up in the middle of the night, eh—Gabi took this horrible ceramic orange ashtray with two people kissing on it, which followed us around for the whole of the war. And I took my doll. I had a lovely big doll, with blue eyes, and so I took my doll.

The doll survived both Drancy and Vittel camps: "she was with me for a very long time," said Danièle, "she even came to Palestine with me." In Palestine, Danièle gave her doll to another little girl, who mistreated and damaged this precious toy. The postwar promised much for Danièle's family, but their hopes were always disappointed. Another Jewish child imprisoned in Drancy, Nicole Kahn, remembered: "I know that someone made me two little dollies." In these recollections, the object exists in memory because it is stuck to an affective state, or to people, places, or events, but no one recounted the more habitual act of playing.

Many children did not have much spare time for playing, particularly outside of cities. Journeys on foot to school took a fair amount of time, and wartime shortages, rural poverty, and absent family members meant that even young children were occupied until bedtime. Sylvette Leclerc, living in the Aube, was eight years old when her father was taken prisoner of war. She had several younger brothers, and her mother was not in good health: "Even though I was very young, I would look after my brothers, wash and bath them. Yes. And it sometimes happened that I'd have to do some cooking, or collect the grass for the rabbits. Well, that wasn't a bad job really, I liked doing it enough." Ginette Renard was twelve in 1942 when her father died in an accident. This brought new responsibilities for Ginette and her sister. Neighboring men might chop logs for the family, but after that, "we'd have to find a way, me and my sister, to saw them up. It was tricky, doing it longways": the wood had to fit the stove, which was the family's only source of heating. Pierre Tainturier and Edmond Magnin were a little older, born in 1927 and 1928, respectively. As young adolescent boys, they had various responsibilities. Edmond's father was ill "so I had to take his place—, because we had chickens and rabbits, and we used wood as fuel, so it was me who had to go to the woods, me who'd look after the rabbits, me who'd cut the grass, who'd make the hay, and then—, I even worked for a little while in the woods with the woodcutters." When Edmond's formal schooling ended at fourteen, he worked to keep his family fed and warm. Pierre Tainturier was still in school:

> PIERRE: I used to go to fetch provisions every Thursday—we didn't have school on Thursdays—so I'd go on Thursday, and I'd bring back milk, butter, eggs, a little bit of butter, not much butter, cream, milk, eggs, all of that.
>
> INTERVIEWER: Did you have to hide it when you brought it back?
>
> PIERRE: Yes, when you came back. You had to be careful not to get caught. I had a little crate on the back of my bike, and I'd come back like that, but I never felt very at ease. I used to go on my own.

Child evacuees were also allocated some of the many chores that occupied all members of farming families. Jacques Kermen recalled that after school in the winter, he and his sister had to cut up the beets to feed the geese; he said "it was so cold!" but afterwards they toasted their stockinged feet on the stove. The other rural occupation for evacuees and local children, always recounted affectionately, was looking after the cows. Mostly a summer holiday occupation, the hours spent in the fields with the cows were also opportunities for playing, exploring the streams and hedgerows, and, later, meeting the opposite sex. Marcel Tatelin commented that rural ponds were one source of entertainment and that a big gang of young people would go there in the summer, but not just to play. The damp environs were good places to look for snails, catch frogs, or hunt mushrooms. Entertaining activities because they were sociable, these were also necessary contributions to household resources.

In rural areas, the practice of the *veillée* was widespread on winter evenings. Rural neighbors would gather in one house, sharing heat and light, exchanging news, playing cards, the women knitting, elderly folk and children perhaps weaving baskets. Odette Journeuaux recollected that her *veillées* had a particular outcome:

> At our house, there would be my parents, of course, and then all the young folks in Perigny—. We'd push the table back—, because there wasn't—, we only had two rooms, the bedroom and the kitchen, so we'd push the table back, and dance in the middle, on the slabs. And, well, our parents, they knew how to dance and so . . . they taught us what do to because we had no idea. And that's how we learned to dance. We did it at our house, and later we'd go to other houses. We had a record player, so we'd take it with us. . . . And we'd dance to the accordion, of course, there was only that. . . . And so once the war was over, we all knew how to dance, when the local dances started up again, we knew how—

With local public dances prohibited by the Germans, the wartime conditions drove young people inside; however, war is really only present in this story at its end. People danced at the liberation, they danced on VE Day, and thanks to their *veillées*, these young people were able to join in. Like many happy memories, these are vague in their details but vivid in their evocation of intergenerational rural sociability.

Many of the male interviewees recalled the war itself as a central interest of their childhood. Toy soldiers and war stories in novels, comics, and films were a popular legacy of the First World War, as was the Franco-German enmity. Max Potter, whose British journalist father was interned in France through the war years, recalled playing journalist with his sister:

> We made a little news report, which is in there [gesturing to a chest containing his wartime papers], on the spot, by describing, we were watching it through binoculars, and all of a sudden we saw the DCA [antiaircraft fire], and the planes were flying up really high, and we saw one of them get hit, there was an explosion, it caught fire, and then we saw a parachute, two parachutes through the binoculars, and then part of the engine which was on fire fell onto the parachute, which caught fire. And the folks down below, "Aaaahhh!" It wasn't hatred [we felt towards them], you understand.

Max, whose father was of the same nationality as the bombers, noticed particularly the sympathy for the RAF parachutists, a relief for a child who risked bullying whenever the Allies bombed Paris. In Lille, Jean Caniot also followed the war closely and, like Max, had retained an archive. I asked him whether he used to watch the Allied planes passing overhead. He said "oh yes, I did! I used to count the English planes. And I found—, I had noted I think it was 36 planes, I'd counted 36 going over. And much later, I got in touch with the Royal Air Force in London to ask for the flight reports, when I received the report from that day . . ., on the report it said 37! So, I said to myself, well, not bad!" Documenting the war as a boy had left him, as an adult, with quantities of contemporary material with which he had written several local history books.[9] It was also common to hear about the interest boys (this was not mentioned by any women) took in the progress of the war. Claude Thomas said "we had maps on the walls with the battlefront, if you like, marked with pins. We'd do that every day." Henri Buc similarly noted "we had maps, with drawing pins, flags, and we'd see how the armies were moving around—, everyone had one at home."

For many boys, of course, the excitement of the war was more actively engaged. Roger Davre described playing at war with his friends:

> **ROGER:** You play at war! Children today, they don't know how to play anymore. There are games but—, playing horses, planes, playing trains, they don't know how to do any of that—
>
> **LINDSEY:** Can you remember playing at war?

ROGER: In planes! Oh, yes, I've even got a memory of having killed two of
my best friends! Michel et Camille! [He laughs and makes the sound of a
machine gun.]

Death, it seems, was part of the game. Serge Holand, a Jewish boy who, with
his parents, found refuge in a rural village, also commented that "we weren't
directly affected by the war, but we were immersed in the atmosphere of war";
he showed me a photograph of a gang of children all clutching mock wooden
rifles held in a salute. Some of the games that older children played involved
real weapons. Indeed, the availability of weapons in and around the countryside
in 1944 made for dangerous adventures. Serge recalled a bullet from his adolescent neighbor's Sten gun narrowly missing his foot; Marie-Madeleine Viguié-
Moreau's eldest brother was killed accidentally while playing with a live weapon.
Jean Caniot hinted at something beyond the fun or excitement of playing at war
as he described his experience of the 1940 exodus: "We used to play evacuees,
me and my cousins, and the cousins, they'd be carrying all the bags and every-
thing. But I'd turned over a chair, me, and I was machine-gunning the refugees!
[He mimes the gesture of firing from the chair legs in his imaginary gun turret,
laughing.]" Jean chuckled at this rather macabre game, which put me in mind of
René Clément's 1952 film Jeux Interdits (Forbidden games), also about the exodus.
He added that playing was the way children worked out what was happening:
"We didn't really realize. We didn't have a house—that belonged to our parents.
We didn't have a past, we didn't have any toys. None of that. So we just played,
and we'd play at war." These games shifted and changed as the war evolved, keeping pace with political, technological, and military developments. Such games
did not just reflect the world; they created the child's world in a way that was
lived, concrete, and meaningful. Playing at war played out real and imagined
scenarios, emotions, and trajectories in assemblages of possibilities and affects.

PAUSE—HENRI PLAYS AT WAR

When recounting his childhood in Gouzon, a large village in the Creuse, Henri
Buc emphasized that he should distinguish three levels of recollections. He
warned me that I would be hearing "my own memory . . ., my memory which

has been reconstructed along with other people, and the way in which that memory has passed into legend." He wanted to give a sense of what his preoccupations had been as a boy, what children had done and understood, and the limits of a known reality that his memories could reveal. Henri, his mother, and his sister had traveled to Gouzon in 1940, leaving his doctor father in the tuberculosis sanitorium where he worked and where he would succumb to the disease. Although Gouzon was far from the battlefront, the games Henri and his local playmates played were their engagement with the wider world: "What was going to happen is that we were going to live the war. We were going to live the war together. And it seems to me that there was a very deep relationship between what the boys were going to invent as their games, the games they were going to play, and the general feeling that now, everything had changed." These games were central: "I would say that [he pauses]—we *had* to play at war [with emphasis]. It became very necessary that we played at war." To play at war required an enemy, territory to defend or attack, weapons, provisions, vehicles, the will to engage in combat, and some kind of plan. For the boys, the plan was found in a favorite novel, *La Guerre des Boutons* (1912) by Louis Pergaud, which described the incessant warfare between gangs of boys from two neighboring villages: "This book really interested us, and we'd get together around it and say 'How are we going to make a war?' But we didn't want to have a war with another village, and that wasn't possible anyway. So there had to be two villages in the village. And so there was *Ceux de la Vouieze* and *Ceux de la Goze* [the Vouieze-ers and the Goze-ers], and from there, we were going to fight." The river Vouieze ran to the south of Gouzon, the Goze to the north. The different armies were named after these rivers, which became territorial markers. The boys also had two differently composed rival gangs if they needed a change: *Ceux de la Campagne* and *Ceux de la Ville* (the country lads and the townies). Thus they created the necessary adversarial context and declaration of intent: "obviously, we all agreed that we would fight." The boys developed resources: "We had to build our huts, our fortresses, and put together our supplies." In their early games, the boys used catapults and hurled horse chestnuts and beets at each other. They kept their provisions in an old combine harvester hopper. Henri remembered these games as ones that united the children:

> We were really happy together. We were a real gang of lads together—, the
> village was full of children, and the social barriers had receded, just for a

moment, and so we'd all go and play in a big property which was over there [gesturing from his window]. We'd go out to play after five o'clock. Not all of our games were war games, but we'd play. And [he pauses for a moment] we knew we were in our own world.

Their war play was influenced by the French situation and their patriotic feeling. When I asked whether the gangs took on the identities of the real adversaries of the war, German or American, he said: "Well, that's an interesting point because, in fact, no. Nobody would have wanted to be German, nobody. Everyone wanted to be French." So while the children played at war, they were not playing out *the* war. Defeated, humiliated France could not be the territory for their war, so they adapted the local terrain. Yet as events unfolded, the French resistance crept into the game. Henri recounted the story of the huts; this story, he said, was told time and again by old men at the village hairdresser—they did not frequent local bars or cafés—where boyhood memories were shared and shaped. One day, the gang found their hut destroyed, their booty gone, and a sinister message: "The Black Bison has destroyed your hut." The children reconstructed their camp, but again one day it was smashed up and the same message communicated. From there, Henri said, the men's reminiscences grew "glorious":

> So now, this has become a myth, because I'm not at all sure which bits of it are true. I wasn't there when it happened. But the third time that he came, so they say—and it's always three times, isn't it, never anything else—he was captured by the children, we were, how old? Perhaps twelve, the oldest boys. And this lad they were chasing, he was about eighteen. They chased him and caught him, and up there, they demasked him and brought him back as a prisoner—! . . . Well, that's how they tell the story, anyway.

Skeptical himself, Henri recounted this myth as part of the story of the past as told by the old men who had been boys: suffering, destruction, and then victorious resistance against unjust oppression.

Henri told me that "these kinds of games evolved as the war went on." He could not say precisely how or why: "It's difficult to piece it all together, but later on, they weren't the same. . . . There was this general awareness that things were changing." Local resistance guerrillas, the maquis, began to appear more regularly in the village, and in the children's games. The maquis held up the post office and scandalized the village with their rough violence. Later, the Germans also entered the children's games: "we understood that the Germans were going to lose, so we did play at the Germans losing." Later, the local resistance and the maquis were better armed, and when the Americans passed through, they left weapons behind. Horse chestnuts were put aside for something more exciting:

> We had access—, we found ourselves having access to more dangerous games. . . . We got hold of gunpowder. It was near the end of the war, right near the end. . . . And we put—our parents knew nothing about it, and I've never really understood—they were older than me, and they'd put a line of gunpowder, like that, with two bullets at either end, you'd set fire to the middle, get out of the way and see if this bullet or that one would go off first!

The boys found bullets and a revolver, and went to fire it in the fields. But the gun was damaged. No bullets emerged and the barrel melted: "we went home with our legs shaking like anything." On another occasion they went fishing using hand grenades. Henri's stories of playing at war were both real and fantastical, self-consciously recounting elements of a happening past negotiated within a community of memory that was constantly rebuilding its own heroic past.

LEARNING

War and its consequences—occupation, ideological change—brought new people, things, ideas, and practices into classrooms.[10] Aspects of school life were often recounted in the memory stories, usually in response to direct questions from interviewers.

Whether mobilized, prisoners of war, or drafted into forced labor, absent male teachers meant that many children experienced inconsistency of staffing in schools. Names were not often recalled, but memories of teachers emerged through anecdotes of singular events often bound together with feeling. Sylvette Leclerc remembered that "we started to run out of primary school teachers, because they'd all gone into the army. We had a retired teacher, who'd come back to work." She said she recalled this because it was the year that she changed classes at primary school from the "little ones" to the "big ones" and was confronted by this unfamiliar man. Marcel Quinet also remembered that their male primary school teacher was mobilized and replaced by a retired female teacher. His memories were of the fun they had at her expense: "because she was a bit deaf—we'd really mess around!" He did not elaborate. Perhaps he barely recalled what they did, yet the return of his original teacher permitted the deduction "and when our teacher came back, he changed the tune, eh!" He told this anecdote in response to a question about discipline during the war. It was the strict male teacher, not the retired woman, who punished the children. Christian Gaillard suffered, he suggested, from the fragmentation of staffing. Taught by the same man between the ages of five and nine, after that "there were comings and goings all the time." His teacher was replaced "by young folks who weren't old enough to join the army . . . and they never stayed long in post." Others benefited in the long term from the disruption. The town of Brest had been evacuated in advance of the siege there in 1944. Against her will, Cécile Bramé's parents left her in the boarding school to which she had been evacuated. Cécile now recognized what she had gained: she was encouraged by the headmistress to train as a teacher, a career she had loved.

Teachers' manuals and education policy testify to the changes Vichy introduced during this period not just to the school system but also to curricula. These changes were barely remarked in the memory stories. A child could not know whether his or her curriculum differed from what had gone before. Daniel Fevre did recall a new introduction, however:

> In the schools, they made us have—it was imposed I think by the *Éducation nationale*—German teachers. And we had a German teacher—, he taught us German. He was called S-----: "Écoutez Monsieur S------!" [Putting on a mock German accent.] He'd say that to us all the time, and of course, because all the French were against them. We didn't listen to him at all [laughing]. But he was very nice, that chap.

Daniel distinguishes his child self who mocked this German teacher from his adult self who pities the man's struggle in front of unruly adolescents. Other teachers were memorable for their political perspectives. Serge Holand remembered his primary school teacher was "very, very Republican." A visual memory gave flesh to the point; he said "Marshal Pétain's photograph, I remember it, hanging there, half torn." Marcel Quinet, on the other hand, said that his teacher "liked the Germans more than the French." Two of the evacuees from Paris to the rural Creuse, Christian Le Goff and Roger Davre, spoke enthusiastically about their outdoors education. Both evoked their Paris schoolrooms in contrast: Roger had been mocked for his stammer by a sarcastic teacher, and Christian, back in the capital after the war, gazed from his classroom window, daydreaming of trees and open spaces. Vichy's anti-intellectual curriculum encouraged more sports and outdoors learning. Whether their teachers were adhering to these new stipulations or not, this style of teaching suited Christian and Roger. The former said "we used to go on walks, we'd get out of school and go into nature to learn things"; the latter recounted studying outside under a large chestnut tree. If a bird started to sing during their history lesson, he said, the teacher would stop and ask them what it was; if a leaf blew across their books, the teacher would stop and discuss the leaf. Consistent with his nostalgic view of the time, Roger was favorable to this method: "We were learning without having to learn. We were learning naturally. You didn't feel that they were trying to force things into your head, like historical dates, for instance." In both stories, school was not a place of constraint, but part of the freedom and growth they both experienced away from Paris and their parents. Even punishment was constructive in this idealized place: Roger was put to work digging the school vegetable patch to pay for his misdemeanors.

School life was affected by the material shortages of war and occupation. A key problem was the lack of physical space, resulting from destruction or requisitioning. In the suburbs of Lille, Sonia Agache's primary school was struck by a bomb. After that, she and her classmates were sent into the city center for their lessons but shared a school with its original inhabitants, each group getting half a day's teaching. Lucien Palisson remembered how his schooling was not just truncated but complicated by distance: "Because they'd requisitioned our school we had to go to the girls' school instead. . . . We'd go to school from seven in the morning to one o'clock, and the girls would go from one o'clock to seven at night. . . . Some children had to walk six kilometers to get to school." Later evenings, long journeys, and dark nights meant that absenteeism grew. Christian Gaillard's class was also reaccommodated:

Our classroom was occupied. The main building, which was also the mayor's office, the mayoral rooms, the teacher's lodging, and the classroom, had been occupied by the Germans. So we were moved into this old house, I'd say it was one that had been abandoned, it was in a pretty sad state. The [mayor] had to convince the inhabitant to lend it to the town temporarily, making a few basic alterations to get the desks in, a blackboard, and a few chairs for the kids.

Few of the interviewees were critical about the extent to which their schooling was disrupted, however. Unlike those Jewish children who hungered for the educational opportunities that persecution had denied them, skipping school, reduced hours, and the lure of mischief often pushed any negative impacts aside.

The prominent place of food in memory stories of wartime childhoods extends into schooling. Matthieu Devigne has written about the dedication of school inspectors and their allies in Marseille who worked to feed the large numbers of children coming to school hungry.[11] In the countryside, children were less likely to be malnourished but often lived several kilometers from schools, which were usually small and did not have canteens. Lucien Palisson spoke of "a lady who heated up our lunch dishes at midday"; it was not quite clear what was in those lunch dishes, though, as he also spoke of a powder mixed with milk which formed part of their lunch—Blédina, perhaps, a wheat-based baby food: "I've got a really good memory of that stuff." In the Dordogne, Robert Bernier's school was staffed by a married couple; the woman taught the younger children, the man the older ones. Each child brought some food from home, perhaps potatoes or leeks, and the woman's mother, who also lived with them, made it into a soup for fifty or sixty children each lunchtime. At Jeannine Graveron's school in the Creuse, children who lived too far from school "each brought a little lunch dish, with whatever their parents had made for them, and that was heated up, there was a wood fire, a stove for heating, on top of that, at around eleven, the teacher would put some water, and they'd put the little things to heat up there in the hot water—."At evacuee Jacques Kermen's school, children participated in making their own midday meal: "When we'd arrive [at school], there were some of us who'd peel the vegetables, others who'd be breaking up the wood to put on the stove, to make the fire, and then, oh, that smelled good, because across the whole morning, there was this [gesturing, a large, round pot]—, of soup, it was as big as that, and it smelled good [laughing]." Marcel Dumas and Roger Davre could not recall whether or not they had to take bread to their school but recalled that children brought what their parents could afford, whether potatoes, vegetables, or eggs.

The arrival of refugee children at rural schools exacerbated all the problems of space and provision. Beyond the material, new interpersonal relations between children in the classroom generated a new set of understandings. Jeannine Graveron commented on the evacuees from Paris who joined her school from 1943:

"[There were] loads of them. Loads, yes. Oh, yes, I remember that there was one family of them, they all had nits. So we were told, well, you'd better not get too close to them because—, oh well, yes. But we still played together!" Geneviève Giraud, also in the Creuse, similarly remarked upon the arrival of the evacuees, who doubled class sizes and made it necessary for local people to bring in tables and desks from home. They were different from local children:

> GENEVIEVE GIRAUD: . . . and the little ones from the Creuse, they
> were—,
> MARIE FAUCONNET: —alongside the others, they were well-behaved—
> GENEVIEVE: They were all so well behaved, I don't know what, a bit
> softer, maybe, while the Parisians, oh, they answered back! So, with the
> schoolteacher . . ., they answered him back like anything, yes, *oh, là!* . . .

I asked her what she thought of their behavior:

> GENEVIEVE: We'd be staring at them a bit, like this [mouth open, eyes
> bulging in disbelief], laughing—
> MARIE FAUCONNET'S DAUGHTER-IN-LAW: —they were a bit more
> brazen than you, you were more reserved—
> GENEVIEVE: Oh, yes, oh, yes, yes, yes, that's for sure. It was like night and
> day [chuckling at the memory] . . . They had an answer for everything!
> Much more than we did. Far more than us.

Genevieve's laugh was gleeful and surprised as she recalled the bold, naughty Parisians and reflected on her sheltered rural world. Evacuee Roger Davre thought that he must have been a little ahead of his rural schoolfriends academically as he recalled a "feeling of superiority" that helped him conquer his stammer. On the other hand, Parisian evacuee Simone Courant found school very challenging:

> She was very badly accepted by the teacher. Because, well, there was an accu-
> mulation of things, eh. A refugee, her poverty, her headlice . . ., so yes, she
> wasn't accepted by the teacher, who always kept her a little bit apart from
> the others, who seemed to have left her out a bit. . . . My mother told me that
> every morning, she'd vomit before going to school. Because the idea of going
> to school made her feel sick.

Simone's daughter made it clear that the problem was not the children but the teacher, who played favorites. Nonetheless, Simone received the highest grade in her School Leaving Certificate—her revenge, her daughter said, on the cruel teacher.

War wove itself into the fabric of experience, creating a mood, a conjuncture, unique to the period and the generation that lived it as schoolchildren. Even more singular are the experiences of individuals, recalled in little anecdotes, inside which events unfolded, objects were encountered, choices were made, and interactions happened. Everyday life is lived through the constant emergence of novelty; every routine may be interrupted to produce a memory of a surprise; every familiar scene may be altered by an event or a chance encounter. As part 1, "Memories Felt," showed, memories cohere around the unusual and the out-of-place and around things that caused anxiety or fear. The clearest traces of everyday life in memory are found not in the humdrum but in the surprising. Yet because the surprising can only emerge from the humdrum, such memories always evoke normality as their foil. Beyond the memories that are recounted are the things that did not stick. These exist simultaneously, but virtually, in a kind of counter-relief with what stuck, giving clues to the expanse of life being lived that overflows the words spoken in the interview.

CHAPTER 9

AFFECTIVE OTHERS

The aim of part 4, "Memories Lived," is to look into the memory stories to observe "where life happens." That spot is populated by the rememberer, of course, but also by many others. Terry Eagleton described "the business of affections and aversions" as central to a social aesthetics; in this chapter I transpose that idea directly onto human relations as related in the stories. I look, first, at the love relations evoked in the oral narratives and, second, at the aversions of war—of named, imagined, and real enemies or adversaries. Love relations were overwhelmingly dominated by parents. Most of the interviewees were older people whose parents had died by the time these memory stories were recorded. Therefore, all evocations of parents in the past were tinged with subsequent loss. It is in the nature of memory stories to be multitemporal, as I showed across previous parts of this study. Memory is never just about the past. Recalling a happy moment with a parent also evokes the later loss of that loved one, for example. War and the conditions of the Occupation also pushed children to form new affective bonds outside of their families. Affect is an orientation away from, as well as toward: affective others were also those feared, despised, or hated. Caroline Williams notes the way affective interactivity gives rise to "many conflicting emotions" and remarks on the "powerful networks of agreement and disagreement that cohere to varying degrees in the imagination."[1] This complexity and conflict is notable in relation to the human objects of aversion in the memory stories. The most obvious enemy, the German, emerges as being complicated by the contingency of everyday coexistence. The second part of this chapter thus explores memories of Germans, Marshal Pétain, the French forces of order (the police, the Milice), the French population, a reckless Resistance, and the Allies to discern threads of dislike, disapproval, and even hatred that intertwine in the assemblage of the recollection.

LOVE AND FAMILY

Parents are prominent across the memory stories. Georgette Transler struggled to remember much of her childhood in detail. The place of her mother, though, stood out and elicited one of her longest passages of continuous speech:

> My mum, she used to do everything. She'd make her own bread, she had cows, we had eight of them, and we even had a bull, and all that. Yes, we had everything you needed, eh. She was pretty gutsy, in any case. I loved my dad, I did, and I loved my mum. . . . Mum knew a lot of people, but people were jealous of her, jealous, they were. There were farmers, but because Mum knew how to do everything, eh, because she was intelligent. Dad too, because Dad, I forgot to tell you, he learned how to make clogs, and he'd sell them to the people there, the farmers, but after he died, Mum was all alone. . . . During the war, it was Mum who made all the food, we had eight cows, there were four horses, we had a bull. . . . We didn't want for anything, because Mum, she'd make her own butter, she'd make her own bread, because she had an oven. We had chickens, cockerels, and all that. There were some calves, but she'd sell them. Calves were for selling. The merchant would come past. She couldn't keep them, she already had the cows, and so she had enough with them.

These memories are neither linear nor clustered into anecdotes. Stubs of stories remain unfinished, with feelings and knowledge arising in a cloud that loops and stutters. At their heart is the figure of a woman so competent that she managed their small farm impeccably, to the extent, Georgette's story suggests, that she incited the jealousy of others. There must have been a story here about what generated their jealousy, but that anecdote did not materialize, even though the feeling did. An attempt to understand Georgette's childhood memories that falters on the unraveled narrative and its frayed edges will miss what remains: the intensity of Georgette's admiration for her mother.

Absent Fathers

Paternal absence is one of the defining characteristics of this period for children.[2] The interviewees Marie-Madeleine Viguié-Moreau, Nancette Blanchou,

Anne-Marie Laurens, and Paul Maubourg saw their fathers killed because of their resistance activity. For the Jewish children, fathers were absent sometimes because they were rounded up and deported separately from the women and children, as with Rachel Jedinak; because they managed to go into hiding successfully, as with Hélène Zytnicki; or because they were interned elsewhere, as with Maurice Goldring, whose father was interned in Switzerland. Some fathers mobilized in 1939 were killed as a result of military duties. Bernard Bauwens's father had fought in the First World War and was called up again. He was sent to Meaux as a military truck driver. Bernard described how, at the very moment of the Nazi invasion, his father fell ill:

> He caught a cold, but it wasn't getting any better, and they left him hanging around there in Meaux, down there, they let him hang around down there in the cold, and it was at the moment of the invasion, it just wasn't getting any better. So they sent him to the military hospital, Versailles, then there was the invasion, and because of that they sent him to—, I think it was Boucicault, I think he was sent to Boucicault in the fifteenth arrondissement, because all the military hospitals cleared out the lads who were already there, and well, of course, it was the invasion, so they didn't look after him, and so he died there.

Bernard's story is a sharp reminder of the sheer contingency of everyday life and death. A combination of chance occurrences—falling ill at a particular moment when the care for noncombatant soldiers degenerated as a result of urgent causalities—led, in Bernard's story, to his father's medical neglect. Jacques Prieur also lost his father in the battle for France. Jacques was born in 1938 and had no memories of him. Jacques's father had volunteered to fight. In our interview, Jacques showed me a document that accompanied the posthumous medal his father had received for leading his group "magnificently" in attack. His death had a big impact on Jacques's life. Jacques surmised that his young mother was unable to cope financially after her husband's death, needed to rebuild her life, and so sent her son away to foster parents. Jacques returned to Paris in 1947, where he was greeted by his mother's new husband and two young half-brothers. Jacques's mother struggled to establish affectionate relations with her eldest son for the rest of her life.

Of the estimated 1.8 million French soldiers taken prisoners of war in 1940, 790,000 were husbands, and maybe 616, 200 were fathers.[3] Sarah Fishman's research focused on their wives, but their children are also central to the problem created by their absence. Lucien Agache's mother had died before the outbreak of war. When I asked him a general question about what war meant for children, he said "well, a war is—, it's going without your father, that's the main thing that I felt, even more so because my mother wasn't around anymore—, and everything that went along with that." For Lucien, war *was* the loss of a father, not a geopolitical struggle for dominance or an ideological combat. Sylvette Leclerc also narrated the events of war through her father's absence:

> As long as my father was there, there weren't any problems. All the problems started when he left to join the army. Er, problems—, my parents didn't have very much money, and the time it took for the military pension to come through, my mother had quickly gone through all of our savings, so for about a year or so we didn't have very much. Afterwards, things did get a bit better. . . . Right away my father was taken prisoner, right at the beginning of the war. I don't know if it was towards the end of '39, the beginning of 1940, I don't know, I was still a bit young. [She laughs.] That sort of thing doesn't stick.

The interviewer asked her if, as a child, she understood what war was. She replied "Oh, yes, even so. For a start, my father was gone." The interviewee later asked how she understood, as a child, that the war was over; again, it was articulated through her father. She responded, "Well, we hoped most of all to see our father come back without too much trouble." When her father did return, he was very ill. He immediately left his family to see his mother, but she died before he arrived. After another long pause, Sylvette commented: "It was such a dreadful sorrow for us all, because he never got to see his mother alive again." I wondered how that distress had manifested itself in the child's daily life. The man who came back was not the one who had been longed for over four or five years, and no joy accompanied the recounting of his return.

Sylvette's experience of a difficult return was not uncommon. A man born in 1934 who was recorded as part of a video made in the 1990s about past childhoods in Romainville, north of Paris, said:

> My father was freed at the end of the war, and he came back in 1945. He'd been in Germany for four years. . . . Obviously, there was a good side, it was good to have a father, but alongside that, when you've lived on your own for

four years with your mother, when a father's authority comes back, there are some ups and downs. You can't do what you like with a father like you can with a mother.

Although the man does not elaborate, much more of this memory focuses on the difficulty of reintegration than the "good side" of having his father back. The "ups and downs" alluded to here made me wonder what "a father's authority" added in real terms to this boy's life. It was not only the return of prisoners of war that provoked tensions. Maurice Goldring's father had been interned in Switzerland through the war. He was not mistreated and was sent to do agricultural work on a farm, where he fell in love with the daughter of the family. At the end of the war, he told his wife that he wanted to leave her: "What a drama. My mother in tears, my sister in tears—and in the end, he stayed." Maurice narrated in such brief terms a period that must have been draining, particularly for his mother. Around this time, Maurice was sent to boarding school; he commented, "I wasn't happy there at all. I cried all the time, I wanted to come home. I was eleven." The period of his father's return was full of emotional agitation. They had survived the Shoah, but war and its consequences had destabilized all of their affective relations.

For very young children, a father's return was the return of a stranger. As soon as I began recording my interview with Danielle Durville, she said:

Well, listen, I was born 30 August 1939, [just] before the declaration of war. And on 3 September, my dad left for the war, and I didn't meet him until 1945 when he came home. So five years passed. . . . That's pretty tough. People spoke to me about him, and Mum had news from him, they wrote to each other, and people spoke about my father. But it was still a shock when he came home, and people said to me "Look, it's your father!"

She did not say much more about it in the interview. However, in these few words that tumbled out, Danielle established the affective shape of her domestic environment. Her brother, also present in the interview, was born in 1946, so the siblings did not share an equivalent relationship with their father. Renée Christian was also born in 1939. Renée's memories of meeting her father for the first time in 1944 or 1945 are full of sorrow and guilt: "Oh, I didn't know him at all, I didn't want to—, when he came home I didn't even want to give him a kiss. Now I feel sick at heart to think of it, because—, he was wearing a big greatcoat, and he was unshaven and everything—, I couldn't accept that that was my daddy. I was five years old." A man, present in her interview, probably Renée's husband, added: " 'You are not my daddy' [using the formal *vous*], she said to him." A very young child at this time and from this kind of background would usually use *tu*, the informal form of "you," to address her father. The story was evidently one that had often been told in this community of memory; it was central to Renée's understanding of how war had reshaped her life. She added: "Oh, it really affected me, it did. Because, when he left, the poor man—, I've often thought about it, I say to myself, 'My God, to think that I wouldn't even give him a—, he just wanted to say hello, he wanted to kiss me.' Afterwards, it was better, but for me, in my head now, I regret having done that—." Renée's discomfort arises from imagining the hurt she may have caused by denying his place in her life and imagining, wishing, a little ashamed, that she might have behaved otherwise. What goes unsaid is the way the new addition to the family unit caused relations between mother and children to alter in the postwar years.

Strained Mothers

Children frequently felt and witnessed their mothers enduring great strain during the war. These women were juggling family provisions, finances, businesses, elderly relatives, fugitive friends and relatives, and their children's well-being, as well as absent husbands and, sometimes, the grief of widowhood. Bernard Lemaire remarked of his mother, who managed eight children and various relatives for certain periods without her husband: "As time has gone by, I really think that my mother must have been extraordinarily courageous!" Of course, Bernard could not speak from her point of view. Perhaps what appeared to him, as for Georgette Transler, as coping admirably was really lurching from crisis to crisis, barely holding on. Children may not have detected distress, although, as I will show, sometimes they did and it was distressing for them too. Mothers' strain was observed, puzzled over, and worried about by their children. It often pained them to speak of it later on.

Marie-Rolande Cornuéjols watched her mother's distress grow through 1940 as they lost contact with her mobilized father:

And slowly, we heard the bad news [about the impending defeat], and what was striking . . . was that we had no more news from my father. And I can just remember one thing, that Mum just lay down on the bed, was just lying down, and she was reading, and reading, and reading, nonstop, she did nothing but read, read, read. Because, in fact, she was completely out of her mind, she thought that perhaps he had died. She had no news at all, and that she would be a widow, with no profession—because she'd got married when she was sixteen—with no profession and two children, of ten and seven, and she must have been in a terrible state. After that she retained—it's strange—a real hatred of church bells. Because we were in a very small village, and you could hear the bells ringing, and for her, those bells . . . well, I don't know, but in short, for her it must have been absolutely atrocious. I remember that my aunt came to see her and said to her "Last night I dreamed of Raymond"—that's my father—"in a coffin, but he said 'no, I'm not dead.'" And that very evening we had a letter from Dad. He'd been taken prisoner . . . and so Mum learned that he wasn't dead but a prisoner. It's also strange, isn't it, that thing—premonition or coincidence? It's that kind of thing you remember.

Marie-Rolande's visual memory is the child's view of her mother defeated, inactive, obsessively reading, and haunted by the church bells as a specter of death. But telling the story, the adult Marie-Rolande can sympathize with her mother. As they waited in ignorance, their father could have been alive or dead; his death and survival were both for them, at that point, virtual but not actual. But his life was also unfolding along its own contingent path. The dream, seen as a premonition, acts as the first step along a line of actualization for the family, when his survival crossed from virtual to actual. So many possibilities must have run through their minds, been tentatively spoken, been overheard by worried children. Yet the premonition sticks because it began the process of making real. He did not die, so any talk of his death—which, had he died, might have been remembered via other premonitions—dissipated as the reality of his survival became actualized.

Memories of watching their mothers disintegrate emotionally resonate painfully. Nancette Blanchou's parents were arrested in September 1943. Her father was deported and her mother imprisoned in France, where she was given electric shocks and released mentally and physically ill. They awaited news of her father.

The day that she learnt of my dad's death, I will never forget it either. I was at the bottom of the garden. I had gone there, I was very proud because in my little garden, I'd grown a cabbage to sell, and there was a lady who wanted it. So I had gone to fetch my cabbage, but at that moment, a man arrived to tell us that Dad was dead. And Mum screamed. She fell to the ground, she became hysterical. And that, for a child to see her mum like that, on the ground—[she pauses]. After having lost her father. It's really something. And well, after that, Mum went downhill. She, pffffff—, she kept trying to commit suicide—. I didn't want to go to school anymore. I didn't want to go. And that wasn't very well understood at the time. Because I followed her around everywhere, I was so [she emphasizes the word] afraid, and as soon as she was out of my sight, I was beside myself with worry. So we always had someone staying at the house, just in case, eh. And we had to take a knife away from her, I had to take her barbiturates off her, I took the knife, but not alone, the knife because—[she sighs] she wanted to slit her wrists. [She sighs again.]

Nancette's mother died in 1950 of tuberculosis. The memory story begins with a moment of pride, placing her firmly in the vegetable patch. It pivots into the distressing events that unfolded from there.

Paul Maubourg's father was arrested, tortured, and killed for his resistance activity. Paul's interview was filled with sadness. He spoke softly, his face turned away from the camera, his body hunched and immobile. He described the impact of his father's death on his mother: "My mother, she lived in her past. . . . She got remarried a few years later, to a former deportee. This new couple, they were always going to meetings of deportee [associations], to inaugurations of memorials—, they were—, and my stepfather bought a lot of books, he had a collection of books about the war, about deportation—. They never came out of it." After his stepfather died, he said, "my mother was always—, she spent her life at the cemetery, between those two tombs, and the tombs of the other war dead who had no family. She was troubled." His mother sought refuge in her second marriage to a man who had lived what her first husband could have lived had things unfolded differently. Although Paul lost only one parent, his mother and stepfather remained haunted and distracted. Marie-Madeleine Viguié-Moreau actively took steps to ensure she found her own way through. Watching as her mother and sister wept, she said "when I saw my mother in that state, I said to myself 'You're going to become just like your mother.'" She asked to be sent to boarding school where she could study better, and her mother agreed.

I told myself "When you're older, you'll be able to help her." But I don't regret having done that. When I left, I felt very guilty, but nobody there [at the school] knew I was the daughter of a deportee, except the headmistress—. We just didn't talk about it. . . . I went to boarding school because I couldn't stand it anymore. And at boarding school, I made good friends, we would laugh, we would sing, nobody knew I was the daughter of a deportee. And in contrast, my sister, she carried on weeping with Mum. . . . But that, that saved me.

Separating herself from obsessive distress, probing questions, and feeling out of place gave her the capacity to recover. A wife's grief is not the same as a child's. Thus, a further affective gap could open between mothers and their children in the aftermath of loss.

PAUSE—DANIÈLE—THE STRAIN OF UNCERTAINTY

Danièle Dubowsky's mother was central to her family's survival. But battling separation from her husband, internment in Drancy and Vittel camps, the long train journey to Palestine, and the disappointment they met there took their toll. The memories are told from twin perspectives: the child witnessing her mother's actions and the adult reflecting on her mother's strength. Danièle's mother was a Jewish Palestinian citizen and thus under British protection. Her three children had been born in France. Danièle's father had an American passport and was interned as an American (not as a Jew) after the attack on Pearl Harbor in 1941. Her mother was able to visit him with her children:

So we used to take the train . . . and we'd go to Gare du Nord, and then Compiègne, and then we'd have to walk through different rooms. And before we got there, Mum would pinch my cheeks, like that, so that I'd have red cheeks. And when we went in, Dad would always say "Oh, thank you Sara, don't the children look well!" And I never felt that Mum was telling a lie, I truly thought she was doing that to make Dad happy.

At this point, the focus was her husband's morale: if he saw they were coping, he too would cope. So began Danièle's mother's struggle under the increasingly difficult circumstances of an uncertain everyday existence.

The family had received a letter of invitation to Palestine from Danièle's grandfather, which would enable them to escape worsening anti-Semitic measures in France. Danièle's father told his wife that she should seek permission to be "repatriated" with the children; he would join them in Palestine as soon as he could. Danièle recalled visiting the Kommandantur with her mother:

> I've got a memory that is very, very vivid, because I recall that we had to go up a grand staircase, and I was holding Mum's hand. I was about seven or eight years old. We went up the staircase, and at the top of the staircase we went into an office—I could film it, eh, re-enact the scene—and there was this little man, I remember thinking that he was very small, a bit like Charlie Chaplin, and he had a whip too, like those we knew [later] at Drancy—, and he spoke to Mum, and Mum said over and over "I demand to be repatriated *with my children*" [Danièle emphasized the last three words]. And this man said, "But Madame, we have *never* [with emphasis] separated a mother from her children!" Oh, oh, oh! I was so relieved, I felt calmer—, no matter what, I won't be separated from my mum! I remember that it was very, very—, and that my mother was relieved too. And so we left with this guarantee. Which was a dreadful lie, but we didn't know that.

Danièle's later knowledge of the Shoah surely recalls to her mind the fate of so many other Jewish children who were separated from their mothers; for her, this virtual future hung over the family like a sword of Damocles. For now, though, all seemed well.

On the night of their arrest in early 1944, Danièle comments again on her mother's astute reading of the situation: "In contrast to other ladies that we saw at Drancy, Mum packed clothes, tea towels, warm things. She didn't take any jewelry, she didn't take any money. . . . She took a can of kerosene, and two liters of pure bleach, and a bag of camphor mothballs." Although Danièle believes her parents had no idea about the existence of the death camps, she acted in the knowledge of her husband's internment: "She had it in mind that her husband had been arrested three years earlier, and she'd seen the camp. So I suppose she knew that we weren't going to the Ritz." Danièle attributes the fact that the children were barely ill—save an ear infection for her brother—in Drancy to her mother's meticulous attention to their hygiene. Every day she rubbed their hair with kerosene to ward off head lice, washed their hands with bleach solution, and hung mothballs around their necks to cleanse their breathing. Danièle spoke of "the transmission of life force, from mother to child" that kept them going. "Mum protected us all that time, I remember," she said. Her protectiveness pre-dated and outlasted their incarceration. Danièle commented: "All she'd ever wanted was to have children. And she had her children, and she became something between a tigress and a mother hen. She was very nice to everyone, but she was a tough old girl, and I think she suffered a lot from loneliness. We didn't talk about it. But she'd become hysterical if anyone touched her children. She was like that all the time, whatever happened to us." When her son's ear infection became known to the guards, he was taken to the infirmary. Danièle's mother would not stand for this. She remembers the guard saying "Madame, you are not allowed [in here]," and her mother responded, with great force, "Yes, I am, that's my son!" The child was given back into his mother's care. Danièle recalls her shouting at him, forbidding him to get ill again, forbidding him to show weakness: "I forbid you to be ill, I forbid you to cry." The infirmary was a dangerous place to be.

But this strong woman could only withstand so much. As D-Day approached, some of the inmates in Drancy were separated from the others. They all had American or British connections. They were taken to Vittel camp, where Danièle recalls conditions were much better. Her mother left Drancy with tea towels wrapped around her feet instead of shoes. They were reaching the end of their physical and emotional resources, but, Danièle said, "we were going to something better." Perhaps believing that she would be reunited with her husband, "Mum was very—, at the same time, she was happy and relieved, as though something had ended, but she had never been so anxious before, she was much more irritable." Her husband was not there, although contacts were renewed. They remained in Vittel for a month and by the middle of July had arrived in Palestine. But still there was no reunion: "What I had understood was that my mum was going to see her dad, we were going to Mum's family to wait for the end of the war, and Dad was going to join us there." The expectation of seeing her husband again and his continued absence tormented Danièle's mother. They lived in Danièle's grandfather's house but did not receive a warm welcome from female relatives there. Disappointment turned to despair. Danièle described "an accident" that put her mother in the hospital for three months: her hair caught fire on a stove and burned her head and shoulders. Danièle said, "I heard the adults talking, and I understood without understanding everything": they insinuated that it was a suicide attempt. Danièle's memories show the desperate strain that was placed on mothers, particularly Jewish mothers. Riven by endless uncertainty, Danièle's mother plunged into crisis. She lurched from difficulty to difficulty, expending so much energy on her children and husband that when hope died, she had nothing left. But she did survive. She always wore a scarf around her head to hide her scars. The family returned to France in 1947.

New Affective Others

Family separation was a major part of the home front experience of the war years in France. Some scholars have argued that because rural child-care solutions were common in early twentieth-century France, whether though relatives, wet nurses, or *colonies de vacances*, the wartime separation of children from parents should not be seen as unusual.[4] Downs suggests that habituation to separation is one reason the evacuation of children from French cities does not feature in national versions of the French wartime past. Yet family separation also came about from fathers' absences and mothers' breakdowns. It also happened in families that had never resorted to such measures previously. Furthermore, from autumn 1939 family separation must be seen through the lens of war, colored by the affective, political, and ideological factors specific to the era. Wartime family separation is part of the conjuncture of war, with its "different rhythm"[5] of mood and feeling. Importantly, and respecting people's capacity to analyze their own experiences, family separation was not understood by interviewees as normal. Cécile Bramé from Brest said: "My father was all alone in Brest, my mother was in Camaret, and I was in Pleyben. It's this separation of families that also created anxiety, I would say." War had caused the separation and war caused this child's anxiety, especially given that her father worked at the port, which was regularly bombed by the Allies. It was not just war and not just separation but family separation in war that mattered. Also in Brest, I asked Yvette Chapalain how she understood the experience of war for a child. She said: "Destruction. First, because they separated children from their parents. Destruction of the house where my grandfather lived, my grandmother, and so on. That was also dramatic. And also separated from childhood friends, because I was—, I didn't have my schoolfriends with me. So yes. A feeling of destruction. Absolutely. Children need to be with their families." Again, family separation is made a root cause of distress and identified as a central dimension of children's lives in war. Yvette was twelve or thirteen when evacuated to a boarding school with her sister, and she desperately missed her mother: "There were no more goodnights, in the evenings, you see. My mother wasn't with us at bedtime. Tears, tears, thinking of home." Yvette is not recounting a prewar pattern of behavior where family separation was so commonplace as to be emotionally negligible. To negate the context of war does a disservice to the particularity of these experiences. Many recalled separation in detail because of its affective intensity, in negative terms but also more positively when new bonds were formed with people and places.

Some interviewees spoke of family separation only briefly. It is difficult to know whether this brevity covered deep feeling, stemmed from a reticence to speak or muted intensity, or was the result of an interview that focused on other matters. Marie-Rolande Cornuéjols spoke of the moment in 1940 when her family returned to Paris after the exodus: "Mum didn't want to go back to our house, so instead she moved in with her sister and she left me with some friends who were primary school teachers, so I stayed there with her friends, who I liked very much. I didn't suffer, eh. And Mum kept my brother with her, and they lived with her sister." Marie-Rolande stipulates that she did not suffer, responding to an unasked question. Perhaps her mother, brother, and aunt were living close by; perhaps she was happy to be away from them. The memory goes no further. Other recollections of separation were truncated by later, more striking events. Marcel Zaidner was nine years old when he was first evacuated in 1939:

> That summer, my parents sent me to Bercq-plage. . . . Before the big [exodus of 1940], there was a first exodus. My father was Polish and he signed up to the French army as a volunteer, so he stayed in Paris, and my mother went to Blois. And so I came back from Bercq-plage on a train, with the Red Cross, with a little label attached to me. That was my first experience of war. And then we went back home. The war receded for a little while, and we came back to Paris. But then there was the collapse, the German army arrived, and I became part of the flood of the exodus with my parents.

At the age of nine, he was not too young to have had memorable experiences, but no further details of Bercq-plage emerged. Marcel described the 1940 exodus in far more detail. This time he was with both of his parents, so memories were anchored through later family talk.[6] Vichy's anti-Semitic measures began in late 1940, with consequences for Marcel and his family. Thus, the first separation from his parents in 1939 was compressed to a sliver of memory by the weight of what followed.

In other cases, bonds formed with carers outside the family are narrated enthusiastically. Denise Algret was sent to the countryside near Lyon when the evacuation of children there became obligatory in 1944. Her brother went elsewhere. Her parents had friends in the countryside, but they lived far away and Denise's parents feared they would be unable to visit. Luckily, a young man who was at that time repainting their shop offered, with his wife, to take the girl. "I loved it," said Denise. "Absolutely loved it! It's one of my really, really lovely memories!" Denise found herself in a "youthful environment, dynamic, we'd go out, have a good time . . . we did things we didn't really do at home with my parents." The young man was involved in the resistance, and Denise witnessed unusual things such as guns stored under a bed. The memories were sticky with exciting or intriguing novel experiences. Evacuee Colette Streicher was integrated into a new family: "Everyone had adopted me so much that I had uncles, aunties, grannies, grandads. And you see, I think that at seven years old, if you give a kid lots of affection and everything, well, I didn't miss my parents." Christian Le Goff was baptized during his evacuation, and the couple who took him in became his godmother and godfather: "Indirectly, I became part of the family afterwards," he said. Roger Davre said of the woman who took him in, "I was her son." Likewise, Colette Streicher stated categorically of her adoptive family, "I was their daughter." War intruded into these children's lives in a strangely constructive way, giving them supplementary families and reshaping futures positively.

Evacuation could complicate relationships with children's own parents. Jacques Prieur was sent by his widowed mother to the Creuse at a young age, brusquely collected by her in 1947, and taken back to a Paris he could not remember. He longed for his adoptive parents and the countryside he knew. His mother had remarried and had two more sons. Jacques found himself in a strange place with a strange family and was forbidden to speak of his former life. Colette Streicher remembered crying when she had to return to Paris:

> I can still hear my own little voice saying "Oh, well, now I go to catechism, I do," and my parents were atheists. There was nothing worse than that! But

my parents—I think this was very good of them—they said, "Alright, well look here," they said to Madame and Monsieur Gadeix, "if you want, we can get her baptized, and you'll be her godfather and godmother." And so in 1946, they came up to Paris and I was baptized, and they came back two years later for my first Communion.

She seemed to feel some shame for her past behavior and how it must have made her mother feel: "Every night, I'd cry and cry, 'Oh, I want my Mummy Gadeix,' and I would even tell my mother that I didn't love her, eh. I would say 'No, no, I want my Mummy Gadeix.' " Unlike in Jacques Prieur's case, her parents chose to send their daughter back to the countryside regularly, maintaining and strengthening the connection. Relations between the two families were very cordial; Madame Gadeix's son spent his honeymoon in Paris with Colette's family.

Thérèse Allglas-Cymmerman was born in 1941. In 1942, as mass roundups of Jews intensified, she was placed with a couple in the countryside outside Paris. She lived with them until she was eight years old:

> I was very lucky, because they taught me how to read, to write, to know how to behave even though I was so young. I was very, very well brought up, in contrast to other hidden children who I've spoken to. . . . They were such altruistic people, they didn't want any money at all. . . . [And as I got older], they were always interested in how I was doing at school, at high school, what I wanted to do in life. They were people who always looked after me, even from a distance, if you see what I mean.

Her own extended family were tailors and tried to pay the foster parents back with good suits and jackets. Thérèse continued to visit them regularly, occasionally with her mother and uncle. But returning to her mother's care at the age of eight was not easy. Her memory story collapses the times of her life together. She remembers through her own experiences of being a mother and a grandmother:

> I think that the hardest thing for me was going back to my mother. Because, I've had children myself, and now I've got grandchildren, and I ask myself how you'd react, having been separated from your parents between the ages of one and eight, how you could build a relationship with someone you've not seen for so many years. . . . I've always asked myself that question—. But I've

always asked myself as well, as I've got no memory of it—the day that I had to leave Monsieur and Madame M------. It must have been totally heart-wrenching for them. They'd always treated me as their granddaughter. And now someone had taken her away from them. It must have been terrible.

She reflects empathetically and imaginatively on what she and her mother lost in their relationship and on what her foster parents lost in losing her. She remarked on her emotional distance from her mother:

it was hard to build a relationship with my mother. I remember that very well. There are things I can't remember any more, but I know that it was a struggle every day, because I'd left her at one year old, I didn't have any memory of her, or of her family, not at all. I know it was hard, and later it was—, indeed, all my life I have had "problems"—in inverted commas, because I don't want to make out that they were serious problems—I've had "problems" communicating with my mother. Because she's a woman who says very little. She never told me that she loved me. Never. I don't recall her kissing me goodnight. All those bonds that you have, or at least I had with my children, that I now have with my grandchildren—.

Her father was deported and killed, and she only began to learn about him when she was a teenager. After her mother's death, Thérèse found her father's papers: his naturalization certificate, his death certificate, and his identity card. She visited Yad Vashem, taking his photo with her, so that he could be among those remembered there. When asked by the interviewer, she replied that she had not found this too difficult psychologically. There, she began the process to have the status of Righteous Among the Nations awarded posthumously to her foster parents. This was granted in 2008 and celebrated in the town where they had lived in 2009.

In Eagleton's words, we live "our sensate lives together";[7] memories reflect the proximity of others inside the unfolding everyday and cohere around important affective bonds. A memory story is always social: it contains the stories of all of those whose lives impress upon our own. In this wartime world, children's love relations were affected by events of the immediate and wider social and political environment, which twisted them in unpredictable ways.

WAR AND HATE

The recollection of negative others in children's lives sits inside the moral framework of behaviors and attitudes that is peculiar to the world of wartime France. These others, who were hated, feared, disliked, or despised, included most obviously the Germans occupying France but also people linked to the Vichy régime including Marshal Pétain, the French police, and the Milice, sometimes the "reckless" resistance, and the Allies. In recounting memories populated by these people, interviewees speak alongside the regimes of memory that structure public understandings of morality in this period. It seems they also speak with imagined audiences beyond the interview in mind and from their positions inside their communities of memory. Rememberers try to articulate the complex moral landscape of their childhoods, making and correcting perceived judgments about past behavior. Morally acceptable or morally reprehensible criteria emerge. These do not belong exclusively to one group or another. What mattered was whether an individual acted independently of orders, whether they abused their power, and whether they were compassionate or cruel. Betrayal and treachery come to the fore as powerful wrongs, with selfishness and recklessness also castigated.

The German Enemy

Knowledge, memories, and myths of the First World War and even the Franco-Prussian War shaped what parents told their children in 1939. The north of France had been occupied by the Germans during the First World War, and atrocities were committed against civilians. Women and girls were particularly at risk, although young children did not understand why. Many learned from older male relatives what the Germans were capable of; Robert Belleuvre commented, "we were afraid of the Germans, and it's because of that that—, being a child, you fear the worst. They said that in 1914, they'd used gas—, and so we were filled with dread, naturally, and we asked ourselves whether this time, there wouldn't be gas again too." Sonia Agache also said, "my father had been gassed during the First World War, and so, it's true, it was a terrifying fear, eh!" Michel Floch in Brest remarked that "they also said that the Boches would cut children's hands off. We were scared witless, it's true," and Raymond Bachelard described the rumors flying as the Wehrmacht advanced across May 1940: "The

Germans kill kids, they'll chop your hands off." This perception was repeated across the interviews. The contrast between this and the Germans' "correct" attitude toward the French population when the occupation began makes this memory worth telling. Despite this surprising turn, many children were still forbidden contact with them. Lola Grynberg said, "we weren't allowed, as children, to take any sweets, any chocolate, that the Germans might give out, because they told us that it was poisoned. You weren't allowed to take anything from them, so we didn't." Feelings other than fear were not impossible, though. Jean-Claude Bourtourault recounted being forbidden to interact with German soldiers: "Of course, our parents told us not to go and see those men there, and they forbade us from taking any of the sweets they might offer us—because that also existed." His comment "that also existed" speaks to an imagined audience or a perception he feels may be held by this audience. He corrects an implicit image of the inhumane German that would not permit the offering of sweets to children. The interviewees make clear distinctions between the different Germans in France that derive from their experience of having been there. Bernard Lemaire's description demonstrates the contingent ways in which affective orientations grow out of interpersonal encounters. Bernard's school in Lille was divided in two. Half was occupied by the Germans. He described going into the playground one day:

> There was this German—to me, he seemed old—sitting on the steps. And he called me over, with two or three other boys, because he wanted to give me a sweet. And I refused. I refused because my mother had told us "Never, ever accept anything from the Germans," people talked about how they poisoned sweets. And that, it really struck me because I saw this fellow there, he just wanted to give me a sweet. Perhaps he had a son about the same age.

Bernard reflects upon his own obedience to his mother's interdiction but also now wonders whether he lacked compassion toward someone he now recognizes as a fellow man and a father.

Across the memory stories, there are many instances of German soldiers being quite pleasant. These men of the earlier period of occupation confounded fearful expectations. Rememberers also characterized them, in some cases, as better behaved than French people, building a didactic point for a modern-day audience. Nancette Blanchou's parents were arrested for their resistance activity.

After her parents were gone, the contents of their family home were taken by the French authorities. Following her mother's release from prison, they went back to the house: "My grandmother told me 'Do you know, there was a German who went up to the house and left a kilo of sugar and some money, for the first—', eh. So I'm telling you, my grandmother told me, there weren't just bad Germans, eh. Some of them were good men, all the same." This was not the only instance in which Nancette remarked that Germans demonstrated more compassion than French people: "I got to know this afterwards from Mum, that when she was in prison, there was a German who brought her wool, and she would knit him socks for his children, to send back to Germany. I know that because she told me herself. She told me that. That there were some nice Germans. Much nicer than the French [prison guards]." Nancette and other interviewees made a distinction between doing good and being bad. Blanket generalizations and stereotypes based on nationality were rejected by those who had experienced such encounters. Christian Gaillard's family had Germans billeted with them. He commented that "they weren't unpleasant, if you like, to the children. They'd give us chocolate—, at the time, I remember—, but they weren't close relationships—. There was the language barrier, of course. Some of them had a few words of French, but it wasn't always the case. So it was very limited really. We were wary of them." While relations were superficially cordial, an underlying tension remained. Arnaud Saunier had Germans billeted in his house too: "The Germans helped me with my homework. . . . I'd be working, like that, at home, and then perhaps the Germans would come back, you see, and would show me, for example, how to do a sum, something like that—." Such encounters with a friendly but nonetheless dominant occupier were far more complicated in relation to arrest or persecution. Marcel Zaidner recalled the evening the Gestapo came to his family's apartment, searching for evidence of his father's communism. He differentiates between the Gestapo and the Feldgendarme who accompanied them:[8]

> [The] Feldgendarme . . . must have been a decent enough chap, I suppose. I was with my sister on the bed while my mother was following these fellows around—and they didn't find anything, by the way, because everything was well hidden—and the Feldgendarme came and sat on the bed with us and played with us. I don't know if he saw his own children in us—, but, in short, that shows the contradictory nature of this period—

Wartime relations unfolded in surprising ways. The memory is sticky because of the incongruity of the scene. In its multitemporality it establishes a sense of foreboding around the unpredictability of these perpetrators. How friendly would a Feldgendarme be when given orders to round up women and children?

Marcel's memory and Bernard Lemaire's highlight a common feature of depictions of the Germans by people who were children during the war: they were fathers. The articulation of German soldiers as fathers serves to humanize them in these memory stories. Nicole Boscariol rejected a fatherly advance one day as she was walking home from school: "He wanted to give me a hug. Mum thought I must have resembled his little sister or his daughter. He was a tall man, a big tall blond man—, I got away quickly. He wanted to hug me." Henri Girardon spoke of the Germans billeted at his family house near to Brest: "I saw another one of them going out into the garden one day, from the house, he went down into the garden. I was with my father. And there, I saw he had some photographs in his hand, and he was crying. And he told my father that his wife and his two children had been killed in an air raid." Henri's account suggests the universality of suffering. Henri's father listened to the bereaved man; the two men were connected by the shared possibility of loss. Danielle Durville had scant memories of an encounter with a German, but the story related by her mother shows an evolving affective orientation:

> Mum said to me, "I'd never been so ashamed in my life," because when I was little, I was blond, I had hair like golden wheat. I looked German, very, very blond, with blue eyes. And she told me that we came out of Marcel Sembat metro station, in Boulogne, and she told me, "Across the way, there was a German, and he came over to us, and took you by the hand. So I was holding one of your hands, and the German the other one. And people turned to stare at us." And he said "me," he spoke a little bit of French, "child like her. But bombs. Kaput!" And he went away in tears. And as my Mum said, "For the first time ever, I pitied a German. Because he was like us." His little girl had been killed by the bombs, and I reminded him of her.

In this community of memory, largely comprising people who were parents, grandparents, and great-grandparents, it was frequently remarked that German lives were also destroyed by the war. In the telling of these stories, being fathers or good family men separated them from those who perpetrated crimes and atrocities; being bereaved fathers pulled them even further away. Yet fathers and good family men were nonetheless responsible for some of the worst crimes of the period.

In some memory stories, German railway workers befriended French railway workers. Railway workers had a very strong professional identity. The French railways were crucial to the occupation and the German war machine, and they were overseen by German personnel, civilians at the lower levels. Not only would this ensure that goods and people could be moved effectively out of France, but it aimed to prevent or reduce theft, sabotage, and other resistance activity. Relations were not always cordial. Anne-Marie Laurens remembered hatred in her father's eyes as his young daughter was greeted by his German overseer: "Naturally, Dad didn't like them at all. I'm telling you, I can still see his—his eyes, as the German came towards me, Dad was behind him, looking daggers at him." The interviewer asked if her father therefore saw them as Germans first and *cheminots* (railwaymen) second. She said emphatically that *he* did but refused to comment on anyone else, saying "there were collaborators everywhere." From her perspective, any friendlier relations between French and German railwaymen were tarred with that brush. In the suburbs of Lille, in districts defined by the working-class politics and identity of their railway workers, André and Josette Dutilleul saw the German railway workers differently:

ANDRÉ: They were railwaymen—
JOSETTE: —they were people like us—
ANDRÉ: —you see, they weren't soldiers—

André said that when his family returned home after the 1940 exodus, they found two German railwaymen living in their apartment, which had been requisitioned: "Well! Apartment gone: taken by the Germans. So my mother spoke to the two men, and they said 'Madame, look, we have placed all of your things into these cupboards. We have locked them. Nothing has gone.' So we thought, 'oh, well, at least they're honest.' Nobody stole anything, nothing was taken. They said 'Because you've come back, we'll look for lodgings elsewhere, and when we find, we leave.'" This considerate attitude is, of course, a striking contrast to the looting experienced by others during the exode and, more systematically, by persecuted French Jews.[9] André also described these Germans as overly friendly: "One day, what should I see at the school gates? The two German railwaymen were there, and they were waiting for me, maybe because they had little kids themselves, and, oh! Pffffff! I blushed from head to toe with the shame of it—Germans had come to pick me up from school! I didn't know where to put myself!" The boy's embarrassment in the happening past had shifted over time to take in these men's search for some kind of normality in the act of collecting a son from school. André explained that one of the men, Konrad, "had been in the First World War and he said 'Sad, war, is sad.' He'd come and listen to Radio London with us!" These Germans—Konrad and Edward—were working-class railwaymen; they were older and not (it seemed) steeped in National Socialism; they had shared the trauma of the Great War; they were fatherly, friendly, worthy of compassion, and interested in a world beyond Nazi propaganda. This complicates the moral framework of enemy-occupier-victim relations considerably.

Some interviewees had their most sustained contact with the enemy after the liberation, when German prisoners of war were put to work in French agriculture.[10] Christian Le Goff, evacuated from Paris to the Creuse, said "the first Germans that I mixed with were German prisoners who came onto the farms." He shared his life on the farm with them and said of one: "I cried when he left, I can remember that. I cried because he was my good pal, that German was." Marie-Josèphe Devaux explained that her family had seven prisoners working for them over the period 1945 to 1947. She remembered that the first one, Ernst—a very thin man, she said—later came back to visit her parents. He joined in their family life, even collecting the children from the station when they returned from school. Claudine Marc recalled German prisoners of war living in barracks in their town and her father having some kind of responsibility for them. Her memory was vague but stuck because of her own small participation in the task: "I remember that he had a stock of tobacco to distribute, and I used to enjoy arranging the packets of tobacco." Evacuee Roger Davre and his friend Marcel Dumas described their relations with German prisoners who were billeted onto local farms. Marcel recalled one "who died a couple of years ago," showing that the relationship had had endured. Roger elaborated:

Charles, yes, Charles. When he arrived at le Grand Breuil, he was only sixteen, I think. And later he married a local girl, from the Creuse. And one day, I met him when I was down for the holidays, and I said "Well, Charles, how come you didn't go back to Germany?" [Putting on a German accent] "What am I going to do with those morons back there? They're all Communists now, it's East Germany. I'm happy in the Creuse!"

In these personal encounters, what is remembered is what was, and is, felt. The friendship that developed between Charles and the locals may not have been easy. Indeed, in Burgundy, Jean-Claude Bourtourault remarked upon lasting tensions between local people and settled Germans. These relationships are an odd outcome of the war, modifying yet again understandings of the enemy through the shifting of affective orientations inside everyday encounters.

Why are there so many positive recollections of Germans? First, many mobilized Germans in the earlier years had not grown up indoctrinated by Nazi ideology. Many were happier to be stationed in France than elsewhere, particularly after the Eastern Front opened. After November 1942, however, the occupiers' manpower crisis brought Germans to France who had been brutalized by action on the Eastern Front. Second, these kinds of memories were not told by the Jewish rememberers. Third, these memory stories typically recount specific interactions with specific Germans rather than the actions of a group. Fourth, as we will see, the Germans of 1944 exhibited very different kinds of behavior in the face of impending defeat. And finally, a great deal of effort in the postwar era went into Franco-German reconciliation. The multitemporality of such memory stories projects postwar reconciliation back into the past. To build lasting peace in Europe, French people had to recognize that German people had also suffered. Denise Algret recounted her visit to Germany immediately after the war and her shock at seeing the ruins of bombed cities. She also emphasized her father's involvement in erecting a monument to Frenchmen killed in Villeurbanne; he ensured that the inscription read "to the victims of Nazi barbarity": this was to be seen as a Nazi atrocity, not a German one. Marie-Madeleine Viguié-Moreau, whose father had died in deportation, remarked that when she was young she had a strong aversion to Germans visiting Cluny: "I used to see the German tourists, speaking German, and it was an instinct, I'd be paralyzed"; however, over time she grew to recognize that "not all Germans were Nazis. . . . Germans are also people like us." Her granddaughter feared Marie-Madeleine would be upset if she took German language at school; Marie-Madeleine was not. Communication was the key, she said, to preventing war. Cécile Bramé became a teacher and organized a class trip to Germany. But the project was personal too:

For me, I tried to forget the war by going to Germany. [I said to the head-teacher] "I want to go to Germany." She stared at me: "To Germany?" "Yes,

I want to go to Germany." She said to me, "Well, as you wish." So we organized a trip to Germany and I said to myself, "this will bring me peace." . . . I wanted to go to Germany with my pupils to put the war behind me, and I did. Because I realized that Germans, you see, they were like us. They'd also suffered a good deal too—

Cécile was proactive in creating her peace. I interviewed her with her friend Serge Aubrée, who was more reticent: "But when I went to Alsace, for instance—, it's a beautiful region, eh, I paint, I painted the grapevines, I thought the Alsatians were really great people, very nice, what have you, but at the edge of Alsace is a river, a river with a bridge over it, to Germany. I didn't go and see it. I didn't go. I said 'No, no, no, I don't even want to go and see it.'" Serge's position had softened over time. He had grandchildren who had studied German at school too. His family had received German exchange students, and he had met German painters through his work. He said: "Now, I would go. . . . . It's a step towards peace. Now I'm proud to be a European, I'm proud. I'm happy. I'm pleased to think we're all Europeans." Remembering the frightening enemy as a man who also thought, loved, and suffered was a retrospective projection of postwar peace building. It could even be done by those whose lives had been devastated by Nazi ambition, although Jewish interviewees did not articulate this kind of memory. When Germans were cruel, they were put into certain groups: they were Gestapo, or SS, or the Das Reich division, not ordinary soldiers, requisitioned railway workers, or good family men.

The French Enemy

The Vichy regime has a low profile in the memory stories. Interviewees rarely offered recollections of the regime's political figures. A few of the oldest remembered participating in orchestrated events in the name of Marshal Pétain. However, most children had little or no awareness of political decisions affecting their day-to-day lives, except in very direct cases. The treatment of Jews by the French authorities is present in several stories, as is the Service de Travail Obligatoire (STO, or Forced Labor Service), and some rememberers link these directly to Vichy. Childhood memory stories can suggest the impressions policies make as they work their way through a population but rarely offer direct reflections on them. In these narratives, comments on Vichy and Pétain are often presented as parents' or teachers' perspectives; children's points of view were shaped in relation to these. Are memories being suppressed because of the shame of having backed Marshal Pétain? Maybe, but not necessarily. The discrediting of Pétain and his government in the immediate postwar period nonetheless ripples back through memories. Léa Duclos remarked, "Pétain, well, I heard more about him after the war than during it." Nonetheless, the memory stories are valuable in their elaboration of a range of positions held at the time or since.

Children's most likely contact with the *maréchaliste* cult was the singing of the song *Maréchal nous voilà!* The song was supposed to be sung every morning in schools at a flag ceremony, just as Pétain's portrait was supposed to replace the republican image of Marianne in all schools.[11] Simone Fauron commented on the omnipresence of the song: "You heard it everywhere," she said. "You didn't need to learn it, it just went in by itself!" Simone also said that she never sang it herself but did not explain why. Experiences of singing the song vary. Eugène commented, "As I was top of the class, it was me who had to lead all my mates in the singing," but offered no reflection on how he felt about this or Marshal Pétain. Sylvette Leclerc did not recall the song being given a special place in the school day. She said they were "obliged" to learn it, but "it was just one of the songs we sang." She was aware of her teacher's disapproval, though: "he didn't like it."[12] In Jacqueline Béné's memory, the song was not privileged either. When her class returned to school in the autumn of 1940, they were urged to give their all to the Marshal. But when asked about singing at school, she said: "*Maréchal nous voilà!* Yes. And *La Marseillaise*. I used to sing *La Marseillaise*, things like that." Do the regimes of memory of the postwar years encourage her to balance *maréchalisme* with a more palatable kind of patriotism? Or did her teacher deliberately put these two songs together on the program? It is impossible to say. Roger Davre was not the only interviewee to burst into song: "*Maréchal, nous voilà—!* [singing loudly] well, I could sing the whole thing to you, I know the words by heart. 'In front of you, the savior,' right." Roger said he learned the song at his holiday camps in 1942 and 1943, not at school. At his school in the Creuse in 1944, he was categorical that the song was not sung. Such was the local mood that the teacher could not have attempted it: "it would have caused a ruckus." Françoise Yessad was also of the same opinion. She had no recollection of having sung it, despite a love of singing: "We sang things, but I don't remember having sung that. Don't forget, the Creuse was a land of resistance." While *Maréchal nous voilà!* was intended to pull children into the *maréchaliste* cult, the singing may not always have been implemented in ways the ideologues hoped—or so it seems from these recollections, which have their own implicit or explicit nuances.

Some children refused to sing for their own reasons. Marie-Madeleine Viguié-Moreau, whose father was arrested with his resistance group in February 1944, said: "The teachers had to do things which were imposed upon them, for example, they'd make us sing *Maréchal nous voilà!*, and well, I remember that I found a way—, you know those people who sing, just opening their mouth, what do they call that?—well I did that. I knew the words by heart, we had to learn it, but like this [she mimes singing the words, but making no sound]." The interviewer asked her why she did this. She continued: "I said to myself that it was Pétain's fault—I got it all a bit muddled up—, I said to myself that it was Marshal Pétain's fault that Dad had been taken away. And I began to be really furious with him. . . . I don't know exactly why, but I didn't like Marshal Pétain at all, that's for sure." Nancette Blanchou's parents were also arrested. Her relation with the song *Maréchal nous voila!* is similar to Marie-Madeleine's:

> Anyway, at home I learned that I mustn't sing *Maréchal nous voila!* I know very well that when we raised the flag, because they made us get in a circle, we'd raise the flag and sing *Maréchal nous voila!* . . . and I always had to keep time, I'd have to start the singing to set the tempo. And I remember very well that I absolutely refused [she emphasizes the word] to sing *Maréchal nous voila!* I used to pretend [she emphasizes the word] to sing [it]. I'd been forbidden from singing it, and I didn't want to sing it. And that's how I know that I understood things quite well.

The memory provides her with evidence that she had an awareness of *something* in relation to Pétain, which oriented her feelings away from him.

Henri Buc recalled that at his school the children were encouraged to write to Pétain "to tell him of our affection for him." He commented wryly that they did so with more enthusiasm than their teacher. He also remembered the older children at his school preparing "to go and see the Marshal in Aubusson." Christian Gaillard, who attended a *lycée* in Troyes, recalled attending "official ceremonies organized by the town of Troyes, all the schools, the high schools, assembled at the Town Hall, for the glory of the Marshal." He commented that their teachers took them "and we just followed them like sheep." Christian nonetheless recalled that his teachers steered clear of political talk in the classroom:

> Our teachers never spoke to us about either the Germans or the Occupation, nothing at all. I don't have any memory of it. No, it was all very neutral on that side of things. . . . I don't remember ever having heard any words in support of the regime, so to speak, from them. I think that was sincere, to some degree, but also because it wasn't in their interest to do it, because they didn't want to create tension.

Even among the boys themselves, "it wasn't something we talked about." Vichy never built a coherent youth movement, in large part because there were so many competing groups young people could join, not least those of various churches.[13] Several interviewees, such as André Dutilleul, Yves Le Roy, and Henri Le Turquais, attended Catholic youth clubs (*patronages*), and Bernard Bauwens and Robert Belleuvre were in other, nonspecified youth groups, possibly linked to local workplaces. Jean-Claude Bourtourault was enrolled in the *maréchaliste* children's group the Coeurs Vaillants: "[I was] recruited, first by the Church and then by the Marshal, eh. They were practically the same thing. So, recruited into all sorts of youth groups, in all these processions that we had to take part in, I was one of the little ones who had to throw rose petals into the streets." He did not remember this fondly. He recalled being told off, punished, and forced to participate in processions and ceremonies. He did not express a specific animosity towards Pétain, however, and his family had the leader's portrait at home, "like everyone," he said.

Memories of Marshal Pétain were, in some cases, stuck to memories of Charles de Gaulle. To remember Pétain evoked de Gaulle and vice versa. As with the *Marseillaise* and *Maréchal nous voila!*, different symbols coexisted, and children listened and tried to understand what each meant. Jacqueline Béné was asked what her parents thought about de Gaulle: "I don't rightly know, because it was difficult to understand. Because on one hand, there was Marshal Pétain who was, how shall I say, honored, respected, the great victor, the great soldier, the great patriot—, and on the other hand, there was General de Gaulle, who was over there, who said we had to continue the fight—, we had no idea, no idea at all what we should do." A question about de Gaulle brings forth the more powerful initial attachment to Marshal Pétain. On the other hand, when Simone Fauron was asked whether there were images of Pétain at her school, she responded: "I don't remember—, the Marshal, yes. And then we put de Gaulle in our schoolbooks, we found some way of getting pictures of General de Gaulle! [Laughing] He was our idol! He was the Johnny Hallyday of our day. Well, it's true, eh! He was a god for us, de Gaulle, a god. . . . That's to tell you that, for me, he wasn't a politician, he was the savior of France!" Here, a question about Marshal Pétain brought forth the stronger attachment to de Gaulle. Pétain was on the walls, consumed passively and without, it seems, much affective intensity. But de Gaulle was actively sought and brought into a greater intimacy with the girls. He appeared to matter in a way that Pétain did not; at least, that is how Simone recounts it.

The interviews echo the evolution of attitudes toward Pétain and his regime: the Vichy of 1940 was very different from the Vichy of 1944 and enjoyed great popular support in the wake of the defeat.[14] Henri Buc said that in 1940, "for a while, I think, the Fren—, we were all for collaborating." His use of the word *collaborateur* as an adjective is ambiguous; did he mean that they were keen to collaborate with the Pétain regime or with the Germans? The latter is the more usual usage. He modifies his initial expression, which would have attributed this quality to French people generally; Henri wanted to be honest. "*Nous*" brought him into complicity, either by dint of being French or by reducing the scale to his own circle, whether local, familial, or schoolboy. He includes a temporal qualification; this was only "for a while." Madame Sauvonnet is similarly circumspect. She said of the new regime: "Everyone, the whole family, all our relatives, they agreed on the spot. Then, well afterwards—". The sentence is left hanging, but the listener understands that early attachments shifted. Simone Fauron recalled her father's opinion in 1940: "At first, my father trusted him, he said 'That old boy, he'll get us out if this,' but he was quickly disenchanted, eh." Pierre Tainturier said that in 1940, "we believed in Marshal Pétain." His tone was defensive. He knew this attitude was discredited. He added: "But that did pass quite quickly, as far as I can recall." Memories of the *maréchaliste* phenomenon are delicate; interviewees strive to make their contemporary and future listeners understand their past position in the unfolding context that shaped attitudes at the time. Pierre continued, speaking of Marshal Pétain: "You can't judge him in 1940 in the same way as you can in 1944 or 1945, because all of what Vichy did didn't yet exist. We clung onto what we could." Robert Bernier emphasized that "we thought he was going to do some good, you know . . ., everyone believed, more or less, that it would get sorted out." His explanation elides, whether through ignorance or design, both the moral and political probity of replacing Republican democracy with an authoritarian, right-wing, exclusionary regime and the many French people suspicious of this new form of government. Robert nonetheless recognizes that early confidence was misplaced, adding immediately, "but in fact, that's not at all what happened, eh."

> I think it rather deteriorated, particularly when we saw everything that people like Pierre Laval—, I can't remember what the others were called, those others, what was the other one called—, it's true, they did some horrific things, eh—, people assassinated, didn't matter who, for—, without motive sometimes, no reason at all. And later on, when we realized that it was the French police that was arresting Jews, all of that, it's certain that then, we started to understand better.

None of the rememberers defend Pétain. They show instead a feeling of betrayal that this veteran hero proved dishonorable and express their disappointment and disgust at the politics of Vichy. Trusting Pétain in 1940 was, for some, justifiable, but attachments to the government evolved continuously. Ultimately, the architects and activists of the French State are positioned in memory as objects of disdain.

For interviewees who had family members involved in resistance work, the epitome of the "bad French"—of cruelty, betrayal, and violence—was the Milice. Created in early 1943 as a counterbalance to the growing influence of the Paris collaborationists, Laval's plan backfired and this violent paramilitary force became the central organ of Franco-German activist collaboration, tracking down terrorists (as resisters were called), Jews, and draft dodgers from the STO.[15] The Milice drew the French State deeper into fascism. It attracted young, unemployed men and was renowned for its brutality. Siblings Luce Terrier and Robert Mignat, whose family was deeply implicated in the resistance in and around Lyon, spoke of a young uncle who had joined the resistance group *Francs-Tireurs et Partisans* in the Ardèche. He was caught by the Germans and, Robert added, "tortured by the Milice, which is even more atrocious." The Milice played a key role in the arrest of Nancette Blanchou's parents:

> So [there were] . . . these two young Miliciens, who had turned up earlier that morning asking to join the maquis. Of course, it wasn't to join the maquis

at all. . . . They'd hidden their suitcases in the barn. . . . And these little Miliciens had come to ensnare my father. So Mum gave them a good meal [she inhales deeply], and [later] the Gestapo, or at least, three Miliciens arrived, and that was the beginning of my parents' arrest. Straight away, the house was surrounded by Germans [she breaths in deeply, and the words come out in a sigh] they were everywhere, everywhere, everywhere. Everywhere, everywhere, everywhere.

This memory is filled not only with sorrow but also with contempt for these false Frenchmen. She repeats that they were young and, later, "little" and describes them as spiteful and cynical. They took advantage of her mother's hospitality, led the Germans straight to the family, and showed no scruples about threatening a child: "He took me out into the fields, he said to me 'You're the one who'll take me to them.' [Pause] He put a revolver into my neck, and he said 'Go on.' " Nancette's memory of this moment is vivid, and the treacherous young Miliciens are at the heart of it.

Jewish memory stories cite the French police more frequently than the Milice as the principal agents of state repression; often the arrests recounted pre-date the formation of the Milice. Keeping a desperate grip on the tattered remains of French sovereignty, an agreement had been signed that placed the policing of Paris in the hands of the French.[16] While the Milice was characterized in memories as brutal and conniving, the moral crime of the French police was to blindly, or zealously, depending who was involved, follow orders. This made a mockery of French republican principles, including a commitment to law and justice. Like many children of Jewish immigrants, Charles Baron described what it meant to choose France: "The Republic—it was great to be French. I could have been born in Poland like my father—, but no, to be French, it was a feeling of pride. But not a feeling of superiority, no. I mean that there was a kind of satisfaction. For us France—, my father had chosen it. And my grandfather too—, for them, it was the land of elections." For Serge Holand's family too, the measures against Jews by the authorities in Paris were simply unbelievable, "especially in France." He said that his parents "came to France as the country of liberty, of the rights of man, a land of philosophers." Marcel Zaidner's parents emigrated to France in the interwar period because it was "the land of liberty," while for Maurice Goldring's parents it was "a country where you could live happily." Charles Baron described his arrest. He, like many of the other Jewish interviewees, insisted that it was the

French police who arrested him and his uncle: "I was sixteen years and nearly two months. His only words were 'If you were two months younger, I wouldn't have arrested you.' Nothing obliged him to arrest me." They were taken to the police station and then on to Drancy. He continued: "And all that time, I never saw any Germans, eh. Only Frenchmen." When he was selected for deportation from Drancy, all he could think to protest was "But I'm French! I'm French!" The French police just seemed satisfied to fill their quota, he added. The aversion toward the Milice across the stories of resistance is derived from the betrayal of one's compatriots; in Jewish memory stories, it is the very idea of France, the land of liberty, equality, and fraternity, that had been betrayed.[17]

Some Jewish interviewees tried to balance a one-sided view of the French police. Some owed their survival partly to individual policemen who acted independently of their orders or showed compassion. Policemen were central in Rachel Jedinak's story of her escape during the roundup of July 16, 1942. The Jews from Rachel's neighborhood were being held in a local theater, waiting for buses that would take them to the Vélodrome d'Hiver. Rachel's mother saw an opportunity for her two daughters to flee. They did not want to leave her, so she slapped their faces and told them to run: "We ran away, us two, towards the emergency exit. But in fact, when we got [there], there were two policemen guarding it, and they turned their heads to not see us escaping. So, do you understand? There were some police who were zealous, who came to get us, and these others who turned their heads so as not to see us escape." The second time Rachel was rounded up with her sister and grandmother in February 1943, the group of Jewish prisoners was again temporarily held in the cellar of the police station. The girls watched what was happening and realized the police were under pressure, with furious people shouting at them. They remembered their mother's words: "try to escape." Rachel said the local police chief seemed ill at ease with what was happening "and after a while he said to us 'Go on, get out of here.' So you see? Get out of here. Sometimes life rests on a few little words. Get out of here." Again, escape depended on a policeman acting independently of his orders. Danièle Dubowsky also described the help her mother received from a local policeman after her father was arrested. This man persuaded the grocer to put food aside for the family, helped them if they needed anything after the curfew, and smuggled their father's letters to them: "I'm saying this because later on, I'm going to talk about the fellow who was the most active in our arrest, and he was also a cop at Vincennes, called Monsieur C------. So it may seem facile to say, but it deserves being said again, there was good and bad on every side." Serge Holand's small family managed to escape Paris via circuitous routes and arrived ultimately together in the Creuse. There, he said, "no policeman ever came to speak to us." Serge speculated on a generalized local orientation toward resistance and away from collaboration. The balancing of zealous with humane policemen serves a didactic purpose as interviewees tell their stories for present and future imagined audiences. They warn against blanket judgments, and, importantly, foreground the agency of individuals who chose to resist their orders.

Discussion of the black market was also steeped in the moral ambiguities of the time. Was everybody doing it, or were most people doing something else to get by? Rememberers took various positions in relation to food and wrongdoing. Marie-Josèphe Devaux was emotional, it seemed with the shame, about her parents' black-market activities. We do not know the extent to which they may have profited or from whom. Despite her shame, Marie-Josèphe added defensively, "nobody would ever tell you everything they were doing." Many who pointed the finger, she suggested, did so with dirty hands. Others speak of collusion between French food providers and the population. This under-the-table commerce benefited neighbors and relied on their complicity. Sylvette Leclerc's family lived in a house rented from a butcher. He kept a room in the house "to come and sell his meat once or twice a week." Interviewees largely tried to distinguish between survival techniques and the black market, which was condemned. Jacqueline Béné noted that her parents had access to wood, which they could exchange for some of the food they needed: "It wasn't black-marketing, it was an exchange—barter, that's it." Edmond Magnin and his wife Ginette were also adamant that there was a moral distinction between what their families did and what, for example, shopkeepers did:

GINETTE: —we once gave some bacon to a shopkeeper in exchange for a coat—

EDMOND: —that's what I was going to say to you, that's how the black market began—

GINETTE: —although, that was barter, if you know what I mean, it wasn't the black market—

EDMOND: —we *bartered* [emphasizing the word]—

GINETTE: —we [echoing the same emphasis] *bartered*–

EDMOND: —but some others—, shopkeepers, that was the black market—

GINETTE: —yes, the black market—

EDMOND: That's what they used to say, they'd say that that was the black market. That's how it began. Because them, they had enough, they were getting by alright, and to get hold of any of it, they'd make us pay a lot, already, and then secondly, they already had enough to eat, they did.

Barter took place between people seen as equal in their needs. Black marketing exploited unequal relations. Edmond's comments stigmatize this behavior. Other interviewees were more ambiguous. Marcel Tatelin was asked whether there was black marketing in his rural village. He said, "Oh yes, on the farms there was, yes. To all of the folks from the towns who'd come." Here, farmers were seen to profit from the more desperate needs of urban people. However, this kind of behavior was seen by others not as black marketing but as a clandestine economy that avoided Vichy's meddling and German-imposed requisitions: selling French to French.

The memory stories consistently condemned other French people who committed crimes for profit or power against their fellow countrymen. In a climate of competition for scarce resources, safety, and security, suspicion reigned. Robert Bernier commented that "at first, there were no denunciations, there were no collaborators . . . but I think that as time went on, yes, there was a kind of mistrust." The specter of denunciation haunted towns and villages. It came in many forms and affected many people. A means to punish neighbors and rivals for long-standing or petty arguments, denunciation ranked highly as an immoral act. Pierre Tainturier commented that "it frightened us, people denouncing each other": unpredictable and malicious, denunciation contributed in large measure to the wartime climate of anxiety. Several interviewees whose families, Jews or resisters, had experienced denunciation knew who was responsible. Nancette Blanchou discovered later in her life which villager had denounced her father; she elaborated no further, but it sounded as though the man had not been punished for it. Nicole Kahn said that her family had been denounced by a woman who "had gone to trial, but nobody cared what had become of her, what the verdict was." The sense I got from each woman was that these people who had caused so much destruction were simply beneath their contempt. Betrayal sits at the heart of these evocations of morally corrupt behavior.

On the other side of the coin was the active, patriotic commitment to the future of France and liberation. Many of the children were fascinated by the resistance, particularly those in rural areas who had contact with the maquis.

Many maquisards were former schoolmates or the sons of neighbors. Serge Holand said of his playmates in the Creuse, "we were completely steeped in the resistance." Pierre Tainturier, a teenager at the time, said "I was a bit enraptured in front of those people who had taken so many risks." And Jacques Kermen recounted how, among his schoolfriends, the exploits of the local maquis were the talk of the playground: "We learned them almost like we learned our times tables at school. Every day, we'd go over the same things." Heroic as such deeds were to schoolboys, they had their own ambiguity. Maquis activity could lead to vicious reprisals against the local population. In such cases people were more circumspect, even critical. Jean-Claude Bourtourault recounted his mother's hesitations about resistance activity: "My mother was against it, because she said it's unfortunate, these resisters, they're doing more harm than good." Bernard Lemaire spoke of a specific incident in Lille when a German soldier was shot in the woods. Bernard did not excuse anything the soldier had done but remarked: "Attacking the railways, all of that, well fine, but there were five poor lads who were killed for that. And that, even though I was a kid, I can still remember it." Yves Le Roy, from Brest, castigated the acts of some young resisters who were not skilled enough to manage their attacks without endangering others: "There were resisters, but there were some who were more like idiots. There were some clashes where there were a fair number of civilians killed. They were too young, too much passion. And the Germans, they'd been trained, they were warriors, they weren't just—, and they had more weapons." Objections were raised about the manner in which rural maquis provisioned itself. Marie-Josèphe Devaux recalled that her parents were on good terms with the local maquisards, but these men nonetheless took from the family, on one occasion commandeering a whole cow. Jacqueline Béné remembered the frightening arrival of some maquisards at her home demanding that her father give them petrol. The interviewer asked if he did. She replied, with a sardonic laugh, "Ah, ha ha, he was pretty much obliged, eh. Otherwise they'd have shot him!" The maquis could be unpredictable and brutal, and their exploits generated mixed feelings. Henri Buc commented on the evolution of the perception of the maquis in the village where he lived: "We're going to see some maquisards, who'll come and, at first, are going to seem like bandits. We're not—, the people were *absolutely not* [he stresses the two words] for the maquisards. I lived opposite the post office, and when I saw them come for the first time and hold up the post office, I thought it was a scandal, it was disorder." Yet, he said, as the Germans began to lose their grip, there was a recognition that the role of the maquis could come to matter. People began to see a purpose in their activities, and, Henri said, "we saw maquisards who were pretty stylish." Even the resistance, then, was a source of fluctuating, ambiguous affects inside the memory stories. These depended greatly on specific, located encounters and the feelings they engendered, whether fear, disdain, shock, or admiration. While the maquis surfaced in various narratives, interviewees rarely if ever mentioned any of the larger resistance networks or movements.

The Allied Enemy

The other group of affective others that was not viewed positively was the Allies, or the Anglo-Saxons as the British and Americans were usually called. I have dealt with this elsewhere.[18] However, it is worth remarking, first, on how the gap across the divide of my interview encounters affected the way hatred or anger toward the Allies was narrated. It is likely that my nationality caused some reticence; yet interviewees could be candid about reactions after destructive air raids. Second, in all of the interviews, there was an understanding that the goal of the Allied air raids was never the civilian population. Nevertheless, strong feelings about the Allied bombers were clear. Marie-Rolande Cornuéjols, whom I did not interview, criticized the national silence around the victims of the Allied bombing, suggesting that "when it's your friends who bomb you, it's terrible." It was hard to construct a narrative of loss and victimhood given that the Allies were acting to defeat Hitler and, in the process, liberate France. Michel Jean-Bart and Bernard Leclercq, both living near Lille and interviewed by me, noted that anger flared up after particularly destructive air raids. Michel said: "Most of all, in the first few days after, for the reason, people said 'what a load of idiots, they should have been more careful, just dropping their bombs and leaving us to clear up.' Because there was this little spike, let's not say of hatred, but of, let's say— with the carnage that they'd caused, you know. It was that, you know. It hurt." Bernard and his wife Thérèse explored their understanding of public sentiment toward the Allies in their collaborative remembering:

> BERNARD: For us, it wasn't that we were angry with them. But we said "they don't know how to aim, they don't know how to aim!" Instead of getting the factories, they got the houses, the schools, what are they playing at?

THÉRÈSE: At the end of the day, really people were mad with the
Germans. This is a region, perhaps my family a bit less, but my husband
grew up with—we should say the world, it's a big word a *hatred*
[emphasizing] for the Germans. Hatred, hatred—

BERNARD: —the Boches, the Boches—

THÉRÈSE: —and the English—

BERNARD: —still even today—

THÉRÈSE: —it's close, because people were saying that it's because of them
that our houses have been destroyed, all of that—

BERNARD: —"they don't know how to aim," that I recall. "They hit the
houses the schools instead of the factories, instead of the—." But, well,
there was a war going on—

THÉRÈSE: They knew that they were here to rescue us, a bit, to set us
free—

BERNARD: We were happy to see them flying over, when they went
overhead, when they were going to Germany. You have to understand,
me, I can remember it, that humming noise, it lasted for years, they were
going to Germany, it was incredible. . . . You have to understand that
the English, they were criticized a bit for their air raids, but more than
anything else, it was the Germans.

Although the speakers appear consensual, there is a slight difference in perspective. Thérèse had experienced an Allied air raid firsthand when her school was
struck and recognized that people on the ground struggled to fully reconcile
themselves with the Allies' actions. Bernard, who was never bombed, said that
there was no hatred toward the Allies. Édith Denhez's brother Jacques was killed
in an Allied air raid in Cambrai in 1944. That fact affected the family's outlook:
"At our house—it's not very nice to say this—we hated the English far more, the
Americans, they'd killed our brother, so we could never forgive them, eh. For my
mother, it was like that. They were worse than the Germans [laughing a little]."
Édith acknowledged, both in her reflexive aside and through her slight laughter
that this was an uncomfortable position to express, particularly to me. Yet given
the circumstances, such feelings are entirely comprehensible.

The creation of affective others across the memory stories depended enormously on how those others were encountered by individuals, their friends, and
their families. Memories are made of feelings, and those feelings are constantly

generated in the "hot mess" of life unfolding. For Édith's mother, regardless of the First World War or the liberation, the Allies were responsible for her son's death. Their bombing was careless, lazy, or reckless, and when it created deeply felt ruptures in individual lives (bereavement, trauma) those characteristics were transferred to the perpetrators themselves. As Sara Ahmed writes, emotions have a political momentum: " 'it hurts' becomes, 'you hurt me,' which might become, 'you are hurtful,' or even 'you are bad.' "[19] Affective others are the human objects of affective relations. In the memory stories, they build the complicated moral landscape of wartime France, where enemies may be friendly, neighbors treacherous, parents incapable, and strangers loving.

PAUSE—ROBERT—THE CONTINGENCY OF MORAL MEANING

The meanings of resistance and collaboration were, and are, continually being defined and redefined. Historians and others have expended a great deal of energy establishing nuanced categorizations of what could and can be defined as either, why, and with what consequences. This mattered in the immediate postwar context when there were medals, titles, and compensation to be awarded and trials, punishments, and prison sentences to be meted out. Resistance (or perhaps active resistance) and collaboration (or perhaps better, collaborationism) were positioned at opposite ends of the moral scale, one to liberate and rebuild, the other to control and profit. Yet as Robert Bernier's explanation of his father's wartime activities shows, among ordinary people and in memory, resistance is more ambiguous. All depended on the contingent evolution of the events in question. Robert had an interest in presenting his father's activities in a way that his audiences, real and imagined, would judge favorably. But the story is more nuanced than a simple defense and highlights the complexity of good and bad in this context.

First, what was resistance against? As Mason Norton suggests, it was not just a case of acting against the German occupiers and in pursuit of liberation.[20] Robert uses the word to describe his father's resistance against the restrictions imposed by the Occupation by flouting laws and quotas. It was resistance, he implied, against Vichy's inadequate rationing system and against German seizures of French produce: "That's how he did, in inverted commas his 'resistance,' if you like. There were still restrictions even though we were in the countryside, you know. So, with his workmates, they set up a clandestine slaughterhouse, and he let it be known that it was resistance—." Robert hesitates to label this as resistance. He makes it clear to his audience that he puts the word in quotes, distancing himself. He knows that this definition of resistance is not the common one and is aware that many would dispute it. However, he notes that his father "let it be known that it was resistance." Robert's father justified what he was doing to himself and to others. If Robert's father was selling illegal meat to local French people, meaning that it was not swallowed up by an unreliable ration system or packed off to Germany, would that be a problem? Perhaps, or perhaps not. For people in urban areas such as nearby Bordeaux, the ration system was unreliable but perhaps entitled some to the protein and fats their diets lacked that they could not get on an open market. Would institutions such as hospitals, schools, or children's homes be deprived because this meat was out of the ration system?

But Robert's father and his colleagues were not selling just to local people: "he was also feeding the Germans too." This is the very nub of everyday economic collaboration. The Germans had the money to buy, generating profit for farmers, slaughterers, and butchers. Robert again unsettled certainties about the morality of his father's actions:

> But not just any Germans. By that I mean, these were older Germans. There was a bridge, up there, and the German army had taken on some old Germans, they were maybe fifty or sixty years old, I don't know, and they were men who'd rather have stayed in Germany, working, looking after their farms, I don't know what, rather than be here, you know, and the problem was that those men there, they had barely anything to eat.

Three points are made in defense of selling meat to Germans: they were older and militarily inactive, they were ideologically uncommitted, and they too were hungry and neglected by the authorities. Was selling food to these men, "who behaved correctly, who paid what they owed," consistent with an understanding, at the time or later, of collaboration? Was it a compassionate act or an act of resistance? Was it unpatriotic to sell meat to men who appeared to be both reluctant occupiers and reluctant Nazis? And were any of these things even true? Were they known at the time or justifications built and maintained to defend a position in the years that followed? The story opens questions to help us think through the past, but it does not offer answers.

Robert described the activity linked to the clandestine slaughterhouse as a "resistance network." Whether the men were doing anything more than slaughtering animals is unknown. Robert said that some of the team would visit local farms to buy the animals. These were slaughtered and butchered, and at night buyers would arrive. French civilians came at nine o'clock, the French police at ten o'clock, and the older Germans at eleven. Robert said: "Well, so, there are people who might believe that that was collaboration, but it wasn't collaboration at all. It was a bit of give-and-take, if you like. There were never any problems, like." It is not clear whether Robert is referring to people who might have characterized it as collaboration at the time or now. Although he hesitated to call it resistance, Robert is clear that it was not collaboration: it was a bit of give-and-take. But if this was give-and-take, what did clandestine slaughterers get in return? Was it just the silence of the Germans who also benefited, allowing them to continue their work and continue to make whatever money they did? Or was there something else at stake? We could see Robert's memory story as an elaborate or weak defense of his father; we do not have to agree with his conclusions. But the story serves as a clear example of the contingency of morality. Right or wrong depended on so many factors beyond our knowledge. Contingency here is about the kind of Germans who happened to be the (remembered) buyers of this meat. It just so happened that they were (remembered as) benign and even pitiable or reluctant enemies. What would have been the case if Robert's father had sold his meat to younger, more ideologically committed Germans? And we might also ask whether the older Germans were as "correct" in other aspects of their work as they were with Robert's father. The memory story only gives us access to some parts of the happening past, filtered through a series of interpretations and moral justifications, contemporary and retrospective.

CHAPTER 10

CONTINGENCY AND RUPTURE

Wartime memories do not just accrete around things and people that mattered but also around events that mattered. A preponderance of memories in the corpus are recounted around 1939/40 and 1944/45. Events such as the outbreak of war and the liberation of France created ruptures in time, shaking up everyday life in physically or emotionally violent ways and generating opportunities for experiencing those intense and novel things that cause memories to stick. The years in between—1941, 1942, and 1943—often collapse together. Precise chronologies are more difficult to recall except where specific events touched lives directly. These created exceptional peaks of detailed remembering, many of which have surfaced across all the previous chapters. Here, though, I will concentrate on 1939/40 and 1944/45. By juxtaposing memories of these nationally significant events, we expose the idiosyncratic, contingent ways such watershed moments in collective memory were lived and remembered. The events of 1939/40 and 1944 underpin national regimes of memory around defeat, collaboration, the birth of resistance, and the triumph of resistance. How things happened, what people did and felt, and what such events looked like are etched into popular understandings of the French experience of the Second World War.[1] Yet, following the arguments of chapter 6, these events are not always evoked in ways that chime with public understandings of the past. In particular, their place in children's everyday lives may render them unfamiliar in both their emphases and their affects. Kathleen Stewart remarks that "little worlds proliferate around everything and anything."[2] The experience of fleeing the German army in 1940 is common to millions, but what happened to *this* family and *this* child is always contingent on the way that "things"—national or local, military or ideological, personal and impersonal—throw themselves together.[3]

AROUND 1939/40

When war broke out in 1939, it was not unexpected. Jacqueline Béné recalled that the partial mobilization around the Sudeten crisis and the Munich Agreement of September 1938 created an affective shift: "it left me with a feeling of uneasiness." The world suddenly caught her attention: "My parents' friends would come to the house, I'd listen to their discussions, and it interested me a great deal." By the later years of the 1930s, war was in the air.[4] The declaration of war in September 1939 was widely remembered. Bernard Lemaire expressed a very precise memory of it because of where he was and how he felt: "I remember that there were these great big billboards on the sides of schools, big wooden billboards with posters on them—declaration of war, calling up the troops—and of course, all the men were looking at that poster. I walked between the billboard and the men who were looking at it, and I got myself told off because I blocked their—, I remember, I got told off because I'd got in their way." Bernard apologized for telling such a mundane anecdote. But without that proprioceptive, affective memory of being trapped, however fleetingly, between the men and the billboards and being told off by them, Bernard may not have had a memory to tell. Madame Gaulthier also recalled the uneasiness of the moment. She and a friend were returning to Burgundy from a trip to Guernsey. The two thirteen-year-old girls got off the boat at Saint-Malo, where they were due to be met:

Nobody was waiting for us on the quayside! . . . We started panicking. Then we noticed that there were lots of people, everywhere, all over the docks, something wasn't right. It was strange. Anyway, so we disembarked from our [trip], straight into war. The declaration was later that evening—. So there we were, both of us, in tears, wondering what we were going to do, to first find a telephone to try to see what was happening, where our families were.

Eventually someone came for them. But the declaration of war, for Madame Gaulthier, was lived anxiously from the start, and this set the tone for the months that followed as her father was mobilized. The declaration itself was only present indirectly, but it nonetheless created a rupture.

The meaning of the declaration of war may not have been fully grasped, but it was understood as a momentous event. It was often recounted as puncturing everyday life and leaving an affective stain. Ginette Renard was nine years old but recalls it vividly:

> Awful. I cried my eyes out. Because—, I remember having gone—, I was in Auvergne because it was the holidays, still the holidays—, and I'd been to Mass. And everyone was at church to pray for—, and afterwards, coming back, two kilometers at least on foot, I came across some horses which had been requisitioned. Oh, that just finished me off. Already, everyone was weeping at Mass eh, because they knew what awaited them—, all of them who'd known 1914–1918, and then I saw those horses. And I kissed them.

Ginette was surrounded by adults' anxiety and their memories of the First World War but the detail of the memory is linked the horses, which affected her deeply. She struggled to hold back tears as she spoke of them. Eugène also learned what to feel about the declaration of war from observing the adults around him. It was perhaps eight or nine o'clock in the evening, just after the cows were milked. Eugène and his brother went as usual to fill their milk churn at a neighboring farm. He recalled passing the cemetery and being terrified to see a light moving around: there was some foreboding here. But it was only "La Berthe," an old lady who "used to go and visit her dead at night with a lantern":

> She brought us a glass of milk each, and we were pretty pleased about that, we drank it up and were about to get going when Old Father D----- said to me "Well, you'd better tell your father that war's been declared." And we were, so happy we were, we went home singing "War's declared, war's declared, war's declared." And all the way home, we sang that, and when we got back up there, we went into the farmyard, all the folks were in the meadow, eh. . . . I remember it, when we said to them "War's been declared," the folks, they . . . [with a loud intake of breath, he acts the shock and horror on the faces of the farmworkers].

In the countryside, news was carried through word of mouth, in this case by two children. The declaration of a world war folds itself into Eugène's everyday life, along with the milk, the cemetery, his brother, La Berthe, Old Father D------, and the farm. This was living news that triggered emotions—the boys' elation, Ginette's sorrow—and muscled its way into lives. What the children learned

sticks in part because the known future projects back to this moment: the trou-
bles of the next six years are simultaneously present in the memory.

More often, it was not the declaration of war that was recalled but its immediate impact inside families. Paul Maubourg, whose memory story centered on his
father's later death under German torture, had a clear memory of 1939:

> My father was mobilized in '39. I was three. But I can still remember when
> he left. Because I can still see him, sitting on a chair, rolling up his puttees.
> I wondered what they were, these bandages he was winding over his calves,
> the bottoms of his trousers, I didn't understand what they were for, but I do
> know that I went with my mother to the station [to see him off], and I asked
> my mother "Why is Daddy crying?" I didn't understand what it was about,
> I was three years old.

The puttees and the tears form surprising memories, which anchor the images
in Paul's mind. These mundane family interactions carry an important national
event; they must also be, for Paul, a precious memory of his father. Nancette
Blanchou also recalls her father joining up. While she could not remember the
declaration of war, she said: "I do have a memory of my father leaving for war. Oh
yes [there is a smile in her voice], yes, I do, I've still got that memory. My father
left, but he was taken prisoner. And he escaped and when he got home, he had a
moustache and a goatee. Yes, I'd forgotten that. And I didn't recognize [him]. And
when he wanted to kiss me, I said 'You're not my Daddy, you're not my Daddy.' "
This memory of her father leaving is in fact the memory of his return. A few years
later, he left again but never returned. It is the returning, therefore, that matters
here. Unlike for Paul Maubourg, it seemed that recounting this memory gave
Nancette pleasure as she added it to her stock of recollections. Memory stories of
fathers leaving for war are the first steps on a common path of paternal absence,
as described in chapter 9, and prefigure difficult emotional territory ahead.

The massive scale of the civilian exodus of 1940, when perhaps eight million
fled their homes, can obscure the earlier evacuation of 1939. At the outbreak of
war in September 1939, warnings were in place for large cities and the eastern
départements bordering Germany. Fear of German air attack prompted the evacuation of many infants, children, mothers, and elderly people.[5] Christian Solet
and his mother left Paris in autumn 1939 to stay with her sister in La Charité-sur-
Loire. He said: "I can remember that we had a very harsh winter, in '39–'40. There

was ice floating down the Loire, and they did a collection to provide mulled wine for the soldiers who were at the front." The winter cold was also present in Serge Holand's memory of 1939: "In '39, Paris was evacuated. The exodus. Well, we didn't have any problems during the exodus, because we were evacuated just like—. I was a child, and women with children were evacuated, so we took the train and we ended up in a little village in the Loiret—I think it was the Loiret—where we spent winter '39–'40 on a farm. It was an extremely cold winter." There is little elaboration, though, perhaps because in 1939 Serge's family could still move around freely, "just like" other French people, and anti-Semitic persecution had not yet begun. The exodus of 1939 exists in memory as a ghostly forerunner of the one that came later. Fathers and husbands, even mobilized, were reasonably safe; there was no sign of the Germans; communication and transport functioned well. Fear was largely absent. In Lyon, Denise Algret's older cousin was garrisoned at the Part-Dieu barracks. Every morning he would come for coffee, saying to her mother "here I am, dearest auntie, the condemned man drinking his coffee," yet every afternoon he would be back to take Denise to the park. But inside these "little worlds," later fears and anxieties, 1940 and after, pressed back upon recollections of a carefree Phoney War.

Memories of 1940 focus almost entirely on the civilian exodus. For some, this was the closest contact they had with the war, but its impacts stretched forward into the future. Memories cluster around dramatic moments on the road. Sylvette Leclerc's story lurches from one accident to the next, in the absence of her father:

> So my grandfather got his car, and he hitched my father's car up behind it, because my mother didn't know how to drive, she just held the wheel. We were completely overloaded, so much stuff piled up inside. We didn't get very far, just to the Yonne, because my grandfather's car, overloaded, pulling the other car, caught fire. The engine caught fire, and his maid—, I'll always remember it—, my father had a maid because my grandmother had died—she wanted to open up the—, I'm not quite sure what—, and her whole arm got really badly burnt by the hot water as it spurted out.

The culmination of the story was a consequence of a set of circumstances peculiar, in their combination, to this family. Christian Gaillard's family's exodus was also complicated by his father's absence. Belongings were piled onto a haycart pulled by two horses and led by a farmworker on foot. Christian and his mother went by bicycle. His sixteen-year-old sister drove their father's car, carrying their belongings and his grandmother. All were aiming for a family-owned farm south of the Loire. Inevitably the cavalcade became separated. When he and his mother arrived, they were greeted by a disaster, which Christian recounted in tears:

> We found that the farm, where we were all supposed to meet up, had burned down [his voice is emotional, he struggles to hold back his tears]. Where is everybody? [Christian is crying. He takes a drink of water.] So we waited—, well, the adults went looking—, the kids were a little bit on the side—, and they found all the people were still alive. But everything had been stolen. Everything they had, their horses killed, the car burned. But at least the people were alive.

But a few days later his uncle's cousin, mending the roof, fell to his death. The exodus was not just the people streaming along the roads; "little worlds" such as this one sprung up around people, families, and journeys, each unique in composition.

Returning home after the 1940 exodus prefigured the new moral landscape of wartime France. Françoise Yessad's family home was damaged while they were away, and Françoise was categorical about who was responsible. Her mother was furious: "The house had been occupied by the Germans, who'd made a—, who'd stolen her records, and damaged her linen." Things were more ambiguous for Charles Magnin and his wife, Ginette. Ginette's family had fled about twenty kilometers when:

> GINETTE: The Germans caught up with us, we were stopped, and then we came back. And when we got home, the whole house had been looted, everything was wide open—
>
> CHARLES: —that was normal—
>
> JULIEN ROCIPON: Looted by whom?
>
> CHARLES: —by the—, we don't know—, there were French people, Germans—
>
> GINETTE: —Germans, yes, and French people too, they took advantage too, eh—
>
> CHARLES: —we had some who'd stayed behind—

Rémy Menigault recalled in detail the mess that greeted his mother and her children when they returned home to the rural railway station where they lived:

> **RÉMY:** We came back by train, of course, and when we arrive at the station, and it's been looted, all our supplies have been looted. We found terrible things, terrible things, like all our poultry had gone, my mother had about forty birds, and rabbits too—and they'd set the rabbits free. Well, we found the rabbits, but the hens, we never got them back. Because, obviously, people lured them in, with a bit of bread, wrung their necks and ate them. All the jam, pots of jam out on the table—. Now those are really vivid memories in my mind.
>
> **INTERVIEWER:** And did you know who'd looted you like that?
>
> **RÉMY:** Oh, no. But it was French refugees—, but there were really terrible things. My mother had unfortunately locked the doors, so all the doors had been smashed in, and it's a strange feeling to see your house like that, eh . . . . My mother had a little diatonic accordion, she really loved playing it, and she found it smashed to pieces in the road. Those are really bad memories, bad memories.

People, he suggested, behaved with cruelty and disregard; there was human excrement in their wardrobes. This began a period that pitted French not just against Germans, but also against French.

Other memories of the exodus are marked by admiration for parents' courage. When asked what the period made her think of, Simone Fauron said in a voice tinged with regret: "I think of my parents, I think that they gave themselves a good deal of trouble." Françoise Yessad remembered her mother, alone with two small children in Orléans as the Germans bombed the town. "And on top of that, she was pregnant! Hugely pregnant!" Roger Davre recalled his exodus in the family car, mattress strapped to the roof, his mother at the wheel, two other women, two girls, a little boy, a cat, and a dog inside. The roads were blocked, and the car ran out of petrol. A French military vehicle offered to tow them, which provoked anger from other refugees. An angry man threatened to slash their tires. Roger recalls his mother leaping from the car, brandishing a knife. She shouted at the man: why was he not on the front line, risking his neck for France? She did not know where *her* husband was, but he was certainly not shouting at women and children in a traffic jam. She threatened him: "If you slash my tires, I'll slash your old lady!" The story of his mother's fury became the stuff of family legend. He chuckled: "Even my grandchildren know that story." Our memories are rarely just our own.

Not everybody participated in the exodus. Lola Grynberg said that in the twentieth arrondissement of Paris, where she lived: "People in my neighborhood, I didn't know any who left. Although, well perhaps I just don't remember it, but I didn't see any of the people who lived around me leaving in the exodus, like you see in photos—, how can I put it, at the cinema or whatever, anyway—no, I didn't see anything like that." Lola's memories do not match the images she has later seen. She questions her memory and doubts it, such is the visual strength of this event in versions of the national past. But for recent immigrants like Lola's family and the very poor, it was harder to leave or to know where to go.[6] Lucienne Scaglia-Chiafi's family were Italian immigrants; they did not leave either. In her district, she said, only three families remained, and all were Italian. Although her neighbors had taken their dogs with them, she said, the dogs soon came back, and Lucienne looked after them until their owners returned. In Lille, Bernard Lemaire's family did not leave either. With eight children in her care and her husband absent, Bernard's mother said, "Well tough luck. With the grace of God, we're staying." Choosing to remain when everyone else had gone created its own problems: "Everything was shut. We had nothing to eat. But there was an engineering college [nearby], everyone had left, but the director Monsieur P----- had left the doors open, there were all the provisions for the students, and so those were distributed among the people who'd stayed—there weren't many of us, eh. So we had lentils, bags of lentils, bags of dried beans. We were eating salted lentils for a long while." It is unclear how official this distribution of supplies was. Bernard recalled that a woman who lived in his street with her brother, a priest, had also remained:

And they were farmers' children, so she knew how to milk cows. So she'd go to Lambersart, well, Lambersart back in those days was still fields, and she'd go and milk the cows, because the cows were crying out from not having been—. The farmers had left, so she'd go and milk the cows. And she'd chop up the carcasses of horses that had been killed in the bombing, and she'd bring us meat and milk—, that's how we were fed, eh.

Bernard justifies what was taken: the cows needed to be milked, and the horses had been killed by bombs. This was not wanton destruction but the fulfilment of need in a situation of abandonment.

Madame Sauvonnet also recalled that her family did not leave, likewise because they were too numerous. Instead, refugees started passing through her village: "We had the refugee trains which would pass just in front of—, so we'd give them something to drink. We were all called upon to give them what we could, but most of all it was water." Jacqueline Béné also recalled "people fleeing": Dutch and Belgian, Parisians, people from the east streaming through her village Ivry-en-Montagne near Beaune. In her opinion, propaganda had created "an intoxication . . . a mad panic," and refugees came "non-stop, non-stop, non-stop." Local people began to ask whether they should leave too, but for many leaving crops and livestock was too great a risk. She believed her father was right in his decision to stay put. Jacqueline Berthou's family gave assistance to refugees arriving in Brittany. She said: "Mum went up there several times to give them milk, things like that, up at the station. My father said, 'Come along, there are children there.' They were arriving from everywhere, from the Somme, coming from that way—." One night her father came home accompanied by a couple, a male banker and a Belgian woman with a small child. Jacqueline realized that the woman was not the man's wife, but they had a child together. The woman stayed at their house for several weeks, although she did not see the man again. She said, "poor folks, . . . they were so shaken up." Whether leaving, staying, or coming home, these memories depend on the feelings evoked in the upheaval.

The other great pole around which memories of 1940 accrete is the arrival of the Germans. These are strongly emplaced visual memories. Marie-Rolande Cornuéjols was on a train heading back to Paris after the signing of the Armistice. "I remember that all the adults were at the windows to see the Germans who—, there were a few Germans, soldiers—, and we were watching the Germans like, not like they were monsters, more like they were curious creatures, that's it." Watching the adults' responses again shaped her own response. Jacqueline Berthou has a stronger memory of their arrival in Morbihan: "I can remember, I can, I was in the courtyard by the station. . . . I was at the bakery. And I saw these enormous motorbikes arriving, with—, helmets, iron collars—." People in the bakery peered out of the shop, she recalls, to take a better look. In the police station in Quimper, where his uncle lived, Henri Girardon was both impressed and afraid: "It's there that I saw the Germans arrive. I have to say, it was kind of impressive, because I already knew I wanted to become a soldier, I already had my own ideas about what an army should be like, already. It was alluring, you could see that it was a professional army. But we were afraid all the same.

Because we said to ourselves 'What's going to happen to us?'" Jean Caniot and his family were staying near Montoire because of the exodus when he witnessed the Germans arrive:

> I saw the first ones coming. . . . We were on a farm. . . . We stayed at that farm for a couple of days, sleeping in the straw, and the road ran alongside the barn where we were, and I saw a motorcyclist going past "brrrrrrrrrrrrrrrrrrrrrrr-rrrrrrrrrrrrrrm!," going past there, and I said "Oh shit, it's the Germans," and I ran, fsssssssh! And he went all around, and entered into the village, and there was a—, I can still see his straw hat—, it must have been a farmer, who came in from his garden, and found himself face to face with this motorcyclist, who took out his revolver and the man, he turned on his heel and ran in the opposite direction! Yes! That's how I saw the first German! Then afterwards, there were columns and columns and columns of them, six abreast at the front, on foot, in cars, on bikes, on horses, and all, it was crazy. I'm not surprised that we were all swept away, the French, the English, swept away. They were perfectly organized.

Like Henri, Jean was struck by the quality of this fighting force. He watched their encounter with the farmer. Excitement ran through his description of this frightening but impressive sight.

Denise Algret later deduced that her first encounter must have been on the Saône embankment in Lyon. The memory was sticky as what she saw was so unusual: "The first sight of the Germans that I had was of men washing and shaving, using little mirrors hanging on the handles of their trucks and lorries. So my first vision—these people, with their mirrors who were doing, well, what my father did every morning, who were shaving." The vision was extraordinary in one sense as dozens of men were shaving in the streets; but they were shaving, just like other men. Things were out of place. For others, the arrival of the Germans was more actively lived. Jacqueline Béné recalled being in a café:

> We hear the sounds of vehicles, of big trucks, something big, so we look out and there were two French soldiers who [had stopped?] . . . to drink a beer, who were going home, no guns, nothing. An enormous tank with everything you'd expect, full, a chap on top, and I saw straight away that it was a German. . . . I said, "they're Boches." Because they were shouting "Ahwa-wa-wa-wa-wa!"

I don't know what, they were shouting that in front of the— . . ., I said to Mum "It's the Boches!" . . . And she said to me "Don't say things like that!"

Her father immediately decided that they should get home. They needed to cross the column of marching Germans. He went to speak to a soldier to ask permission to pass. At that moment, one of the Germans took offence: "I had this lovely French flag [pinned to my jacket], crossed over, like that, with an English flag—, I was so proud of it, so, so proud of my flags! . . . And he took his knife, and he cut my flags off, and they fell on the—. I can still see them, my poor flags." With this act, they sealed their reputation. They were both extraordinary and dangerous and were fixed in Jacqueline's memory through her shock and fear.

Both Yvette Chapalain and Serge Aubrée recounted a sudden realization that defeat meant subjugation. Both were in Brest, far from the German frontier. Serge and other townspeople were assembled on a beach, having fled the town, "seeing the Germans, with all their arrogance, the fear we had of the Germans! Because, if you like, all the rumors—, going back to '14–'18, people spoke about the Germans, they were Prussians, they were the Boches who'd do a thousand things to you." Yvette suggested a similar response of diminishment and helplessness: "And so, with our Mum, we went to the countryside, and there we saw the occupiers arrive. There you have it. They had motorbikes, tanks, lorries. But I have a memory of these warriors, they were downright arrogant warriors. It really struck me. They stared at us, they were the victors, you see, it's like—. And us, we looked on, from afar. Because they frightened us all the same." Yvette describes a mutual regard: the gaze of the victor fell on the defeated, and the defeated looked back afraid but defiant. Just as the memory of pillage during the exodus set the tone for Franco-French relations to come, so the first encounter with the Germans in Brest presaged the way that all interviewees from that town described Franco-German relations there: the occupiers occupied, and the French—subjugated, afraid, and angry—resisted.

Interviewees recount the beginning of the war knowing its middle, its end, and its future; echoes of how reality unfolded are necessarily present in the account of the past. This holds particularly true for memories of the Armistice. The Armistice acts as a pivot: it ended the terrible ordeal of the exodus and began occupation and collaboration. No memory of the Armistice is free of its past and its future. Marie-Rolande Cornuéjols said: "And one day, the Armistice [was signed]. . . . And it's true that everybody was happy. I'm not going to say we toasted it with champagne, it wasn't like that at all, but the relief, the relief, because everybody had had enough, everybody wanted to get home, everybody had had bad news, their folks taken prisoner, people killed and missing, and we didn't know what would become of us—." Relief was the strongest feeling associated with the Armistice, in relation to what had gone before. Henri Buc described emotions around Marshal Pétain's speech to the nation on June 17, 1940, in which he announced the end of combat:

> First of all, there was a feeling that we'd come to this, that the French army was demolished. It was a feeling that ran very deep—. . . . On the Champs de Foire, out there [gesturing to the green space beyond his window], there was a defeated army. . . . So hearing Pétain saying "I give to France the gift of my person," for everyone, that seemed the only possible way. . . . What I remember is the voice of that man, a trembling voice, who wanted to comfort us. And it's out of this, it's out of this, we couldn't—, we were naturally collaborating [*collaborateur*], in a certain way.

His village, Gouzon, was bombed by the Germans on June 19, killing several civilians including refugees. From his window, as we spoke in the interview, Henri revisualized the debris of national humiliation. Marshal Pétain, the victor of Verdun, would become the savior of France, restoring order and pride. At the time, of course, nobody knew how Vichy's reforms would unroll. But Henri and the other interviewees know what happened next. They knew the shame that the Armistice brought in the longer term, through collaboration and anti-Semitism. Jacqueline Béné commented of Marshal Pétain: "He didn't manage things well, but another man in his place, would he have done any better? Unlikely." She mentioned Charles de Gaulle—"a great man," even to his political enemies— immediately afterward, but did not suggest that de Gaulle had the right answer in June 1940 either. The Armistice highlights the multitemporal nature of these memories: a necessary measure to end the chaos of defeat, it was also a yoke of shame. Given that such memories simultaneously and uncomfortably evoke complex compounds of feeling, it is unsurprising that some people have been reticent to talk about certain aspects of these years.

AROUND 1944/45

Memories also accrete around events from mid-1944 through to the liberation and on toward the end of the war. While the Normandy landings in June and the liberation of Paris in August 1944 are important sites of national memory, every town or region has its own liberation chronology and commemorative practices. These vertical regimes of memory orient ways of thinking about the past. In the interviews, they get folded into the everyday lives of the children who lived through them. In Cluny, Marie-Madeleine Viguié-Moreau associated the D-Day landings with "an extraordinary feeling of hope, really extraordinary." Her family life was dominated at the time by another hope: that her father would return from deportation. The two hopes intertwined: "It gave us hope. Because at that point we still didn't know if our fathers and mothers would return from that nightmare." Although 1944 is frequently associated with hope and celebration, many public versions of this part of the past fail to account fully for the marked increase in violence leading up to liberation. Yet for some, the only contact they had with violence across the war years was in summer 1944. Anxiety, fear, distress, terror, hope, and joy cause intense memories to accrete around these events because memories are suffused with these feelings.

The Allies were on the move, but so were the Germans. Some divisions advanced northward to engage with the Allies while others scrambled to leave. Some people recalled their undignified departure gleefully, with echoes of 1940. Jean-Claude Bourtourault said that by late August 1944 in Burgundy, "they were on their bikes, in prams, on scooters, however they could, eh. It was a complete debacle." Arrogance gave way to absurdity, quite the opposite of their arrival four years previously. Daniel Fèvre in Beaune told a similar tale: "Afterwards, of course, there was the German debacle. . . . A German company, going back up on foot, where to I don't know, they were going on foot. They had tanks and horses, they had the cannons . . . and they were sleeping on the ground, they didn't even have any blankets, they didn't have anything. It was really the debacle, but the other way around." The word *débâcle*, a name frequently given to the French defeat of 1940, builds a temporal bridge. Neither Daniel nor Jean-Claude references much more than the disarray of the German army. However, Raymond Févrat added a crucial detail: "And then of course the Germans who came in 1940 . . . well, back then we weren't afraid of the Germans, no. . . . They'd won, so it was fine. It wasn't the same as in 1944 when they left." Putting aside the widely circulating fears about Germans cutting people's hands off and the bombing of refugees on the roads, the conquering Germans are often remembered, as by Raymond here, as behaving "correctly" once they had installed themselves. Now humiliated rather than victorious, they became more dangerous.

As the Allies fought out of Normandy, German reinforcements moved up from the south, passing through the rural interior. The Germans of 1944 were different men from those of 1940. As John Sweets emphasizes, "all Germans . . . were not alike."[7] The younger men who arrived after the occupation of the whole of France in November 1942 had grown up indoctrinated by Nazi ideology, and many had been brutalized by time spent on the Eastern Front.[8] The pursuit of Jews became fanatical, as the targeting of the Jewish children's home at Izieu (Ain) in April 1944 testifies. Later judged a crime against humanity, the arrest, deportation, and murder of forty-four Jewish refugee children, the youngest four years old, from Izieu shows the single-minded fanaticism of men like Klaus Barbie.[9] Recruitment to rural maquis guerrilla units was increasing, and Allied arms drops meant that there were more weapons everywhere. Early summer 1944 was marked by the destruction and dislocation caused by the Allied landings and intensified air raids as well as by vicious battles between the Germans and the resistance.[10] These led to reprisals against the civilian population, of which the massacre of the village Oradour-sur-Glane is the best known. Many others exist.[11] Marie-Josèphe Devaux described the intrusion of this violence into her family's smallholding in the Dordogne:

My mother heard some singing in the woods, a soldiers' song, and then some moments later, we heard machine gun fire. My father was in the middle of sowing his Jerusalem artichokes with my brother and my sister, and I was ironing. I also heard the machine gun, so I came outside. I could see the mare there, in the other field, she raised her head, frightened. Guns fired several times. And my father, he always said afterwards that there was a German motorbike which got away, which went towards Périgueux, and my father always said "that bike's going to denounce the others. There's going to be reprisals."

Marie-Josèphe's memories are often rather vague, but this is recounted in detail—not that she saw much. She heard gunshots, went outside, and saw the mare look up in alarm. Marie-Josèphe witnessed no violence. The following day the nearby village of Rouffignac was razed to the ground by the Germans, and several men were shot and arrested. Other accounts tell us that the ambush referred to by Marie-Josèphe was not the trigger for this reprisal.[12] Yet her memory stakes a claim to these events.

The Second SS Panzer Division "Das Reich" was stationed in southern France on June 6, 1944, when the Normandy landings happened, but swiftly moved northward to reinforce the new frontline. As it moved, it killed. On June 9, the division was responsible for hanging ninety-nine men in the town of Tulle and on June 10 murdered 642 villagers in Oradour-sur-Glane. The name "Das Reich" is associated in memories with all sightings of Germans troops moving northward across this period. Whether they were the same men is beside the point here: memory stakes a claim to bearing witness and to knowledge. Memories dwell on hiding, awe, and fear, with later knowledge projecting back, making the men who martyred Oradour and Tulle more terrifying. Jeannine Graveron recalled her mother's concern as the Germans passed their house, which was near a main road. Madeleine, the Parisian evacuee living with them, added to their anxiety:

> We had climbed up onto a little wall, and then she said, just like that, "Oh, it's the Boches!" My mother, I remember that she was angry, "Don't say that, don't say that!" But I didn't understand what it meant. . . . And they were—, they went past, and they'd just shot up a little village a bit further away. I remember that my mother said, "Oh, if they come, we'll give them anything we can, we'll give them eggs, we'll give them whatever we can." . . . We were really frightened, oh yes, we were.

Jeannine's words suggest how her mother conceived of the threat at the time. If news of their crimes had not yet reached her, perhaps she thought eggs might be enough to pacify them. Jacques Prieur had one strong memory of the Germans passing through his village in the Creuse in 1944:

> One day, in front of that house there were some railings . . . and there, in the road, there were the Germans. With automatic machine guns, trucks, other things, and the Germans, I can still remember it, there, a child at the gate and there, in the road—, I will always remember this German, sitting on the steps of his truck, waxing his boots. Waxing his boots, like that, shining, gleaming,

tch tch tch [making the noise and movement of holding a brush waxing a boot], and then "Get inside, get inside, because the Germans—".

The little boy watched with no real understanding of what the men represented. He supposed it was different for the adults: "*they* [he emphasizes the word] knew, but us, the children, we didn't know." Jacques has since researched the movements of the "Das Reich" division and discovered that a detachment did indeed pass through his village on the way from Oradour and Limoges to Guéret. The child watched in awe as a soldier shined his boots. The man knew where those boots had trodden.

Such brushes with danger were not limited to the "Das Reich" division. Yves Le Roy had been evacuated to a children's colony in the rural interior of Finistère, where they were looked after by two seminarists (the other staff, he said, had joined the maquis). Yves recalled that the children slept in their clothes, such was the anxiety after D-Day:

One morning, we heard noises, machine gun fire, cannons. . . . We heard a noise, and one of the priests—the future priests—went to look out of the window. He saw the Germans, coming back. . . . There was another house in front, and a little courtyard, and the Germans were coming in there, as though they were in retreat. There was no question of us leaving. It was five o'clock in the morning. And we stayed like that. There was nothing to eat, because the refectory was on the other side, but I can assure you, we made no noise at all. Nobody had to tell us to be quiet. We just sat on our beds. At midday, there was no lunch, no dinner, nothing to eat. At five o'clock in the afternoon, one of the seminarists said "I'm going to ask them if we can leave." He opened the door, and there was a concrete staircase. At the bottom, there were some officers sitting on the steps. He'd hardly opened the door when one came in with his machine gun. They were parachutists, and below, down there, was Ramcke, who commanded Brest. He was down there. And the seminarist asked, "Can we go and fetch some bread for the children?"—"Have you got children up there?"—"Yes", he said "they're very well behaved." "Where have the people from the village gone?" That was his question. "Er, well, I don't know," he said. "We're from Brest, we're all refugees from Brest here." "No, you can't go and fetch bread. We will be gone soon, and after that you can do what you like."

If this was indeed General Hermann-Bernhard Ramcke and his men, it was June 1944 and his Second Parachute Division was moving from Normandy to Brest. Ramcke's men held the port during the siege, surrendering on September 19, 1944. As with encounters with the "Das Reich" division, Yves's memory has particular resonance because of the reputation of those involved. The "Das Reich" soldiers already had blood on their hands; Ramcke's men were on the brink of destroying Yves's home town.[13] Future echoes reinforce the significance of a memory, making it both memorable and worth telling.

The liberation of France has its own iconography. Leaning from their tanks, smiling Americans kiss young French women who offer them flowers, and everyone dances in the streets.[14] Not surprisingly, these images resonate across the memory stories. But before such moments arrived, some children witnessed the worst violence they had yet seen. For Denise Algret in Villeurbanne, on the outskirts of Lyon, the night of August 26–27 left her with memories "which are a bit more difficult for me to relive." Denise recounted a violent engagement between the insurrectionary resistance and the Germans. "For me," she said, "the liberation of Lyon was first and foremost the tragic shootout in the Place de la Bascule": "We'd been woken up—in the accounts I've read of it later they say it's 4:45 A.M., but I'd be completely unable to tell you it was 4:45, but it was towards the end of the night—by a German operation on the Place de la Bascule, the square was completely surrounded. My father tried to get to grips with the situation and wanted to see what was going on." As he adjusted the blind at the window, "a bullet came in right past his neck and lodged in the kitchen wall." Several resisters were executed in the square, but the Germans were also firing at onlookers. The family moved onto the landing outside their flat, hoping they could climb out and escape across the rooftops, but there was a German posted downstairs. Once on the landing, they were too afraid to move: "That moment was very, very hard to bear. We stayed there, trapped, for two or three hours, maybe more, at least, I don't know exactly. . . . We didn't dare speak, we couldn't move, so it was really a moment that was very, very hard to bear." Violence escalated outside, and shops and buildings were set alight. Denise remembered being afraid that the flames would reach them. She recalled the cacophony of noise coming from below, as the German trucks stood with their engines running, and "we could hear gunfire, we could hear shooting, we could hear screaming." Then all of a sudden, the Germans left. Her father ran out to help. Buildings were on fire, bodies lined up on the pavement. The fire brigade, she said, was reluctant to come. The insurrection lasted until liberation on September 3, 1944. The Germans were at the river, "armed to the teeth," Denise said; "it really was horrific." She continued:

> Well, it was there that fear took a hold of me. I was seeing—, I was hearing gunfire everywhere, the Germans, they were going to come back, they were going to kill us, they were going to set fire to—, I was intolerable, well, I don't know if I received a couple of slaps to calm me down. . . . I was really on the edge of a nervous breakdown, and I have a very, very clear memory of it.

Memories of stressful experiences are likely to be better remembered. Having witnessed violence, Denise became hypervigilant, expecting an attack again at any moment. Fear projects into the future because it is about what *could* happen. As chapter 3 showed, the weirdness of memory time makes the virtual crucial to understanding the actual.

Denise was not alone in witnessing violence during the liberation. Yvette Cadiou, her mother, and her sister had found refuge in a Finistère village for much of the war. After the Americans passed through, she said, "everyone was saying, that's it, that's it! The war's over, the war's over!" But a vicious reprisal followed: "This group of Germans started firing at people. They even went into some of the houses [and] dragged people out of their homes and killed them. And among the people killed like that was my primary school teacher, who'd taught me to read. . . . And I remember that I was deeply, deeply affected by that, because it was someone I knew personally and very, very well." Simone Fauron in Troyes witnessed the horrible death of an enemy. Her voice trembled as she recounted a visual memory: "At the liberation, I saw them, I did, chained to their motorbike, they'd been burned, burned alive, but they were tied, they were still on their motorbike and attached with chains. They had SS badges on them, young people, enrolled through force. [She swallows audibly.] It was terrible, that. It really made a strong impression on me. [Her voice trembles.]" Affects flow as Simone seeks to justify, to herself and to a listener, what she feels. Her revulsion forces her into a position of compassion for these men, and yet they were SS men. She balances her compassion and revulsion using the fact of their youth: they must have been recruited by force, she thinks (rather than being committed Hitler Youth, as may have also been the case). A major national and international event, the liberation, was thus lived as millions of "little worlds," little ruptures and little occurrences, sensory and affective lived experiences in the spaces and places of everyday life. Liberation was not only troops, tanks, and celebrations. It was an escalation of capricious, contingent violence.

The arrival of the Americans signaled a shift from anxious anticipation to the reality of liberation. Paul Maubourg said that his first thoughts were not necessarily of freedom: "So there, I have a memory of being in the street, I was with a schoolfriend, and all of a sudden, trucks and men in helmets. Fear. We ran into the corridor of the friend's house, next door. Fear. But straight away we realized that outside, what was happening, it wasn't an act of war, it was something else. It was the Americans." Despite the presence of the Americans, the liberation was, first and foremost, a French affair. Luce Terrier said that whenever anyone asked her to name the best moments of her life, she replied: her wedding day, the birth of her children, and the liberation. Serge Holand recalled taking a bus from the Creuse to Paris. He and his friends hung out of the windows and made the V sign for victory as they passed through towns and villages. Bernard Lemaire recalled the festivities in Lille: "Ah, the liberation! I still talk about it! I remember very well, on the Grande-Place of Lille we danced a wonderful farandole! Just wonderful. Everyone held hands, strangers were kissing each other. I was fourteen at the time. . . . That farandole was incredible, really incredible." Simone Fauron recalled dancing to "In the Mood" with American GIs, who were "correct" with the young women of her town, she said, "we danced with them, we danced with each other, we even danced with people we didn't know!"[15] Yvette Chapalain from Brest was sixteen years old; together with schoolfriends, "we sang, we danced, in the stones, in the rubble, in the debris. We had our whole lives ahead of us, we were full of hope." Whether the girls literally danced in the ruins was less the point than the symbolic act. So, although the liberation era was full of fear and pain, it was also remembered in ways that resonated strongly with the wider memory regimes and their imagery.

Food resurfaces across these stories. The American arrival signaled not just plenty but novelty and modernity. In the town of Sorcy (Meuse), the Americans camped on the football pitch. Nadine Padovani listed with enthusiasm the bounty that appeared: "They gave us chocolate, now that I do remember! [She says it triumphantly.] Great big packets of chocolate, as thick as that. Corned beef [she says the words in English]. Cigarettes, which my father was pleased with. . . . And I remember his name, he was called Charles, an American who'd always come and spoil us all. Little bars of soap, cigarettes, boxes of candy [again in English], I can still see it all—." Also in Sorcy, Nicole Boscariol remembered a feeding station set up by the Americans: "There were pouches of soup, tins, and cheese, and white bread, tomato sauce, pears in syrup. I ate condensed milk for the very first time." Chewing gum proved a very sticky memory. Danielle Durville recalled, smiling broadly: "The Americans, when they came up route de la Reine, with their tanks, their trucks, I can still see it, I can! Ah! And I held up my hands for chocolates, biscuits, chewing gum. And afterwards, when I'd see them, the Americans, I'd go up and ask them—because I didn't know how to say chewing gum, I'd say 'chum chum gum, please, chum chum gum!' " Rémy Meningault was also flummoxed by this desirable delicacy: "We'd say semsemgum"; Nicole Boscariot simply swallowed it. Paul Maubourg and Simone Fauron also remembered Americans tossing packets of chewing gum from their tanks, along with sweets, chocolate, and cigarettes. There were no dissonant memories recounted of bad American behavior or negative attitudes toward their arrival.

In French memories, liberation often takes precedence over the end of the Second World War (May 8, 1945 for Europe and August 15, 1945 when Japan surrendered).[16] Sometimes the two became entangled. Claudine Meyer said: "I remember hearing the big boys shouting 'the war's finished, atomic bomb.' I've also got some memories of fireworks, but it's quite vague, it's a long time ago." When the interviewer asked if that was perhaps the moment of liberation, in spite of Claudine's mention of the atom bomb, she added: "For me, it's all mixed up. It's mixed up." A similar contraction of the two events was evident in Ginette Renard's memories:

And I was wearing—, you see, everyone was laughing when I was dancing at the liberation—, we were dancing Swing, I don't know, "La Bombe Atomique," it was "Tharama-boum-di-hé" [singing], we were dancing "La Danse Atomique," and, well, everyone was laughing and I thought that perhaps it was because I was dancing so well, but no, every time my skirt went up, they'd see these shirt tails, because I was wearing a man's shirt—[she laughs heartily].

Ginette mixes the liberation of 1944 with the events beyond the end of war, associating the 1946 song "La Danse Atomique" with the bombing of Japan in August 1945.[17] The events of May 1945 simply did not seem meaningful to some children. Roger Davre lived 1944 and 1945 happily evacuated in the rural Creuse. He said: "For me, the end of the war was just a half day off school, nothing more. . . . There wasn't any 'We've won, we're the winners, we're the best.' No, no, no. There was none of that kind of patriotism. . . . It was, *hup*, ah, the war's over. Well, perhaps for the adults, perhaps it meant something to them." In a larger village than Roger's, Henri Buc also recalled the end of the war, emphasizing new friendships between the Allies:

> There was a great celebration, we didn't have school, the bells were ringing, we were so happy. We understood what the end of the war meant because we'd been so afraid. And I recall, there was a boy who was an evacuee, who was there, and he was riding around on his bike, and he had a trailer on the back full of chestnuts. And on each of the four corners of the trailer there were the four flags, French, English, American, Russian.[18]

Denise Algret in Lyon, whose liberation had been so frightening, recalled the end of the war positively. Her family went to the Place Bellecour to watch Allied troops parading in an atmosphere she described as "euphoric." She admired the Russian soldiers and felt excited about the "friendship between peoples" it promised.

Instead of this blossoming hope, other children in other situations were forced to accept the permanence of their losses. For Jacques Prieur, who had been cared for in the Creuse since he was very young, and Thérèse Allglas-Cymmerman, protected by a couple in Mandres-les-Roses, the end of war broke stable relationships. New domestic regimes also began for those whose prisoner-of-war fathers returned. Pupils from Denise Algret's school were taken to the Gare de Brotteaux in Lyon to welcome back trainloads of deportees. These men and women who had survived work camps, concentration camps, or even death camps were in a terrible state. The children took cherries to offer as gifts, but they were confused by what they encountered. Denise said:

> You felt as though you were dealing with ghosts. And as well, we couldn't understand why, and our teachers were just the same. And that's where I have a very clear memory, that more than the horror—and this shows children can be a bit unfair—of the sight that greeted us, it was a huge disappointment. They had the cheek not to accept our cherries. We'd gone to get them, we'd carried them with us, we spent our money, we'd had a collection, and they didn't want them. We went home very disappointed.

Denise feels a little ashamed of her child self, but her memory recognizes the gap that had opened between the deportees and the rest of the population.

Children awaited the return of loved ones arrested months or years before. For Nancette Blanchou, whose father had been deported, the end of the war changed little: "When all the bells rang out at the end of the war, that also really affected me, because I still hadn't got my dad back. I still didn't have my dad. I'd got my mum back, but I didn't have my dad." Marie-Madeleine Viguié-Moreau also recounted the return of deportees to Cluny, hoping that her father would be among them. She was shocked to see them: "You didn't know if it was a man or a woman, it was horrific, they were, they were just skeletons." Every time a truck arrived bringing more home, local people "would come to try and understand, would come to try and recognize, because you couldn't recognize them. Most of them were in their striped pajamas. . . . It was a nightmare, really a nightmare. We'd go home each time muttering 'But our Dad . . .?' " The situation had something in common with the experience of Jewish children who awaited the return of their family and friends. Marie-Madeleine had in later years become friendly with various Jewish memorial associations. She said that she and the Jewish members felt they shared a great deal.

Rachel Jedinak lost both of her parents in the Shoah. She remembered taking photographs of her family members to the station where the deportees were returning to try to gain information about them: " 'Did you ever meet these—?' And I didn't finish my sentence. The people I saw really frightened me. Ghosts. Imagine the thinness of these men who probably weighed only thirty kilos. Their eyes were sticking out, it was true horror. They lived what was unsayable, the horror—. As far as possible, they didn't talk about it—. What could they have told us?" Silence began in those moments. For some of the returned deportees, the truth was too horrible to say; for children, the questions too difficult to ask. For a while Rachel and her sister still had hope. They invented reasons why their parents had not yet returned. Perhaps they had lost their memories, but one day they would remember. But eventually, hope ceased: "and as the months went by, we had to surrender to the evidence. They weren't ever coming back. You had to accept your new status as an orphan." As the war ended, France had to reconstruct itself. Morally, physically, and politically, the years of occupation, collaboration, resistance, Franco-French conflict, suspicion, violence, and lawlessness had deeply damaged the nation. For the children of this study, reconstruction was not a matter of infrastructure or political regime; it was closer to home. Families reconfigured themselves, affective relations were reestablished and reworked, but there were gaping absences. A shroud of silence covered many losses, imposed from both inside and outside. Experiences of fear, anger, shame, and pride shaped themselves into a regime of memory that validated certain experiences and not others. For children, the psychological consequences could be profound and long-lasting. But this is also a story of resilience, survival, and self-belief. Without any psychological support, many children who grew up in these difficult and unusual circumstances built happy and balanced lives, burying their pain for some years but attending to it thoughtfully in later life. What is abundantly clear from all of these interviews, however, is that it has mattered enormously to them to speak about love and loss: to speak and to be heard.

CONCLUSION

A PALETTE OF HAECCEITIES

his work began as a book project about children's lives in wartime France to be told, it was hoped, from a place called "the inside out." It ended up as something more than, or perhaps just different from, that: an experiment in bringing affect and oral history together. This conclusion concerns the reorientation of thought that has come to stand in place of an argument or narrative arc. Collective memory as a concept of structure and transmission has never excited me; at heart I have always been more interested in individuals: the singular teller of autobiographical tales, tragic tales, tall tales, tales of chewing gum and dancing and funerals, simultaneously separate from and connected to others. That word *individual* has become more complex to me in its relation to collectivities or to multiplicities of wildly diverse things as I have shifted away from the binary frameworks—individual/collective, child/adult, subject/object, agency/passivity, past/present—that underpin not only my previous work but that of many others.

Discovering the world of affect, its literatures, traditions, and language, I experienced the "shock to thought" that Elizabeth Adams St. Pierre described when she encountered, among other things, concepts such as haecceity and rhizome in the work of Gilles Deleuze and Félix Guattari.[1] Whether or not my work in *Feeling Memory* reads well and whether or not I have engaged sensibly with the ideas I have encountered, I will struggle to regard conventional historical scholarship or memory studies work in the same light as I did before. It is as though I have walked into a slightly different dimension where the things of the world speak differently to one another and seem pressingly, but realistically, overflowing and abundant. I like it, but you do not have to. This dimension holds more scope for thinking about reality through fabulation, virtuality, imagination, and playfulness; its language overuses words like imbricate, rupture, and entangle; its scholarly brief is to suggest, try, and wonder, not to state, follow, and know. Thinking about affective methodologies, affective knowledge, affective listening, affective writing, and their unknowable potential has already led me into new collaborative territory. I have tended toward and into other bodies; I have become something else. I had never before come across scholarship that said, boldly, let's make something new. Quite the opposite. Academic disciplinary conventions shape house styles, reviewing practices, research censuses, funding opportunities, and teaching curricula: these tell us *not* to make something new. They tell us to make an iteration of what has already been done, to be novel by filling a gap. They tell us to trace, not to draw. Interdisciplinarity is a fashionable trend, but to meld together at an epistemological level is risky and rarely attempted. Academic disciplines can be very stratified with hard-edged boundaries. But oral history is not quite a discipline, is it? It is something like a method. Or it is something like an ethos. As a nonassigned entry point into past-present relationships, it can still permit experimentation—and will do so as long as its gatekeeping practices (journals, publishers, reviewers) remain open to innovation.

Feeling Memory: Remembering Wartime Childhoods in France could have had a narrative arc, perhaps the chronology of the wartime years, or the process of growing up from toddler to adolescent, or the different places and spaces of children's everyday lives. Things could always have been different. But none of those categories, various of which I sketched out in earlier plans for the book, seemed sufficient to account for the overwhelming feeling of *feeling* that I had when working with the memory stories. Feeling when remembering, feeling when listening, feeling when writing, feeling when recounting, feeling when doing, feeling about people, feeling about the past, feeling emotions, feeling about emotions, feeling about objects, feeling about places, feeling about events, about people, feeling during events, feeling in places, feeling at times, feeling for others, feeling space, feeling objects, feeling angry, feeling scared, feeling shocked, feeling ashamed— feeling was inescapable. It was ubiquitous, intense, concerning, and surprising.

Part 1, "Memories Felt," mapped the contours of the felt realm in the memory stories. It considered sensory memories, emotional memories, and qualities of affect that were generated relationally, between things, and that, becoming intense, burned brightly in memory. Memories were seen to be sticky with affect, to leap and skitter along affective lines. It sought to establish that these memories were indeed made of feeling. Feeling did not need to be articulated as emotion for the felt quality of experience to press itself into the story. Parts 2 and 3, "Memories Located" and "Memories Told," concerned themselves with assemblages: the first brought trauma and locatedness together, the other brought remembering and discourse together. They observed parts of experience entering into composition with one another: place, happening, mother, feeling, pain, fence, train, truck, gun, story, defensiveness, desire, assumption, indignation. When things enter into combination, they make other things happen: memories stick, memories become intense, memories get told, histories get written. These assemblages were contingent, fleeting, and fundamentally unique, even when they had commonalities of expression, emphasis, or theme. This singularity is not just a question of everybody being different; such a statement does not get us very far and attaches too much weight to the person. An experience comprises much more than the person having it. Singularity came about through the heterogenous combinations that each instance of remembering generated. A recorded oral narrative is deep and wide, and it can only be *this* singular instance. Part 4 "Memories Lived," dwelt in the happening past. At its core was the proliferation of contingent possibilities that shaped children's realities; it fanned that multiplicity out like a deck of playing cards. For every child who liked, there was one who disliked; for every child who saw, there was one who did not see; for every child who suffered, there was one who did not, who looked on, who did not know, who did not care, who cried later. I can impose an extrinsic logic, my own post hoc logic, onto these experiences by highlighting commonality or contrast, but intrinsically they are a flow of remembering, events unfolding in their various presents, unknowable in their potential. Dipping the brush into this palette of haecceities creates a canvas shimmering with their multiplicity.

Does this book, then, point to a kind of hyperindividualism? Individualism is often treated with opprobrium as the mainstay of modern capitalism, conjuring ideas of self-reliance or self-isolation at best and selfishness, competitiveness, and social Darwinian destruction at worst. Alexis de Tocqueville pondered what might be the result of American democracy, noting that the individualist man "withdrawn apart, is like a stranger to the destiny of all the others; his children and his particular friends form for him the entire human species; as for the remainder of his fellow citizens, he is next to them, but he does not see them; he touches them without feeling them; he exists only in himself and for himself alone."[2] There *is* an isolationary, self-interested, protective dimension to the war years in France, and probably elsewhere. Fear, anxiety, and danger were frequently present, hunger too. Waiting it out, looking after one's own, perhaps ignoring the peril of others—certainly these behaviors existed. Yet time and again the memory stories suggest just how far, in spite of the precarious conditions of life, sociality and association continued, both interpersonally and politically. This is the case in the happening past, across the memory stories, and in the listening encounter. Individualism is not the outcome of these memory stories, taken together.

That said, I can perceive a kind of individuality here that recognizes each person as the final, indivisible state of being human: particular, singular, connected upstream to family, neighborhood, town, region, nation, religion, but nonetheless a discrete iteration of human difference. But that difference is not simply a condition belonging to the subject, to this or that person; indeed, this book is not really *about* subjects. It is not about actors or agents, or about getting to know this person from that person, deeply, their quirks, their whole life stories, their social worlds. It is not prosopography. It is about memories. What could be taken for hyperindividualism is a function of multiplicity: of individuation, not individualism. And that individuation exists at the level of the memory story: each interviewee is in their story as one element of an assemblage. Deleuze and Guattari write: "There is a mode of individuation very different from that of a person, subject, thing, or substance. . . . A season, a winter, a summer, an hour, a date have perfect individuality lacking nothing, even though this individuality is different from that of a thing or a subject."[3] Memory stories—oral histories, recorded autobiographical narratives, thoughts spoken, recorded, heard, referring to but never fully representing reality—are events. They are haecceities. They are instances of perfect individuality that "belong to no kind"; they are not just declensions of this or that.[4] They are deep pools of themselves, made of themselves, singular combinations of multiple other singularities, including the researcher who jumped in a while back. With this conceptual approach, we can turn away from the predeterminations that act as roadblocks to taking it *all* in and become differently attuned to what we understand of its constituent parts— when *it* is anything, *this* thing, *this* story—its connections and its potential to affect and be affected. This is a book about memories. Those memories are made of feeling. But it is also a book of haecceities, and by reading it and engaging with it, we keep on remaking it a haecceity.

Has that helped me find answers to the two questions that underpinned the research from the start: what was it like to be a child in Second World War

France, and how can we get at that experience "from the inside out"? My attempt to respond to the first rejected earlier ideas about listening for the "voice of the child"[5] but instead experimented with using affect as a medium for perceiving something of the past. Something of that past seemed, on occasion, perceptible because I tried to listen affectively: I tried to follow the affective lines and make sense of the connections the adult made between parts of their remembered childhood, to discern what was intense as a marker of what had captured the child's attention. Listening for the intensities that emerged around traumatic memory revealed something not only of ongoing affects but also of the past itself. By taking affect as not just an object of study but also its means, it was possible sometimes to look and feel alongside the child, imaginatively and sympathetically. It was very clear too that the child and the adult rememberer were one and the same. Thinking with ideas of multitemporality situated the child as a thinking, wondering, assuming, guessing person: fear projects a future, and fear could not happen without a concept of what might happen next. Thinking with the idea of surprise or shock also helped define the contours of the normal; such memories exist because they rupture normality. Shame too permitted something similar, with a moral drive.

Being differently attuned to the affectivity of these stories also meant I was less likely to discard parts of the memories that did not fit into preconceived categories; this meant that my task was to take in everything, potentially, or at least anything that was said in an interview. Being differently attuned made me more open to the mundanity, triviality, and ordinariness that comprise the vast majority of experience, of life, even in an extraordinary war. The German invasion was also cherries in eau-de-vie. Drancy was also a nightdress. Liberation was a funeral. These stories were told from the inside out to the degree that this can be possible. But is there a separate inside? Deleuze and Guattari cite Virginia Woolf's *Mrs. Dalloway*: "she sliced like a knife through everything: at the same time was outside, looking on."[6] The world strikes people—me, you, the rememberers—and we are inserted into the world. The memory stories reveal these zones of contact and encounter between the inner worlds of people in the past and the present—their desires, assumptions, motivations, anxieties, projections, beliefs—which are never insulated from the outside, the material world, the gaze of others, the pressure of discourse, and so on. It is impossible to know another's perspective from the inside out; this is why empathy is always a false promise. Instead, this book attempts to walk, if only for a moment, alongside the rememberers rather than step into their shoes. If we think we glimpse the past, or we think we glimpse the inner world of someone else, it is probably an illusion, but that is fine: after all, it is impossible to represent reality precisely as it is or was.

The Council on Foreign Relations, a U.S. think tank, lists armed conflicts and the potential for violence in territories across the world.[7] As I write in summer 2022, according to its definitions, there is "instability" in Venezuela, Pakistan, Myanmar, Iraq, Lebanon, Egypt, Libya, Mali, the Central African Republic, and the Democratic Republic of Congo; there is "conflict" in India and Pakistan, Ukraine, Nagorno-Karabakh, Syria, Israel and Palestine, and with Boko Haram in Nigeria and Al-Shabab in Somalia; there is "war" in Afghanistan, Yemen, Ethiopia, and South Sudan. In April 2022, Watchlist on Children and Armed Conflict made its recommendations for the UN Secretary-General's 2022 Annual Report on Children and Armed Conflict, listing grave violations against children in the Central African Republic, Colombia, Myanmar, Sudan, Yemen, and Israel/ Palestine; requesting further investigations in Colombia, Sudan, Burkina-Faso, Cameroon, and Israel/Palestine; and noting "other situations of concern" requiring action to determine where grave violations are being committed against children in Ethiopia, Mozambique, Niger, and Ukraine.[8] In each of these places, it should go without saying, children and their carers live with fear, anxiety, shock, and shame as they register, record, process, and store memories of what they witness and experience. Whether they are bystanders, implicated subjects, targets, or victims, whether they are active or passive in the conflicts around them, the affective dimensions of these situations are live, profound, and enduring. Their presents are unfolding on that knife-edge where their inner world of childish sense making, shock, fear, and anxiety collides with the material world in all its forms. Some will be asked to recount their experiences—whether to courtrooms, truth and reconciliation committees, psychiatrists, statisticians, NGOs, politicians, counselors, grandchildren, oral historians, doctors, journalists, or television cameras—which will be combinations of fact, impression, and emotion, with peaks of intensity, with objects and events made sticky by deep feeling, but perhaps not chronological or comprehensible though extrinsic forms of logic. Stories of emotion will be of great interest to some, but those held together by cobwebs of feeling may well be discounted by others, particularly if the speakers are deemed suspect in their emotional control.

To ignore the importance and value of affective knowledge, what we know by and through feeling and the felt realm, in favor of something purportedly free of contaminating emotional content is a high-stakes gamble. All researchers should be developing tools to understand the affective realm better, on its own terms. It is a shameful failing of conventional academic research culture, of competitive and quantifiable research strategies, and of the monetized education systems that they prop up that affective methodologies and epistemologies are so often overlooked. As arts and humanities research and teaching facilities around the world are shrinking and closing, disciplinary frontiers must yield. Not to recognize the affective quality of our lives is to ignore our common humanity; it is to stunt our capacity to enter into combination with one another, to make positive change, and to imagine this fragile world anew.

THE INTERVIEWEES

Surname	Name	Birth year*	Year of interview*	Source of interview	Key places	Notes
Agache	Lucien	1934	2009	Interviewer Lindsey Dodd. Archived in the Archives municipales de Lille.	Hellemmes, near Lille (Nord)	Mother died in 1938. Interviewed with his wife, Sonia Agache. Dodd's bombing research.
Agache	Sonia	1933	2009	Interviewer Lindsey Dodd. Archived in the Archives municipales de Lille.	Hellemmes, near Lille (Nord)	Interviewed with her husband, Lucien Agache. Dodd's bombing research. Evacuated child.
Algret	Denise	1935	1996	Centre d'Histoire de la Résistance et de la Déportation, Lyon, HRT 136.	Villeurbanne, near Lyon (Rhône)	
Allglas-Cymmerman	Thérèse	1941	2009	Interviewer unknown. Archives départementales du Val-de-Marne, 11AV 335.	Mandres-les-Roses (Seine-et-Oise, now Val-de-Marne)	Jewish child fostered by a non-Jewish couple while very young. Father was killed during the Holocaust but mother survived.
Aubrée	Serge	1928	2009	Interviewer Lindsey Dodd. Archived in the Archives municipales et communautaires de Brest.	Brest (Finistère)	Interviewed with his friend Cécile Bramé. Dodd's bombing research.
Bachelard	Raymond	1925?	Not given	Interviewer unknown. Archives municipales de Beaune, file number not given.	Beaune, Dijon (Côte-d'Or)	Father taken prisoner of war.
Baron	Charles	1926	1983	Interviewer Jean-Patrick Lebel. Archives départementales de Seine-Saint-Denis, 2AV 032/334.	Belleville, Paris; Drancy (Seine, now Seine-Saint-Denis); Auschwitz	Filmed interview, for Jean-Patrick Lebel's 1986 film *Cité de la Muette*. Deported Jewish child. Parents killed in the Holocaust.
Bauwens	Bernard	1928	2009	Interviewer Lindsey Dodd. Archived in the Archives municipales de Boulogne-Billancourt.	Boulogne-Billancourt (Seine, now Hauts-de-Seine)	Dodd's bombing research. Father became ill and died after having been mobilised.

Surname	First name	Birth year	Year	Source	Location	Notes
Becherel	Jean-Pierre	1936	2017	Interviewer Lindsey Dodd. Interview not yet archived.	Mallerat-Boussac (Creuse)	Refugee during 1940 civilian exodus. Father taken prisoner of war but quite soon released. Interviewed with his friends Denis and Jeannine Graveron and their daughter.
Belleuvre	Robert	1927	2009	Interviewer Lindsey Dodd. Archived in the Archives municipales de Boulogne-Billancourt.	Boulogne-Billancourt (Seine, today Hauts-de-Seine)	Dodd's bombing research. Evacuated child.
Béné	Jacqueline	1929	Not given	Interviewer unknown. Archives municipales de Beaune. File number not given.	Ivry-en-Montagne (Côte-d'Or)	Interviewer and interviewee address each other using the familiar form *tu* rather than *vous*. Father requisitioned into Forced Labor Service (STO).
Berland	Daniel	1929?	Not given	No interviewer. Archives départementales du Val-de-Marne, 4 AV 2558.	L'Haÿ-les-Roses (Seine), Oradour-sur-Vayres (Haute-Vienne)	Filmed monologue to camera. Family became refugees during 1940 civilian exodus. Only this period of his wartime experience is narrated.
Bernier	Robert	1939	2012	Interviewer Cécile Hochard. Rails et histoire: AHICF**, AV1 AT B072/E01.	Coutras (Gironde); Saint-Julien-sur-Cher (Loir-et-Cher), Dordogne	Father ran a clandestine abattoir.
Berthou	Jacqueline	1931	2013	Interviewer Cécile Hochard. Rails et histoire: AHICF**, AV1 AT B152/E01.	Auray (Morbihan); Nantes (Loire-Inférieure, now Loire-Atlantique)	

(continued)

Surname	Name	Birth year*	Year of interview*	Source of interview	Key places	Notes
Blanchou	Nancette	1936	2009	Archives départementales de la Dordogne, 14 AV 61.	La Coquille (Dordogne)	Part of the Mémoires De Résistances series: http://memoires-resistances. dordogne.fr/temoignages-audio/1008 -temoignages-integraux/52-jean-dolet -blanchou-resistant-deporte-nancette -blanchou.html. Child of resister. Father died at Mittelbau-Dora.
Boscariol	Nicole	1936	2008	Interviewers Françoise Dose, Vincent Lacorde, Lydiane Gueit-Montchal. Archives départementales de la Meuse, FAD055_J_059J0139.	Sorcy (Meuse)	
Bourrourault	Jean-Pierre	1938	Not given	Archives municipales de Beaune. No file number given.	Beaune (Côte-d'Or); Saint-Romain (Côte-d'Or)	
Bramé	Cécile	1929	2009	Interviewer Lindsey Dodd. Archived in the Archives municipales et communautaires de Brest.	Brest (Finistère)	Evacuated to a boarding school. Interviewed with her friend Serge Aubrée. Dodd's bombing research.
Buc	Henri	1934	2017	Interviewer Lindsey Dodd. Interview not yet archived.	Gouzon (Creuse)	Dodd's evacuation research. Family displaced in 1940. Father died of tuberculosis during the war.
Cadiou	Yvette	1936	2009	Interviewer Lindsey Dodd. Archived in the Archives municipales et communautaires de Brest.	St-Pierre-Quilbignon, near Brest (Finistère); Huelgoat (Finistère)	Dodd's bombing research. Family evacuated to rural area.
Caniot	Jean	1929	2009	Interviewer Lindsey Dodd. Archived in the Archives municipales de Lille.	Lambersart, near Lille (Nord)	Dodd's bombing research.

Surname	First name	Birth year	Year	Source	Location	Notes
Chapalain	Yvette	1929	2009	Interviewer Lindsey Dodd. Archived in the Archives municipales et communautaires de Brest.	St-Pierre-Quilbignon, near Brest (Finistère)	Dodd's bombing research. Evacuated with younger sister to a boarding school.
Christian	Renée	1939	2010	Interviewer Julien Rocipon, *Le Son des Choses* (https://lesondeschoses.org/).	Bar-sur-Aube (Aube)	Father was taken prisoner of war and was absent for the whole war.
Cornuéjols	Marie-Rolande	1930?	2002?	Unknown interviewer. Archives municipales de Beaune.	Antibes (Alpes-Maritimes), Peyrat-le-Château (Haute-Vienne), Paris (Seine)	Family became refugees during 1940 exodus. Father was taken prisoner of war but soon released.
Courant	Simone	1935	2017	Interviewer Lindsey Dodd. Interview not yet archived.	Saint-Denis, Paris (Seine, now Seine-Saint-Denis); Saint-Marc-à-Loubaud (Creuse)	Dodd's evacuation research. Interview takes place with Simone's daughter, Yolande, and Simone's widower, Eugène (b. 1933). Simone died in 2010.
Cousteaux	Andréa	1927	2009	Interviewer Lindsey Dodd. Archived in the Archives municipales et communautaires de Brest.	Brest (Finistère)	Evacuated from Paris region. Dodd's bombing research.
Davre	Roger	1933	2017	Interviewer Lindsey Dodd. Interview not yet archived.	Saint-Priest-la-Feuille (Creuse); fourteenth arrondissement, Paris	Dodd's evacuation research. Interviewed with his friend Marcel Dumas. Evacuated from Paris region. Father taken prisoner of war.
de la Bachellerie	Christian	1924	2009	Interviewer Lindsey Dodd. Archived in the Archives municipales de Boulogne-Billancourt.	Boulogne-Billancourt (Seine, now Hauts-de-Seine)	Dodd's bombing research.
Debarre	René	1938?	2012?	Interviewer unknown. Archives départementales du Val-de-Marne, 14 AV 962.	Montreuil-Bellay (Loire)	Interned Traveler child.

(continued)

Surname	Name	Birth year*	Year of interview*	Source of interview	Key places	Notes
Demont	Suzanne	1925–1929	2009	Interviewers unknown. Archives départementales de Saône-et-Loire, 25 AV 1.	Saint-Martin-en-Bresse; Chalon-sur-Saône (Saône-et-Loire)	Film *J'avais 15 ans sous l'occupation*, made by students at the Collège Olivier de la Marche, Saint-Martin-en-Bresse.
Denhez	Edith	1935	2009	Interviewer Lindsey Dodd. Archived in the Archives municipales de Lille.	Cambrai (Nord)	Dodd's bombing research. Family became refugees in 1940. Older brother killed by Allied bombs. Family bombed out 1944. Interviewed with her husband, Jean Denhez.
Denhez	Jean	1934	2009	Interviewer Lindsey Dodd. Archived in the Archives municipales de Lille.	Aulnoye (Nord)	Dodd's bombing research. Family became refugees in 1940. Interviewed with his wife, Edith Denhez
Devaux	Marie-Josèphe	1933	2009	Archives départementales de la Dordogne, 14 AV 15	Milhac-d'Auberoche (Dordogne)	Part of the Mémoires de Résistances series: http://memoires-resistances. dordogne.fr/temoignages-audio/1008-temoignages-integraux/36-souvenirs-de-temoignages-integraux/36-souvenirs-de-l-occupation-marie-josephe-devaux.html.
Dubowsky	Danièle	1936	2005	Interviewer unknown. Archives départementales du Val-de-Marne, 11AV 245-8.	Paris; Drancy; Vittel (Vosges); Palestine	Jewish child, interned at Drancy and Vittel. Father interned (U.S. national). Family emigrated to Palestine and then returned to France. Parents both survived the Holocaust.
Duclos	Léa	1934	2017	Interviewer Lindsey Dodd. Interview not yet archived.	Champigny (Seine, now Val-de-Marne); Lourdoueix (Creuse)	Dodd's evacuation research. Family became refugees.
Dumas	Marcel	1939	2017	Interviewer Lindsey Dodd. Interview	Creuse (near Saint-Priest-	Dodd's evacuation research. Interviewed

Surname	First name	Birth year	Interview/archive details	Place	Notes
Durville	Danielle	1939	Interviewer Lindsey Dodd. Archived in the Archives municipales de Boulogne-Billancourt.	Boulogne-Billancourt	Dodd's bombing research. Bombed out in 1942. Father taken prisoner of war and absent for the whole war.
Dutilleul	André	1929	Interviewer Lindsey Dodd. Archived in the Archives municipales de Lille.	Mont de Terre district of Fives, near Lille (Nord)	Dodd's bombing research. Interviewed with his wife, Josette Dutilleul.
Dutilleul	Josette	1932	Interviewer Lindsey Dodd. Archived in the Archives municipales de Lille.	Mont de Terre district of Fives, near Lille (Nord)	Dodd's bombing research. Interviewed with her husband, André Dutilleul.
Falchetto	Elvina	1937	Interviewers Françoise Dose, Vincent Lacorde, Lydiane Gueit-Montchal. Archives départementales de la Meuse, FRAD055_J_059J0134.	Sorcy (Meuse)	
Fauconnet	Marie-Madeleine	1928	Interviewer Lindsey Dodd. Interview not yet archived.	Le Cherchet (Creuse)	Dodd's evacuation research. Family received an evacuee from Paris. Interviewed with her friend and neighbor Genevieve Giraud, with other family members present. Father died early in the wartime period.
Fauron	Simone	1925	Interviewer Julien Rocipon, Le Son des Choses (https://lesondeschoses.org/).	Troyes (Aube)	
Févrat	Raymond	1925–1929	Interviewers unknown. Archives départementales de Saône-et-Loire, 25 AV 1.	Saint-Martin-en-Bresse; Chalon-sur-Saône (Saône-et-Loire)	Film J'avais 15 ans sous l'occupation, made by students at the Collège Olivier de la Marche, Saint-Martin-en-Bresse.
Fèvre	Daniel	1927	Interviewer unknown. Archives municipales de Beaune. File number not given.	Beaune (Côte-d'Or)	

(continued)

Surname	Name	Birth year*	Year of interview*	Source of interview	Key places	Notes
Floch	Michel	1927	2009	Interviewer Lindsey Dodd. Archived in the Archives municipales et communautaires de Brest.	Saint-Pierre-Quilbignon, near Brest (Finistère)	Dodd's bombing research.
Frugier	Raymond	1940	2001	Centre d'Histoire de la Résistance et de la Déportation, Lyon, HRT 395.	Oradour-sur-Glane	Escaped the massacre at Oradour-sur-Glane in 1944.
Gaillard	Christian	1930	2010	Interviewer Julien Rocipon, Le Son des Choses (https://lesondeschoses.org/).	Le Chêne (Aube)	Father taken prisoner of war.
Gaulthier	Madame	1926	Not given	Interviewer unknown. Archives municipales de Beaune. File number not given.	Beaune (Côte-d'Or)	
Ghisolfo	Madame	1930	2014	Interview team Jérôme Daeron, Simon Morin, and Pauline Orain. Paroles libérées de Sète (http://parolesliberees.org/).	Sète (Hérault)	Edited oral history extracts: http://parolesliberees.org/madame-ghisolfo/.
Girardon	Henri	1928	2009	Interviewer Lindsey Dodd. Archived in the Archives municipales et communautaires de Brest.	Lambézellec, near Brest; Quimper (Finistère)	Dodd's bombing research. Evacuated away from Brest to relatives.
Giraud	Geneviève	?	2017	Interviewer Lindsey Dodd. Interview not yet archived.	Le Cherchet (Creuse)	Dodd's evacuation research. Family took in an evacuee child from Paris. Interviewed with her friend and neighbor Marie-Madeleine Faucomnet.

Gobert	Suzanne	Later 1930s	2002	Centre d'Histoire de la Résistance et de la Déportation, Lyon, HRT 376.	Oradour-sur-Glane; Alsace	Video interview. Recorded with her sister, Marie-Louise Linder. Family were refugees near Oradour-sur-Glane, but escaped the massacre there in 1944.
Goldring	Maurice	1933	2005	Interviewer unknown. Archives départementales du Val-de-Marne, 11AV 235, 236.	Saint-Quentin (Aisne); Vidaillat (Creuse)	Jewish child. Parents survived the Holocaust.
Graveron	Denis	1931	2017	Interviewer Lindsey Dodd. Interview not yet archived.	Near Mallerat-Boussac (Creuse)	Dodd's evacuation research. Interviewed with his friend Jean-Pierre Becherel and his wife, Jeannine Graveron. Family took in Jean-Pierre Becherel's family during 1940 exodus.
Graveron	Jeannine	1938	2017	Interviewer Lindsey Dodd. Interview not yet archived.	Near Mallerat-Boussac (Creuse)	Dodd's evacuation research. Interviewed with her friend Jean-Pierre Becherel and her husband, Denis Graveron. Family took in an evacuee child from Paris.
Grynberg	Lola	1935	2005	Archives départementales du Val-de-Marne, 11 AV 251.	Paris; Nice, Berre-les-Alpes (Alpes-Maritimes)	Jewish child, hidden, housed in several different places in the south of France. Parents survived the Holocaust.
Guendjian	Grégoire	1934	2012	Interviewer Myriam Fellous-Sigrist. Rails et histoire: AHICF**, AV1 AT GO37/EO1.	Bron, near Lyon (Rhône)	Survived a near-miss in an air raid. Family of Armenian origins. Available at: http://www.memoire-orale.org/notice.php?id=142
Haigneré	Pierre	1935	2009	Interviewer Lindsey Dodd. Archived in the Archives municipales de Lille.	La Délivrance, Lomme, near Lille (Nord)	Dodd's bombing research. Family bombed out in 1944.

Surname	Name	Birth year*	Year of interview*	Source of interview	Key places	Notes
Holand	Serge	1934	2017	Interviewer Lindsey Dodd. Interview not yet archived.	Saint-Priest-la-Feuille (Creuse)	Jewish child. Crossed demarcation line, family "hid" in village. Parents survived the Holocaust.
Jean-Bart	Madame	Later 1930s?	2009	Interviewer Lindsey Dodd. Archived in the Archives municipales de Lille.	Lille (Nord)	Dodd's bombing research. Interviewed with her husband, Michel Jean-Bart, who was the main interviewee. Brother killed by Germans.
Jean-Bart	Michel	1934	2009	Interviewer Lindsey Dodd. Archived in the Archives municipales de Lille.	La Délivrance, Lomme, near Lille (Nord)	Dodd's bombing research. Interviewed with his wife, Madame Jean-Bart. Family bombed out in 1944.
Jedinak	Rachel	1934	2008	Archives départementales du Val-de-Marne, 11AV 310.	Paris; Brittany	Jewish child, hidden. Author of *Nous étions seulement des enfants* (Paris: Fayard, 2018). Father was taken prisoner of war but was soon released. Parents killed during the Holocaust.
Jossent	André	1933	2017	Interviewer Lindsey Dodd. Interview not yet archived.	Faux-la-Montagne (Creuse)	Dodd's evacuation research. Evacuated to an aunt's house in the countryside with his cousin. Interviewed with his cousin Michel Pauty and their wives.
Journeuaux	Odette	1925–1929	2009	Interviewers unknown. Archives départementales de Saône-et-Loire, 25 AV 1.	Perigny (Saône-et-Loire)	Film *J'avais 15 ans sous l'occupation*, made by students at the Collège Olivier de la Marche, Saint-Martin-en-Bresse.
Kahn	Nicole	1933	1983	Interviewer Jean-Patrick Lebel. Archives départementales de Seine-Saint-Denis, 2AV 032/328.	Marseille (Bouches-du-Rhone); Drancy	Filmed interview, for Jean-Patrick Lebel's 1986 film *Cité de la Muette*. Interned Jewish child. Parents survived

Surname	First name	Born	Interview	Place	Archive / Interviewer	Notes
Kermen	Jacques	1932	2017	Dontreix (Creuse), Suresnes (Seine, now Hauts-de-Seine)	Interviewer Lindsey Dodd. Interview not yet archived.	Dodd's evacuation research. Evacuated from the Paris region.
Krouck	Sam	1933	2008	Third arrondissement, Paris; Limoges (Haute-Vienne); Douadic (Indre)	Interviewer unknown. Archives départementales du Val-de-Marne, 11 AV 302.	Jewish child. Temporarily interned in Douadic camp. Family then "hid" in the countryside. Parents survived the Holocaust.
Laurens	Anne-Marie	1935	2012	Châlons-sur-Marne (Marne, now Châlons-en-Champagne)	Interviewer Cécile Hochard. Rails et histoire: AHICF**, AV1 AT L020/E01	Child of resister. Father died in Dachau. http://www.memoire-orale.org/notice.php?id=145.
Lazard	Guy	1932	[after 2000]	Mâcon (Saône-et-Loire)	Recorded presentation to schoolchildren. Archives départementales de Saône-et-Loire, 596 J.	Jewish child. Filmed recording of Guy Lazard talking to a group of schoolchildren (c. 11 years old) at the archive. Family "hid" in the countryside. Parents survived the Holocaust.
Leclerc	Sylvette	1932	2010	Saint-Mesmin (Aube)	Interviewer Julien Rocipon, Le Son des Choses (https://lesondeschoses.org/).	Father was taken prisoner of war and absent for the whole war.
Leclercq	Bernard	1936?	2009	Hellemmes, near Lille (Nord)	Interviewer Lindsey Dodd. Archived in the Archives municipales de Lille.	Dodd's bombing research. Bernard's wife was the main interviewee. Father taken prisoner of war, released in 1941.
Leclercq	Thérèse	1938	2009	Hellemmes, near Lille (Nord)	Interviewer Lindsey Dodd. Archived in the Archives municipales de Lille.	Dodd's bombing research. Interviewed with her husband, Bernard Leclercq.
Lefèvre	Christian	1930	2008	Sorcy (Meuse)	Interviewers Françoise Dose, Vincent Lacorde, and Lydiane Gueit-Montchal. Archives départementales de la Meuse, FRAD055_J_059J0136.	

(continued)

Surname	Name	Birth year*	Year of interview*	Source of interview	Key places	Notes
Lemaire	Bernard	1930	2009	Interviewer Lindsey Dodd. Archived in the Archives municipales de Lille.	Lille (Nord)	Dodd's bombing research.
Le Goff	Christian	1937	2017	Interviewer Lindsey Dodd. Interview not yet archived.	Colombes, Paris (Seine, now Hauts-de-Seine); Issoudun-Létrieix (Creuse)	Dodd's evacuation research. Evacuated from the Paris region.
Le Roy	Yves	1931	2009	Interviewer Lindsey Dodd. Archived in the Archives municipales et communautaires de Brest.	Saint-Pierre-Quilbignon, near Brest (Finistère)	Dodd's bombing research. Evacuated away from Brest to a boarding school.
Le Turquais	Henri	1930	2009	Interviewer Lindsey Dodd. Archived in the Archives municipales et communautaires de Brest.	Saint-Pierre-Quilbignon, near Brest (Finistère)	Dodd's bombing research. Evacuated away from Brest. Mother died of an illness partway through the wartime period.
Liévin	Blanche	1934	2011	Interviewer unknown. Archives municipales de Dunkerque. File number not given.	Dunkerque (Nord)	Transcript only made available.
Linder	Marie-Louise	Late 1930s	2002	Centre d'Histoire de la Résistance et de la Déportation, Lyon, HRT 376.	Oradour-sur-Glane (Haute-Vienne); Alsace	Video interview. Recorded with her sister, Suzanne Gobert. Family were refugees near Oradour-sur-Glane, but escaped the massacre there in 1944.
Magnin	Edouard	1925	2010	Interviewer Julien Rocipon, Le Son des Choses (https://lesondeschoses.org/).	Ville-sous-la-Ferré (Aube)	

Surname	First name	Birth	Interview	Source / Archive	Location	Notes
Marc	Claudine	1939	2008	Interviewers Françoise Dose, Vincent Lacorde, and Lydiane Gueit-Montchal. Archives départementales de la Meuse, FRAD055_J_059J0131.	Sorcy (Meuse)	Dodd's bombing research. Evacuated to a boarding school in Normandy.
Martin	Michèle	1931	2009	Interviewer Lindsey Dodd. Archived in the Archives municipales de Boulogne-Billancourt.	Boulogne-Billancourt (Seine); Normandy	Filmed interview. Child of resister. Father tortured and killed by Nazis.
Maubourg	Paul	1936?	1992	Centre d'Histoire de la Résistance et de la Déportation, Lyon, HRT 130.	Oyannax (Ain); Chateau Dortan (Ain)	
Ménigault	Rémy	1937	2013	Interviewer unknown. Rails et histoire: AHICF**, interview unnumbered at the time of access.	Audeville (Loiret)	
Meppiel	Jacqueline	1928	1982	Archives départementales de Seine-Saint-Denis, 2AV 032 / 244	Saint-Denis (Seine, now Seine-Saint-Denis); Chateauroux (Indre)	Filmed interview.
Mingat	Robert	1928	1995	Centre d'Histoire de la Résistance et de la Déportation, Lyon, HRT 454.	Lyon (Rhône)	Filmed interview, recorded with his cousin Luce Terrier. Child of resisters.
Millot	Lucien	1930	2008	Interviewers Françoise Dose, Vincent Lacorde, and Lydiane Gueit-Montchal. Archives départementales de la Meuse, AD055_J_059J0133.	Sorcy (Meuse)	
Muller	Madame	1929	2014	Interview team Jérôme Daeron, Simon Morin, and Pauline Orain. Paroles libérées de Sète (http://parolesliberees.org/).	Sète (Hérault)	Edited oral history extracts, available online at: http://parolesliberees.org/madame-muller/

(continued)

Surname	Name	Birth year*	Year of interview*	Source of interview	Key places	Notes
Padovani	Nadine	1937	2008	Interviewers Françoise Dose, Vincent Lacorde, Lydiane Gueit-Montchal. Archives départementales de la Meuse, FRAD055_J_059J0130.	Sorcy (Meuse)	
Palisson	Lucien	1933	2012	Interviewer Myriam Fellous-Sigrist. Rails et histoire: AHICF**, interview unnumbered at the time of access.	Sancergues (Cher)	Evacuated to grandparents' house during the war.
Pauty	Michel	1933	2017	Interviewer Lindsey Dodd. Interview not yet archived.	Paris; Faux-la-Montagne (Creuse)	Dodd's evacuation research. Interviewed with his cousin André Jossent; for a part of the interview his wife, Madame Pauty, and André Jossent's wife, Madame Jossent, were also present. Evacuated from Paris region to stay with aunt in the countryside.
Pochart	Jean	1931	2009	Interviewer Lindsey Dodd. Archived in the Archives municipales et communautaires de Brest.	Brest (Finistère)	Dodd's bombing research.
Potiquet	Robert	1925-1929	2009	Interviewers unknown. Archives départementales de Saône-et-Loire, 25 AV 1.	Saint-Martin-en-Bresse; Chalon-sur-Saône (Saône-et-Loire)	Film *J'avais 15 ans sous l'occupation*, made by students at the Collège Olivier de la Marche, Saint-Martin-en-Bresse.
Potter	Max	1929	2009	Interviewer Lindsey Dodd; interview not archived.	La Chapelle district, eighteenth arrondissement, Paris	Dodd's bombing research. Father interned (British national).

Prieur	Jacques	1938	2016	Interviewer Lindsey Dodd. Interview not yet archived.	St-Dizier-Leyrennes (Creuse); Paris	Dodd's evacuation research. Evacuated from the Paris region. Father killed fighting during the German invasion.
Puech	Madame	1928	2014	Interview team Jérôme Daeron, Simon Morin, Pauline Orain. Aout 1944: Paroles libérées sur Sète (http://parolesliberees.org/).	Sète (Hérault)	Edited oral history extracts: http://parolesliberees.org/madame-puech/.
Quinet	Marcel	1925–1929	2009	Interviewers unknown. Archives départementales de Saône-et-Loire, 25 AV 1.	Saint-Martin-en-Bresse; Chalon-sur-Saône (Saône-et-Loire)	Film *J'avais 15 ans sous l'occupation*, made by students at the Collège Olivier de la Marche, Saint-Martin-en-Bresse.
Rémeur	Lucienne	1930	2009	Interviewer Lindsey Dodd. Archived in the Archives municipales et communautaires de Brest.	Brest (Finistère)	Dodd's bombing research. Escaped the explosion in the Sadi-Carnot bomb shelter in 1944.
Renard	Ginette	1930	2012	Interviewer Cécile Hochard. Rails et histoire: AHICF**, AV/AT RO51/E01.	Villeneuve-Saint-Georges (Seine-et-Oise); Riom (Puy-de-Dôme); Neuvy-Sautour (Yonne)	Father died in an accident during the war.
Richard	Irène	1932	2008	Interviewers Françoise Dose, Vincent Lacorde, and Lydiane Gueit-Montchal. Archives départementales de la Meuse, FRAD055_J_059J0129.	Sorcy (Meuse)	Interviewed with her husband, Yves Richard.

(continued)

Surname	Name	Birth year*	Year of interview*	Source of interview	Key places	Notes
Richard	Yves	1930	2008	Interviewers Françoise Dose, Vincent Lacorde, and Lydiane Guéit-Montchal. Archives départementales de la Meuse, FRAD055_J_059J0129.	Sorcy (Meuse)	Interviewed with his wife, Irène Richard.
Saunier	Arnaud	1934	2012	Interviewer unknown. Rails et histoire: AHICF**, AV1 AT S122/E01.	Lamballe (Côtes-d'Armor)	This is a pseudonym, used at the interviewee's request.
Sauvonnet	Madame	1930?	Not given	Archives municipales de Beaune. No file number given.	Beaune (Côte-d'Or)	
Scaglia-Chiaffi	Lucienne	1931	Not given	Interviewer unknown. Archives départementales du Val-de-Marne, 11 AV 286–92.	Fontenay-sous-Bois (Seine)	
Solet	Christian	1932	2009	Interviewer Lindsey Dodd. Archived in the Archives municipales de Boulogne-Billancourt.	Boulogne-Billancourt (Seine); La Charité-sur-Loire (Nièvre)	Dodd's bombing research. Refugee during 1940 exodus.
Streicher	Colette	1937	2017	Interviewer Philippe Béquia. Interview not known to be publicly archived.	La Cellette (Creuse); Suresnes (Seine, now Hauts-de-Seine)	Dodd's evacuation research. Evacuated from the Paris region.
Tatelin	Marcel	1925–1929	2009	Interviewers unknown. Archives départementales de Saône-et-Loire, 25 AV 1.	Saint-Martin-en-Bresse; Chalon-sur-Saône (Saône-et-Loire)	Film *J'avais 15 ans sous l'occupation*, made by students at the Collège Olivier de la Marche, Saint-Martin-en-Bresse.
Tainturier	Pierre	1928	Not given	Archives municipales de Beaune. No file number given.	Beaune (Côte-d'Or)	

Surname	First name					
Termote	Marie-Thérèse	1930	2009	Interviewer Lindsey Dodd. Archived in the Archives municipales de Lille.	Hellemmes, near Lille (Nord)	Dodd's bombing research. Interviewed with her husband, Paul Termote.
Termote	Paul	1935	2009	Interviewer Lindsey Dodd. Archived in the Archives municipales de Lille.	Hellemmes, near Lille (Nord)	Dodd's bombing research. Interviewed with his wife, Marie-Thérèse Termote.
Terrier	Luce	1932	1995	Interviewer unknown. Centre d'Histoire de la Résistance et de la Déportation, Lyon, HRT 454.	Lyon (Rhône)	Filmed interview recorded with her cousin Robert Mingat. Child of resisters.
Th	Madame	1927	2009	Interviewer Lindsey Dodd. Archived in the Archives municipales de Boulogne-Billancourt.	Boulogne-Billancourt (Seine)	Dodd's bombing research. Interviewee opted to be anonymized via this pseudonym.
Thomas	Claude	1931	2009	Interviewer Lindsey Dodd. Archived in the Archives municipales de Boulogne-Billancourt.	Boulogne-Billancourt (Seine)	Dodd's bombing research. Evacuated to relatives in the countryside. Interviewed with his brother, Michel Thomas.
Thomas	Michel	1929	2009	Interviewer Lindsey Dodd. Archived in the Archives municipales de Boulogne-Billancourt.	Boulogne-Billancourt (Seine)	Dodd's bombing research. Evacuated to relatives in the countryside. Interviewed with his brother, Claude Thomas.
Transler	Georgette	1928	2010	Interviewer Julien Rocipon, Le Son des Choses (htps://lesondeschoses. org/).	Grange l'Eveque (Aube)	Memories quite muddled across the interview.
Valade	Albert	1930	2001	Interviewer unknown. Centre d'histoire de la résistance et de la déportation, Lyon, HRT391.	Oradour-sur-Glane (Haute-Vienne)	

(continued)

Surname	Name	Birth year*	Year of interview*	Source of interview	Key places	Notes
Viguié-Moreau	Marie-Madeleine	1934	After 2004	Interviewers unknown. Archives départementales de Saône-et-Loire, 14 NUM [non coté].	Cluny (Saône-et-Loire)	The archived version to which I was given access was the unedited rushes of a filmed interview. Child of resisters. Father died at Mauthausen. Author of *Les orphelins de la Saint-Valentin: Histoire vraie d'une enfance brisée le 14 février 1944* (Paris: L'Harmattan, 2004).
Yessad	Françoise	1937	2017	Interviewer Lindsey Dodd. Interview not yet archived.	Saint-Sulpice-le-Guérétois (Creuse); Orléans (Loiret)	Dodd's evacuation research. Her family received an evacuee from Paris.
Zaidner	Marcel	1930	2010	Interviewer unknown. Archives départementales du Val-de-Marne, 1 AV 430.	Belleville, Paris; Grenoble (Isère)	Jewish child. Parents survived the Holocaust.
Zytnicki	Hélène	1932	1983	Interviewer Jean-Patrick Lebel. Archives départementales de Seine-Saint-Denis, 2AV 032/357, 358.	Paris; Drancy (Seine, now Seine-Saint-Denis; Beaune-la-Rolande (Loiret)	Filmed interview, for Jean-Patrick Lebel's 1986 film *Cité de la Muette*. Interned Jewish child. Mother killed during the Holocaust, father and brother survived.

*Sometimes the year of birth and/or the year in which the interview was conducted were not available. Approximations are marked with a question mark or via an explanation.

**AHICF, Association pour l'histoire des chemins de fer.

NOTES

INTRODUCTION

1. Susan J. Matt, "Current Emotion Research in History: Or, Doing History from the Inside Out," *Emotion Review* 3, no. 1 (2011): 117–124.
2. Some scholars of childhood see children as a subaltern group because of their subordination to adult power. Kristine Alexander describes them as "a colonized group, frequently seen as primitive or not fully realized, who are more often spoken for and about than they are allowed to speak." Kristine Alexander, "Can the Girl Guide Speak? The Perils and Pleasures of Looking for Children's Voices in Archival Records," *Jeunesse: Young People, Texts, Cultures* 4, no. 1 (2012): 134.
3. Claire Langhamer, " 'Who the Hell Are Ordinary People?' Ordinariness as a Category of Historical Analysis," *Transactions of the Royal Historical Society* 28 (2018): 175–95.
4. Keith Jenkins, *Re-Thinking History* (London: Routledge, 1991), 6–29.
5. See, for example, Alan Prout, *The Future of Childhood* (London: Routledge, 2005); Mary Jane Kehily, ed., *An Introduction to Childhood Studies*, 2nd ed. (New York: Open University Press, 2009); Paula S. Fass, ed., *The Routledge History of Children in the Western World*, 2nd ed. (Abingdon, UK: Routledge, 2015).
6. Mark Salber Phillips, "On the Advantage and Disadvantage of Sentimental History for Life," *History Workshop Journal* 65 (2008): 50.
7. Lawrence Grossberg, "Affect's Future: Rediscovering the Virtual in the Actual," in *The Affect Theory Reader*, ed. Gregory J. Seigworth and Melissa Gregg (Durham, NC: Duke University Press, 2010), 313.
8. Matt, "Current Emotion Research."
9. See, for example, Manon Pignot, *La guerre des crayons. Quand les petits Parisiens dessinaient la Grande Guerre* (Paris: Parigramme, 2004); for children's letter writing in Second World War France, see Lindsey Dodd, " 'Mon Petit Papa Chéri': Children, Fathers, and Family Separation in Wartime France," *Essays in French Literature and Culture* 54 (2017): 97–116; and Lindsey Dodd, "Children's Citizenly Participation in the National Revolution: The Instrumentalization of Children in Vichy France," *European Review of History/Revue d'Histoire Européenne* 24, no. 5 (2017): 759–80.

10. Ludmilla Jordanova, "Children in History: Concepts of Nature and Society," in *Children, Parents, and Politics*, ed. Geoffrey Scarre (Cambridge: Cambridge University Press, 1989), 5, discussed in Lindsey Dodd, *French Children Under the Allied Bombs, 1940–1944: An Oral History* (Manchester: Manchester University Press, 2016), 41.

11. Harald Welzer, "Communicative Memory," in *A Companion to Cultural Memory Studies: An International and Interdisciplinary Handbook*, ed. Astrid Erll and Ansgar Nünning (Berlin: Walter de Gruyter, 2008), 285–298. Welzer writes that there are "considerable gaps in the research on the non-intentional, casual, social procedures of memory. The texture of memory seems so complex and so ephemeral that scientific instruments simply fail in attempting to determine what memory is made of and how it is created every day" (286).

12. Keith Jenkins, "Nobody Does It Better: Radical History and Hayden White," *Rethinking History: The Journal of Theory and Practice* 12, no. 1 (2008): 63; also Jenkins, *Re-Thinking History*, 12–15.

13. Ewa Domanska, "A Conversation with Hayden White," *Rethinking History: The Journal of Theory and Practice* 12, no. 1 (2008): 16.

14. Owain Jones, "Geography, Memory and Non-Representational Geographies," *Geography Compass* 5, no. 2 (2011): 881–882.

15. These questions originate with Sara Ahmed's interrogation of emotion: "So rather than asking 'What are emotions?,' I will ask, 'What do emotions do?' " Sara Ahmed, *The Cultural Politics of Emotion*, 2nd ed. (Edinburgh: Edinburgh University Press, 2014), 4. I am also influenced by Deleuze and Guattari's rhizomatic approach to knowledge, as discussed clearly in Brent Adkins, *Deleuze and Guattari's* A Thousand Plateaus: A Critical Introduction and Guide (Edinburgh: Edinburgh University Press, 2015), 22–33. These ideas are also inspired by Deleuze and Guattari's assemblage thinking: "For each assemblage, Deleuze and Guattari ask: what is the manner of its composition? What combinations can it enter into that compose and decompose it?" Adkins, *Deleuze and Guattari's* A Thousand Plateaus, 245.

16. Grossberg, "Affect's Future," 318.

17. Shane Vogel emphasizes the important "critical work" done by the phrase "or something" in Kathleen Stewart's *Ordinary Affects* (Durham, NC: Duke University Press, 2007), which seems pertinent here: "The phrase evokes the reach of the imagination as it attempts to understand an encounter or scene. At the same time, it undoes the authority of the possible interpretations offered and refuses the fixing of experiences that are always fluid and in formation. . . . 'Or something' is a placeholder for other possibilities." Shane Vogel, "By the Light of What Comes After: Eventologies of the Ordinary," *Women and Performance: A Journal of Feminist Theory* 19, no. 2 (2009), 257.

18. Gregory J. Seigworth and Melissa Gregg, "An Inventory of Shimmers," in *The Affect Theory Reader*, 4.

19. Kathleen Stewart, "Weak Theory in an Unfinished World," *Journal of Folklore Research* 45, no. 1 (2008): 72.

20. Jones, "Geography, Memory," 876.

21. Marianne Hirsch and Leo Spitzer, "The Witness in the Archive," in *Memory: History, Theories, Debates*, ed. Susannah Radstone and Bill Schwartz (New York: Fordham University Press, 2010), 405.

22. Hirsch and Spitzer, "The Witness," 403–405.

23. For a study illustrating the embeddedness of Jewish citizens in French society, see Daniel Lee, *Pétain's Jewish Children: French Jewish Youth and the Vichy Regime, 1940–1942* (Oxford: Oxford University Press, 2014).

24. Seigworth and Gregg, "An Inventory," 3; emphasis in original.

25. Interviews will not be referenced in the endnotes after each citation; consult the appendix.

26. The Mémorial de Caen has a large collection of oral history interviews that I did not consult because the Mémorial did not respond to my inquiries, the region has already had attention from scholars, and practical reasons of finance and time precluded a visit. My current research is taking in children's experiences of internment in the southwest, in the departments of Pyrénées-Atlantiques and Pyrénées-Orientales.

27. See, for example, Anindya Raychaudhuri, " 'This, Too, Is History': Oral History, the 1947 India-Pakistan Partition and the Risks of Archival Re-Ordering," *Oral History* 49, no. 2 (2021): 69–80.

28. These were conducted for Dodd, *French Children*, 2016.

29. Until 1941, the E (up to two years old), J1 (three to six years old) and J2 (seven to thirteen years old) ration cards were the only three categories for children. After that age, young people were classed as A (adult) until the age of seventy; calories and protein intake for the A category were the lowest of all ration groups except V (over seventy). From 1941, in recognition of the serious nutritional deficiencies among young people, the J3 ration category was introduced for ages fourteen to twenty-one. J3 provided a higher caloric and protein intake for this group, a little above that allocated to a manual worker (T category). Michel Cépède, *Agriculture et alimentation en France, durant la Seconde Guerre Mondiale* (Paris: Génin, 1961), 389.

30. Alistair Thomson, "Indexing and Interpreting Emotion: Joy and Shame in Oral History," *Studies in Oral History* 41 (2018): 1.

31. Alessandro Portelli, *The Death of Luigi Trastulli and Other Stories: Form and Meaning in Oral History* (Albany: State University of New York Press, 1991); Alessandro Portelli, *The Battle of the Valle Giulia: Oral History and the Art of Dialogue* (Madison: University of Wisconsin Press, 1997).

32. Sherna Berger Gluck, "Has Oral History Lost Its Radical/Subversive Edge?," *Oral History* 39, no. 2 (2011): 63–72.

33. Alistair Thomson, "Four Paradigm Transformations in Oral History," *Oral History Review* 34, no. 1 (2007): 49–70.

34. Gluck, "Has Oral History Lost," 66.

35. An excellent example of sharing authority can be seen in Alistair Thomson, *Moving Stories: An Intimate History of Four Women Across Two Countries* (Manchester, UK: Manchester University Press, 2011). The term derives from Michael Frisch, *A Shared Authority? Essays on the Craft and Meaning of Oral and Public History* (Albany: State University of New York Press, 1990).

36. Gluck, "Has Oral History Lost," 66.

37. Sherna Berger Gluck and Daphne Patai, eds., *Women's Words: The Feminist Practice of Oral History* (New York: Routledge, 1991); Katrina Srigley, Stacey Zembrzycki, and

Franca Iacovetta, eds., *Beyond Women's Words: Feminisms and the Practices of History in the Twenty-First Century* (New York: Routledge, 2018). Other recent collections bringing affect more clearly into focus for oral historians include Nan Alamilla Boyd and Horacio N. Roque Ramírez, eds., *Bodies of Evidence: The Practice of Queer Oral History* (New York: Oxford University Press, 2012); and Anna Sheftel and Stacey Zembrzycki, eds., *Oral History Off the Record: Toward an Ethnography of Practice* (New York: Palgrave, 2013). Additionally, *plática* research methodologies, coming out of Chicana studies, embed interaffectivity into conversational practices of encounter, exchange, and respect, which shift the dynamics of oral history interviewing in productive ways. See, for example, Dolores Delgado Bernal, "Disrupting Epistemological Boundaries: Reflections on Feminista Methodological and Pedagogical Interventions," *Aztlán: A Journal of Chicano Studies* 45, no. 1 (2020): 155–169; also María Eugenia Cotera, "Fleshing the Archive: Reflections on Chicana Memory Practice," *Oral History* 49, no. 2 (2021): 49–56.

38. Kevin P. Murphy, Jennifer L. Pierce, and Jason Ruiz, "What Makes Queer Oral History Different," *Oral History Review* 43, no. 1 (2016): 1–24.

39. Gluck, "Has Oral History Lost," 63–72.

40. Murphy, Pierce, and Ruiz, "What Makes Queer Oral History," 3.

41. Examples could include Amy Starecheski, "South Bronx Soundwalks as Embodied Archiving Practice," *Oral History* 48, no. 2: 102–112, or the interpretative performative work of E. Patrick Johnson in relation to his *Sweet Tea: Black Gay Men of the South* (Chapel Hill: University of North Carolina Press, 2012), epatrickjohnson.com.

42. Carrie Hamilton, "Moving Feelings. Nationalism, Feminism and the Emotions of Politics," *Oral History* 38, no. 2 (2010): 86.

43. Jenny Harding, "Looking for Trouble: Exploring Emotion, Memory and Public Sociology: Inaugural Lecture, 1 May 2014, London Metropolitan University," *Oral History* 42, no. 2 (2014): 101.

44. Thomson, "Indexing and Interpreting Emotion."

45. See, for example, Jeff Friedman, "Oral History, Hermeneutics and Embodiment," *Oral History Review* 41, no. 2 (2014): 290–300.

46. Horacio N. Roque Ramírez and Nan Alamilla Boyd, "Close Encounters: The Body and Knowledge in Queer Oral History," in Boyd and Ramírez, *Bodies of Evidence*, 1–20.

47. Naomi Greyser, "Beyond the 'Feeling Woman': Feminist Implications of Affect Studies," *Feminist Studies* 38, no. 1 (2012): 85–86.

48. Some of these discussions can be found, for example, in Joanna Bornat, "A Second Take: Revisiting Interviews with a Different Purpose," *Oral History* 31, no. 1: 47–53; Peter Jackson, Graham Smith, and Sarah Olive, "Families Remembering Food: Reusing Secondary Data," working paper, 2007, accessed June 25, 2021, https://www.researchgate.net/publication/260351319_Families_remembering_food_reusing_secondary_data; Steven High, Elizabeth Tasong, Felipe Lalinde Lopera, and Hussain Almahr, "The Pedagogy and Practice of Listening to Rwandan Exiles and Genocide Survivors," *Oral History* 50, no. 1 (2022): 115–126.

49. Ronald Grele, "History and the Languages of History in the Oral History Interview: Who Answers Whose Questions and Why," University of the Witwatersrand, Johannesburg, *History Workshop*, 146 (1990): 1–35. http://wiredspace.wits.ac.za/bitstream/handle/10539/7815/HWS-146.pdf?sequence=1&isAllowed=y.

50. Jackson, Smith, and Olive, "Families Remembering Food."

51. Joanna Bornat, "Crossing Boundaries with Secondary Analysis: Implications for Archived Oral History Data," paper given at the ESRC National Council for Research Methods Network for Methodological Innovation, University of Essex, 2008, https://www.researchgate.net/profile/Joanna_Bornat/publication/237258161_Crossing_Boundaries_with_Secondary_Analysis_Implications_for_Archived_Oral_History_Data/links/00463531975a38bb5b000000.pdf, 2.

52. Jackson, Smith and Olive, "Families Remembering Food," drawing on Jennifer Mason, " 'Re-Using' Qualitative Data: On the Merits of an Investigative Epistemology," *Sociological Research Online* 12, no. 3 (2007), https://www.socresonline.org.uk/12/3/3.html.

53. Jodie Matthews, "Romani Pride, *Gorja* Shame: Race and Privilege in the Archive," *Oral History* 49, no. 2 (2021): 57–68; see also Elena Trivelli, "Exploring a 'Remembering Crisis': 'Affective Attuning' and 'Assemblage Archive' as Theoretical Frameworks and Research Methodologies," in *Affective Methodologies: Developing Cultural Research Strategies for the Study of Affect*, ed. Britta Timm Knudsen and Carsten Stage (London: Palgrave Macmillan, 2015), 133–135.

54. Portelli, *The Death of Luigi Trastulli*, 130.

55. Michael Roper argues that the historian is part of his or her own toolkit through the "enlistment" of emotions in his or her attempt to understand the past. He writes that the emotions of the people of the past are not just "historically situated statements" but were and are "located in the structures of desire, conflict, defence" that are "revivified in the historian's mind in the process of understanding the past." Michael Roper, "The Unconscious Work of History," *History Workshop Journal* 11, no. 2 (2014): 172–173.

56. Jones, "Geography, Memory," 882, 877.

57. Jones, "Geography, Memory," 877.

58. See, for example, Maurice Halbwachs, *On Collective Memory*, ed. and trans. Lewis Coser (Chicago: University of Chicago Press, 1992); Jan Assmann, "Communicative and Cultural Memory," in *Cultural Memory Studies: An International and Interdisciplinary Handbook*, ed. Ansgar Nünning and Astrid Erll (Berlin: Walter de Gruyter, 2008), 109–119; Erika Apfelbaum, "Halbwachs and the Social Properties of Memory," in *Memory: History, Theories, Debates*, ed. Susannah Radstone and Bill Schwartz (New York: Fordham University Press, 2010), 77–92.

59. Brief details of Paul Mouton's record can be found on the website of the Anciens des Services Spéciaux de la Défense nationale, accessed August 1, 2022, http://www.aassdn.org/araMnbioMf-Mz.html.

60. Françoise Laborde, *Ça va mieux en le disant!* (Paris: Fayard, 2008), 95–98. My translation.

61. One example often cited about how communist memory bled into the railway memory of resistance is via the popular film by René Clément, *La Bataille du Rail* (1946); for further information, see https://fresques.ina.fr/jalons/fiche-media/InaEdu01207/la-bataille-du-rail-rene-clement-1946.html (accessed August 1, 2022).

62. For press coverage, see "Guillaume Pepy reconnait le rôle de la SNCF dans la Shoah," *Le Monde*, January 25, 2011, https://www.lemonde.fr/societe/article/2011/01/25/bobigny-la-sncf-doit-s-expliquer-sur-son-role-dans-la-shoah_1470065_3224.html.

63. Kathleen Stewart, *Ordinary Affects* (Durham, NC: Duke University Press, 2007), 2.

64. Kaitlin M. Murphy, "Memory Mapping: Affect, Place, and Testimony in *El Lugar Más Pequeño* (2011)," *Journal of Latin American Cultural Studies* 25, no. 4 (2016): 573.

POSITIONING

1. Sara Ahmed, "Happy Objects," in *The Affect Theory Reader*, ed. Gregory J. Seigworth and Melissa Gregg (Durham, NC: Duke University Press, 2010), 31–32.

2. Ahmed, "Happy Objects."

3. Scholarly works specifically dealing with children in wartime France remain few, and most deal with propaganda. They include Gilles Ragache, *Les Enfants de la guerre; vivre, survivre, lire et jouer en France (1939–1949)* (Paris: Perrin, 1997); Judith Proud, *Children and Propaganda: Il Était une Fois . . . Fiction and Fairy Tale in Vichy France* (Bristol, UK: Intellect, 1999); F. Thuin, *Pétain et la dictature de l'image: Enfance et jeunesse, cinq ans de propagande* (Clermont-de-l'Oise, France: Éditions Daniel Bordet, 2011); Thierry Crépin, " 'Il était une fois un maréchal de France . . .': Presse enfantine et bande dessinée sous le régime de Vichy," *Vingtième Siècle* 28 (1990): 77–82. For children's experiences, the best sources are memoirs such as Paul Le Melledo, *Lorient à l'heure de l'évacuation: Itinéraire d'un Gavroche lorientais* (La Faouët, France: Liv'éditions, 2004); Nicole Roux, *C'est la guerre les enfants* (Cherbourg-Octeville, France: Isoète, 2007); Louis Mexandeau, *Nous, nous ne verrons pas la fin: Un enfant dans la guerre (1939–1945)* (Paris: Éditions Le Cherche-midi, 2003); Maria Carrier, ed., *Maréchal nous voilà . . . 1940–1944: Souvenirs d'enfances sous l'Occupation* (Paris: Éditions Autrement, 2004). Children are not absent from work on the family and on women's lives during this period but rarely appear as subjects in their own right. See, for example, Christophe Capuano, *Vichy et la famille: Réalités et faux-semblants d'une politique publique* (Rennes, France: Presses Universitaires de Rennes, 2009); Sarah Fishman, *We Will Wait: Wives of French Prisoners of War, 1940–1945* (New Haven, CT: Yale University Press, 1991); Sarah Fishman, *The Battle for Children: World War II, Youth Crime, and Juvenile Justice in Twentieth-Century France* (Cambridge, MA: Harvard University Press, 2002); or Matthieu Devigne, *L'École des Années Noires: Une histoire du primaire en temps de guerre* (Paris: Presses Universitaires de France, 2018).

4. My publications pull children as historical actors back into the frame. See, for example, *French Children Under the Allied Bombs, 1940–45: An Oral History* (Manchester, UK: Manchester University Press, 2016); "Children's Citizenly Participation in the National Revolution: The Instrumentalization of Children in Vichy France," *European Review of History/Revue d'Histoire Européenne* 24, no. 5 (2017): 759–780; " 'Mon petit papa chéri': Children, Fathers and Family Separation in Wartime France," *Essays in French Literature and Culture* 54 (2017): 97–116; "Wartime Rupture and Reconfiguration in French Family Life: Experience and Legacy," *History Workshop Journal* 88 (2019): 134–152; and "Rural Lives, Urban Lives and Children's Evacuation," in *Vichy France and Everyday Life: Confronting the Challenges of Wartime*, ed. Lindsey Dodd and David Lees (London: Bloomsbury, 2018), 123–139. In the Dodd and Lees volume, these chapters all deal with aspects of childhood: Camille Mahé, "Children and Play in Occupied France," 17–34; Matthieu Devigne, "Coping in the Classroom: Adapting Schools to Wartime, 1940–45," 35–50; Isabelle von

Bueltzingsloewen, "Reconstructing the Daily Life of a Lyonnaise Family," 51–68; Shannon L. Fogg, "The American Friends Service Committee and Wartime Aid to Families," 107–122.

5. Chief among these works is Serge Klarsfeld's monumental *Le Mémorial des enfants juifs déportés de France* (Paris: Les Fils et filles des déportés juifs de France, 1994). Historical research continues to document the history and the consequences of being deported, orphaned, imprisoned, or hidden. Recent works include Antoine Rivière, "Des pupilles ordinaires: Les enfants juifs recueillis par l'Assistance publique de Paris sous l'Occupation (1940–1944)," *Revue d'histoire de l'enfance "irrégulière"* 19 (2017): 87–117; Laura Hobson Faure, "Orphelines ou sœurs? Penser la famille juive pendant et après la Shoah en France et aux États-Unis," *Revue d'histoire* 145, no. 1 (2020): 91–104; Daniella Doron, *Jewish Youth and Identity in Postwar France: Rebuilding Family and Nation* (Bloomington: Indiana University Press, 2015); Katy Hazan, "Enfants cachés, enfants retrouvés," *Les Cahiers de la Shoah* 9, no. 1 (2007): 181–212. Nathalie Zajde and Marion Feldman have brought psychological expertise to bear on the subject; see, for example, Nathalie Zajde, *Les Enfants cachés en France* (Paris: Odile Jacob, 2012); Nathalie Zajde, *Qui sont les enfants cachés? Penser avec les grands témoins* (Paris: Odile Jacob, 2014); Marion Feldman, *Entre trauma et protection: Quel devenir pour les enfants juifs cachés en France (1940–1944)?* (Paris: Érès, 2013); Marion Feldman, "Enfants juifs cachés (1940–1944): Une littérature récente," *Psychologie française* 54, no. 2 (2009): 191–209. Beyond academic research, it is worth pointing out that Jewish children have been at the heart of commemorative programs, such as the placing of plaques on school buildings to remember former pupils deported and killed (via the Comité national pour la mémoire des enfants juifs déportés, COMEJD). Other vectors of memory, such as children's books, graphic novels, and feature films have also told Jewish children's stories to wider publics across the years.

6. Colin Nettelbeck, "A Forgotten Zone of Memory? French Primary School Children and the History of the Occupation," *French History and Civilization* 14 (2011): 165; emphasis in the original.

7. Nettelbeck, "Forgotten Zone," 164.

8. Laurent Douzou and Pierre Laborie, "Le rôle des historiens dans la transmission de la mémoire des comportements collectifs," in *Images des comportements sous l'Occupation: Mémoires, transmission, idées reçues*, ed. Jacqueline Sainclivier, Jean-Marie Guillon, and Pierre Laborie (Rennes, France: Presses Universitaires de Rennes, 2016), 157. All translations are my own.

9. Michael Rothberg, *The Implicated Subject: Beyond Victims and Perpetrators* (Stanford, CA: Stanford University Press, 2019); also, Susanne C. Knittel and Sofia Forchieri, "Navigating Implication: An Interview with Michael Rothberg," *Journal of Perpetrator Research* 3, no. 1 (2020): 8.

10. Knittel and Forchieri, "Navigating Implication," 14.

11. Elizabeth Adams St. Pierre, "Post Qualitative Inquiry, the Refusal of Method, and the Risk of the New," *Qualitative Inquiry* 27, no. 1 (2021): 5.

12. "Introduction," in Sainclivier, Guillon, and Laborie, *Images des comportements*, 14.

13. See Henry Rousso, *The Vichy Syndrome: History and Memory in France Since 1944*, trans. Arthur Goldhammer (Cambridge, MA: Harvard University Press, 1991). Arguably this

chronological pattern of commemorative practice around trauma and guilt is not specific to France. See, for example, Wulf Kansteiner, *In Pursuit of German Memory: History, Television and Politics after Auschwitz* (Athens: Ohio University Press, 2006).

14.   See Popular Memory Group, "Popular Memory: Theory, Politics, Method," in *The Oral History Reader*, ed. Robert Perks and Alistair Thomson (London: Routledge, 1998), 75–86.

15.   The sociologist Marie-Claire Lavabre draws critical attention to the amount of scholarly attention paid to *mémoire* (national, collective) over *souvenirs* (personal, lived experiences), particularly among historians; however, she neglects the work of the international oral history community. Marie-Claire Lavabre, "Paradigmes de la mémoire," *Transcontinentales: Société, idéologies, système mondiale* 5 (2007): 139–147.

16.   Robert Gildea, "The Long March of Oral History: Around 1968 in France," *Oral History* 38, no. 1 (2010): 68–80. Gildea's detailed study of the French resistance, *Fighters in the Shadows* (London: Faber and Faber, 2015) draws almost exclusively on testimony—oral, filmed, written—which, he says, is the only source capable of revealing subjectivity, experience, and meaning. He notes the "new confidence" of French historians in the 2000s to turn, once again, to testimonies of former resisters which had been cast aside as unreliable sources two decades earlier (12–15).

17.   Michael Roper, "Re-remembering the Soldier Hero: The Psychic and Social Construction of Memory in Personal Narratives of the Great War," *History Workshop Journal* 50, no. 1 (2000): 184.

18.   Graham Dawson, "Trauma, Place and the Politics of Memory: Bloody Sunday, Derry, 1972–2004," *History Workshop Journal* 59, no. 1 (2005): 154, 164.

19.   Popular Memory Group, "Popular Memory," 77.

20.   Graham Dawson provides an excellent example of this process in "Trauma, Place."

21.   Ruth Kitchen, *A Legacy of Shame: French Narratives of War and Occupation* (Oxford: Peter Lang, 2013), 1.

22.   Kathleen Stewart, "Weak Theory in an Unfinished World," *Journal of Folklore Research* 45, no. 1 (2008): 75.

23.   John D. Dewsbury, Paul Harrison, Mitch Rose, and John Wylie, "Introduction: Enacting Geographies," *Geoforum* 33 (2002): 437.

24.   Stuart Hall, *Cultural Studies 1983: A Theoretical History*, ed. Jennifer Daryl Slack and Lawrence Grossberg (Durham, NC: Duke University Press, 2016), 71.

25.   Dewsbury, Harrison, Rose, and Wylie, "Introduction," 437.

26.   Hayden Lorimer, "Cultural Geography: Worldly Shapes, Differently Arranged," *Progress in Human Geography* 31, no. 1 (2007): 89; Michael Jackson, ed., *Things As They Are: New Directions in Phenomenological Anthropology* (Washington, DC: Georgetown University Press, 1996), 8, cited in Anita Kumar, "The Play Is Now the Reality: Affective Turns, Narrative Struggles, and Theorising Emotion as Practical Experience," *Culture, Medicine & Psychiatry* 37 (2013): 712.

27.   Ben Highmore, "Aesthetic Matters: Writing and Cultural Studies," *Cultural Studies* 32, no. 2 (2018): 245.

28.   Kumar, "The Play Is Now the Reality," 713n1.

29.   Harald Welzer, "Communicative Memory," in *Cultural Memory Studies: An International and Interdisciplinary Handbook*, ed. Ansgar Nünning and Astrid Erll (Berlin: Walter de

Gruyter, 2008), 285. Ideas of communicative and cultural memory derive from the work of Jan Assmann; see, for example, Jan Assmann, "Communicative and Cultural Memory," in Nünning and Erll, *Cultural Memory Studies*, 109–119.

30. Jonathan Flatley, *Affective Mapping: Melancholia and the Politics of Modernism* (Cambridge MA: Harvard University Press, 2008), 25, citing Raymond Williams, *Marxism and Literature* (New York: Oxford University Press, 1977), 132.

31. Ewa Domanska, "A Conversation with Hayden White," *Rethinking History: The Journal of Theory and Practice* 12, no. 1 (2008): 16.

32. Keith Jenkins, "Nobody Does It Better: Radical History and Hayden White," *Rethinking History: The Journal of Theory and Practice* 12, no. 1 (2008): 61.

33. Stewart, "Weak Theory," 71.

34. Stewart, "Weak Theory," 75.

35. Ann Cvetkovich, *An Archive of Feelings* (Durham, NC: Duke University Press, 2003).

36. Lorimer, "Cultural Geography: Worldly Shapes," 90.

37. Stewart, "Weak Theory," 73; Luisa Passerini, "Memories Between Silence and Oblivion," in *Contested Pasts: The Politics of Memory*, ed. Katharine Hodgkin and Susannah Radstone (London: Routledge, 2003), 249.

38. Gilles Deleuze and Félix Guattari, *A Thousand Plateaus: Capitalism and Schizophrenia*, trans. Brian Massumi (Minneapolis: University of Minnesota Press, 1988), 372.

39. Andrea Doucet, "Decolonizing Family Photographs: Ecological Imaginaries and Nonrepresentational Ethnographies," *Journal of Contemporary Ethnography* 47, no. 6 (2018): 736.

40. Lorraine Code, *Ecological Thinking: The Politics of Epistemic Location* (New York: Oxford University Press, 2006), 41, cited in Doucet, "Decolonizing Family Photographs," 734–735.

41. Doucet, "Decolonizing Family Photographs," 731.

42. Highmore, "Aesthetic Matters," 247.

43. Devigne, *L'École des Années Noires*, 12. All translation is my own.

44. Vincent Duclert, "Archives orales et recherche contemporaine: Une histoire en cours," *Sociétés et Représentations* 13, no. 1 (2002): 75; see also comments by Dominique Aron Schnapper cited in "Archives orales et entretiens ethnographiques: Un débat entre Florence Descamps et Florence Weber, animé par Bertrand Müller," *Genèses* 62, no. 1 (2006): 93–109. The contention appears not to have gone away. While asserting that "oral history is very much alive and well in France," Ariane Mak reported from a French oral history conference in April 2019 that Florence Descamps emphasized "the success of the 'oral archives' concept and its deep impact on the way the field has established itself in France." Ariane Mak, "France: Oral History Conference," *Oral History* 47, no. 2 (2019): 21.

45. Paul Thompson, "The Voice of the Past: Oral History," in *Oral History Reader*, ed. Perks and Thomson, 24.

46. Olivier Wieviorka, *La Mémoire désunie: Le souvenir politique des années sombres, de la Libération à nos jours* (Paris: Seuil, 2010), 20–23. All translations are my own.

47. Henry Rousso, *Face au passé: Essais sur la mémoire contemporaine* (Paris: Belin, 2016), 18–19. All translations are my own.

48. Michael Rothberg has argued, in *Multidirectional Memory: Remembering the Holocaust in the Age of Decolonization* (Stanford, CA: Stanford University Press, 2009), that a competitive model of memory is unhelpful for understanding patterns of remembering and

commemoration. Instead he proposes memory as a complex, intercultural, and dynamic web, "subject to on-going recognition, cross referencing, and borrowing" (3). Just because there is a lot of attention given to one object of memory (e.g., the Holocaust), it does not follow there is less memory around others (e.g., decolonization).

49. Rousso, *Face au passé*, 16.

50. Wieviorka, *La Mémoire désunie*, 17–19.

51. Henry Rousso, *La Hantise du passé* (Paris: Textuel, 1998), 22–23; all translations are mine. In a similar vein, he writes in *Face au passé* (22) that "contemporary memory is often active in an emotional register" because it is "essentially a victim memory (*une mémoire essentiellement victimaire*)." Memory is emotional *because* we are speaking of victims' memories. My position is rather that memories are emotional *whether or not* they are victims' memories.

52. Douzou and Laborie, "Le rôle des historiens," 157.

53. Michael Roper, "The Unconscious Work of History," *History Workshop Journal* 11, no. 2 (2014): 177.

54. Owain Jones, "Geography, Memory and Non-Representational Geographies," *Geography Compass* 5, no. 2 (2011): 882.

55. Lindsey Dodd, *French Children Under the Allied Bombs, 1940–1944: An Oral History* (Manchester, UK: Manchester University Press, 2016), 41.

56. Domanska, "A Conversation with Hayden White," 16.

57. Jenkins, 'Nobody Does It Better," 65, 64.

58. Code, *Ecological Thinking*, 41, cited in Doucet, "Decolonizing Family Photographs," 734–735.

59. Nigel Thrift, *Non-Representational Theory: Space, Politics, Affect* (London: Routledge, 2007), 12.

60. Flatley, *Affective Mapping*, 7.

61. Steve Pile, "Emotions and Affects in Recent Human Geography," *Transactions of the Institute of British Geographers* 35, no. 1 (2010): 5, cited in Roy Huijsmans, " 'Knowledge That Moves': Emotions and Affect in Policy and Research with Young Migrants," *Children's Geographies* 16, no. 6 (2018): 629.

62. Jenkins, 'Nobody Does It Better," 71.

63. Stewart, "Weak Theory," 71, 72; *Ordinary Affects* (Durham, NC: Duke University Press, 2007), 4.

64. Hayden Lorimer, "Cultural Geography: The Busyness of Being 'More-Than-Representational,' " *Progress in Human Geography* 29, no. 1 (2005): 84, discussing Nigel Thrift, "Summoning Life," in *Envisioning Human Geographies*, ed. Paul Cloke, Philip Crang, and Mark Goodwin (London: Arnold, 2014): 81–103.

65. Stewart, "Weak Theory," 72, citing Eve Kosofsky Sedgwick's idea of weak theory from her essay "Paranoid Reading and Reparative Reading: Or, You're So Paranoid, You Probably Think This Introduction Is About You," in *Novel Gazing: Queer Readings in Fiction*, ed. Eve Kosofsky Sedgwick, Michèle Aina Barale, Jonathan Goldberg, and Michael Moon (Durham, NC: Duke University Press), 1–40.

66. Philippe Vannini, "Non-Representational Ethnography: New Ways of Animating Lifeworlds," *Cultural Geographies* 22, no. 2 (2015): 319, cited in Doucet, "Decolonizing Family Photographs," 737.

67. Maurice Halbwachs, *On Collective Memory*, ed. and trans. Lewis Coser (Chicago: University of Chicago Press, 1992); Sarah Gensburger, "Halbwachs' Studies in Collective Memory: A Founding Text for Contemporary 'Memory Studies'?" *Journal of Classical Sociology* 16, no. 4 (2016): 396–413.

68. Nick J. Fox, "Emotions, Affects and the Production of Social Life," *British Journal of Sociology* 66, no. 2 (2015): 305, drawing on, for example, Deleuze and Guattari, *A Thousand Plateaus*, 261.

69. Gregory J. Seigworth and Melissa Gregg, "An Inventory of Shimmers," in *The Affect Theory Reader*, 8.

70. Emma Renold and David Alan Mellor, "Deleuze and Guattari in the Nursery: Towards an Ethnographic Multi-Sensory Mapping of Gendered Bodies and Becomings," in *Deleuze and Research Methodologies*, ed. Rebecca Coleman and Jessica Ringrose (Edinburgh: Edinburgh University Press, 2013), cited in Fox, "Emotions, Affects," 305.

71. Fox, "Emotions, Affects," 306.

72. Deleuze and Guattari, *A Thousand Plateaus*, 19–21; Brent Adkins, *Deleuze and Guattari's A Thousand Plateaus: A Critical Introduction and Guide* (Edinburgh: Edinburgh University Press, 2015), 22–23.

73. Adkins, *Deleuze and Guattari's* A Thousand Plateaus, 31.

74. Stephanie Trigg, "Introduction: Emotional Histories—Beyond the Personalization of the Past and the Abstraction of Affect Theory," *Exemplaria* 26, no. 1 (2014): 11.

75. Donovan Schaefer, "The Promise of Affect: The Politics of the Event in Ahmed's *The Promise of Happiness* and Berlant's *Cruel Optimism*," *Theory and Event* 16, no. 2 (2013), muse.jhu.edu/article/509908.

76. Trigg, 'Introduction: Emotional Histories," 3–4. Affect seems to be at the heart of oral history, yet few oral historians deal explicitly with it; some recent works that do so include Jeff Friedman, "Oral History, Hermeneutics and Embodiment," *Oral History Review* 41, no. 2 (2014): 290–300, and Katie Holmes, "Does It Matter If She Cried? Recording Emotion and the Australian Generations Oral History Project," *Oral History Review* 44, no. 1 (2017): 56–76. Holmes refers to emotion, but the article might better be described as being about affect. Similarly, in the history of childhood and youth, there are recent developments around analyzing affect, but still often through the lens of emotion. See, for example, two review articles: Chris Brickell, "Histories of Adolescence and Affect: Setting an Agenda," *History Compass* 13, no. 8 (2015): 385–395; Stephanie Olsen, "The History of Childhood and the Emotional Turn," *History Compass* 15, no. 11 (2017), unpaginated.

77. Schaefer, "The Promise of Affect."

78. Ben Highmore, *Cultural Feelings: Mood, Mediation and Cultural Politics* (London: Routledge, 2017) is situated in cultural studies, despite chapters focusing on the feelings circulating in Britain during the Second World War, bomb sites in the British postwar urban landscape, migration in twentieth-century Britain, punk and postpunk, and despite providing analysis based—among other things—on archives. To my mind, it could also be framed as history, but it does not conform to the analytical norms of academic history writing.

79. Sara Ahmed, *The Cultural Politics of Emotion*, 2nd ed. (Edinburgh: Edinburgh University Press, 2014), 204, 230n8; emphasis in the original.

80. Highmore, *Cultural Feelings*, specifically chap. 2.

81. Fox, 'Emotions, Affects," 304; here, Fox draws on Ahmed, *The Cultural Politics of Emotion*, 8–10.

82. Lawrence Grossberg, "Affect's Future: Rediscovering the Virtual in the Actual," in *The Affect Theory Reader*, 318.

83. Highmore, *Cultural Feelings*, 47, 48; here he is referring to the work of Lauren Berlant, *Cruel Optimism* (Durham, NC: Duke University Press, 2011), 54.

84. Stewart, "Weak Theory," 76. See Introduction, n17, for Shane Vogel's evaluation of Stewart's important critical use of the phrase "or something."

85. Berlant, *Cruel Optimism*, 54, cited in Highmore, *Cultural Feelings*, 48.

86. Huijsmans, " 'Knowledge That Moves,' " 629.

87. Ahmed, *The Cultural Politics of Emotion*, 4.

88. Patricia T. Clough, "The Affective Turn: Political Economy, Biomedia, and Bodies," in *The Affect Theory Reader*, 206–225.

89. Brian Massumi, "Autonomy of Affect," *Cultural Critique* 31 (1995): 87.

90. Massumi, "Autonomy of Affect', discussed in Kumar, 'The Play Is Now the Reality," 732.

91. Seigworth and Gregg, "Inventory of Shimmers," 14.

92. Gilles Deleuze, *Two Regimes of Madness: Texts and Interviews, 1975–1995* (Cambridge, MA: MIT Press, 2007), 177, cited in Yannis Hamilakis, "Sensorial Assemblages: Affect, Memory and Temporality in Assemblage Thinking," *Cambridge Archaeological Journal* 27, no. 1 (2017): 172.

93. Stewart, "Weak Theory," 72.

94. Deleuze, *Two Regimes of Madness*, 177, in Hamilakis, "Sensorial Assemblages," 172.

95. Fox, 'Emotions, Affects," 306, drawing on Manuel DeLanda, *A New Philosophy of Society* (London: Continuum, 2006), 5.

96. Kevin Grove and Jonathan Pugh, "Assemblage Thinking and Participatory Development: Potentiality, Ethics, Biopolitics," *Geography Compass* 9, no. 1 (2015): 2.

97. Fox, "Emotions, Affects," 306, drawing on Ben Anderson, "Becoming and Being Hopeful: Towards a Theory of Affect," *Environment and Planning D: Space and Society* 24, no. 5 (2006): 736, and Deleuze and Guattari, *A Thousand Plateaus*, 257.

98. Grove and Pugh, "Assemblage Thinking," 3.

99. Grossberg, "Affect's Future," 320.

100. Stewart, "Weak Theory," 72.

101. Deleuze and Guattari, *A Thousand Plateaus*, 261–263; Elizabeth Adams St. Pierre, "Haecceity: Laying Out a Plane for Post Qualitative Inquiry," *Qualitative Inquiry* 23, no. 9 (2017): 686–698.

102. Stewart, "Weak Theory," 72, 76; Ahmed, "Happy Objects," 30.

103. Alessandro Portelli, *The Death of Luigi Trastulli and Other Stories: Form and Meaning in Oral History* (Albany: State University of New York Press, 1991), 99–116.

104. Kumar, "The Play Is Now the Reality," 712, drawing on Cheryl Mattingly, "Emergent Narratives," in *Narrative and the Cultural Construction of Illness and Healing*, ed. Cheryl Mattingly and Linda C. Garro (Berkeley: University of California Press, 2010), 181–211.

105. Hamilakis, "Sensorial Assemblages," 174.

106. Hamilakis, "Sensorial Assemblages," 173.

107. Fox, 'Emotions, Affects," 307. Fox takes the phrase "politics of affect" from Nigel Thrift, "Intensities of Feeling: Towards a Spatial Politics of Affect," *Geografiska Annaler: Series B, Human Geography* 86, no. 1 (2004): 64.

108. Hamilakis, "Sensorial Assemblages," 175.

PART 1. MEMORIES FELT

1. Naomi Norquay, "Identity and Forgetting," *Oral History Review* 26, no. 1 (1999): 11.

2. Megan Watkins, "Desiring Recognition, Accumulating Affect," in *The Affect Theory Reader*, ed. Gregory J. Seigworth and Melissa Gregg (Durham, NC: Duke University Press, 2010), 269.

3. Gregory Hollin, Isla Forsyth, Eva Giraud, and Tracy Potts, "(Dis)entangling Barad: Materialisms and Ethics," *Social Studies of Science* 47, no. 6 (2017): 927. Barad's point, more specifically, is that "we can learn something about the dropping of the stones by examining the ripples in the pool": the diffraction pattern reveals the diffraction apparatus. The cause and effect, doer and action, subject and object are *intra*affective.

4. Yi-Fu Tuan, *Space and Place: The Perspective of Experience* (Minneapolis: University of Minnesota Press, 1977), 10.

5. The expression "structures of feeling" derives from the work of Raymond Williams. For useful explanations, see Jonathan Flatley, *Affective Mapping: Melancholia and the Politics of Modernism* (Cambridge MA: Harvard University Press, 2008), 24–27, and Ben Highmore, *Cultural Feelings: Mood, Mediation and Cultural Politics* (London: Routledge, 2017), 20–37.

6. Eduardo Bericat, "The Sociology of Emotions: Four Decades of Progress," *Current Sociology* 64, no. 3 (2015): 491; emphasis in the original.

7. Linda J. Levine, Heather C. Lench, and Martin A. Safer, "Functions of Remembering and Misremembering Emotion," *Applied Cognitive Psychology* 23, no. 8 (2009): 1068.

8. Michael Roper, "Re-remembering the Soldier Hero: The Psychic and Social Construction of Memory in Personal Narratives of the Great War," *History Workshop Journal* 50, no. 1 (2000): 181–204.

9. Brian Massumi, "The Autonomy of Affect," *Cultural Critique* 31 (1995): 88.

10. Ben Highmore, "Bitter After Taste: Affect, Food, and Social Aesthetics," in *The Affect Theory Reader*, 118–137.

11. Robert Desjarlais and Jason C. Throop, "Phenomenological Approaches in Anthropology," *Annual Review of Anthropology* 40 (2011): 89, cited in Anita Kumar, "The Play Is Now the Reality: Affective Turns, Narrative Struggles, and Theorising Emotion as Practical Experience," *Culture, Medicine & Psychiatry* 37 (2013): 712–713.

12. Tuan, *Space and Place*, 10.

13. Sara Ahmed, *The Cultural Politics of Emotion*, 2nd ed. (Edinburgh: Edinburgh University Press, 2014), 208.

1. ARTICULATED FEELING

1. On memory and the senses, see, for example, Joy Damousi and Paula Hamilton, eds., *A Cultural History of Sound, Memory, and the Senses* (Abingdon, UK: Routledge, 2017); Paula

Hamilton, "The Proust Effect: Oral History and the Senses," in *The Oxford Handbook of Oral History*, ed. Donald Ritchie (Oxford: Oxford University Press, 2012), 219–232; Sue Bradley, "Hobday's Hands: Recollections of Touch in Veterinary Oral History," *Oral History* 49, no. 1 (2021): 35–48.

2. Yannis Hamilakis, "Sensorial Assemblages: Affect, Memory and Temporality in Assemblage Thinking," *Cambridge Archaeological Journal* 27, no. 1 (2017): 177, drawing on Yannis Hamilakis, *Archaeology and the Senses: Human Experience, Memory, and Affect* (Cambridge: Cambridge University Press, 2013).

3. Hamilakis, "Sensorial Assemblages," 177.

4. For more on this topic, see Lindsey Dodd, *French Children Under the Allied Bombs, 1940–1945: An Oral History* (Manchester, UK: Manchester University Press, 2016), chap. 4, "Being Bombed," 87–100.

5. See, for example, Marloes J. A. G. Henckens, Erno J. Hermans, Zhenwei Pu, Marian Joëls, and Guillén Fernández, "Stressed Memories: How Acute Stress Affects Memory Formation in Humans," *Journal of Neuroscience* 29, no. 32 (2009): 10111–10119.

6. Dana Jack describes a meta-statement as a moment in the interview "where people spontaneously stop, look back, and comment about their own thoughts or something just said," which "alert[s] us to the individual's awareness of a discrepancy within the self—or between what is expected and what is being said." Dana C. Jack and Kathryn Anderson, "Learning to Listen: Interview Techniques and Analyses," in *The Oral History Reader*, ed. Robert Perks and Alistair Thomson (London: Routledge, 1998), 167–168.

7. Linda J. Levine, Heather C. Lench, and Martin A. Safer, "Functions of Remembering and Misremembering Emotion," *Applied Cognitive Psychology* 23, no. 8 (2009): 1063.

8. On the value of sympathy in historical analysis, see Lindsey Dodd, "Fellow Feeling in Childhood Memories of Second World War France: Sympathy, Empathy and the Emotions of History," *Close Encounters in War* 4 (2021): 123–147.

9. In *French Children*, I compare perceptions of the American and British bombers. Americans were typically characterized as selfish, careless, and cowardly, while the British were (largely) seen as the opposite. Differences in bombing techniques stemmed from the different technologies available to each national air force, which meant the Americans could bomb from a higher altitude. Accuracy was not much different. See also Lindsey Dodd and Andrew Knapp, " 'How Many Frenchmen Did You Kill?' British Bombing Policy Towards France (1940–1945)," *French History* 22, no. 4 (2008): 480, 488–490.

10. Toward the end of spring 1941, as the RAF bombed the German warships docked in the port of Brest, the decision was taken to construct two deep underground shelters in the center of Brest. One had an entrance on the Place Sadi-Carnot. During the siege of Brest (August–September 1944), the civilians who had not been evacuated stayed day and night in the shelter. It was also being used by the occupying Germans, who stored ammunition and explosives there. On September 9, 1944, an accidental fire caused a huge explosion in the shelter, killing 371 French civilians and between 500 and 600 Germans. The Abri Sadi-Carnot is now a commemorative museum. See Dodd, *French Children*, 15–16, 213–214.

11. Some psychological evidence suggests that happy memories are more malleable over time, remolding and shaping themselves to fit later or present concerns, whereas stressed

memories may well be more accurate, detailed representations of past events. See, for example, Christie Napa Scollon, Amanda Hiles Howard, Amanda E. Caldwell, and Sachiyo Ito, "The Role of Ideal Affect in the Experience and Memory of Emotions," *Journal of Happiness Studies* 10, no. 3 (2009): 257–269, and Henckens et al., "Stressed Memories."

12. Brian Massumi, "The Autonomy of Affect," *Cultural Critique* 31 (1995): 103.

13. Carrie Hamilton, "Happy Memories," *New Formations* 63 (2007): 66–67. Hamilton makes the point that nostalgia is neither necessarily regressive nor neutral in the telling of autobiographical stories. She stresses its agential quality, noting that by listening carefully to nostalgic, happy memories "we can position [rememberers] as agents in the construction of their own histories [who . . .] have some choice in their feelings about the past" (67).

14. Sara Ahmed writes that "fear opens up past histories of association"; that is, fear is multitemporal: "the response of fear is itself dependent on particular narratives of what and who is fearsome that are already in place." Sara Ahmed, *The Cultural Politics of Emotion*, 2nd ed. (Edinburgh: Edinburgh University Press, 2014), 69.

15. Ahmed, *The Cultural Politics of Emotion*, 65.

16. The historian of emotions William Reddy has used neuropsychological research in his work but counsels against a too-ready acceptance of this research into the humanities, given the different aims, objectives, and operational methodologies of the different disciplines. Jan Plamper, "The History of the Emotions: An Interview with William Reddy, Barbara Rosenwein and Peter Stearns," *History & Theory* 49, no. 2 (2010): 240. It could be added that many experiments on memory and emotion decontextualize remembering, setting up controlled environments to test precise parts of the memory process. Typically, the items to be remembered and the "emotions" to be tested are artificially induced, and the lapses between the experience and the remembering are usually rather short, not the forty to seventy-plus years of the memory corpus used in this study. Furthermore, the subject is conscious of the experiment. The emotions being tested have to be identifiable and their boundaries delineated. Psychological research on memory often has juridical applications; as such, its aims are frequently bound up with assessing remembered events (or emotions) for their veracity in relation to the item to be remembered. On the latter point, Sutton, Harris, and Barnier ask whether truth is ever an appropriate ideal for memory. John Sutton, Celia B. Harris, and Amanda Barnier, "Memory and Cognition," in *Memory: Histories, Theories, Debates*, ed. Susannah Radstone and Bill Schwartz (New York: Fordham University Press, 2010), 209–226.

17. Gilles Deleuze and Félix Guattari, *A Thousand Plateaus: Capitalism and Schizophrenia*, trans. Brian Massumi (Minneapolis: University of Minnesota Press, 1988), 361; Brent Adkins, *Deleuze and Guattari's* A Thousand Plateaus: *A Critical Introduction and Guide* (Edinburgh: Edinburgh University Press, 2015), 197.

18. Kathleen Stewart, *Ordinary Affects* (Durham, NC: Duke University Press, 2007), 128. Stewart writes that this process is transpersonal; it is "not about one person's feelings becoming another's but about bodies literally affecting one another and generating intensities: human bodies, discursive bodies, bodies of thought, bodies of water."

19. As I will discuss in chapter 9, paternal absence was a common childhood experience in Second World War France. Absent fathers mattered both materially, given reduced

resources, and emotionally. See Lindsey Dodd, " 'Mon petit papa chéri': Children, Fathers and Family Separation in Wartime France," *Essays in French Literature and Culture* 54 (2017): 97–116.

20. Ian Burkitt, *Emotions and Social Relations* (Thousand Oaks, CA: Sage, 2014), 11–12. Burkitt uses the work of Brian Massumi and Seigworth and Gregg, specifically, to make his critique.

21. Sutton, Harris, and Barnier, "Memory and Cognition"; Roger Kennedy, "Memory and the Unconscious," in *Memory: Histories, Theories, Debates*, ed. Susannah Radstone and Bill Schwartz (New York: Fordham University Press, 2010), 179–197.

22. Scollon et al., "The Role of Ideal Affect."

23. Rebecca Clifford, *Survivors: Children's Lives After the Holocaust* (New Haven, CT: Yale University Press, 2020). For literature on child and young survivors in France, see "Positioning," n5. On the rejected, untreated, and unrecognized trauma of bombing, see Dodd, " 'It Did Not Traumatise Me At All': Childhood 'Trauma' in French Oral Narratives of Wartime Bombing," *Oral History* 42, no. 2 (2013): 37–48.

24. Marianne Hirsch and Leo Spitzer, "The Witness in the Archive," in *Memory: History, Theories, Debates*, 397.

25. The interview encounter will be discussed in greater depth in chapter 7.

26. For further detail on Rémy's story, see Dodd, "Fellow Feeling."

27. Interviewees Pierre Haigneré and Michel Jean-Bart both became visibly emotional as they described their mothers' words during the air raid at Lille-Délivrance in April 1944; for more, see Lindsey Dodd, *French Children Under the Allied Bombs, 1940–1944: An Oral History* (Manchester, UK: Manchester University Press, 2016), 87, 97.

2. AFFECTS AND INTENSITIES

1. Kathleen Stewart, "Weak Theory in an Unfinished World," *Journal of Folklore Research* 45, no. 1 (2008): 71.

2. Gregory J. Seigworth and Melissa Gregg, "An Inventory of Shimmers," in *The Affect Theory Reader*, ed. Gregory J. Seigworth and Melissa Gregg (Durham, NC: Duke University Press, 2010), 3.

3. Lorraine Code, *Ecological Thinking: The Politics of Epistemic Location* (New York: Oxford University Press, 2006).

4. Gilles Deleuze and Félix Guattari, *A Thousand Plateaus: Capitalism and Schizophrenia*, trans. Brian Massumi (Minneapolis: University of Minnesota Press, 1988), 372.

5. Sara Ahmed, *The Cultural Politics of Emotion*, 2nd ed. (Edinburgh: Edinburgh University Press, 2014), 65.

6. Ahmed, *The Cultural Politics of Emotion*, 105–107.

7. See, for example, Pieter Lagrou, "Victims of Genocide and National Memory: Belgium, France and the Netherlands," *Past & Present* 154, no. 1 (1997): 181–222. Lagrou notes of Jewish deportees: "Persecuted for something they had not chosen, for the simple reason of being born Jews, they were placed at the bottom of the hierarchy of martyrs" (222).

8. Ahmed, *The Cultural Politics of Emotion*, 105–107.

PART 2. MEMORIES LOCATED

1. Edward S. Casey, *The Fate of Place: A Philosophical History* (Berkeley: University of California Press, 1997), 9.
2. Edward S. Casey, "How to Get from Space to Place in a Fairly Short Stretch of Time: Phenomenological Prolegomena," in *Senses of Place*, ed. Steven Feld and Keith S. Basso (Santa Fe, NM: School of American Research Press, 1996), 24.
3. Levine and colleagues cite a number of studies suggesting that "memory for the emotions elicited by life-threatening trauma and social rejection show notable persistence over time." Linda J. Levine, Heather C. Lench, and Martin A. Safer, "Functions of Remembering and Misremembering Emotion," *Applied Cognitive Psychology* 23, no. 8 (2009): 1071. See also Marloes J. A. G. Henckens, Erno J. Hermans, Zhenwei Pu, Marian Joëls, and Guillén Fernández, "Stressed Memories: How Acute Stress Affects Memory Formation in Humans," *Journal of Neuroscience* 29, no. 32 (2009): 10111–10119.
4. Brian Massumi writes of the importance of what he calls "affective facts," which may put "actual facts aside": what is felt to be true, by individuals or groups, and what one is encouraged to believe is true may alter behavior and shape personal and social trajectories as much as what is or was actually true. Brian Massumi, "The Future Birth of the Affective Fact: The Political Ontology of Threat," in *The Affect Theory Reader*, ed. Gregory J. Seigworth and Melissa Gregg (Durham, NC: Duke University Press, 2010), 53–54.
5. Graham Dawson, "Trauma, Place and the Politics of Memory: Bloody Sunday, Derry, 1972–2004," *History Workshop Journal* 59, no. 1 (2005): 156.
6. Pirjo Lyytikäinen and Kirski Saarikangas, "Introduction: Imagining Spaces and Places," in *Imagining Spaces and Places*, by Saija Isomaa, Pirjo Lyytikäinen and Renja Suominen-Kokkonen (Newcastle-Upon-Tyne, UK: Cambridge Scholars, 2003), x.
7. Casey, "How to Get from Space to Place," 19.
8. Keith S. Basso, *Wisdom Sits in Places: Landscape and Language Among the Western Apache* (Albuquerque: University of New Mexico Press, 1996), 15–16.
9. Yi-Fu Tuan, *Space and Place: The Perspective of Experience* (Minneapolis: University of Minnesota Press, 1977), 12.
10. Casey, "How to Get from Space to Place," 24–25; emphasis in original.
11. Tuan, *Space and Place*, 6.
12. Lyytikäinen and Saarikangas, "Introduction: Imagining Spaces and Places," xi–xiii.
13. Owain Jones, "Geography, Memory and Non-Representational Geographies," *Geography Compass* 5, no. 2 (2011): 878, referencing Ash Amin and Nigel Thrift, *Cities: Reimagining the Urban* (Cambridge: Polity, 2002), and Doreen Massey and Nigel Thrift, "The Passion of Place," in *A Century of British Geography*, ed. Ron Johnston and Michael Williams (Oxford: Oxford University, 2003), 275–299.
14. Jones, "Geography, Memory," 882.
15. Yannis Hamilakis, "Sensorial Assemblages: Affect, Memory and Temporality in Assemblage Thinking," *Cambridge Archaeological Journal* 27, no. 1 (2017): 174. Henri Bergson's important idea of durational time underpins all of the ideas of memory, the virtual, and

actualization here. For Bergson, as Middleton and Brown explain, " 'virtual' is synonymous with 'potential,' and opposed to 'actual.' . . . The virtual is that which does not currently act. The virtual is potentiality, rather than possibility and so is no less real than the actual, in the way that a seed is no less real than the tree it may potentially become. There is always 'more' in the virtual than in the actual, meaning that 'actualization' is a diminution or 'contraction' of the virtual. . . . The virtual is not that which precedes the actual—as we might erroneously assume if we understand potential as possibility—but, rather, our existence 'unrolls' simultaneously in each register." David Middleton and Steven Brown, *The Social Psychology of Experience: Studies in Remembering and Forgetting* (Thousand Oaks, CA: Sage, 2005), 74–75. They draw here on Henri Bergson, *The Creative Mind: An Introduction to Metaphysics*, trans. Mabelle L. Andison (New York: Citadel, 1992), 99–102, and Henri Bergson, *Key Writings*, ed. Keith Ansell-Pearson and John Mullarky (London: Continuum, 2002), 147.

16. Hamilakis, "Sensorial Assemblages," 174.

17. John Sutton, Celia B. Harris, and Amanda Barnier, "Memory and Cognition," in *Memory: Histories, Theories, Debates*, ed. Susannah Radstone and Bill Schwartz (New York: Fordham University Press, 2010), 209–226.

18. Carrie Hamilton, "Happy Memories," *New Formations* 63 (2007): 65–81. Hamilton emphasizes that thinking about happy memories in this way "does not make the events themselves less devastating, or the perpetrators less guilty" (66).

19. Christie Napa Scollon, Amanda Hiles Howard, Amanda E. Caldwell, and Sachiyo Ito, "The Role of Ideal Affect in the Experience and Memory of Emotions," *Journal of Happiness Studies* 10, no. 3 (2009): 257–269.

20. Yi-Fu Tuan, *Space and Place: The Perspective of Experience* (Minneapolis: University of Minnesota Press, 1977), 12.

21. Tuan, *Space and Place*, 4.

3. THE WEIRDNESS OF MEMORY TIME

1. The General Jewish Labor Bund in Poland, where Serge's family originated from, was a Jewish socialist party established in 1917. In 1922, about a quarter of the Polish Bund left to form the Communist Bund, which merged into the Communist Party as part of the International in 1923. See Bernard K. Johnpoll, *The Politics of Futility: The General Jewish Workers Bund of Poland, 1917–1943* (Ithaca, NY: Cornell University Press, 1967); also Nick Underwood, "Lending Identity: Circulating Literacy, Current Events, Yiddish Culture, and Politics in Interwar France," *Contemporary French Civilization* 45, no. 1 (2020): 71–88.

2. Ben Highmore, *Cultural Feelings: Mood, Mediation and Cultural Politics* (London: Routledge, 2017), 44. The second quotation Highmore takes from Jonathan Flatley, *Affective Mapping: Melancholia and the Politics of Modernism* (Cambridge, MA: Harvard University Press, 2008), 17. Highmore draws on Heidegger's ideas of mood or *Stimmung* as elaborated, particularly, in Martin Heidegger, *Being and Time*, trans. Joan Stambaugh (Albany: State University of New York Press, 1996).

3. Judith Proud notes that the metaphor of a storm was frequently used to evoke the defeat of France in 1940 in children's books of the era. *Children and Propaganda* (Bristol, UK: Intellect, 1995), 59.

4. Time has been a central concern in several of Alessandro Portelli's essays, yet there is still more to say. See, for example, " 'The Time of My Life': Functions of Time in Oral History," 59–80, and "The Best Garbage Man in Town: Life and Times of Valtàro Peppoloni, Worker,' 117–138, both in Alessandro Portelli, *The Death of Luigi Trastulli and Other Stories: Form and Meaning in Oral History* (Albany: State University of New York Press, 1991).

5. Kathleen Stewart, *Ordinary Affects* (Durham, NC: Duke University Press, 2007), 128.

6. John D. Dewsbury, Paul Harrison, Mitch Rose, and John Wylie, "Introduction: Enacting Geographies," *Geoforum* 33 (2002): 439.

4. PLACES IN TRAUMATIC MEMORY

1. Graham Dawson, "Trauma, Place and the Politics of Memory: Bloody Sunday, Derry, 1972–2004," *History Workshop Journal* 59, no. 1 (2005): 155, drawing on Pamela J. Stewart and Andrew Strathern, "Introduction," in *Landscape, Memory and History: Anthropological Perspectives*, ed. Pamela J. Stewart and Andrew Strathern (London: Pluto, 2003), 3–6.

2. Sigmund Freud, *Mourning and Melancholia* (1917), referenced in Eva Hoffman, "The Long Afterlife of Loss," in *Memory: History, Theories, Debates*, ed. Susannah Radstone and Bill Schwartz (New York: Fordham University Press, 2010): 411.

3. There is no discernible body of scholarship on resistance deportees and their descendants making "pilgrimages" to the sites of former camps. There is some scholarship on visits to former camps by Holocaust survivors and their families. See for example, Tim Cole, "Crematoria, Barracks, Gateway: Survivors' Return Visits to the Memory Landscapes of Auschwitz," *History and Memory* 25, no. 2 (2013): 102–131; Anne Grynberg, "La pédagogie des lieux," *Les Cahiers de la Shoah* 8, no. 1 (2005): 15–56; Florence Heymann, "Tourisme des mémoires blessées: Traces de Transnistrie," *Revue d'Histoire de la Shoah* 194, no. 1 (2011): 319–341; Carol A. Kidron, "Being There Together: Dark Family Tourism and the Emotive Experience of Co-Presence in the Holocaust Past," *Annals of Tourism Research* 41 (2013): 175–194; Natalie C. Polzer, "Durkheim's Sign Made Flesh: The 'Authentic Symbol' in Contemporary Holocaust Pilgrimage," *Canadian Journal of Sociology* 39, no. 4 (2014): 697–718; Brigitte Sion, "Memorial Pilgrimage or Death Tourism? A Jewish Perspective," *Liturgy* 32, no. 3 (2017): 23–28. On so-called dark tourism, see John Lennon and Malcolm Foley, *Dark Tourism* (London: Continuum, 2000).

4. Kathleen Stewart, *Ordinary Affects* (Durham, NC: Duke University Press, 2007), 42.

5. Henri Bergson, *Matter and Memory*, trans. Nancy Margaret Paul and W. Scott Palmer (New York: Zone, 1991), 150, cited in David Middleton and Steven Brown, *The Social Psychology of Experience: Studies in Remembering and Forgetting* (Thousand Oaks, CA: Sage, 2005), 74.

5. SPACES IN TRAUMATIC MEMORY

1. Yi-Fu Tuan, *Space and Place: The Perspective of Experience* (Minneapolis: University of Minnesota Press, 1977), 6. See also, for example, Michel Foucault with Jay Miskowiec, "Of Other Spaces," *Diacritics* 16, no. 1 (1986): 22–27; Michel Foucault, *Surveiller et punir: Naissance de la prison* (Paris: Gallimard, 1975); Maurice Merleau-Ponty, *Phénoménologie de la perception*

(Paris: Gallimard, 1945); Henri Lefebvre, *De la production de l'espace* (Paris: Anthropos, 1974); Michel de Certeau, *L'Invention du quotidien 1: Arts de faire* (Paris: Gallimard, 1980).

2. Michael Rothberg, *The Implicated Subject: Beyond Victims and Perpetrators* (Stanford, CA: Stanford University Press), 2019.

3. Lindsey Dodd, " 'It Did Not Traumatise Me At All': Childhood 'Trauma' in French Oral Narratives of Wartime Bombing," *Oral History* 42, no. 2 (2013): 38–41.

4. Leyla Vural, "Potter's Field as a Heterotopia: Death and Mourning at New York City's Edge," *Oral History* 47, no. 2 (2019): 108. Vural cites Foucault, who writes that heterotopias "have the curious property of being in relation with all the other sites, but in such a way as to suspect, neutralise, or invent the set of relations that they happen to designate, mirror or reflect" (Foucault with Miskowiec, "Of Other Spaces," 24).

5. Julian Jackson writes: "Assessing the impact of the Occupation on the French population is difficult because a unified France no longer existed: there were at least six Frances," to which, he says, "one could add three more"; here, he is speaking of the physical carving up of territory across the whole period. He continues that this new map "must be fitted over a much older map of French memories and traditions." Julian Jackson, *France: The Dark Years, 1940–1944* (Oxford: Oxford University Press, 2001), 246–248.

6. For more on Sylvette's story, see Lindsey Dodd, "Fellow Feeling in Childhood Memories of Second World War France: Sympathy, Empathy and the Emotions of History," *Close Encounters in War* 4 (2021): 123–147.

7. See Annette Wieviorka and Michel Laffitte, *À l'intérieur du camp de Drancy* (Paris: Perrin, 2012); Maurice Rajsfus, *Drancy: Un camp de concentration très ordinaire, 1941–1944* (Paris: Le Cherche-midi, 1996). On internment camps in France more generally, see Denis Pechanski, *La France des camps: L'internement, 1938–46* (Paris: Gallimard, 2002). On the case of British "enemy aliens" interned in Vittel and Besançon camps, see Ayshka Sené, "The Orphan Story of British Women in Occupied France: History, Memory, Legacy" (PhD diss., Cardiff University, 2018).

8. See Lindsey Dodd, *French Children Under the Allied Bombs, 1940–1945: An Oral History* (Manchester, UK: Manchester University Press, 2016), chap. 3; Claudia Baldoli and Andrew Knapp, *Forgotten Blitzes: France and Italy Under Allied Air Attack, 1940–1945* (London: Continuum, 2012), chap. 3, for more on preparations for bombing.

PART 3. MEMORIES TOLD

1. Gilles Deleuze and Félix Guattari, *A Thousand Plateaus: Capitalism and Schizophrenia*, trans. Brian Massumi (Minneapolis: University of Minnesota Press, 1988), 256.

2. Deleuze and Guattari, *A Thousand Plateaus*, 25. In reference to the idea of the rhizome, Deleuze and Guattari write: "The tree imposes the verb 'to be,' but the fabric of the rhizome is the conjunction, 'and . . . and. . . . and. . . .' " See also Brent Adkins, *Deleuze and Guattari's* A Thousand Plateau: *A Critical Introduction and Guide* (Edinburgh: Edinburgh University Press, 2015), 24. Using their imagery, I tend to see memory as what they describe as "vortical," "operat[ing] in an open space throughout which things-flows are distributed," while recording an oral history interview, for example, plots "a closed space for linear and solid things" (Deleuze and Guattari, *A Thousand Plateaus*, 361).

3.   On intersubjectivity in oral history interviewing, see Lynn Abrams, *Oral History Theory* (London: Routledge, 2010), chap. 4., "Subjectivity and Intersubjectivity"; Donald A. Ritchie, ed., *The Oxford Handbook of Oral History* (Oxford: Oxford University Press, 2011), part 1, "The Nature of Interviewing."

4.   Lawrence Grossberg, "Affect's Future: Rediscovering the Virtual in the Actual," in *The Affect Theory Reader*, ed. Gregory J. Seigworth and Melissa Gregg (Durham, NC: Duke University Press, 2010), 318.

5.   Andrea Doucet, "Decolonizing Family Photographs: Ecological Imaginaries and Non-representational Ethnographies," *Journal of Contemporary Ethnography* 47, no. 6 (2018): 729–757.

6.   Yannis Hamilakis, "Sensorial Assemblages: Affect, Memory and Temporality in Assemblage Thinking," *Cambridge Archaeological Journal* 27, no. 1 (2017): 175.

7.   Nick J. Fox, "Emotions, Affects and the Production of Social Life," *British Journal of Sociology* 66, no. 2 (2015): 310.

8.   Hamilakis, "Sensorial Assemblages," 175.

9.   The ideas of regimes of affect, machines of affect, and structures of affect draw on Grossberg, "Affect's Future."

10. Jan Assmann, "Collective Memory and Cultural Identity," trans. John Czaplicka, *New German Critique* 65 (1995): 128–129, cited in Harald Welzer, "Communicative Memory," in *Cultural Memory Studies: An International and Interdisciplinary Handbook*, ed. Ansgar Nünning and Astrid Erll (Berlin: Walter de Gruyter, 2008), 285–298.

11. On such cultural scripts, see, for example, Lindsey Dodd, "Small Fish, Big Pond: Using a Single Oral Narrative to Reveal Broader Social Change," in *Memory and History: Understanding Memory as Source and Subject*, ed. Joan Tumblety (London: Routledge, 2013), 37–38.

12. Grossberg, "Affect's Future," 324–325.

13. Grossberg, "Affect's Future," 324. See, for example, Julie Fette, "Apology and the Past in Contemporary France," *French Politics, Culture & Society* 26, no. 2 (2008): 78–113. On poppy wearing, see James Fox, "Poppy Politics: Remembrance of Things Past," in *Cultural Heritage Ethics: Between Theory and Practice*, ed. Constantine Sandis (Cambridge: Open Book, 2014), 21–30; Victoria M. Basham, "Gender, Race, Militarism and Remembrance: The Everyday Geopolitics of the Poppy," *Gender, Place & Culture* 23, no. 6 (2016): 883–896.

14. Welzer, "Communicative Memory," 286.

15. Welzer, "Communicative Memory," 285.

16. Raymond Williams's concept of "structures of feeling" is valuable when discussing emotion, affect, culture, and society, but scholars find it notoriously slippery. Useful explanations can be found in Jennifer Harding and E. Deirdre Pribram, "The Power of Feeling: Locating Emotions in Culture," *European Journal of Cultural Studies* 5, no. 4 (2002): 407–426; Jonathan Flatley, *Affective Mapping: Melancholia and the Politics of Modernism* (Cambridge, MA: Harvard University Press, 2008); Ben Highmore, *Cultural Feelings: Mood, Mediation and Cultural Politics* (London: Routledge, 2017).

17. Flatley, *Affective Mapping*, 26.

18. Concerning his term *structure of feeling*, Raymond Williams wrote: "We are concerned with meanings and values as they are actively lived and felt, and relations between these

and formal or systematic beliefs are in practice variable. . . . We are talking about characteristic elements of impulses or restraint and tone; specifically affective elements of consciousness and relationships: not feeling against thought, but thought as felt and feeling as thought: practical consciousness of a present kind, in a living and interrelating continuity." Raymond Williams, *Marxism and Literature* (New York: Oxford University Press, 1977), 132, cited in Flatley, *Affective Mapping*, 25–26.

19. Stuart Hall, *Cultural Studies 1983: A Theoretical History*, ed. Jennifer Daryl Slack and Lawrence Grossberg (Durham, NC: Duke University Press, 2016), 31.

20. Graham Smith, "Remembering in Groups: Negotiating Between 'Individual' and 'Collective' Memories," in *The Oral History Reader*, 3rd ed., ed. Robert Perks and Alistair Thomson (London: Routledge, 2016), 193–211.

21. Kevin Buchanan and David Middleton, "Voices of Experience: Talk, Identity and Membership in Reminiscence Groups," *Ageing & Society* 15, no. 4 (1995): 457–491.

22. Megan Watkins, "Desiring Recognition, Accumulating Affect," in *The Affect Theory Reader*, 278.

23. Buchanan and Middleton, "Voices of Experience," 468.

24. Ronald Grele, "History and the Languages of History in the Oral History Interview: Who Answers Whose Questions and Why," University of the Witwatersrand, Johannesburg, History Workshop, February 6–10, 1990, https://wiredspace.wits.ac.za/bitstream/handle/10539/7815/HWS-146.pdf?sequence=1&isAllowed=y, 18.

25. Gregory Hollin, Isla Forsyth, Eva Giraud, and Tracy Potts, "(Dis)entangling Barad: Materialisms and Ethics," *Social Studies of Science* 47, no. 6 (2017): 923.

26. Lorraine Code, *Ecological Thinking: The Politics of Epistemic Location* (New York: Oxford University Press, 2006), 229, cited in Doucet, "Decolonizing Family Photographs," 748.

27. Optimistic approaches include those outlined in Joanna Bornat, "A Second Take: Revisiting Interviews with a Different Purpose," *Oral History* 31, no. 1 (2003): 47–53; and Steven High, Elizabeth Tasong, Felipe Lalinde Lopera, and Hussain Almahr, "The Pedagogy and Practice of Listening to Rwandan Exiles and Genocide Survivors," *Oral History* 50, no. 1 (2022): 115–126.

28. Ronald Grele, "History and the Languages of History in the Oral History Interview: Who Answers Whose Questions and Why," University of the Witwatersrand, Johannesburg, History Workshop, February 6–10, 1990, https://wiredspace.wits.ac.za/bitstream/handle/10539/7815/HWS-146.pdf?sequence=1&isAllowed=y, 11–19. A lot of contemporary practices of archiving oral history strive to contextualize the interview as much as possible, as though knowing more about the recording provides the key to interpreting meaning at a later date.

29. Gilles Deleuze and Félix Guattari, *A Thousand Plateaus: Capitalism and Schizophrenia*, trans. Brian Massumi (Minneapolis: University of Minnesota Press, 1988) make the difference between "reproducing" as an analytical trope, which "implies the permanence of a fixed point of view" that is "external to what is reproduced: watching the flow from the bank," and jumping in, "following" rather than reproducing, being "carried away by a vortical flow," when one "engages in a continuous variation of variables, instead of extracting constants from them" (372).

30. Grele, "History and the Languages of History," 26.

31. Deleuze and Guattari, *A Thousand Plateaus*, 502.

32. Deleuze and Guattari, *A Thousand Plateaus*, 371.

6. REGIMES OF MEMORY, REGIMES OF FEELING

1. Laurent Douzou and Pierre Laborie, "Le rôle des historiens dans la transmission de la mémoire des comportements collectifs," in *Images des comportements sous l'Occupation: Mémoires, transmission, idées reçues*, ed. Jacqueline Sainclivier, Jean-Marie Guillon, and Pierre Laborie (Rennes, France: Presses Universitaires de Rennes, 2016), 158–159. Translations are my own.

2. Susannah Radstone and Katharine Hodgkin understand "both history and memory [as] 'regimes' in a number of senses; that is, that what is understood as history and as memory is produced by historically specific and contestable systems of knowledge and power and that what history and memory produce as knowledge is also contingent upon the (contestable) systems of knowledge and power that produce them." This stance, they write, is different from that taken by many memory studies scholars, who typically treat memory as acting in opposition to a public "regime" of history and capable of destabilizing the "grand narratives" history has authoritatively constructed. They continue: "This is of course not to deny that memory may contest history, but it is to insist that neither memory nor history is 'outside' systems of knowledge and power." Susannah Radstone and Katharine Hodgkin, introduction to *Regimes of Memory*, ed. Susannah Radstone and Katharine Hodgkin (London: Routledge, 2003), 10–11.

3. The interview can be found on the Mémoires de Résistances website: http://memoires -resistances.dordogne.fr/temoignages-audio/1008-temoignages-integraux/52-jean -dolet-blanchou-resistant-deporte-nancette-blanchou.html (accessed August 2, 2022).

4. For more about Nancette's story, see Lindsey Dodd, "The Disappearing Child: Observations on Oral History, Archives and Affects," *Oral History* 49, no. 2 (2021): 37–48.

5. See, for example, Martin Parsons, ed., *Children: The Invisible Victims of War: An Interdisciplinary Study* (Peterborough, UK: DSM, 2008).

6. Eva M. MacMahon, *Elite Oral History Discourse: A Study of Cooperation and Coherence* (Tuscaloosa: University of Alabama, 1989), cited in Ronald Grele, "History and the Languages of History in the Oral History Interview: Who Answers Whose Questions and Why," University of the Witwatersrand, Johannesburg, History Workshop, February 6–10, 1990, https://wiredspace.wits.ac.za/bitstream/handle/10539/7815/HWS-146.pdf?sequence =1&isAllowed=y, 5.

7. Lindsey Dodd, " 'It Did Not Traumatise Me at All': Childhood 'Trauma' in French Oral Narratives of Wartime Bombing," *Oral History* 42, no. 2 (2013): 44–46.

8. Jacques Sémelin, *The Survival of the Jews in France, 1940–1944*, trans. Cynthia Schoch and Natasha Lehrer (London: Hurst, 2018).

9. In 2007, the Allied bombing of France was described as "the last 'black hole' of French collective memory of the Second World War." Jean-François Muracciole, "Les bombardements stratégiques en France durant la Seconde Guerre Mondiale: Premier bilan et pistes de recherche," in *Les Bombardements alliés sur la France durant la Seconde Guerre*

Mondiale: stratégies, bilans matériels et humains, ed. Michèle Battesti and Patrick Facon (Vincennes, France: Cahiers du CEHD no. 37, 2007), 174. For more on this question, see Lindsey Dodd, *French Children Under the Allied Bombs, 1940–1945: An Oral History* (Manchester, UK: Manchester University Press, 2016), particularly the conclusion.

10. A great deal has been written about the swing away from the Gaullist myth of a "nation of resisters," not least Henry Rousso, *The Vichy Syndrome: History and Memory in France Since 1944*, trans. Arthur Goldhammer (Cambridge, MA: Harvard University Press, 1991). See also, for example, Moshik Temkin, " 'Avec Un Certain Malaise': The Paxtonian Trauma in France, 1973–74," *Journal of Contemporary History* 38, no. 2 (2003): 291–306; Richard J. Golsan, *Vichy's Afterlife: History and Counterhistory in Postwar France* (Lincoln: University of Nebraska Press, 2000).

11. Popular Memory Group, "Popular Memory: Theory, Politics, Method," in *The Oral History Reader*, ed. Robert Perks and Alistair Thomson (London: Routledge, 1998), 75–86; for a worked example, see also Graham Dawson, "Trauma, Place and the Politics of Memory: Bloody Sunday, Derry, 1972–2004," *History Workshop Journal* 59, no. 1 (2005): 151–178. Popular memory theory describes the process by which new hegemonies develop in practices of remembering as memorial regimes shift; what is interesting in relation to the French resistance is the way it has been both valued and discredited.

7. COMMUNITIES OF MEMORY, COMMUNITIES OF FEELING

1. Sara Ahmed, *The Cultural Politics of Emotion*, 2nd ed. (Edinburgh: Edinburgh University Press, 2014).

2. A classic example in which the oral historian critiques her own practice of imposing an interpretation on a memory story is Katherine Borland, " 'That's Not What I Said': Interpretive Conflict in Oral Narrative Research," in *The Oral History Reader*, ed. Robert Perks and Alistair Thomson (London: Routledge, 1998), 320–332. Borland found it to be both uncomfortable and damaging to trust when a researcher interprets an interview (in her case, with her grandmother) in a way with which the interviewee disagrees. She concluded that a "true exchange" was ultimately reached when "each of us granted the other interpretative space." Yet the goal of "sharing authority," which has animated a great deal of oral history, should not govern research practices so far as to deny the researcher's legitimacy in contributing to, and even leading, the interpretive project. Michael Frisch, *A Shared Authority? Essays on the Craft and Meaning of Oral and Public History* (Albany: State University of New York Press, 1990).

3. United Nations High Commissioner for Refugees, "Monthly Arrivals by Nationality to Greece, Italy and Spain," *Refugees/Migrants Emergency Response—Mediterranean*, March 31, 2016, https://europadreaming.eu/open-data/20160122-Dec_Nationality_of_arrivals_to_Greece _Italy_and_Spain-Monthly_Jan-Dec_2015.pdf.

4. My interviews about the evacuation of children from the Paris region as a measure of protection against the Allied bombing from 1943 were overlaid with a later story of displacement. Between 1962 and 1984, around two thousand children from the island of Réunion were forcibly "evacuated" (or deported) to France as part of a racist politics of so-called child protection. The children were often taken against the will of their

families. The line was given that this measure intended to improve their quality of life and reduce population pressure on the island. Unlike the many stories of evacuated French children during the Second World War found either in the archives or in memory, the "petits réunionnais" were not, on the whole, well treated. Interviewees and their family members often made reference to this later shameful case, which showed the Creuse in a very bad light. See Gilles Gauvin, "L'affaire des enfants de la Creuse: Entre abus de mémoire et nécessité de l'histoire," *Revue d'histoire* 3, no. 143 (2019): 85–98.

5. Kevin Buchanan and David Middleton, "Voices of Experience: Talk, Identity and Membership in Reminiscence Groups," *Ageing & Society* 15, no. 4 (1995): 457–491.

6. Nicole Dombrowski Risser, *France Under Fire: German Invasion, Civilian Flight and Family Survival During the Second World War* (Cambridge: Cambridge University Press, 2012); Sharif Gemie and Fiona Reid, "Chaos, Panic and Historiography of the Exode (France, 1940)," *War & Society* 26, no. 2 (2007): 73–97; Hanna Diamond, *Fleeing Hitler: France, 1940* (New York: Oxford University Press, 2007).

7. See, for example, Jean-Michel Chaumont, *La concurrence des victimes: Génocide, identité, reconnaissance* (Paris: Éditions de la Découverte, 1997), 334.

8. Ronald Grele, "History and the Languages of History in the Oral History Interview: Who Answers Whose Questions and Why," University of the Witwatersrand, Johannesburg, History Workshop, February 6–10, 1990, https://wiredspace.wits.ac.za/bitstream/handle/10539/7815/HWS-146.pdf?sequence=1&isAllowed=y, 5, 11.

9. For the concept of actualization in memory and time, drawing on Henri Bergson, see David Middleton and Steven Brown, *The Social Psychology of Experience: Studies in Remembering and Forgetting* (Thousand Oaks, CA: Sage, 2005), 74–75; also Yannis Hamilakis's useful explanation and diagram in "Sensorial Assemblages: Affect, Memory and Temporality in Assemblage Thinking," *Cambridge Archaeological Journal* 27, no. 1 (2017): 174.

10. Sean Field states: "I am making a plea for oral historians to think more deeply about how subjects construct dissonant 'inter-views' of each other (and the dialogue) and the unfolding intersubjective production of alterity i.e. recognizing (and misrecognizing) the other as other." Sean Field, "Critical Empathy," *Continuum: Journal of Media and Cultural Studies* 31, no. 5 (2017): 664.

11. Grele, 'History and the Languages of History," 9.

12. On the "duty of memory," see Sébastien Ledoux, *Le devoir de mémoire: Une formule et son histoire* (Paris: CNRS Éditions, 2016).

13. Nicolas Sarkozy was president of the French Republic between 2007 and 2012, the period during which a fair number of the memory stories in this corpus were recorded. Sarkozy became notorious for interventions in history making. He was highly criticized for attempts to instrumentalize the memory and history of the Second World War in France. See Nicolas Bancel and Herman Lebovics, "Building the History Museum to Stop History: Nicolas Sarkozy's New Presidential Museum of French History," *French Cultural Studies* 22, no. 4 (2011): 271–288; Paul Smith, "*L'Histoire Bling-Bling*—Nicolas Sarkozy and the Historians," in *The Use and Abuse of Memory: Interpreting World War II in Contemporary European Politics*, ed. Christian Karner and Bram Mertens (New Brunswick, NJ: Transaction, 2013), 121–136.

14. Rachel Jedinak was founder of the Comité École de la rue Tlemcen. Since 1997, this group has been active in commemorating Jewish children from Paris. The group campaigned

for plaques to be placed on the walls of Paris schools to remember the children from each one who were deported and killed. Rachel has been active in upholding one of the group's aims: to educate the next generation about hatred, fascism, anti-Semitism, persecution, forgetting, and Holocaust denial by speaking out about the past and telling their stories. Her memoir is *Nous étions seulement des enfants* (Paris: Fayard, 2018). She participated in the documentary film *Nous étions des enfants* produced by Jean-Gabriel Carasso in 2011. She was interviewed on Franco-German TV channel Arte's leading current affairs program, *28 Minutes*, in September 2018.

15. It was common for French men who had been boys during the Second World War to be doing their National Service or to be conscripted during the Indochina War (1946–1954) and/or the Algerian War of Independence (1954–1962). For a brief discussion of this, see Lindsey Dodd, " 'It Did Not Traumatise Me at All': Childhood 'Trauma' in French Oral Narratives of Wartime Bombing," *Oral History* 42, no. 2 (2013): 45–46. See also Michael Rothberg, *Multidirectional Memory: Remembering the Holocaust in the Age of Decolonization* (Stanford, CA: Stanford University Press, 2009).

16. Nick J. Fox, "Emotions, Affects and the Production of Social Life," *British Journal of Sociology* 66, no. 2 (2015): 310.

PART 4. MEMORIES LIVED

1. Ben Highmore, "Bitter After Taste: Affect, Food, and Social Aesthetics," in *The Affect Theory Reader*, ed. Gregory J. Seigworth and Melissa Gregg (Durham, NC: Duke University Press, 2010), 118–137. He makes reference to Alexander Baumgarten, "Aesthetics" (1750), in *Art in Theory, 1648–1815: An Anthology of Changing Ideas*, ed. Charles Harrison, Paul Wood, and Jason Gaiger (Oxford: Blackwell, 2000), 489–491.

2. Terry Eagleton, *The Ideology of the Aesthetic* (Oxford: Blackwell, 1990), 13, cited in Highmore, "Bitter After Taste," 121.

3. Owain Jones, "Geography, Memory and Non-Representational Geographies," *Geography Compass* 5, no. 2 (2011): 876. The idea of present moments of practice derives from nonrepresentational theory.

4. Harald Welzer, "Communicative Memory," in *Cultural Memory Studies: An International and Interdisciplinary Handbook*, ed. Ansgar Nünning and Astrid Erll (Berlin: Walter de Gruyter, 2008), 295.

5. "Memory . . . is fundamental to becoming, and a key wellspring of agency, practice/habit, creativity, imagination, and thus of the potential of the performative moment." Jones, "Geography, Memory," 875–876.

6. Stuart Hall and Les Back, "At Home and Not at Home: Stuart Hall in Conversation with Les Back," *Cultural Studies* 23, no 4 (2009): 665, cited in Ben Highmore, "Aesthetic Matters: Writing and Cultural Studies," *Cultural Studies* 32, no. 2 (2018): 254.

8. MATERIALITIES OF THE EVERYDAY

1. Terry Eagleton, *The Ideology of the Aesthetic* (Oxford: Blackwell, 1990), 13, cited in Ben Highmore, "Bitter After Taste: Affect, Food, and Social Aesthetics," in *The Affect Theory*

Reader, ed. Gregory J. Seigworth and Melissa Gregg (Durham, NC: Duke University Press, 2010), 121–122.

2. See, for example, Ramon F. Minioli, "Food Rationing and Mortality in Paris, 1940–41," *Milbank Memorial Fund Quarterly* 20, no. 3 (1942): 213–220; Harold C. Stuart and Daniel Kuhlmann, "Studies of the Physical Characteristics of Children in Marseilles, France, in 1941," *Journal of Pediatrics* 20, no. 4 (1942): 424–453; Harold C. Stuart, "Review of the Evidence as to the Nutritional State of Children in France," *American Journal of Public Health* 35, no. 4 (1945): 299–307; Robert Debré, "Condition of Children in France Under the Occupation," *Proceedings of the Royal Society of Medicine: Section for the Study of Disease in Children* 38 (1945), 447–449. Also see Dominique Veillon, *Vivre et survivre en France, 1939–1947* (Paris: Éditions Payot, 1995); John F. Sweets, *Choices in Vichy France: The French Under Nazi Occupation* (New York: Oxford University Press, 1994), 15; and chapters by Matthieu Devigne, Shannon Fogg, and Jean-Pierre Le Crom in Lindsey Dodd and David Lees, eds., *Vichy France and Everyday Life: Confronting the Challenges of Wartime* (London: Bloomsbury, 2018).

3. Examples of authors using rutabaga symbolically include Jean-Luc Besson's illustrated memoir for children, *Paris rutabaga: Souvenirs d'enfance 1939–45* (Paris: Éditions-Jeunesse, Gallimard, 2005), as well as Louis Valentin's children's adventure, *Les années rutabagas* (Paris: Olivier Orban, 1994). Claire Hsu Accomando's memoir is titled *Love and Rutabaga: A Remembrance of the War Years* (New York: St. Martin's, 1993).

4. See, for example, Annie Ernaux's description of her father in *La Place* (Paris: Gallimard, 1983): "Jusqu'à la fin des années cinquante, il a mangé de la soupe le matin, après il s'est mis au café au lait, avec réticence, comme s'il sacrifiait à une délicatesse féminine" (68). (My translation: "Right up until the end of the 1950s, he would eat soup in the morning. After that, he reluctantly took to having milky coffee, as though making a concession to feminine delicacy.")

5. Robert Bichet, *Célébration des gaudes: Autrefois plat national comtois* (Besançon, France: Éditions Cêtre, 2000), 168.

6. Isabelle von Bueltzingsloewen notes that the term *gray market* (*marché gris*) is used by historians but is usually unfamiliar to others, including those who lived through the period. Isabelle von Bueltzingsloewen, "Reconstructing the Daily Life of a Lyonnaise Family," in *Vichy France and Everyday Life: Confronting the Challenges of Wartime*, ed. Lindsey Dodd and David Lees (London: Bloomsbury, 2018), 66–67n28. Typically, the black market is seen as motivated by profit and involves a trafficker selling on at much inflated prices from a producer. The gray market is motivated by the supplementing of basic rations (rather than more luxurious products) and brings together consumer and producer, the latter selling directly to the former below the black-market price but above the official price. The term *brown market* has been used to describe selling to the Germans at high prices for very large profits, again usually through traffickers. Fabrice Grenard, *La France du marché noir, 1940–1949* (Paris: Payot, 2008)). The term *pink market* has been used to describe the exchange of goods among friends, family, and acquaintances.

7. Robert Debré, "Condition of Children in France Under the Occupation," *Proceedings of the Royal Society of Medicine: Section for the Study of Disease in Children* 38 (1945): 447–449.

8. Camille Mahé's research describes cutout and coloring books that venerated Marshal Pétain; masks of Pétain's and Laval's faces were also on sale for dressing up. The Great Game of French History inculcated nationalistic ideals, and games like The Game of Life embedded traditional gendered values about life trajectories. Camille Mahé, "Children and Play in Occupied France," in *Vichy France and Everyday Life*, 17–33.

9. For example, Jean Caniot, *Lille 1939–1945* (Lambersart, France: Author, 2009).

10. Matthieu Devigne, *L'École des Années Noires: Une histoire du primaire en temps de guerre* (Paris: Presses Universitaires de France, 2018).

11. Devigne, *L'École des Années Noires.*

9. AFFECTIVE OTHERS

1. Caroline Williams, "Thinking the Political in the Wake of Spinoza: Power, Affect and Imagination in *The Ethics*," *Contemporary Political Theory* 6, no. 3 (2007): 358.

2. Lindsey Dodd, " 'Mon petit papa chéri': Children, Fathers and Family Separation in Wartime France," *Essays in French Literature and Culture* 54 (2017): 97–116.

3. Sarah Fishman, *We Will Wait: Wives of French Prisoners of War, 1940–1945* (New Haven, CT: Yale University Press, 1991), xv. The children of prisoners of war received special treatment, including an increased child allowance. Fishman notes that in 1941, a prisoner's wife living in Paris received 5f 50 per day for a first child; this had risen to 10f 50 by March 1942, and in July 1942 she received 15f per day for her first child (52, 193). They were also offered special events such as Christmas parties, tea parties, and gifts. These children were made a national object of pity and patriotic duty. None of the interviewees commented on having received any of these benefits, however; their stories reflected more directly the loss of their fathers.

4. Laura Lee Downs writes that the only difference between the family separation of prewar *colonies de vacances* and wartime evacuations was that the latter "occurred under the shadow of war," which, I believe, somewhat underplays the nature of that shadow. Laura Lee Downs, "Milieu Social or Milieu Familial? Theories and Practices of Childrearing Among the Popular Classes in Twentieth-Century France and Britain: The Case of Evacuation (1939–45)," *Family and Community History* 8, no. 1 (2005): 58. Von Bueltzingsloewen notes: "Not living permanently with one's parents was quite a widespread experience in interwar France, especially for the younger children of working-class families in which both parents worked." Isabelle von Bueltzingsloewen, "Reconstructing the Daily Life of a Lyonnaise Family," in *Vichy France and Everyday Life: Confronting the Challenges of Wartime*, ed. Lindsey Dodd and David Lees (London: Bloomsbury, 2018), 56. While this is undoubtedly the case (archival data tell us so), the fact remains that, as with the *colonies de vacances*, if this particular child had never been separated from his or her parents before, it would be a novel experience regardless of whether it had been a common social practice in the recent past.

5. Stuart Hall and Les Back, "At Home and Not at Home: Stuart Hall in Conversation with Les Back," *Cultural Studies* 23, no. 4 (2009): 665, cited in Ben Highmore, "Aesthetic Matters: Writing and Cultural Studies," *Cultural Studies* 32, no. 2 (2018): 254.

6. On family memory, see, for example, Astrid Erll, "Locating Family in Cultural Memory Studies," *Journal of Comparative Family Studies* 42, no. 3 (2011): 303–318.

7. Terry Eagleton, *The Ideology of the Aesthetic* (Oxford: Blackwell, 1990), 13, cited in Ben Highmore, "Bitter After Taste: Affect, Food, and Social Aesthetics," in *The Affect Theory Reader*, ed. Gregory J. Seigworth and Melissa Gregg (Durham, NC: Duke University Press, 2010), 121.

8. Elisabeth Meier details the range of different branches of the German occupation and their activities in "Les services d'occupation et de répression allemandes à Lyon (1942–1944)," in *Lyon dans la Seconde Guerre Mondiale: Villes et métropoles à l'épreuve du conflit*, ed. Isabelle von Bueltzingsloewen, Laurent Douzou, Jean-Dominique Durand, Hervé Joly and Jean Solchany (Rennes, France: Presses Universitaires de Rennes, 2016), 37–50. It is worth noting that "the Gestapo" was the name commonly given by French people to members of the Sicherheitsdienst (SD). John F. Sweets, *Choices in Vichy France: The French Under Nazi Occupation* (New York: Oxford University Press, 1994), 181. Historians tend to write of the Sipo-SD complex in relation to Nazi policing; this was the amalgamation, from 1936, of the Sicherheitspolizei (Sipo, the security police, which incorporated the Kripo, the criminal investigative police, and the Gestapo, the political police) with the Sicherheitsdienst (the security service of the Third Reich) under Reinhard Heydrich. See, for example, George C. Browder, *Foundations of the Nazi Police State: The Formation of Sipo and SD* (Lexington: University Press of Kentucky, 1990); also Tal Bruttmann, "La Sipo-SD de Lyon et la chasse aux juifs," in *Lyon dans la Seconde Guerre Mondiale*, 51–60.

9. On the looting of Jewish property, see Shannon L. Fogg, *Stealing Home: Looting, Restitution, and Reconstructing Jewish Lives in France, 1942–1947* (Oxford: Oxford University Press, 2016).

10. See Hanna Diamond, "'Prisoners of the Peace': German Prisoners-of-War in Rural France, 1944–48," *European History Quarterly* 43, no. 3 (2013): 442–463.

11. For a discussion of Pétain's relationship with children, see Lindsey Dodd, "Children's Citizenly Participation in the National Revolution: The Instrumentalization of Children in Vichy France," *European Review of History/Revue d'Histoire Européenne* 24, no. 5 (2017): 759–780. The song *Maréchal, nous voilà!* appeared in 1941, with lyrics by André Montagard and music attributed to Charles Courtioux.

12. Roger Austin, "Political Surveillance and Ideological Control in Vichy France: A Study of Teachers in the Midi," in *Vichy France and the Resistance: Culture and Ideology*, ed. Rod Kedward and Roger Austin (London: Croom Helm, 1985), 13–35. See also Nicholas Atkin, "Church and Teachers in Vichy France, 1940–1944," *French History* 4, no. 1 (1990): 1–22; W. D. Halls, *The Youth of Vichy France* (Oxford: Clarendon, 1981).

13. See, for example, Halls, *Youth of Vichy France*; Pierre Giolitto, *Histoire de la jeunesse sous Vichy* (Paris: Perrin, 1991).

14. Stanley Hoffman identified Vichy as a "pluralist dictatorship"; this was elaborated by Robert Paxton as the Vichy of the National Revolution, the Vichy of the technocrats, and the Vichy of the fascists. See Stanley Hoffman, *Decline or Renewal? France Since the 1930s* (New York: Viking, 1974), 3–4; Robert O. Paxton, *Vichy France: Old Guard and New Order, 1940–1944* (New York: Knopf, 1972), 231, 262–283.

15. Julian Jackson, *France: The Dark Years, 1940–1944* (Oxford: Oxford University Press, 2001), 230–231.

16. An agreement signed between René Bousquet and Karl Oberg in August 1942 promised autonomy to the French police but also made them responsible for fighting "terrorism, anarchism, and communism" alongside the Germans, which effectively meant they would act in pursuit of goals established by the Germans. Julian Jackson notes that by August 1943, French Prime Minister Pierre Laval refused to supply French police to conduct and support the roundups of Jews in Paris (*The Dark Years*, 216, 228–229).

17. See Claire Zalc, *Les Dénaturalisés: Les retraits de nationalité sous Vichy* (Paris: Seuil, 2016). See also Michael Marrus and Robert O. Paxton, *Vichy France and the Jews* (Stanford, CA: Stanford University Press, 1995); Angela Kershaw, *Before Auschwitz: Irène Némirovsky and the Cultural Landscape of Inter-War France* (London: Routledge, 2009); Nick Underwood, "Lending Identity: Circulating Literacy, Current Events, Yiddish Culture, and Politics in Interwar France," *Contemporary French Civilization* 45, no. 1 (2020): 71–88.

18. Lindsey Dodd, *French Children Under the Allied Bombs, 1940–1945: An Oral History* (Manchester, UK: Manchester University Press, 2016), chap. 10, "Friends, Enemies and the Wider War."

19. Sara Ahmed, *The Cultural Politics of Emotion*, 2nd ed. (Edinburgh: Edinburgh University Press, 2014), 28.

20. Mason Norton, "Counter-Revolution? Resisting Vichy and the National Revolution," *Vichy France and Everyday Life: Confronting the Challenges of Wartime*, ed. Lindsey Dodd and David Lees (London: Bloomsbury, 2018), 197–211.

10. CONTINGENCY AND RUPTURE

1. Wendy Michallat, "Madeleine Blaess: An Emotional History of a Long Liberation," in *Vichy France and Everyday Life: Confronting the Challenges of Wartime*, ed. Lindsey Dodd and David Lees (London: Bloomsbury, 2018), 181.

2. Kathleen Stewart, *Ordinary Affects* (Durham, NC: Duke University Press, 2007), 42.

3. Stewart, *Ordinary Affects*, 29.

4. Lindsey Dodd, "Are We Defended? Conflicting Representations of War in Pre-War France," *University of Sussex Journal of Contemporary History* 12 (2008), https://www.sussex.ac.uk/webteam/gateway/file.php?name=article-dodd-12&site=15).

5. For discussions of prewar and interwar planning for evacuation, see, for example, Nicole Dombrowski Risser, *France Under Fire: German Invasion, Civilian Flight, and Family Survival During World War II* (Cambridge: Cambridge University Press, 2012), chap. 1; Hanna Diamond, *Fleeing Hitler: France 1940* (Oxford: Oxford University Press, 2008), 16–24; Lindsey Dodd and Marc Wiggam, 'Civil Defence as a Harbinger of War in France and Britain During the Interwar Period,' *Synergies Royaume-Uni et Irlande* 4 (2011): 139–150.

6. Gemie and Reid stress hereditary patterns of behavior that were triggered in 1940 and that depended on prior, territorially distinct experiences in 1870 and 1914–1918. "Many French people, especially those on the northern and eastern borders, had grown up with the ever-present notion of a German attack. . . . This enabled them to develop coping mechanisms and organising strategies in 1940. Memories, whether individual or collective, also affected the direction they took. Many refugees had no specific destination in mind, but the majority of them believed that they would be safe south of the Loire."

Sharif Gemie and Fiona Reid, "Chaos, Panic and Historiography of the Exode (France, 1940)," *War & Society* 26, no. 2 (2007): 79.

7. John F. Sweets, *Choices in Vichy France: The French Under Nazi Occupation* (New York: Oxford University Press, 1994), 176. He adds, however, that the brutal behavior of the Germans toward the end of the Occupation made it impossible afterward "to distinguish between the 'bad' Nazis and the 'good' Germans" (190).

8. For example, from spring 1943, Werner Knab arrived in Lyon, where he was head of the Sipo-SD and thus the superior of Klaus Barbie. Knab had been a member of the Einsatzgruppe C in 1941 and head of section IV of the Sipo-SD in Kiev, where he had overseen the mass murder of Jews. Elisabeth Meier, "Les services d'occupation et de répression allemandes à Lyon (1942–1944)," in *Lyon dans la Seconde Guerre Mondial: Villes et métropoles à l'épreuve du conflit*, ed. Isabelle von Bueltzingsloewen, Laurent Douzou, Jean-Dominique Durand, Hervé Joly, and Jean Solchany (Rennes, France: Presses Universitaires de Rennes, 2016), 38.

9. Kathel Houzé and Jean-Christophe Bailly, *La Colonie des enfants d'Izieu* (Lyon, France: Éditions Libel, 2012).

10. Andrew Knapp records the severity of the Allied bombing in its impact on the French population during 1944. In 1943, there had been 788 air raids on France; in 1944 there were 7,482. This equates to 8.4 percent compared 79.3 percent of all Allied raids on France during the war. In 1943, there were 7,446 civilian deaths as a result of bombing; in 1944 there were 38,158. This equates to 13.6 percent compared with 69.8 percent of all civilian deaths in France from bombing. Andrew Knapp, *Les Français sous les bombes alliées, 1940–1945* (Paris: Tallandier, 2014), 19.

11. Robert Gildea, "Resistance, Reprisals and Community in Occupied France," *Transactions of the Royal Historical Society* 13 (2003): 163–185; Sarah Farmer, *Martyred Village: Commemorating the 1944 Massacre at Oradour-sur-Glane* (Berkeley: University of California Press, 1999).

12. For events in Rouffignac, see the account on the pages of the association Anonymes, Justes et Persécutés Durant la Période Nazie dans les communes de France, accessed August 2, 2022, https://www.ajpn.org/commune-Saint-Cernin-de-Reilhac-24356.html; http://rouffignac-perigordnoir.fr/le-31-mars-1944-guerre-mondiale-rouffignac-saint-cernin-perigord-noir/.

13. Patrick Galliou, *Histoire de Brest* (Paris: Éditions Jean-Paul Gisserot, 2007), 103; François Péron, *Brest sous l'occupation* (Rennes, France: Ouest-France, 1981), 101–104; Hervé Le Boterf, *La Bretagne dans la guerre (1938–1945)* (Paris: France-Empire, 2000), 530.

14. Alain Brossat, *Libération fête folle, 6 juin 1944–8 mai 45: Mythes et rites ou le grand théâtre des passions populaires* (Paris: Éditions Autrement, 1994); Susan Keith, "Collective Memory and the End of Occupation: Remembering (and Forgetting) the Liberation of Paris in Images," *Visual Communication Quarterly* 17, no. 3 (2010): 134–146; also H. R. Kedward and Nancy Wood, eds., *The Liberation of France* (Oxford: Berg, 1995); Michallat, "Madeleine Blaess."

15. Not all were correct in their behavior. See, for example, J. Robert Lilly, *La face cachée des GIs: Les viols commis par des soldats Américains en France, en Angleterre et en Allemagne pendant la Seconde Guerre mondiale* (Paris: Payot, 2003).

16. This is despite the fact that in France May 8th has been a national day of commemoration to mark VE day since 1953.

17. The song "Thamara-boum-di-hé! C'est la danse atomique," by Henri Bazin (music E. Deransart) is dated as first appearing in 1946.

18. On how the Allies are depicted in children's literature of the liberation era, see Judith K. Proud, "Plus Ça Change . . .? Propaganda Fiction for Children, 1940–1945," in *The Liberation of France: Image and Event*, ed. H. R. Kedward and Nancy Wood (Oxford: Berg, 1995), 57–74.

CONCLUSION: A PALETTE OF HAECCEITIES

1. Elizabeth Adams St. Pierre, "Haecceity: Laying Out a Plane for Post Qualitative Inquiry," *Qualitative Inquiry* 23, no. 9 (2017): 686, citing *A Shock to Thought: Expression After Deleuze and Guattari*, ed. Brian Massumi (London: Routledge, 2002).

2. Alexis de Toqueville, *Democracy in America*, ed. Eduardo Nolla, trans. James Schleifer (Indianapolis, IN: Liberty Fund, 2012), 663, cited in *Individualism: A Reader*, ed. George H. Smith and Marilyn Moore (Libertarianism.org Press, 2015), 10.

3. Gilles Deleuze and Félix Guattari, *A Thousand Plateaus: Capitalism and Schizophrenia*, trans. Brian Massumi (Minneapolis: University of Minnesota Press, 1988), 261.

4. Deleuze and Guattari, *A Thousand Plateaus*, 261; John Rajchman, *The Deleuze Connections* (Cambridge, MA: MIT Press, 2001), 85, cited in St. Pierre, "Haecceity," 688.

5. Ludmilla Jordanova, "Children in History: Concepts of Nature and Society," in *Children, Parents and Politics*, ed. Geoffrey Scarre (Cambridge: Cambridge University Press, 1989): 5, discussed in Lindsey Dodd, *French Children Under the Allied Bombs, 1940–1944: An Oral History* (Manchester, UK: Manchester University Press, 2016), 41.

6. Deleuze and Guattari, *A Thousand Plateaus*, 263.

7. Council on Foreign Relations, Center for Preventative Action, https://www.cfr.org/programs/center-preventive-action.

8. Watchlist on Children and Armed Conflict, https://watchlist.org.

BIBLIOGRAPHY

ARCHIVAL COLLECTIONS

File references for individual interviews where available; see appendix.

DEPARTMENTAL ARCHIVES CONSULTED

Archives départementales de la Creuse
Archives départementales de la Dordogne
Archives départementales de la Meuse
Archives départementales du Nord
Archives départementales de Saône-et-Loire
Archives départementales de Seine-Saint-Denis
Archives départementales du Val-de-Marne

MUNICIPAL ARCHIVES CONSULTED

Archives municipales de Beaune
Archives municipales de Boulogne-Billancourt
Archives municipales et communautaires de Brest
Archives municipales de Dunkerque
Archives municipales de Lille

OTHER ORGANIZATIONS

Aout 1944: Paroles libérées sur Sète, http://parolesliberees.org/, ville de Sète
Centre d'Histoire de la Résistance et de la Déportation, Lyon
Le Son des Choses, https://lesondeschoses.org/ former Champagne-Ardenne region
Maison d'Izieu (Ain)
Mémoires de résistances, https://memoires-resistances.dordogne.fr/, département de la Dordogne
Rails et histoire—Association pour l'histoire des chemins de fer (AHICF)

WEB RESOURCES

Anciens des Services Spéciaux de la Défense nationale: http://www.aassdn.org/araMnbioMf-Mz
.html

Anonymes, Justes et Persécutés Durant la Période Nazie: http://www.ajpn.org/

Council on Foreign Relations, Center for Preventative Action: https://www.cfr.org/programs
/center-preventive-action

Institut national de l'audiovisuel: https://www.ina.fr/

Watchlist on Children and Armed Conflict: https://watchlist.org,

PUBLISHED MATERIAL: BOOKS, CHAPTERS, ARTICLES

Abrams, Lynn. *Oral History Theory*. London: Routledge, 2010.

Accomando, Claire Hsu. *Love and Rutabaga: A Remembrance of the War Years*. New York: St.
Martin's, 1993.

Adkins, Brent. *Deleuze and Guattari's* A Thousand Plateaus: *A Critical Introduction and Guide*.
Edinburgh: Edinburgh University Press, 2015.

Ahmed, Sara. *The Cultural Politics of Emotion*. 2nd ed. Edinburgh: Edinburgh University Press, 2014.

——. "Happy Objects." In *The Affect Theory Reader*, ed. Gregory J. Seigworth and Melissa Gregg,
29–51. Durham, NC: Duke University Press, 2010.

Alexander, Kristine. "Can the Girl Guide Speak? The Perils and Pleasures of Looking for Children's Voices in Archival Records." *Jeunesse: Young People, Texts, Cultures* 4, no. 1 (2012): 132–145.

Amin, Ash, and Nigel Thrift. *Cities: Reimagining the Urban*. Cambridge: Polity, 2002.

Apfelbaum, Erika. "Halbwachs and the Social Properties of Memory." In *Memory: History, Theories, Debates*, ed. Susannah Radstone and Bill Schwartz, 77–92. New York: Fordham University Press, 2010.

Assmann, Jan. "Communicative and Cultural Memory." In *Cultural Memory Studies: An International and Interdisciplinary Handbook*, ed. Ansgar Nünning and Astrid Erll, 109–119. Berlin:
Walter de Gruyter, 2008.

Atkin, Nicholas. "Church and Teachers in Vichy France, 1940–1944." *French History* 4, no. 1
(1990): 1–22.

Austin, Roger. "Political Surveillance and Ideological Control in Vichy France: A Study of
Teachers in the Midi." In *Vichy France and the Resistance: Culture and Ideology*, ed. Rod Kedward and Roger Austin, 13–35. London: Croom Helm, 1985.

Baldoli, Claudia, and Andrew Knapp, *Forgotten Blitzes: France and Italy Under Allied Air Attack,
1940–1945*. London: Continuum, 2012.

Bancel, Nicolas, and Herman Lebovics. "Building the History Museum to Stop History: Nicolas
Sarkozy's New Presidential Museum of French History." *French Cultural Studies* 22, no. 4
(2011) 271–288.

Basham, Victoria M. "Gender, Race, Militarism and Remembrance: The Everyday Geopolitics
of the Poppy." *Gender, Place & Culture* 23, no. 6 (2016): 883–896.

Basso, Keith S. *Wisdom Sits in Places: Landscape and Language Among the Western Apache*. Albuquerque: University of New Mexico Press, 1996.

Baumgarten, Alexander. "Aesthetics" (1750). In *Art in Theory, 1648–1815: An Anthology of Changing
Ideas*, ed. Charles Harrison, Paul Wood and Jason Gaiger, 489–491. Oxford: Blackwell, 2000.

Bergson, Henri. *The Creative Mind: An Introduction to Metaphysics*. Trans. Mabelle L. Andison. New York: Citadel, 1992.

Bergson, Henri. *Key Writings*. Ed. Keith Ansell-Pearson and John Mullarky. London: Continuum, 2002.

Bericat, Eduardo. "The Sociology of Emotions: Four Decades of Progress." *Current Sociology* 64, no. 3 (2015): 491–513.

Berlant, Lauren. *Cruel Optimism*. Durham, NC: Duke University Press, 2011.

Bernal, Dolores Delgado. "Disrupting Epistemological Boundaries. Reflections on Feminista Methodological and Pedagogical Interventions." *Aztlán: A Journal of Chicano Studies* 45, no. 1 (2020): 155–169.

Besson, Jean-Luc. *Paris Rutabaga: Souvenirs d'enfance 1939–45*. Paris: Éditions-Jeunesse, Gallimard, 2005.

Borland, Katherine. " 'That's Not What I Said': Interpretive Conflict in Oral Narrative Research." In *The Oral History Reader*, ed. Robert Perks and Alistair Thomson, 320–332. London: Routledge, 1998.

Bornat, Joanna. "Crossing Boundaries with Secondary Analysis: Implications for Archived Oral History Data." Paper given at the ESRC National Council for Research Methods Network for Methodological Innovation, University of Essex, 2008. https://www.researchgate.net /profile/Joanna_Bornat/publication/237258161_Crossing_Boundaries_with_Secondary_Analysis _Implications_for_Archived_Oral_History_Data/links/00463531975a38bb5b000000.pdf.

——. "A Second Take: Revisiting Interviews with a Different Purpose." *Oral History* 31, no. 1 (2003): 47–53.

Boyd, Nan Alamilla, and Horacio N. Roque Ramírez, eds. *Bodies of Evidence: The Practice of Queer Oral History*. New York: Oxford University Press, 2012.

Bradley, Sue. "Hobday's Hands: Recollections of Touch in Veterinary Oral History." *Oral History* 49, no. 1 (2021): 35–48.

Brickell, Chris. "Histories of Adolescence and Affect: Setting an Agenda." *History Compass* 13, no. 8 (2015): 385–395.

Brossat, Alain. *Libération fête folle, 6 juin 1944–8 mai 45: Mythes et rites ou le grand théâtre des passions populaires*. Paris: Éditions Autrement, 1994.

Browder, George C. *Foundations of the Nazi Police State: The Formation of Sipo and SD*. Lexington: University Press of Kentucky, 1990.

Bruttmann, Tal. "La Sipo-SD de Lyon et la chasse aux juifs." In *Lyon dans la Seconde Guerre Mondiale: Villes et métropoles à l'épreuve du conflit*, ed. Isabelle von Bueltzingsloewen, Laurent Douzou, Jean-Dominique Durand, Hervé Joly, and Jean Solchany, 51–60. Rennes, France: Presses Universitaires de Rennes, 2016.

Buchanan, Kevin, and David Middleton. "Voices of Experience: Talk, Identity and Membership in Reminiscence Groups." *Ageing & Society* 15, no. 4 (1995): 457–491.

Bueltzingsloewen, Isabelle von. "Reconstructing the Daily Life of a Lyonnaise Family." In *Vichy France and Everyday Life: Confronting the Challenges of Wartime*, ed. Lindsey Dodd and David Lees, 51–68. London: Bloomsbury, 2018.

Bueltzingsloewen, Isabelle von, Laurent Douzou, Jean-Dominique Durand, Hervé Joly, and Jean Solchany, eds. *Lyon dans la Seconde Guerre Mondiale: Villes et métropoles à l'épreuve du conflit*. Rennes, France: Presses Universitaires de Rennes, 2016.

Burkitt, Ian. *Emotions and Social Relations*. Thousand Oaks, CA: Sage, 2014.

Caniot, Jean. *Lille 1939–1945*. Lambersart, France: Author, 2009.

Capuano, Christophe. *Vichy et la famille: Réalités et faux-semblants d'une politique publique*. Rennes, France: Presses Universitaires de Rennes, 2009.

Carrier, Maria, ed. *Maréchal nous voilà . . . 1940–1944: Souvenirs d'enfances sous l'Occupation*. Paris: Éditions Autrement, 2004.

Casey, Edward S. *The Fate of Place: A Philosophical History*. Berkeley: University of California Press, 1997.

——. "How to Get from Space to Place in a Fairly Short Stretch of Time: Phenomenological Prolegomena." In *Senses of Place*, ed. Steven Feld and Keith S. Basso, 13–52. Santa Fe, NM: School of American Research Press, 1996.

Cépède, Michel. *Agriculture et alimentation en France, durant la Seconde Guerre Mondiale*. Paris: Génin, 1961.

Certeau, Michel de. *L'Invention du quotidien 1: Arts de faire*. Paris: Gallimard, 1980.

Chaumont, Jean-Michel. *La Concurrence des victimes : Génocide, identité, reconnaissance*. Paris: Éditions de la Découverte, 1997.

Clifford, Rebecca. *Survivors: Children's Lives After the Holocaust*. New Haven, CT: Yale University Press, 2020.

Clough, Patricia T. "The Affective Turn: Political Economy, Biomedia, and Bodies." In *The Affect Theory Reader*, ed. Gregory J. Seigworth and Melissa Gregg, 206–225. Durham, NC: Duke University Press, 2010.

Code, Lorraine. *Ecological Thinking: The Politics of Epistemic Location*. New York: Oxford University Press, 2006.

Cole, Tim. "Crematoria, Barracks, Gateway: Survivors' Return Visits to the Memory Landscapes of Auschwitz." *History and Memory* 25, no. 2 (2013): 102–131.

Cotera, María Eugenia. "Fleshing the Archive: Reflections on Chicana Memory Practice." *Oral History* 49, no. 2 (2021): 49–56.

Crépin, Thierry. " 'Il était une fois un maréchal de France': Presse enfantine et bande dessinée sous le régime de Vichy." *Vingtième Siècle* 28 (1990): 77–82.

Cvetkovich, Ann. *An Archive of Feelings*. Durham, NC: Duke University Press, 2003.

Damousi, Joy and Paula Hamilton, *A Cultural History of Sound, Memory, and the Senses*. Abingdon, UK: Routledge, 2017.

Dawson, Graham. "Trauma, Place and the Politics of Memory: Bloody Sunday, Derry, 1972–2004." *History Workshop Journal* 59, no. 1 (2005): 151–178.

Debré, Robert. "Condition of Children in France Under the Occupation." *Proceedings of the Royal Society of Medicine: Section for the Study of Disease in Children* 38 (1945): 447–449.

DeLanda, Manuel. *A New Philosophy of Society*. London: Continuum, 2006.

Deleuze, Gilles. *Two Regimes of Madness: Texts and Interviews, 1975–1995*. Cambridge, MA: MIT Press, 2007.

Deleuze, Gilles, and Félix Guattari. *A Thousand Plateaus: Capitalism and Schizophrenia*. Trans. Brian Massumi. Minneapolis: University of Minnesota Press, 1988.

Desjarlais, Robert, and Jason C. Throop. "Phenomenological Approaches in Anthropology." *Annual Review of Anthropology* 40 (2011): 87–102.

Devigne, Matthieu. "Coping in the Classroom: Adapting Schools to Wartime, 1940–45." In *Vichy France and Everyday Life: Confronting the Challenges of Wartime*, ed. Lindsey Dodd and David Lees, 35–50. London: Bloomsbury, 2018.

——. *L'École des Années Noires: Une histoire du primaire en temps de guerre*. Paris: Presses Universitaires de France, 2018.

Dewsbury, John D., Paul Harrison, Mitch Rose, and John Wylie. "Introduction: Enacting Geographies," *Geoforum* 33 (2002): 437–440.

Diamond, Hanna. *Fleeing Hitler: France, 1940*. New York : Oxford University Press, 2007.

——. " 'Prisoners of the Peace': German Prisoners-of-War in Rural France, 1944–48." *European History Quarterly* 43, no. 3 (2013): 442–463.

Dodd, Lindsey, "Fellow Feeling in Childhood Memories of Second World War France: Sympathy, Empathy and the Emotions of History." *Close Encounters in War* 4 (2021): 123–147.

——. "The Disappearing Child: Observations on Oral History, Archives and Affects," *Oral History* 49, no. 2 (2021): 37–48.

——. "Wartime Rupture and Reconfiguration in French Family Life: Experience and Legacy." *History Workshop Journal* 88 (2019): 134–152.

——. "Rural Lives, Urban Lives and Children's Evacuation." In *Vichy France and Everyday Life: Confronting the Challenges of Wartime*, ed. Lindsey Dodd and David Lees, 123–139. London: Bloomsbury, 2018.

——. " 'Mon Petit Papa Chéri': Children, Fathers and Family Separation in Wartime France." *Essays in French Literature and Culture* 54 (2017): 97–116.

——. "Children's Citizenly Participation in the National Revolution: The Instrumentalization of Children in Vichy France." *European Review of History/Revue d'Histoire Européenne* 24, no. 5 (2017): 759–780.

——. *French Children Under the Allied Bombs, 1940–1944: An Oral History*. Manchester, UK: Manchester University Press, 2016.

——. " 'It Did Not Traumatise Me at All': Childhood 'Trauma' in French Oral Narratives of Wartime Bombing." *Oral History* 42, no. 2 (2013): 37–48.

——. "Small Fish, Big Pond: Using a Single Oral Narrative to Reveal Broader Social Change." In *Memory and History: Understanding Memory as Source and Subject*, ed. Joan Tumblety, 44–59. London: Routledge, 2013.

——. "Are We Defended? Conflicting Representations of War in Pre-War France." *University of Sussex Journal of Contemporary History* 12 (2008). https://www.sussex.ac.uk/webteam/gateway/file.php?name=article-dodd-12&site=15.

Dodd, Lindsey, and Andrew Knapp. " 'How Many Frenchmen Did You Kill?' British Bombing Policy Towards France (1940–1945)." *French History* 22, no. 4 (2008): 469–492.

Dodd, Lindsey, and Marc Wiggam. 'Civil Defence as a Harbinger of War in France and Britain During the Interwar Period." *Synergies Royaume-Uni et Irlande* 4 (2011): 139–150.

Domanska, Ewa. "A Conversation with Hayden White." *Rethinking History: The Journal of Theory and Practice* 12, no. 1 (2008): 3–21.

Doron, Daniella. *Jewish Youth and Identity in Postwar France: Rebuilding Family and Nation*. Bloomington: Indiana University Press, 2015.

Doucet, Andrea. "Decolonizing Family Photographs: Ecological Imaginaries and Nonrepresentational Ethnographies." *Journal of Contemporary Ethnography* 47, no. 6 (2018): 729–757.

Douzou, Laurent and Pierre Laborie. "Le rôle des historiens dans la transmission de la mémoire des comportements collectifs." In *Images des comportements sous l'Occupation: Mémoires, transmission, idées reçues*, ed. Jacqueline Sainclivier, Jean-Marie Guillon, and Pierre Laborie, 151–160. Rennes, France: Presses Universitaires de Rennes, 2016.

Downs, Laura Lee. "Milieu Social or Milieu Familial? Theories and Practices of Childrearing Among the Popular Classes in Twentieth-Century France and Britain: The Case of Evacuation (1939–45)." *Family and Community History* 8, no. 1 (2005): 49–65.

Duclert, Vincent. "Archives orales et recherche contemporaine: Une histoire en cours." *Sociétés et Représentations* 13, no. 1 (2002): 69–86.

Eagleton, Terry. *The Ideology of the Aesthetic*. Oxford: Blackwell, 1990.

Erll, Astrid. "Locating Family in Cultural Memory Studies." *Journal of Comparative Family Studies* 42, no. 3 (2011): 303–318.

Erll, Astrid, and Ansgar Nünning, eds. *A Companion to Cultural Memory Studies: An International and Interdisciplinary Handbook*. Berlin: Walter de Gruyter, 2008.

Ernaux, Annie. *La Place*. Paris: Gallimard, 1983.

Farmer, Sarah. *Martyred Village: Commemorating the 1944 Massacre at Oradour-sur-Glane*. Berkeley: University of California Press, 1999.

Fass, Paula S., ed. *The Routledge History of Children in the Western World*. 2nd ed. Abingdon, UK: Routledge, 2015.

Faure, Laura Hobson. "Orphelines ou sœurs? Penser la famille juive pendant et après la Shoah en France et aux États-Unis." *Revue d'histoire* 145, no. 1 (2020): 91–104.

Feldman, Marion. "Enfants juifs cachés (1940–1944): Une littérature récente." *Psychologie française* 54, no. 2 (2009): 191–209.

Feldman, Marion. *Entre trauma et protection: Quel devenir pour les enfants juifs cachés en France (1940–1944)?* Paris: Érès, 2013.

Fette, Julie. "Apology and the Past in Contemporary France." *French Politics, Culture & Society* 26, no. 2 (2008): 78–113.

Field, Sean. "Critical Empathy." *Continuum: Journal of Media and Cultural Studies* 31, no. 5 (2017): 660–670.

Fishman, Sarah. *The Battle for Children: World War II, Youth Crime, and Juvenile Justice in Twentieth-Century France*. Cambridge, MA: Harvard University Press, 2002

——. *We Will Wait: Wives of French Prisoners of War, 1940–1945*. New Haven, CT: Yale University Press, 1991.

Flatley, Jonathan. *Affective Mapping: Melancholia and the Politics of Modernism*. Cambridge, MA: Harvard University Press, 2008.

Fogg Shannon L. "The American Friends Service Committee and Wartime Aid to Families." In *Vichy France and Everyday Life: Confronting the Challenges of Wartime*, ed. Lindsey Dodd and David Lees, 107–122. London: Bloomsbury, 2018.

——. *Stealing Home: Looting, Restitution, and Reconstructing Jewish Lives in France, 1942–1947*. Oxford: Oxford University Press, 2016.

Foucault, Michel. *Surveiller et punir: Naissance de la prison*. Paris: Gallimard, 1975.

Foucault, Michel, with Jay Miskowiec. "Of Other Spaces." *Diacritics* 16, no. 1 (1986): 22–27.

Fox, James. "Poppy Politics: Remembrance of Things Past." In *Cultural Heritage Ethics: Between Theory and Practice*, ed. Constantine Sandis, 21–30. Cambridge: Open Book, 2014.

Fox, Nick J. "Emotions, Affects and the Production of Social Life." *British Journal of Sociology* 66, no. 2 (2015): 301–318.

Friedman, Jeff. "Oral History, Hermeneutics and Embodiment." *Oral History Review* 41, no. 2 (2014): 290–300.

Frisch, Michael. *A Shared Authority? Essays on the Craft and Meaning of Oral and Public History.* Albany: State University of New York Press, 1990.

Galliou, Patrick. *Histoire de Brest.* Paris: Éditions Jean-Paul Gisserot, 2007.

Gauvin, Gilles. "L'affaire des enfants de la Creuse: Entre abus de mémoire et nécessité de l'histoire." *Revue d'histoire* 3, no. 143 (2019): 85–98.

Gemie, Sharif, and Fiona Reid. "Chaos, Panic and Historiography of the Exode (France, 1940)." *War & Society* 26, no. 2 (2007): 73–97.

Gensburger, Sarah. "Halbwachs' Studies in Collective Memory: A Founding Text for Contemporary 'Memory Studies'?" *Journal of Classical Sociology* 16, no. 4 (2016): 396–413.

Gildea, Robert. "The Long March of Oral history: Around 1968 in France." *Oral History* 38, no. 1 (2010): 68–80.

——. "Resistance, Reprisals and Community in Occupied France." *Transactions of the Royal Historical Society* 13 (2003): 163–185.

——. *Marianne in Chains: In Search of the German Occupation, 1940–1945.* Basingstoke, UK: Macmillan, 2002.

Giolitto, Pierre. *Histoire de la jeunesse sous Vichy.* Paris: Perrin, 1991.

Gluck, Sherna Berger. "Has Oral History Lost Its Radical/Subversive Edge?" *Oral History* 39, no. 2 (2011): 63–72.

Gluck, Sherna Berger, and Daphne Patai, eds. *Women's Words: The Feminist Practice of Oral History.* New York: Routledge, 1991.

Golsan, Richard J. *Vichy's Afterlife: History and Counterhistory in Postwar France.* Lincoln: University of Nebraska Press, 2000.

Grele, Ronald. "History and the Languages of History in the Oral History Interview: Who Answers Whose Questions and Why." University of the Witwatersrand, Johannesburg, History Workshop, February 6–10, 1990. https://wiredspace.wits.ac.za/bitstream/handle/10539/7815/HWS-146.pdf?sequence=1&isAllowed=y.

Grenard, Fabrice. *La France du marché noir, 1940–1949.* Paris: Payot, 2008.

Greyser, Naomi. "Beyond the 'Feeling Woman': Feminist Implications of Affect Studies." *Feminist Studies* 38, no. 1 (2012): 84–112.

Grossberg, Lawrence. "Affect's Future: Rediscovering the Virtual in the Actual." In *The Affect Theory Reader*, ed. Gregory J. Seigworth and Melissa Gregg, 309–338. Durham, NC: Duke University Press, 2010.

Grove, Kevin, and Jonathan Pugh. "Assemblage Thinking and Participatory Development: Potentiality, Ethics, Biopolitics." *Geography Compass* 9, no. 1 (2015): 1–13.

Grynberg, Anne. "La pédagogie des lieux." *Les Cahiers de la Shoah* 8, no. 1 (2005): 15–56.

Halbwachs, Maurice. *On Collective Memory.* Ed. and trans. Lewis Coser. Chicago: University of Chicago Press, 1992.

Hall, Stuart. *Cultural Studies 1983: A Theoretical History*, ed. Jennifer Daryl Slack and Lawrence Grossberg. Durham, NC: Duke University Press, 2016.

Halls, W. D. *The Youth of Vichy France.* Oxford: Clarendon, 1981.

Hamilakis, Yannis. "Sensorial Assemblages: Affect, Memory and Temporality in Assemblage Thinking." *Cambridge Archaeological Journal* 27, no. 1 (2017): 169–182.

——. *Archaeology and the Senses: Human Experience, Memory, and Affect.* Cambridge: Cambridge University Press, 2013.

Hamilton, Carrie. "Moving Feelings. Nationalism, Feminism and the Emotions of Politics." *Oral History* 38, no. 2 (2010): 85–94.

——. "Happy Memories." *New Formations* 63 (2007): 65–81.

Hamilton, Paula. "The Proust Effect: Oral History and the Senses," in *The Oxford Handbook of Oral History*, ed. Donald Ritchie, 219–232. Oxford: Oxford University Press, 2012.

Harding, Jenny. "Looking for Trouble: Exploring Emotion, Memory and Public Sociology: Inaugural Lecture, 1 May 2014, London Metropolitan University." *Oral History* 42, no. 2 (2014): 94–104.

Harding, Jennifer, and E. Deirdre Pribram. "The Power of Feeling: Locating Emotions in Culture." *European Journal of Cultural Studies* 5, no. 4 (2002): 407–426.

Hazan, Katy. "Enfants cachés, enfants retrouvés." *Les Cahiers de la Shoah* 9, no. 1 (2007): 181–212.

Henckens, Marloes J. A. G., Erno J. Hermans, Zhenwei Pu, Marian Joëls, and Guillén Fernández. "Stressed Memories: How Acute Stress Affects Memory Formation in Humans." *Journal of Neuroscience* 29, no. 32 (2009): 10111–10119.

Heymann, Florence. "Tourisme des mémoires blessées: Traces de Transnistrie." *Revue d'Histoire de la Shoah* 194, no. 1 (2011): 319–341.

High, Steven, Elizabeth Tasong, Felipe Lalinde Lopera, and Hussain Almahr. "The Pedagogy and Practice of Listening to Rwandan Exiles and Genocide Survivors." *Oral History* 50, no. 1 (2022): 115–126.

Highmore, Ben. "Aesthetic Matters: Writing and Cultural Studies." *Cultural Studies* 32, no. 2 (2018): 240–260.

——. *Cultural Feelings: Mood, Mediation and Cultural Politics*. London: Routledge, 2017.

——. "Bitter After Taste: Affect, Food, and Social Aesthetics." In *The Affect Theory Reader*, ed. Gregory J. Seigworth and Melissa Gregg, 118–137. Durham, NC: Duke University Press, 2010.

Hirsch, Marianne, and Leo Spitzer. "The Witness in the Archive." In *Memory: History, Theories, Debates*, ed. Susannah Radstone and Bill Schwartz, 390–405. New York: Fordham University Press, 2010.

Hodgkin, Katharine, and Susannah Radstone, eds. *Contested Pasts: The Politics of Memory*. London: Routledge, 2003.

Hoffman, Eva. "The Long Afterlife of Loss." In *Memory: History, Theories, Debates*, ed. Susannah Radstone and Bill Schwartz, 406–415. New York: Fordham University Press, 2010.

Hoffman, Stanley. *Decline or Renewal? France Since the 1930s*. New York: Viking, 1974.

Hollin, Gregory, Isla Forsyth, Eva Giraud, and Tracy Potts. "(Dis)entangling Barad: Materialisms and Ethics." *Social Studies of Science* 47, no. 6 (2017): 918–941.

Holmes, Katie. "Does it Matter If She Cried? Recording Emotion and the Australian Generations Oral History Project." *Oral History Review* 44, no. 1 (2017): 56–76.

Houzé, Kathel, and Jean-Christophe Bailly. *La Colonie des enfants d'Izieu*. Lyon, France: Éditions Libel, 2012.

Huijsmans, Roy. "'Knowledge That Moves': Emotions and Affect in Policy and Research with Young Migrants." *Children's Geographies* 16, no. 6 (2018): 628–641.

Jack, Dana C., and Kathryn Anderson. "Learning to Listen: Interview Techniques and Analyses." In *The Oral History Reader*, ed. Robert Perks and Alistair Thomson, 157–171. London: Routledge, 1998.

Jackson, Julian. *France: The Dark Years, 1940–1944*. Oxford: Oxford University Press, 2001.

Jackson, Michael, ed. *Things As They Are: New Directions in Phenomenological Anthropology*. Washington, DC: Georgetown University Press, 1996.

Jackson, Peter, Graham Smith, and Sarah Olive. "Families Remembering Food: Reusing Secondary Data," working paper, 2007. https://www.researchgate.net/publication/260351319 _Families_remembering_food_reusing_secondary_data.

Jedinak, Rachel. *Nous étions seulement des enfants*. Paris: Fayard, 2018.

Jenkins, Keith. "Nobody Does It Better: Radical History and Hayden White." *Rethinking History: The Journal of Theory and Practice* 12, no. 1 (2008): 59–74.

——. *Re-Thinking History*. London: Routledge, 1991.

Johnpoll, Bernard K. *The Politics of Futility: The General Jewish Workers Bund of Poland, 1917–1943*. Ithaca, NY: Cornell University Press, 1967.

Johnson, E. Patrick. *Sweet Tea: Black Gay Men of the South*. Chapel Hill: University of North Carolina Press, 2012.

Jones, Owain. "Geography, Memory and Non-Representational Geographies." *Geography Compass* 5, no. 2 (2011): 875–885.

Jordanova, Ludmilla. "Children in History: Concepts of Nature and Society." In *Children, Parents and Politics*, ed. Geoffrey Scarre, 3–24. Cambridge: Cambridge University Press, 1989.

Kansteiner, Wulf. *In Pursuit of German Memory: History, Television, and Politics After Auschwitz*. Athens: Ohio University Press, 2006.

Kehily, Mary Jane. *An Introduction to Childhood Studies*. 2nd ed. New York: Open University Press, 2009.

Keith, Susan. "Collective Memory and the End of Occupation: Remembering (and Forgetting) the Liberation of Paris in Images." *Visual Communication Quarterly* 17, no. 3 (2010): 134–146.

Kennedy, Roger. "Memory and the Unconscious." In *Memory: Histories, Theories, Debates*, ed. Susannah Radstone and Bill Schwartz, 179–197. New York: Fordham University Press, 2010.

Kershaw, Angela. *Before Auschwitz: Irène Némirovsky and the Cultural Landscape of Inter-War France*. London: Routledge, 2009.

Kidron, Carol A. "Being There Together: Dark Family Tourism and the Emotive Experience of Co-Presence in the Holocaust Past." *Annals of Tourism Research* 41 (2013): 175–194.

Kitchen, Ruth. *A Legacy of Shame: French Narratives of War and Occupation*. Oxford: Peter Lang, 2013.

Klarsfeld, Serge. *Le Mémorial des enfants juifs déportés de France*. Paris: Les Fils et filles des déportés juifs de France, 1994.

Knapp, Andrew. *Les Français sous les bombes alliées, 1940–1945*. Paris: Tallandier, 2014.

Knittel, Susanne C., and Sofia Forchieri. "Navigating Implication: An Interview with Michael Rothberg." *Journal of Perpetrator Research* 3, no. 1 (2020): 6–19.

Laborde, Françoise. *Ça va mieux en le disant!* Paris: Fayard, 2008.

Lagrou, Pieter. "Victims of Genocide and National Memory: Belgium, France and the Netherlands." *Past & Present* 154, no. 1 (1997): 181–222.

Langhamer, Claire. " 'Who the Hell Are Ordinary People?' Ordinariness as a Category of Historical Analysis." *Transactions of the Royal Historical Society* 28 (2018): 175–195.

Lavabre, Marie-Claire. "Paradigmes de la mémoire." *Transcontinentales: Société, idéologies, système mondiale* 5 (2007): 139–147.

Le Boterf, Hervé. *La Bretagne dans la guerre (1938–1945)*. Paris: France-Empire, 2000.

Ledoux, Sébastien. *Le Devoir de mémoire: Une formule et son histoire*. Paris: CNRS Éditions, 2016.

Lee, Daniel. *Pétain's Jewish Children: French Jewish Youth and the Vichy Regime, 1940–1942*. Oxford: Oxford University Press, 2014.

Lefebvre, Henri. *De la production de l'espace*. Paris: Anthropos, 1974.

Le Melledo, Paul. *Lorient à l'heure de l'évacuation: Itinéraire d'un Gavroche lorientais*. La Faouët, France: Liv'éditions, 2004.

Lennon, John, and Malcolm Foley. *Dark Tourism*. London: Continuum, 2000.

Levine, Linda J., Heather C. Lench, and Martin A. Safer. "Functions of Remembering and Mis-remembering Emotion." *Applied Cognitive Psychology* 23, no. 8 (2009): 1059–1075.

Lilly, J. Robert. *La face cachée des GIs: Les viols commis par des soldats Américains en France, en Angleterre et en Allemagne pendant la Seconde Guerre mondiale*. Paris: Payot, 2003.

Lorimer, Hayden. "Cultural Geography: Worldly Shapes, Differently Arranged." *Progress in Human Geography* 31, no. 1 (2007): 89–100.

——. "Cultural Geography: The Busyness of Being 'More-Than-Representational.'" *Progress in Human Geography* 29, no. 1 (2005): 83–94.

Lyytikäinen, Pirjo, and Kirski Saarikangas. "Introduction: Imagining Spaces and Places." In *Imagining Spaces and Places*, by Saija Isomaa, Pirjo Lyytikäinen, and Renja Suominen-Kokkonen, ix–xx. Newcastle-Upon-Tyne, UK: Cambridge Scholars, 2003.

MacMahon, Eva M. *Elite Oral History Discourse: A Study of Cooperation and Coherence*. Tuscaloosa: University of Alabama, 1989.

Mahé, Camille. "Children and Play in Occupied France." In *Vichy France and Everyday Life: Confronting the Challenges of Wartime*, ed. Lindsey Dodd and David Lees, 17–33. London: Bloomsbury, 2018.

Mak, Ariane. "France: Oral History Conference." *Oral History* 47, no. 2 (2019): 21.

Marrus, Michael, and Robert O. Paxton, *Vichy France and the Jews*. Stanford, CA: Stanford University Press, 1995.

Mason, Jennifer. "'Re-Using' Qualitative Data: On the Merits of an Investigative Epistemology." *Sociological Research Online* 12, no. 3 (2007). https://www.socresonline.org.uk/12/3/3.html.

Massey, Doreen, and Nigel Thrift. "The Passion of Place." In *A Century of British Geography*, ed. Ron Johnston and Michael Williams, 275–299. Oxford: Oxford University Press, 2003.

Massumi, Brian. "The Future Birth of the Affective Fact: The Political Ontology of Threat." In *The Affect Theory Reader*, ed. Gregory J. Seigworth and Melissa Gregg, 52–70. Durham, NC: Duke University Press, 2010.

——, ed. *A Shock to Thought: Expression After Deleuze and Guattari*. London: Routledge, 2002.

——, "The Autonomy of Affect." *Cultural Critique* 31 (1995): 83–109.

Matt, Susan J. "Current Emotion Research in History: or, Doing History from the Inside Out." *Emotion Review* 3, no. 1 (2011): 117–124.

Matthews, Jodie. "Romani Pride, *Gorja* Shame: Race and Privilege in the Archive." *Oral History* 49, no. 2 (2021): 57–68.

Mattingly, Cheryl. "Emergent Narratives." In *Narrative and the Cultural Construction of Illness and Healing*, ed. Cheryl Mattingly and Linda C. Garro, 181–211. Berkeley: University of California Press, 2010.

Meier, Elisabeth. "Les services d'occupation et de répression allemandes à Lyon (1942–1944)." In *Lyon dans la Seconde Guerre Mondiale: Villes et Métropoles à l'épreuve du conflit*, ed. Isabelle von

Bueltzingsloewen, Laurent Douzou, Jean-Dominique Durand, Hervé Joly, and Jean Solchany, 37–50. Rennes, France: Presses Universitaires de Rennes, 2016.

Merleau-Ponty, Maurice. *Phénoménologie de la perception*. Paris: Gallimard, 1945.

Mexandeau, Louis. *Nous, nous ne verrons pas la fin: Un enfant dans la guerre (1939–1945)*. Paris: Éditions Le Cherche-midi, 2003.

Michallat, Wendy. "Madeleine Blaess: An Emotional History of a Long Liberation." In *Vichy France and Everyday Life: Confronting the Challenges of Wartime*, ed. Lindsey Dodd and David Lees, 179–196. London: Bloomsbury, 2018.

Middleton, David, and Steven Brown. *The Social Psychology of Experience: Studies in Remembering and Forgetting*. Thousand Oaks, CA: Sage, 2005.

Minioli, Ramon F. "Food Rationing and Mortality in Paris, 1940–41." *Milbank Memorial Fund Quarterly* 20, no. 3 (1942): 213–220.

Muracciole, Jean-François. "Les bombardements stratégiques en France durant la Seconde Guerre Mondiale: Premier bilan et pistes de recherche." In *Les Bombardements alliés sur la France durant la Seconde Guerre Mondiale: Stratégies, bilans matériels et humains*, ed. Michèle Battesti and Patrick Facon, 173–178. Vincennes, France: Cahiers du CEHD no. 37, 2007.

Murphy, Kaitlin M. "Memory Mapping: Affect, Place, and Testimony in *El Lugar Más Pequeño* (2011)." *Journal of Latin American Cultural Studies* 25, no. 4 (2016): 571–595.

Murphy, Kevin P., Jennifer L. Pierce, and Jason Ruiz. "What Makes Queer Oral History Different." *Oral History Review* 43, no. 1 (2016): 1–24.

Nettelbeck, Colin. "A Forgotten Zone of Memory? French Primary School Children and the History of the Occupation." *French History and Civilization* 14 (2011): 157–166.

Norquay, Naomi. "Identity and Forgetting." *Oral History Review* 26, no. 1 (1999): 1–21.

Norton, Mason. "Counter-Revolution? Resisting Vichy and the National Revolution." In *Vichy France and Everyday Life: Confronting the Challenges of Wartime*, ed. Lindsey Dodd and David Lees, 197–211. London: Bloomsbury, 2018.

Olsen, Stephanie. "The History of Childhood and the Emotional Turn." *History Compass* 15, no. 11 (2017): e12410.

Parsons, Martin. *Children: The Invisible Victims of War: An Interdisciplinary Study*. Peterborough, UK: DSM, 2008.

Passerini, Luisa. "Memories Between Silence and Oblivion." In *Contested Pasts: The Politics of Memory*, ed. Katharine Hodgkin and Susannah Radstone, 238–250. London: Routledge, 2003.

Paxton, Robert O. *Vichy France: Old Guard and New Order, 1940–1944*. New York: Knopf, 1972.

Pechanski, Denis. *La France des camps: l'internement, 1938–46*. Paris: Gallimard, 2002.

Perks, Robert, and Alistair Thomson. *The Oral History Reader*. 3rd ed. London: Routledge, [1998] 2016.

Péron, François. *Brest sous l'occupation*. Rennes, France: Ouest-France, 1981.

Phillips, Mark Salber. "On the Advantage and Disadvantage of Sentimental History for Life." *History Workshop Journal* 65, no. 1 (2008): 49–64.

Pignot, Manon. *La Guerre des crayons: Quand les petits Parisiens dessinaient la Grande Guerre*. Paris: Parigramme, 2004.

Pile, Steve. "Emotions and Affects in Recent Human Geography." *Transactions of the Institute of British Geographers* 35, no. 1 (2010): 5–20.

Plamper, Jan. "The History of the Emotions: An Interview with William Reddy, Barbara Rosenwein and Peter Stearns." *History & Theory* 49, no. 2 (2010): 237–265.

Polzer, Natalie C. "Durkheim's Sign Made Flesh: The 'Authentic Symbol' in Contemporary Holocaust Pilgrimage." *Canadian Journal of Sociology* 39, no. 4 (2014): 697–718.

Popular Memory Group. "Popular Memory: Theory, Politics, Method." In *The Oral History Reader*, ed. Robert Perks and Alistair Thomson, 75–86. London: Routledge, 1998.

Portelli, Alessandro. *The Battle of the Valle Giulia: Oral History and the Art of Dialogue.* Madison: University of Wisconsin Press, 1997.

——. *The Death of Luigi Trastulli and Other Stories: Form and Meaning in Oral History.* Albany: State University of New York Press, 1991.

Proud, Judith, *Children and Propaganda.* Bristol, UK: Intellect, 1995.

Prout, Alan. *The Future of Childhood.* London: Routledge, 2005.

Radstone, Susannah, and Bill Schwartz. *Memory: History, Theories, Debates.* New York: Fordham University Press, 2010.

Ragache, Gilles. *Les Enfants de la guerre; vivre, survivre, lire et jouer en France (1939–1949).* Paris: Perrin, 1997.

Rajsfus, Maurice. *Drancy: un camp de concentration très ordinaire, 1941–1944.* Paris: Le Cherche-midi, 1996.

Ramírez, Horacio N. Roque, and Nan Alamilla Boyd. "Close Encounters: The Body and Knowledge in Queer Oral History." In *Bodies of Evidence: The Practice of Queer Oral History*, ed. Nan Alamilla Boyd and Horacio N. Roque Ramírez, 1–20. New York: Oxford University Press, 2012.

Raychaudhuri, Anindya. " 'This, Too, Is History': Oral History, the 1947 India-Pakistan Partition and the Risks of Archival Re-Ordering." *Oral History* 49, no. 2 (2021): 69–80.

Renold, Emma, and David Alan Mellor. "Deleuze and Guattari in the Nursery: Towards an Ethnographic Multi-Sensory Mapping of Gendered Bodies and Becomings." In *Deleuze and Research Methodologies*, ed. Rebecca Coleman and Jessica Ringrose, 23–41. Edinburgh: Edinburgh University Press, 2013.

Risser, Nicole Dombrowski. *France Under Fire: German Invasion, Civilian Flight and Family Survival During the Second World War.* Cambridge: Cambridge University Press, 2012.

Ritchie, Donald A. *The Oxford Handbook of Oral History.* Oxford: Oxford University Press, 2011.

Rivière, Antoine. "Des pupilles ordinaires: Les enfants juifs recueillis par l'Assistance publique de Paris sous l'Occupation (1940–1944)." *Revue d'histoire de l'enfance "irrégulière"* 19 (2017): 87–117.

Roper, Michael. "The Unconscious Work of History." *History Workshop Journal* 11, no. 2 (2014): 169–193.

——. "Re-remembering the Soldier Hero: The Psychic and Social Construction of Memory in Personal Narratives of the Great War." *History Workshop Journal* 50, no. 1 (2000): 181–204.

Rothberg, Michael. *The Implicated Subject: Beyond Victims and Perpetrators.* Stanford, CA: Stanford University Press, 2019.

——. *Multidirectional Memory: Remembering the Holocaust in the Age of Decolonization.* Stanford, CA: Stanford University Press, 2009.

Rousso, Henry. *Face au passé: Essais sur la mémoire contemporaine.* Paris: Belin, 2016.

——. *La Hantise du passé.* Paris: Textuel, 1998.

——. *The Vichy Syndrome: History and Memory in France Since 1944.* Trans. Arthur Goldhammer. Cambridge, MA: Harvard University Press, 1991.

Roux, Nicole. *C'est la guerre les enfants*. Cherbourg-Octeville: Isoète, 2007.

Schaefer, Donovan. "The Promise of Affect: The Politics of the Event in Ahmed's *The Promise of Happiness* and Berlant's *Cruel Optimism*." *Theory and Event* 16, no. 2 (2013). https://muse.jhu.edu/article/509908.

Scollon, Christie Napa, Amanda Hiles Howard, Amanda E. Caldwell, and Sachiyo Ito. "The Role of Ideal Affect in the Experience and Memory of Emotions." *Journal of Happiness Studies* 10, no. 3 (2009): 257–269.

Sedgwick, Eve Kosofsky. "Paranoid Reading and Reparative Reading: Or, You're So Paranoid, You Probably Think This Introduction Is About You." In *Novel Gazing: Queer Readings in Fiction*, ed. Eve Kosofsky Sedgwick, Michèle Aina Barale, Jonathan Goldberg, and Michael Moon, 1–40. Durham, NC: Duke University Press, 1997.

Seigworth, Gregory J., and Melissa Gregg. "An Inventory of Shimmers," in *The Affect Theory Reader*, ed. Gregory J. Seigworth and Melissa Gregg, 1–25. Durham, NC: Duke University Press, 2010.

Sémelin, Jacques. *The Survival of the Jews in France, 1940–1944*. Trans. Cynthia Schoch and Natasha Lehrer. London: Hurst, 2018.

Sené, Ayshka. "The Orphan Story of British Women in Occupied France: History, Memory, Legacy." Unpublished PhD diss., Cardiff University, 2018.

Sheftel, Anna, and Stacey Zembrzycki, eds. *Oral History Off the Record: Toward an Ethnography of Practice*. New York: Palgrave, 2013.

Sion, Brigitte. "Memorial Pilgrimage or Death Tourism? A Jewish Perspective." *Liturgy* 32, no. 3 (2017): 23–28.

Smith, George H., and Marilyn Moore, eds. *Individualism: A Reader*. Libertarianism.org Press, 2015.

Smith, Graham. "Remembering in Groups: Negotiating Between 'Individual' and 'Collective' Memories." In *The Oral History Reader*, ed. Robert Perks and Alistair Thomson, 193–211. 3rd ed. London: Routledge, 2016.

Smith, Paul. "*L'histoire bling-bling*—Nicolas Sarkozy and the Historians." In *The Use and Abuse of Memory: Interpreting World War II in Contemporary European Politics*, ed. Christian Karner and Bram Mertens, 121–136. New Brunswick, NJ: Transaction, 2013.

Srigley, Katrina, Stacey Zembrzycki, and Franca Iacovetta, eds. *Beyond Women's Words: Feminisms and the Practices of History in the Twenty-First Century*. New York: Routledge, 2018.

Starecheski, Amy. "South Bronx Soundwalks as Embodied Archiving Practice." *Oral History* 48, no. 2 (2020): 102–112.

Stewart, Kathleen. "Weak Theory in an Unfinished World." *Journal of Folklore Research* 45, no. 1 (2008): 71–82.

Stewart, Kathleen. *Ordinary Affects*. Durham, NC: Duke University Press, 2007.

Stewart, Pamela J., and Andrew Strathern. "Introduction." In *Landscape, Memory and History: Anthropological Perspectives*, ed. Pamela J. Stewart and Andrew Strathern, 3–6. London: Pluto, 2003.

St. Pierre, Elizabeth Adams. "Post Qualitative Inquiry, the Refusal of Method, and the Risk of the New." *Qualitative Inquiry* 27, no. 1 (2021): 3–9.

——. "Haecceity: Laying Out a Plane for Post Qualitative Inquiry." *Qualitative Inquiry* 23, no. 9 (2017): 686–698.

Stuart, Harold C. "Review of the Evidence as to the Nutritional State of Children in France." *American Journal of Public Health* 35, no. 4 (1945): 299–307.

Stuart, Harold C., and Daniel Kuhlmann. "Studies of the Physical Characteristics of Children in Marseilles, France, in 1941." *Journal of Pediatrics* 20, no. 4 (1942): 424–453.

Sutton, John, Celia B. Harris, and Amanda Barnier. "Memory and Cognition." In *Memory: Histories, Theories, Debates*, ed. Susannah Radstone and Bill Schwartz, 209–226. New York: Fordham University Press, 2010.

Sweets, John F. *Choices in Vichy France: The French Under Nazi Occupation*. New York: Oxford University Press, 1994.

Temkin, Moshik. " 'Avec Un Certain Malaise': The Paxtonian Trauma in France, 1973–74." *Journal of Contemporary History* 38, no. 2 (2003): 291–306.

Thompson, Paul. "The Voice of the Past: Oral History." In *The Oral History Reader*, ed. Robert Perks and Alistair Thomson, 21–28. London: Routledge, 1998.

Thomson, Alistair. "Indexing and Interpreting Emotion: Joy and Shame in Oral History." *Studies in Oral History* 41 (2018): 1–11.

——. *Moving Stories: An Intimate History of Four Women Across Two Countries*. Manchester, UK: Manchester University Press, 2011.

——. "Four Paradigm Transformations in Oral History." *Oral History Review* 34, no. 1 (2007): 49–70.

Thrift, Nigel. "Summoning Life." In *Envisioning Human Geographies*, ed. Paul Cloke, Philip Crang, and Mark Goodwin, 81–103. London: Arnold, 2014.

——. *Non-Representational Theory: Space, Politics, Affect*. London: Routledge, 2007.

——. "Intensities of Feeling: Towards a Spatial Politics of Affect." *Geografiska Annaler: Series B, Human Geography* 86, no. 1 (2004): 57–78.

Toqueville, Alexis de. *Democracy in America*. Ed. Eduardo Nolla. Trans. James L. Schleifer. Indianapolis, IN: Liberty Fund, 2012.

Trigg, Stephanie. "Introduction: Emotional Histories—Beyond the Personalization of the Past and the Abstraction of Affect Theory." *Exemplaria* 26, no. 1 (2014): 3–15.

Trivelli, Elena. "Exploring a 'Remembering Crisis': 'Affective Attuning' and 'Assemblage Archive' as Theoretical Frameworks and Research Methodologies." In *Affective Methodologies: Developing Cultural Research Strategies for the Study of Affect*, ed. Britta Timm Knudsen and Carsten Stage, 119–139. London: Palgrave Macmillan, 2015.

Tuan, Yi-Fu. *Space and Place: The Perspective of Experience*. Minneapolis: University of Minnesota Press, 1977.

Underwood, Nick. "Lending Identity: Circulating Literacy, Current Events, Yiddish Culture, and Politics in Interwar France." *Contemporary French Civilization* 45, no. 1 (2020): 71–88.

United Nations High Commissioner for Refugees. "Monthly Arrivals by Nationality to Greece, Italy and Spain." *Refugees/Migrants Emergency Response—Mediterranean*, March 31, 2016. https://europadreaming.eu/open-data/20160122-Dec_Nationality_of_arrivals_to_Greece_Italy_and_Spain-Monthly_Jan-Dec_2015.pdf.

Valentin, Louis. *Les Années rutabagas*. Paris: Olivier Orban, 1994.

Vannini, Philippe. "Non-Representational Ethnography: New Ways of Animating Lifeworlds." *Cultural Geographies* 22, no. 2 (2015): 317–327.

Veillon, Dominique. *Vivre et survivre en France, 1939–1947*. Paris: Éditions Payot, 1995.

Vogel, Shane. "By the Light of What Comes After: Eventologies of the Ordinary." *Women and Performance: A Journal of Feminist Theory* 19, no. 2 (2009): 247–260.

Vural, Leyla. "Potter's Field as a Heterotopia: Death and Mourning at New York City's Edge." *Oral History* 47, no. 2 (2019): 106–116.

Watkins, Megan. "Desiring Recognition, Accumulating Affect." In *The Affect Theory Reader*, ed. Gregory J. Seigworth and Melissa Gregg, 269–285. Durham, NC: Duke University Press, 2010.

Welzer, Harald. "Communicative Memory." In *A Companion to Cultural Memory Studies: An International and Interdisciplinary Handbook*, ed. Astrid Erll and Ansgar Nünning, 285–298. Berlin: Walter de Gruyter, 2008.

Wieviorka, Annette, and Michel Laffitte. *À l'intérieur du camp de Drancy*. Paris: Perrin, 2012.

Wieviorka, Olivier. *La Mémoire désunie: Le souvenir politique des années sombres, de la Libération à nos jours*. Paris: Seuil, 2010.

Williams, Caroline. "Thinking the Political in the Wake of Spinoza: Power, Affect and Imagination in *The Ethics*." *Contemporary Political Theory* 6, no. 3 (2007): 349–369.

Williams, Raymond. *Marxism and Literature*. New York: Oxford University Press, 1977.

Wood, Nancy. *Vectors of Memory: Legacies of Trauma in Postwar Europe*. Oxford: Berg, 1999.

Zajde, Nathalie. *Qui sont les enfants cachés? Penser avec les grands témoins*. Paris: Odile Jacob, 2014.

——. *Les Enfants cachés en France*. Paris: Odile Jacob, 2012.

Zalc, Claire. *Les Dénaturalisés: Les retraits de nationalité sous Vichy*. Paris: Seuil, 2016.

INDEX